**Other Kaplan Books on Graduate Admissions**

Graduate School Admissions Adviser
GRE Biology
GRE Exam Verbal Workbook
GRE/GMAT Math Workbook

# GRE*
## Exam
## 2003

**By the Staff of Kaplan, Inc.**

**Simon & Schuster**

New York · London · Singapore · Sydney · Toronto

Kaplan Publishing
Published by Simon & Schuster
1230 Avenue of the Americas
New York, NY 10020

Contributing Editors: Trent Anderson and Albert Chen
Project Editor: Eileen Mager
Cover Design: Cheung Tai
Production Editor: Maude Spekes
Editorial Coordinator: Déa Alessandro
Executive Editor: Del Franz

Special thanks to: Martha Arango, Megan Duffy, Larissa Shmailo, and Grace Begany

Manufactured in the United States of America
Published simultaneously in Canada

July 2002

10 9 8 7 6 5 4 3 2 1

ISBN: 0-7432-3029-9

# Contents

The information in this book is up-to-date at the time of publication. The Educational Testing Service may have instituted changes in the test after this book was published. Please read carefully all material you receive from this organization regarding the GRE exam.

If there are any important late-breaking developments—or any changes or corrections to the Kaplan test preparation materials in this book—we will post that information online at **kaptest.com/publishing**. Check to see if there is any information posted there regarding this book.

# Important Test Changes

**E**ffective October 1, 2002, the GRE General Test will no longer include the multiple-choice Analytical section. **The multiple-choice Analytical section will be replaced by a mandatory Analytical Writing Measure (AWM) essay section.** The multiple-choice Verbal and Quantitative sections will remain unchanged.

The AWM—currently offered as a separate, optional exam called the Analytical Writing Assessment (AWA)—consists of two essays: one requiring the test taker to express and support a position on an issue, and one requiring the test taker to critique the logic of an argument.

Unlike the Verbal and Quantitative sections, the AWM will not use computer scoring. Instead, the essays will be scored by two readers, using a 6-point holistic scale. While you will still receive your unofficial Verbal and Quantitative scores at the test center, you will not receive your AWM score for 10–15 days following the test administration.

## If you are taking the GRE General Test BEFORE October 1, 2002

### Test Format

| | |
|---|---|
| Verbal | 30 minutes<br>30 multiple-choice questions |
| Quantitative | 45 minutes<br>28 multiple-choice questions |
| Analytical | 60 minutes<br>35 multiple-choice questions |

### Your Study Materials

- All of the chapters, exercises, and appendixes in this book
- The paper-based GRE Practice Test in this book
- All of the practice tests and exercises on the CD-ROM

# If you are taking the GRE General Test ON or AFTER October 1, 2002

## Test Format

| | |
|---|---|
| Verbal | 30 minutes |
| | 30 multiple-choice questions |
| Quantitative | 45 minutes |
| | 28 multiple-choice questions |
| Analytical Writing Measure (AWM) | 75 minutes |
| | 2 essay questions |

## Your Study Materials

- All of the chapters, exercises, and appendixes in this book EXCEPT Chapter 4, "Test Content: Analytical"
- Chapter 8, "The GRE Writing Assessment," can be used to prepare for the new Analytical Writing Measure, which is identical to the old Analytical Writing Assessment
- Section One and Section Two of the paper-based GRE Practice Test in this book
- The Verbal and Quantitative practice tests and exercises on the CD-ROM
- The special Analytical Writing Measure document (GRE AWM.pdf) on the CD-ROM

# About the Authors

**Eric Goodman** has been teaching the Kaplan GRE, GMAT, and LSAT courses for over a decade and also works for Kaplan as a product consultant. When not teaching or writing for Kaplan, Eric works as a composer and musician in New York City.

**Ingrid Multhopp** is Senior Curriculum Manager for Kaplan's Graduate Programs, where she has worked extensively on Kaplan's GRE, GMAT, and LSAT courses, researching changes to the tests and developing effective and innovative test-taking strategies. Before writing curriculum for Kaplan, she spent nine years teaching thousands of students how to score high on the GRE and get into the graduate schools of their choice. She has taken the CAT version of the GRE many times and always scored in the ninety-ninth percentile. She graduated from the University of Chicago with a B.A. in English Language and Literature.

**Ray Ojserkis** is Manager of GRE and GMAT Curriculum for Kaplan. During his tenure at Kaplan, he has researched the GRE extensively, and trained many students seeking entrance to graduate programs in classes and one-to-one sessions. He has a B.S. in Economics from Lehigh University, and a Masters and a Doctorate in International History from the London School of Economics and Political Science. He lives in New York City.

**Bob Verini** is currently Director of Academic Excellence for the western United States and a national training associate for Kaplan Educational Centers. Since joining Kaplan in 1980, Bob has taught thousands of students how to ace the GRE. He also trains new Kaplan instructors nationally, works in course development, and serves as academic counselor in Kaplan's one-on-one Admissions Consulting program. He holds a B.A. from SUNY/Albany and an M.F.A. from Indiana University. In his spare time, Bob is a writer, actor, and director, with several films and extensive stage experience to his credit. He is also one of the biggest money winners in the history of the game show *Jeopardy*™ and was a winner of the 1987 Tournament of Champions.

# Readers' Comments

Here's what some of our readers have to say about previous editions of Kaplan's *GRE Exam*:

"I never would have scored so well on my first computer adaptive test without the chance Kaplan gave me to practice taking them. Getting used to the timer, the types of questions, even just training to sit at the screen and test for three full hours made a positive difference in my ability to take the GRE."
—*Sarah Whitesel, Annapolis, Maryland*

"I feel prepared to take the GRE. The CD-ROM was entertaining and informative. Thank you for having the book and CD-ROM available. Peace of mind before a test is priceless."
—*Karen Mosher, Rowlett, Texas*

"A big thank you to the support staff at the Kaplan Test program. With your help, via the GRE preparation book and CD-ROM, I was able to get a good score in the GRE test that I took in September 2001."
—*Saty Satyamuri, P.E., Grand Prairie, Texas*

"All explanations were incredibly easy to understand, and the relaxed language of the book actually made it an enjoyable read. Thank you!"
—*Kim D'Ardenne, Roswell, Georgia*

"I loved this book. It raised two of my scores up approximately 200 points after studying from it. Thanks, Kaplan. I knew just what to expect from the test on test day."
—*Marla Ross, Dieppe, New Brunswick, Canada*

"I felt completely prepared for the test. My computer scores were much higher than I had anticipated. I felt confident—when I am usually a nervous test taker! Thank you!"
—*Andrea L. Walton, Somers Point, New Jersey*

# How to Use This Book

## The Classic Plan

Ideally, you should take a couple of months to work through the book and CD-ROM in this package, though it's certainly possible to do so in far less time. Below you'll find some suggestions as to how you can effectively use both the book and CD-ROM in your GRE exam preparation. (Refer to the installation instructions at the back of this book for help in installing the software.)

1. On the CD-ROM, fill out the student profile and take the diagnostic test. This will allow the software to assign you a personalized study plan that is customized to your individual needs. Follow this study plan as you work through the interactive lessons and practice tests, review the reference sections and flashcards, and play games that will help reinforce the skills you'll need to perform well on the GRE.

2. Read through each chapter in the book completely, learning from the example problems and trying the practice sets at the end of each chapter. Spend sufficient time reviewing the questions you get wrong by reading carefully through the explanations to the practice set questions at the end of each Test Content section.

3. Study the appendixes at the back of the book for help with word roots and important math concepts.

4. Read the "Test Mechanics" and "Test Mentality" chapters to set the stage for your training and testing success.

5. Take a full-length practice test under strictly timed conditions. You can take the Practice Test in the book or one of the full-length CATs on the CD-ROM, depending on your preference.

6. Score your Practice Test. Find out where you need help and then review the appropriate chapters and/or appendixes in the book, as well as the lessons on the CD-ROM.

7. Try your luck at section tests and the other CATs on the CD-ROM. Repeat the process of reviewing your areas of weakness.

8. Give yourself a day of rest right before the real exam.

## Note

The GRE is changing! To determine how this will affect your study plan, see page vii.

If you have time, do just two or three chapters and/or CD-ROM practice lessons a week, and let the material sink in slowly. Don't hesitate to take some time off from your GRE preparation when you need to. Nobody can take this stuff day in and day out for weeks at a time without a break.

## The Emergency Plan

Maybe you have only two or three weeks—or even less time than that. Don't freak! Kaplan's *GRE Exam* has been designed to work for students in your situation, too. If you go through a chapter or two every day, you can finish this book in a couple of weeks. If you have limited time to prepare for the GRE (fewer than six weeks), we suggest you do the following:

1. Take a slow, deep breath. Read the "Test Mechanics" and "Test Mentality" chapters to set the stage for your training and testing success.

2. Fill out the student profile on the CD-ROM and follow the personalized study plan which is customized to your individual needs and time constraints.

3. Based on your performance on the first practice test you take and the requirements of the graduate programs to which you are applying, concentrate your review on those areas of greatest need. Keep your eyes on the ultimate prize—study only those Test Content chapters you need to in order to maximize your score and get into the program of your choice.

4. Look at the important math concepts, grouped by level of difficulty, in Appendix B. Review any Level 1 or Level 2 math concepts you don't know.

5. Take as many of the Practice Tests as you can—especially those on the CD-ROM—under timed conditions.

6. Review your results, paying special attention to the questions you missed.

7. Give yourself the day before the test off.

To help keep you on track, we've placed a Highlights box containing the most important test concepts at the beginning of each Test Content chapter. You'll also find important points regarding the GRE and invaluable Kaplan teacher advice in easy-to-read sidebars throughout the book.

# A Special Note for International Students

About a quarter million international students pursue advanced academic degrees at the master's or Ph.D. level at U.S. universities each year. This trend of pursuing higher education in the United States, particularly at the graduate level, is expected to continue. Business, management, engineering, and the physical and life sciences are popular areas of study for students coming to the United States from other countries. Along with these academic options, international students are also taking advantage of opportunities for research grants, teaching assistantships, and practical training or work experience in U.S. graduate departments.

If you are not from the United States, but are considering attending a graduate program at a university in the United States, here is what you'll need to get started.

- If English is not your first language, start there. You will probably need to take the Test of English as a Foreign Language (TOEFL) or show some other evidence that you're proficient in English prior to gaining admission to a graduate program. Graduate programs will vary on what is an acceptable TOEFL score. For degrees in business, journalism, management, or the humanities, a minimum TOEFL score of 600 (250 on the computer-based TOEFL) or better is expected. For the hard sciences and computer technology, a TOEFL score of 550 (213 on the computer-based TOEFL) is a common minimum requirement.

- You may also need to take the Graduate Record Exam (GRE).

- Since admission to many graduate programs is quite competitive, you may want to select three or four programs you would like to attend and complete applications for each program.

- Selecting the correct graduate school is very different from selecting a suitable undergraduate institution. You should research the qualifications and interests of faculty members teaching and doing research in your chosen field. Look for professors who share your specialty.

- You need to begin the application process at least a year in advance. Be aware that many programs offer only August or September start dates. Find out application deadlines and plan accordingly.

- Finally, you will need to obtain an 1-20 Certificate of Eligibility in order to obtain an F-1 Student Visa to study in the United States.

# Kaplan International Programs

If you need more help with the complex process of graduate school admissions, or assistance preparing for the TOEFL or GRE, you may be interested in Kaplan's programs for international students.

Kaplan International Programs were designed to help students and professionals from outside the United States meet their educational and career goals. At locations throughout the United States, international students take advantage of Kaplan's programs to help them improve their academic and conversational English skills, raise their scores on the TOEFL, GRE, and other standardized exams, and gain admission to the schools of their choice. Our staff and instructors give international students the individualized instruction they need to succeed. Here is a brief description of some of Kaplan's programs for international students:

### General Intensive English

Kaplan's General Intensive English classes are designed to help you improve your skills in all areas of English and to increase your fluency in spoken and written English. Classes are available for beginning to advanced students, and the average class size is 12 students.

### TOEFL and Academic English

This course provides you with the skills you need to improve your TOEFL score and succeed in an American university or graduate program. It includes advanced reading, writing, listening, grammar and conversational English. You will also receive training for the TOEFL using Kaplan's exclusive computer-based practice materials.

## GRE Test Preparation Course

The Graduate Record Exam (GRE) is required for admission to many graduate programs in the United States. Nearly one-half million people take the GRE each year. A high score can help you stand out from other test takers. This course includes the skills you need to succeed on each section of the GRE, as well as access to Kaplan's exclusive computer-based practice materials.

## Other Kaplan Programs

Since 1938, more than 3 million students have come to Kaplan to advance their studies, prepare for entry to American universities, and further their careers. In addition to the above programs, Kaplan offers courses to prepare for the SAT, GMAT, LSAT, MCAT, DAT, USMLE, NCLEX, and other standardized exams at locations throughout the United States.

## Applying to Kaplan International Programs

To get more information, or to apply for admission to any of Kaplan's programs for international students and professionals, contact us at:

Kaplan International Programs
700 South Flower, Suite 2900
Los Angeles, CA 90017  USA
Phone (if calling from within the United States): 800-818-9128
Phone (if calling from outside the United States): 213-452-5800
Fax: 213-892-1364
Website: www.kaplaninternational.com
Email: world@kaplan.com

Kaplan is authorized under federal law to enroll nonimmigrant alien students.

Kaplan is authorized to issue Form IAP-66 needed for a J-1 (Exchange Visitor) visa.

Kaplan is accredited by ACCET (Accrediting Council for Continuing Education and Training).

Test names are registered trademarks of their respective owners.

# Getting a Higher Score on the GRE

# CHAPTER ONE

# An Introduction to the GRE

## HIGHLIGHTS

- Understand how the GRE CAT is constructed
- Get acquainted with the Kaplan Three-Level Master Plan

This test preparation section will explain more than just a few basic strategies. It will cover practically everything that's ever on the GRE.
No kidding.

We can do this because we don't explain questions in isolation or focus on particular problems. Instead, we explain the underlying principles behind all of the questions on the GRE. What a particular question is *really* testing. We give you the big picture.

## Understanding the GRE CAT

One of the keys to getting the big picture is knowing how the test is constructed. Why should you care how the GRE is constructed? Because if you understand the difficulties that the people at ETS have when they make this test, you'll understand what it is you have to do to overcome it. As someone famous once said, "Know thine enemy." And you need to know firsthand the way this test is put together if you want to take it apart.

**Kaplan Tip**

You can't cram for the GRE, but you can prepare for it by learning to think the GRE way.

**Note**

About half a million people take the GRE each year. By reading the following chapters, you'll learn the underlying principles of GRE questions and acquire test strategies that will help increase your score.

Before you begin, though, remember that the test makers sometimes change the content, administration, and scheduling of the GRE too quickly for a published guide to keep up with. For the latest, up-to-the-minute news about the GRE, contact Kaplan's Website at kaptest.com, or use AOL keyword: Kaplan.

### The Secret Code

There is a sort of unwritten formula at the heart of the GRE. First, there's psychometrics, a peculiar kind of science used to write standardized tests. Also, ETS bases its questions on a certain body of knowledge, which doesn't change. ETS tests the same concepts in every GRE. The useful thinking skills and shortcuts that succeed on one exam—the exam that you're signing up to take, for instance—have already succeeded and will continue to succeed, time and time again.

### Play the Game

If you're like the authors of this book, you weren't too crazy about the idea of taking the SAT back in high school. It seemed unfair that our entire future—where we went to college and where that took us after—would be based on our performance on an unfeeling exam one dreary Saturday morning. Some of us weren't too crazy about our GPAs, which we could no longer do much about.

There are a great many people who think of these exams as cruel exercises in futility, as the oppressive instruments of a faceless societal machine. People who think this way usually don't do very well on these tests.

The key discovery that people who ace standardized tests have made, though, is that fighting the machine doesn't hurt it. If that's what you choose to do, you will just waste your energy. So, instead, they choose to think of the test as a game. Not an instrument of punishment, but an opportunity for reward. And like any game, if you play it enough times, you get really good at it.

### Acquire the Skills

You may think that the GRE isn't fair or decent, but that attitude won't help you get into graduate school.

None of the GRE experts who work at Kaplan were *born* acing the GRE. No one is. That's because these tests do not measure innate skills; they measure *acquired* skills. People who are good at standardized tests are, quite simply, people who've already acquired the necessary skills. Maybe they acquired them in math class, or by reading a lot, or by studying logic in college, or perhaps the easiest way—in one of Kaplan's GRE classes. But they have, perhaps without realizing it, acquired the skills that bring success on tests like the GRE. And if *you* haven't, you have nothing whatsoever to feel bad about. You simply must acquire them now.

**Kaplan Tip**

By learning how the GRE is created, you can better understand how to beat it.

**Kaplan Tip**

Think of the GRE as a game—one that you can improve at the more times you play.

**Kaplan Tip**

Standardized tests measure acquired skills. The people who succeed on them are those who have acquired the skills that the test measures.

## Same Problems—but Different

We know it sounds incredible, but it's true: The test makers use the same problems on every GRE. Only the words and the numbers change. They test the same principles over and over.

Here's an example: This is a type of math problem known as a Quantitative Comparison. Look familiar? These are also on the SAT. Your job is to pick (A) if the term in Column A is bigger, (B) if the term in Column B is bigger, (C) if they're equal, or (D) if there is not enough information given to solve the problem.

| Column A | Column B |
|----------|----------|
| $2x^2 = 32$ | |
| $x$ | 4 |

Most people answer (C), that they're equal. They divide both sides of the equation by 2 and then take the square root of both sides.

Wrong. The answer isn't (C), because $x$ doesn't have to be 4. It could be 4 *or* –4. Both work. If you just solve for 4 you'll get this problem—and every one like it—wrong. ETS figures that if you get burned here, you'll get burned again next time. Only next time it won't be $2x^2 = 32$; it will be $y^2 = 36$ or $s^4 = 81$.

The concepts that are tested on any particular GRE—Pythagorean triangles, simple logic, word relationships, and so forth—are the underlying concepts at the heart of *every* GRE.

Basically, every GRE is the same as every other one administered that year. In fact, the GREs being given today are extremely similar to those given a decade ago. For instance, most of the math problems you are going to get on the test that you've signed up for are just superficially different from the math problems that have been on every other GRE. To guarantee scores that are almost perfectly consistent, ETS writes tests that are almost perfectly consistent.

## Why Don't They Just Start Testing Something New?

If ETS started testing different principles, it would have to compromise score consistency. Even when it makes very minor changes in test structure or content, it does so between school years, introducing the revisions in October, so that everyone who takes the exam that school year has the same kind of test. That's important, because it means that Kaplan knows what every GRE is going to look like, before it's administered.

### Note

The GRE tests the same principles over and over. Every GRE is virtually the same as every other one because the tests must be consistent from year to year to yield dependable results.

### Teacher Tip

"Students have to become aware of all the common mistakes that can be made on a question. If they do this, they will be more careful not to make these errors."
—Derek Veazey
Fort Worth, Texas

ETS makes these minor changes only after testing them exhaustively. This process is called *norming*, which means taking a normal test and a changed test and administering them to a random group of students. As long as the group is large enough for the purposes of statistical validity and the students get consistent scores from one test to the next, then the revised test is just as valid and consistent as any other GRE.

That may sound technical, but norming is actually quite an easy process. We do it at Kaplan all the time—for the tests that we write for our students. The test at the back of this book, for instance, is a normed exam.

### They Like Their Test

Another major reason they don't rework most or all of the GRE is that they think it's really a pretty good test. (We know what you're thinking.) To be more specific, they feel that the GRE tests what it's designed to test: various fundamental concepts of algebra, geometry, verbal ability, reasoning ability, and so on. So what if people learn all those principles and get better at the test? That doesn't mean the test is rotten. Quite the opposite: To improve your score, you have to learn a lot of important things.

### Let Them Think That

If ETS and the Graduate School Admissions Council want you to learn a bunch of simple concepts and improve your vocabulary, why fight it?

We don't think any of Kaplan's students, after they took the GRE, ever said to themselves, "Now that it's all over, I just wish I hadn't learned all that vocabulary!" Let's face it, none of us would mind being able to read dense, confusing material better and faster. Or being more logical and analytical thinkers. Or improving our vocabulary.

All those things are good things, and they translate into success on the day of the test. The first step is to take a close look at the setup of this test that you'll be taking.

## Kaplan Tip

Your opinion of the test doesn't matter. Your score on it does.

## The Sections

The GRE computer-adaptive test (CAT) consists of three scored sections, with different amounts of time allotted for you to complete each section:

| VERBAL | |
|---|---|
| Time | 30 minutes |
| Format | 30 questions |
| | Question types include: Analogies, sentence completion, antonyms, and reading comprehension |
| Content | Tests vocabulary, verbal reasoning skills, and the ability to read with understanding and insight |

| QUANTITATIVE | |
|---|---|
| Time | 45 minutes |
| Format | 28 questions |
| | Question types include: Problem solving, quantitative comparison, and graph problems |
| Content | Tests basic mathematical skills, ability to understand mathematical concepts, and quantitative reasoning skills |

| ANALYTICAL | |
|---|---|
| Time | 60 minutes |
| Format | 35 questions |
| | Question types include: Logical reasoning and logic games |
| Content | Tests ability to understand and analyze arguments and to understand and draw logical conclusions |

### Note

Starting October 1, 2002, the multiple-choice Analytical section will be replaced by the **Analytical Writing Measure** essay section. See chapter 8 for more info on the essay section.

You'll get a one-minute break after each section, and an optional 10-minute break in the middle of the test. There are also up to two non-scored sections: an Experimental section and a "Research" section.

The Experimental section is unscored. That means that if you could identify the Experimental section, you could doodle for half an hour, guess in a random pattern, or daydream and still get exactly the same score on the GRE. However, the Experimental section is disguised to look like a real section—there is no way to identify it. All you will really know on the day of the test is that one of the subject areas will have two sections instead of one.

Naturally, many people try to figure out which section is Experimental. But because ETS really wants you to try hard on it, they do their best to keep you guessing. If you guess wrong you could blow the whole test, so we urge you to treat all sections as scored unless you are told otherwise. (Besides, a nap in the middle of the test is pretty unlikely to help you one way or the other.)

The Research section on the CAT is also unscored, and is not always included in the GRE. If you see a Research section on Test Day, ETS will be kind enough to tell you when it appears. So there is no reason whatsoever for you to complete it, unless you feel like doing ETS a favor, or unless they offer you some reward (which they have been known to do).

## Pointing and Clicking

The computer on which you will take the GRE has a keyboard and a mouse. You won't use the keyboard to answer questions; instead, you will use the mouse to point at your answer choices and "click" to select them. Also, the test makes use of computer functions, such as HELP and QUIT, which may take some getting used to. For these reasons, make sure you go through the information in the Test Mechanics chapter carefully.

## Test Registration

You should first obtain a copy of the *GRE Registration Bulletin*. This booklet contains information on scheduling, pricing, repeat testing, cancellation policies, and more. You can receive the booklet by calling the Educational Testing Service at (609) 771-7670, or by downloading it from www.gre.org.

To register for and schedule your GRE General Test, use one of the options below.

---

**Kaplan Tip**

Don't try to figure out which section of your test is experimental. Even if you guess right, it can hurt your score. If you guess wrong . . .

**Note**

You can't score higher than 800 or lower than 200 on any of the three sections (Verbal, Quantitative, and Analytical).

---

**KAPLAN**

## Register by Phone

Call (800) GRE-CALL or (800) 529-3590 (TTY). A confirmation number, reporting time, and test center location will be given to you when you call. Though you can register by phone up to two days before the exam, registering earlier is strongly recommended since spaces often fill quickly. Payments can be made with a VISA, MasterCard, or American Express card.

## Register by Mail

Complete the Authorization Voucher Request Form found in the *GRE Registration Bulletin*. Mail the request form, along with your payment (by check or money order), to:

Computer-Based Testing Program
Graduate Record Examinations
Educational Testing Service
P.O. Box 6020
Princeton, NJ 08541-6020

ETS advises that you allow two to four weeks for processing before you receive your voucher in the mail. Vouchers are valid for one year from the date of issue.

# Scoring

Each of the three sections on the GRE yields a scaled score within a range of 200 to 800. You cannot score higher than 800 on any one section, no matter how hard you try! Similarly, it's impossible (again, no matter how hard you try) to have a score lower than 200 on any of the three sections. Scaled scores are much like the old scores that you received if you took the SAT, the major difference being the addition of a score for the Analytical measure, which isn't tested on the SAT.

But you don't receive *only* scaled scores. You will also receive a percentile rank, which will place your performance relative to those of a large sample population of other GRE takers. Percentile scores tell graduate schools just what your scaled scores are worth. For instance, even if everyone got very high scaled scores, universities would still be able to differentiate candidates by their percentile score.

Percentile ranks match with scaled scores differently, depending on the measure. Let's imagine that our founder, Stanley H. Kaplan, were to take the GRE this year. He would (no doubt) get a perfect 800 on each measure type, but that would translate into different percentile ranks. In Verbal, he'd

### Definition

The **percentile figure** tells you how many other test takers scored at or below your level. In other words, a percentile figure of 80 means than 80 percent did as well or worse than you did and that only 20 percent did better.

be scoring above 99 percent of the population, so that would be his percentile rank. But in the Quantitative and Analytical sections, many other people will score very high as well. Difficult as these sections may seem, so many people score so well on them that high scaled scores are no big deal. Mr. Kaplan's percentile rank for Quantitative, even if he doesn't miss a single question, would be in only the 96th percentile. So many other people are scoring that high in Quantitative that no one can score above the 96th percentile! Similarly, his Analytical percentile would be 98th.

What this means is that it's pretty easy to get good scaled scores on the GRE and much harder to get good percentile ranks. A Quantitative score of 600, for example, is actually not all that good; if you are applying to science or engineering programs, it would be a handicap at most schools. Even a score of 700 in Quantitative is relatively low for many very selective programs in the sciences or engineering—after all, it's only the 79th or 80th percentile.

The relative frequency of high scaled scores means that universities pay great attention to percentile rank. What you need to realize is that scores that seemed good to you when you took the SAT might not be all that good on the GRE. It's important that you do some real research into the programs you're thinking about. Many schools have cut-off scores below which they don't even consider applicants. But be careful! If a school tells you they look for applicants scoring 600 average per section, that doesn't mean they think those are good scores. That 600 may be the baseline. You owe it to yourself to find out what kinds of scores *impress* the schools you're interested in and work hard until you get those scores. You can definitely get there if you want to and if you work hard enough. We see it every day.

A final note about percentile rank: The sample population that you are compared against in order to determine your percentile is not everyone else who takes the test the same day as you do. ETS doesn't want to penalize an unlucky candidate who takes the GRE on a date when everyone else happens to be a rocket scientist. So they compare your performance with those of a random three-year population of recent GRE test takers. Your score will not in any way be affected by the other people who take the exam on the same day as you. We often tell our students, "Your only competition in this classroom is yourself."

## Canceling

When you finish the GRE you will be given the opportunity to cancel your scores, but the only time you can cancel is immediately after the test. That's the only chance you'll have, because if you don't cancel your scores they will be recorded immediately as they are given to you. If you do cancel, you won't be able to undo it.

## The Kaplan Three-Level Master Plan

To give your best performance on the GRE, you'll need to have the right kind of approach for the entire test as a whole. We've developed a plan to help you, which we call (cleverly enough) "The Kaplan Three-Level Master Plan for the GRE." You should use this plan as your guide to preparing for and taking the GRE. The three levels of the plan are: test content, test mechanics, and test mentality.

### Level 1: Test Content

In the first part of the test prep section, we'll talk about how to deal with individual short verbal questions, reading passages, math problems, logic games, and logical reasoning questions. For success on the GRE, you'll need to understand how to work through each of these question types. What's the difference between antonym and analogy questions? What are the best ways of handling each? What's a sentence completion and how do I approach it? How should I read a reading comprehension passage and what should I focus on? What's the best way to approach the math section? Is there a secret to logic games? How do I solve logical reasoning questions? Our instruction in Level 1 will provide you with all of the information, strategies, and techniques you'll need to answer these questions and more.

### Level 2: Test Mechanics

Next, we'll move up the ladder from individual question types to a discussion of how to handle the GRE's unique computer-adaptive testing format. We'll reveal the test mechanics that will help you to use the strategies you learned in Level 1 to maximum effect.

### Level 3: Test Mentality

On this final level, we'll help you pull everything you've learned together. By combining the question strategies and test mechanics, you'll be in control of the entire test experience. With a good test mentality, you can have everything at your fingertips—from building good bridges to gridding techniques, from sequencing game strategies to pacing methods. We'll also outline all of the subtle attitudinal factors that will help you perform your absolute best on the day of the test.

Understanding the three levels, and how they interrelate, is the first step in taking control of the GRE. We'll start, in the next chapter, with the first level: test content.

---

**Teacher Tip**

"Learn the process of question creation. Always ask, 'why did the test maker do it this way?' when going over explanations. And don't forget that the test is only a part (albeit an important part) of the overall application experience."
—Chris Skinner
Santa Barbara, California

---

**Kaplan Rules**

The three levels of the Kaplan Master Plan are:

1. Test content
2. Test mechanics
3. Test mentality

# CHAPTER TWO

# Test Content: Verbal

## HIGHLIGHTS

- Study the Kaplan Word Families and the Top 100 GRE Words
- Learn the Basic Principles and the Kaplan Method for answering Sentence Completions, Analogies, Antonyms, and Reading Comp questions
- Focus on the different types of Reading Comp questions and targeted strategies for answering each type
- Complete the Verbal Practice Set

In this chapter and the two chapters that follow, we'll give you the nuts and bolts of GRE preparation—the strategies and techniques for each of the individual question types on the test. For each of the multiple-choice sections—Verbal, Quantitative, and Analytical—we'll present you with the following:

- **Directions and General Information**
  The specific directions for each section will introduce you to the question types. We'll also give you some ground rules for each question type.

- **Basic Principles**
  These are the general rules-of-thumb that you need to follow to succeed on this section.

- **Common Question Types**
  Certain types of questions appear repeatedly on each section. We'll show you what these question types are and how best to deal with each one.

**Kaplan Tip**

The Verbal section tests your vocabulary and your ability to read passages quickly and efficiently.

### At a Glance

There are four types of verbal questions:

- Sentence completions
- Analogies
- Antonyms
- Reading comprehension

- **The Kaplan Method**

  This is a step-by-step way of organizing your work on every question in the section. The Kaplan Method will allow you to orchestrate all of the individual strategies and techniques into a flexible, powerful modus operandi.

Now let's begin with an important part of the GRE, the Verbal Section. You'll have 30 minutes to complete 30 questions, which are broken down into four types: sentence completion, analogies, reading comprehension, and antonyms. The chart below shows roughly how many questions correspond to each question type and how much time you should spend on each question type.

|  | SENTENCE COMPLETION | ANALOGIES | READING COMPREHENSION | ANTONYMS |
|---|---|---|---|---|
| Number of Questions | about 6 | about 7 | about 8 | about 9 |
| Time per Question | 20–45 seconds | 30–45 seconds | > 1 minute | 30 seconds |

The computer determines the sequence and difficulty of the questions, so you will not be able to tell what sort of question you will get next, or how hard it will be.

There are two basic things that the Verbal section tests: your vocabulary and your ability to read a particular kind of passage quickly and efficiently. You may have wondered how the material we covered earlier about test construction is going to help you in the GRE Verbal sections. Well, just like the math questions, which are the same from test to test (just with different numbers), the verbal questions are the same (just with different words). Have you ever heard the expression, "That's an SAT word"? It's a commonly used phrase among high school students, and it refers to any member of a very particular class of prefixed and suffixed words derived from Latin or Greek. For instance, *profligate* is a great SAT word. It's also a great GRE word.

# Vocabulary—the Most Basic Principle for Verbal Success

Many of the same kinds of words that would commonly show up on the SAT are likely candidates for the GRE as well, though GRE words tend to be harder.

The GRE tests the same kinds of words over and over again. (Remember, for ETS, consistency is key.) We'll call these words "GRE words," and we're going to make a point of including them in the rest of this chapter. That way, you can get a feel for what they look and sound like, and you can see them used in context. So if you see a word in this book that's unfamiliar, take a moment to look it up in the dictionary and reread the sentence with the word's definition in mind. Learning words in context is one of the best ways for the brain to retain their meanings.

The GRE words used in context in this vocabulary section will appear in **boldface.** Look them up while you read. We'll give you an example of what we mean by "the same kinds of words over and over again." The words in the list below all mean nearly the same thing. They all have something to do with the concept of criticism, a concept often tested on the GRE. The GRE that you take could well test you on one of these words or one of the other synonyms for *criticize.* A great way to prepare for GRE Vocabulary, then, is to learn which word concepts are tested most frequently and learn all those words.

### Kaplan Tip

The same kinds of vocabulary words that you saw on the SAT may well appear on your GRE.

CRITICIZE/CRITICISM
calumny
castigate
chastise
deride/derisive
derogate
diatribe
harangue
lambaste
oppugn
pillory
rebuke
remonstrate

### Kaplan Rules

Learning words in context is a good way to retain their meanings.

On the test, for instance, you might see an antonym question like this:

REMONSTRATE:

- (A) show
- (B) atone
- (C) vouchsafe
- (D) laud
- (E) undo

Or an analogy question that looks something like this:

VITUPERATE : DISPARAGE ::

- (A) profligate : bilk
- (B) equivocate : reduce
- (C) parody : excuse
- (D) lie : prevaricate
- (E) brave : succeed

There are many such families of word synonyms whose members appear frequently on the GRE. We'll run across more as we proceed.

## What You Need to Know

The GRE does not test whether you know exactly what a particular word means. If you have only an idea what the word means, you will get just as many points for that question as you will if you know the precise dictionary definition of the word. That's because ETS isn't interested in finding out whether you're a walking dictionary. They want to see if you have a broad and diverse (but, of course, classically based) vocabulary.

## 20% × 500 > 100% × 50

This means, simply, that it's better to know 20 percent of the definition of 500 words than it is to know the exact definition of 50 words. Or, more generally put, it's better to know a little bit about a lot of words than to know a lot about just a few. In fact, it's a lot better. And it's a lot easier.

## Thesaurus > Dictionary

The *criticize* family is not the only family of synonyms whose members appear frequently on the GRE. There are plenty of others. And lists of synonyms are much easier to learn than many words in isolation. So don't learn words with a dictionary; learn them with a thesaurus. Make synonym index cards based on the common families of GRE words (listed at the end of this chapter) and **peruse** those lists periodically. It's like weight-lifting for vocabulary. Pretty soon you will start to see results.

If you think this might be **fallacious,** then check this out. The words in the list below all have something to do with the concept of falsehood. Their precise meanings vary: *erroneous* means "incorrect," whereas ***mendacious*** means "lying." But unless you're shooting for a very high verbal score (720 or higher), you don't need to know the exact meanings of these words. You will most likely get the question right if you simply know that these words have something to do with the concept of falsehood.

FALSE

| | |
|---|---|
| apocryphal | guile |
| dissemble | mendacious |
| duplicity | mendacity |
| equivocate | prevaricate |
| equivocation | prevarication |
| erroneous | specious |
| ersatz | spurious |
| fallacious | |

The way that you should use a list like this is to look it over once or twice a week for 30 seconds every week until the test. If you don't have much time until the exam date, look over your lists more frequently. Then, by the day of the test, you should have a rough idea of what most of the words on your lists mean. If you get an antonym question such as:

HONESTY:

- Ⓐ displeasure
- Ⓑ mendacity
- Ⓒ disrepute
- Ⓓ resolution
- Ⓔ failure

you might not know exactly what **mendacity** means, but you'll know that it's "one of those *false* words," which will be enough to get the question right. Your subconscious mind has done most of the work for you!

It might be **vexatious** to learn word meanings the slow way, but you'll be amazed how easy and **facile** vocabulary building can be when you do it this way. Here are some more word families:

| ANNOY | BEGINNER | FOUL |
|---|---|---|
| aggravate | acolyte | festering |
| irk | neophyte | fetid |
| irritate | novice | fulsome |
| perturb | proselyte | invidious |
| vex | tyro | noisome |

You may not know exactly what **invidious** means, but if you study the last list, pretty soon you will know that it refers to something foul.

We're now going to give you a lot of common GRE words grouped together by meaning. This isn't high-stress learning. All you have to do is make flash cards from these lists and look over your cards a few times a week from now until the day of the test. You'll find that your subconscious mind does much of the work for you.

## Kaplan Word Families

Note: The categories in which these words are listed are general and should not be understood as the exact definitions of the words.

DIFFICULT TO
UNDERSTAND
abstruse
arcane
enigmatic
esoteric
inscrutable
obscure
opaque
rarefied
recondite
turbid

DEBAUCHED/
DEBAUCHERY
bacchanalian
depraved
dissipated
iniquity
libertine
libidinous
licentious
reprobate
ribald
salacious
sordid
turpitude

CRITICIZE/CRITICISM
aspersion
belittle
berate
calumny
castigate
decry
defamation
deride/derisive
diatribe
disparage
excoriate
gainsay
harangue
impugn
inveigh
lambaste
obloquy
objurgate
opprobrium
pillory
rebuke
remonstrate
reprehend
reprove
revile
vituperate

PRAISE
accolade
aggrandize
encomium
eulogize
extol
laud/laudatory
venerate/veneration

## FALSEHOOD
apocryphal
dissemble
duplicity
equivocate
equivocation
erroneous
ersatz
fallacious
guile
mendacious/mendacity
prevaricate
prevarication
specious
spurious

## BITING (as in wit or temperament)
acerbic
acidulous
acrimonious
asperity
caustic
mordant
mordacious
trenchant

## RENDER USELESS/ WEAKEN
enervate
obviate
stultify
undermine
vitiate

## HARMFUL
baleful
baneful
deleterious
inimical
injurious
insidious
minatory
perfidious
pernicious

## TIMID/TIMIDITY
craven
diffident
pusillanimous
recreant
timorous
trepidation

## STUBBORN
froward
implacable
inexorable
intractable
intransigent
obdurate
obstinate
pertinacious
recalcitrant
refractory
renitent
untoward

## BEGINNING/YOUNG
burgeoning
callow
inchoate
incipient
nascent

## Kaplan Tip

Make flash cards from these lists and look over your cards a few times a week from now until the day of the test.

## OVERBLOWN/WORDY
bombastic
circumlocution
garrulous
grandiloquent
loquacious
periphrastic
prolix
turgid

## HOSTILE/ONE WHO IS HOSTILE
antithetic
churlish
curmudgeon
irascible
malevolent
misanthropic
truculent
vindictive

## CLICHÉD/BORING
banal
fatuous
hackneyed
insipid
mundane
pedestrian
platitude
prosaic
quotidian
trite

## Kaplan Tip

Lists of synonyms are easier to learn than long lists of unrelated words.

## The Top 100
While we're at it, here, gathered together for easy reference, are the 100 difficult words that appear most frequently on the GRE. You will notice that many of these words are also in the preceding lists of word families.

1. Equivocal/Equivocate/Equivocation—ambiguous, open to two interpretations
2. Tractable (Intractable)—obedient, yielding
3. Placate (Implacable)—to soothe or pacify
4. Miser—person who is extremely stingy
5. Engender—to produce, cause, bring out
6. Dogma(tic)(tism)(tist)—rigidly fixed in opinion, opinionated
7. Garrulous (Garrulity)—very talkative
8. Homogeneous (Homogenize)—composed of identical parts
9. Laconic—using few words
10. Quiescence (Quiescent)—inactivity, stillness
11. Anomalous—irregular or deviating from the norm
12. Venerate (-ion)—to respect
13. Assuage—to make less severe, ease, relieve
14. Misanthrope (-ic)—person who hates human beings

15. Digress(ive)—to turn aside; to stray from the main point
16. Corroborate (-ion)—to confirm, verify
17. Buttress—to reinforce or support
18. Antipathy—dislike, hostility, extreme opposition or aversion
19. Disabuse—to free from error or misconception
20. Feigned (Unfeigned)—pretended
21. Banal(ity)—trite and overly common
22. Desiccate (-ion)—to dry completely, dehydrate
23. Diatribe—bitter verbal attack
24. Pedant(ic)(ry)—uninspired, boring academic
25. Guile(less)—trickery, deception
26. Eulogy (-ize)—high praise, often in public
27. Fawn(ing)—to flatter excessively, seek the favor of
28. Aberrant/Aberration—different from the usual or normal
29. Heresy/Heretic(al)—an act opposed to established religious orthodoxy
30. Obdurate—stubborn
31. Prevaricate (-ion)—to lie, evade the truth
32. Embellish(ment)—to ornament; make attractive with decoration or details; add details to a statement
33. Pragmatic/Pragmatism—practical; moved by facts rather than abstract ideals
34. Precipitate—to cause to happen; to throw down from a height
35. Proximity—nearness
36. Profundity—depth (usually depth of thought)
37. Adulterate—to corrupt or make impure
38. Sanction—permission, support; law; penalty
39. Ameliorate (-ion)—to make better, improve
40. Anachronism/Anachronistic—something chronologically inappropriate
41. Vindictive—spiteful, vengeful, unforgiving
42. Propitiate—to win over, appease
43. Aver—to declare to be true, affirm
44. Burgeon (-ing)—to sprout or flourish
45. Commensurate—proportional
46. Mitigate/Mitigation—to soften, or make milder
47. Culpability—guilt, responsibility for wrong
48. Specious(ness)—having a false appearance of truth; showy
49. Turpitude—inherent baseness, depravity
50. Diffident/Diffidence—shy, lacking confidence
51. Repudiate—to reject as having no authority
52. Discrete—individually distinct; consisting of unconnected elements

## Kaplan Tip

Pencil a check mark by each word you don't know. Quiz yourself on them, erasing check marks as you learn words.

53. Obviate—to make unnecessary; to anticipate and prevent
54. Dissemble—to pretend, disguise one's motives
55. Implacable—inflexible, incapable of being pleased
56. Emulate—to copy, imitate
57. Complaisance/Complaisant—disposition to please or comply
58. Enervate—to weaken, sap strength from
59. Latency—the condition of being present but hidden
60. Erudite (-ition)—learned, scholarly
61. Espouse—to support or advocate; to marry
62. Florid(ness)—gaudy, extremely ornate; ruddy, flushed
63. Occlude—to shut, block
64. Harangue—a ranting writing or speech; lecture
65. Hieroglyph(ic)—pictorial character
66. Iconoclast—one who attacks traditional beliefs
67. Impervious—impossible to penetrate; incapable of being affected
68. Efficacy/Efficacious—effectiveness, efficiency
69. Inchoate—imperfectly formed or formulated
70. Loquacity/Loquacious—talkative
71. Irascible (-ility)—easily angered
72. Ephemeral—momentary, transient, fleeting
73. Laudable (-tory)—deserving of praise
74. Insipid—bland, lacking flavor; lacking excitement
75. Magnanimity/Magnanimous—generosity
76. Precarious(ly)—uncertain
77. Endemic—belonging to a particular area; inherent
78. Mollify—to calm or make less severe
79. Rarefy/Rarefaction—to make thinner, purer, or more refined
80. Disinterest(ed)(edness)—unbiased; not interested
81. Foster—to nourish, cultivate, promote
82. Perennial—present throughout the years; persistent
83. Malevolent—ill-willed; causing evil or harm to others
84. Defer(ence)—to show respect or politeness in a submissive way
85. Precursor(y)—forerunner, predecessor
86. Lucid—clear and easily understood
87. Probity—honesty, high-mindedness
88. Abscond—to depart secretly
89. Propensity—inclination, tendency
90. Audacious—bold, daring, fearless
91. Wheedle—to influence or entice by flattery
92. Prudent—careful, cautious
93. Mundane—worldly; commonplace
94. Diffuse—widely spread out
95. Aggrandize—to make larger or greater in power

96. Decimate—to reduce drastically; to destroy a large part of
97. Succinct—terse, brief, concise
98. Enigma(tic)—a puzzle, something inexplicable
99. Unfettered—free, unrestrained
100. Ascetic—self-denying, abstinent, austere

## Roots

You knew that this dreaded word from grade school was going to come up sooner or later. Because GRE words are so heavily drawn from Latin and Greek, roots can be extremely useful, both in deciphering words with obscure meanings and in guessing intelligently.

Use the Kaplan Root List in the back of this book to pick up the most valuable GRE roots. Target these words in your vocabulary prep. Learn a few new roots a day, familiarizing yourself with the meaning.

## Learning Vocabulary

In review, the three best ways (in no particular order) to improve your GRE vocabulary are:

- Learning words in context
- Learning families of words
- Deciphering words by their roots

A broader vocabulary will serve you well on all four Verbal question types on the GRE. Now let's look at the four Verbal question types, starting with Sentence Completions.

### Kaplan Tip

The more roots you know, the better you'll be at deciphering perplexing words on the GRE and at coming up with smart guesses.

# Sentence Completions

The directions for this question type look like this:

> **The question includes a sentence that has either one or two blanks. The blanks indicate that a piece of the sentence is missing. Each sentence is followed by five answer choices that consist of words or phrases. Select the answer choice that completes the sentence <u>best</u>.**

The difficulty of the sentence completions you will see on the CAT depends on how many questions you get right.

## The Four Basic Principles of Sentence Completion

*1. Every Clue Is Right in Front of You*

Each sentence contains a few crucial clues that determine the answer. In order for a sentence to be used on the GRE, the answer must already be in the sentence. Clues *in the sentence* limit the possible answers, and finding these clues will guide you to the correct answer.

For example, could the following sentence be on the GRE?

> The student thought the test was quite _____ .
>
> (A) long
> (B) unpleasant
> (C) predictable
> (D) ridiculous
> (E) indelible

No. Because nothing in the sentence hints at which word to choose, it would be a terrible test question. You would *never* see a question like this on the GRE. Now let's change the sentence to get a question that *could* be answered:

> Since the student knew the form and content of the questions in advance, the test was quite _____ for her.
>
> (A) long
> (B) unpleasant
> (C) predictable
> (D) ridiculous
> (E) indelible

What are the important clues in this question? Well, the word *since* is a great structural clue. It indicates that the missing word follows logically from part of the sentence. Specifically, the missing word must follow from "knew the form and content . . . in advance." That means the test was predictable.

## 2. Look for What's Directly Implied and Expect Clichés

We're not dealing with poetry here. These sentences aren't excerpted from the works of Toni Morrison or William Faulkner. The correct answer is the one most directly implied by the meanings of the words in the sentence.

## 3. Don't Imagine Strange Scenarios

Read the sentence literally, not imaginatively. Pay attention to the meaning of the words, not associations or feelings that you have.

## 4. Look for Structural Roadsigns

Structural roadsigns, such as *since,* are keywords that will point you to the right answer. The missing words in sentence completions will usually have a relationship similar or opposite to other words in the sentence. Keywords, such as *and* or *but,* will tell you which it is.

On the GRE, a semicolon by itself always connects two closely related clauses. If a semicolon is followed by another roadsign, then that roadsign determines the direction. Just like on the highway, there are roadsigns on the GRE that tell you to go ahead and that tell you to take a detour.

"Straight ahead" signs are used to make one part of the sentence support or elaborate another part. They continue the sentence in the same direction. The positive or negative charge of what follows is not changed by these clues. Straight-ahead clues include: *and, similarly, in addition, since, also, thus, because, ; (semicolon),* and *likewise.*

"Detour" signs change the direction of the sentence. They make one part of the sentence contradict or qualify another part. The positive or negative charge of an answer is changed by these clues. Detour signs include: *but, despite, yet, however, unless, rather, although, while, unfortunately,* and *nonetheless.*

In the following examples, test your knowledge of sentence completion roadsigns by finding the right answers (in the parentheses):

1. The winning argument was _____ *and* persuasive. (cogent, flawed)

2. The winning argument was _____ *but* persuasive. (cogent, flawed)

3. The play's script lacked depth and maturity; *likewise,* the acting was altogether _____. (sublime, amateurish)

4. The populace _____ the introduction of the new taxes, *since* they had voted for them overwhelmingly. (applauded, despised)

## Kaplan Rules

When working through a sentence completion question:

- Look for clues in the sentence.
- Focus on what's directly implied.
- Pay attention to the meanings of the words.
- Keep an eye out for structural roadsigns.

## Definition

"Straight ahead" road-signs—such as *because,* *thus,* and *consequently*—continue the sentence in the same direction.

## Definition

"Detour" signs—such as *but, however,* and *on the other hand*—change the direction of the sentence.

5. *Despite* your impressive qualifications, I am _____ to offer you a position with our firm. (unable, willing)

6. Scientists have claimed that the dinosaurs became extinct in a single, dramatic event; *yet* new evidence suggests a _____ decline. (headlong, gradual)

7. The first wave of avant-gardists elicited _____ from the general population, *while* the second was completely ignored. (indifference, shock)

By concentrating on the roadsigns, wasn't it easy to find your way through the question and arrive at the right answer? (See the "Answers to the Roadsign Questions" sidebar when you turn the page.)

### The Kaplan Four-Step Method for Sentence Completions
Now that you have the basics, here's how to combine skills.

1. Read the sentence strategically, looking for structural roadsigns and other clues to see where the sentence is heading.
2. In your own words, anticipate its answer.
3. Look for answers close in meaning to yours and eliminate tempting wrong answers using the clues.
4. Read your choice back into the sentence to make sure it fits.

### Using Kaplan's Four-Step Method
Try the following sentence completion questions using the Kaplan Four-Step Method. These are more difficult, but you should be able to do them. Time yourself: you only have 30–45 seconds to do each question.

1. The yearly financial statement of a large corporation may seem _____ at first, but the persistent reader soon finds its pages of facts and figures easy to decipher.

  (A) bewildering
  (B) surprising
  (C) inviting
  (D) misguided
  (E) uncoordinated

2.  Usually the press secretary's replies are terse, if not downright
    _____, but this afternoon his responses to our questions were
    remarkably comprehensive, almost _____.

    - (A) rude . . . concise
    - (B) curt . . . verbose
    - (C) long-winded . . . effusive
    - (D) enigmatic . . . taciturn
    - (E) lucid . . . helpful

3.  Organic farming is more labor intensive and thus initially more
    _____, but its long-term costs may be less than those of con-
    ventional farming.

    - (A) uncommon
    - (B) stylish
    - (B) restrained
    - (D) expensive
    - (E) difficult

4.  Unfortunately, there are some among us who equate tolerance
    with immorality; they feel that the _____ of moral values in a
    permissive society is not only likely, but _____.

    - (A) decline . . . possible
    - (B) upsurge . . . predictable
    - (C) disappearance . . . desirable
    - (D) improvement . . . commendable
    - (E) deterioration . . . inevitable

Think about how you solved these sentence completion questions. You
should use the same method when you encounter sentence completion
questions on the GRE.

Now let's move to the next question type: Analogies.

## Review

Answers to the roadsign
questions:

1. cogent
2. flawed
3. amateurish
4. applauded
5. unable
6. gradual
7. shock

## Kaplan Rules

The Kaplan Sentence
Completion Method:

- Focus on where the sen-
  tence is heading.
- Anticipate the answer in
  your own words.
- Look for answers that are
  similar to yours.
- Plug your choice into the
  sentence to see if it fits.

## Review

Answers to the sentence completion questions:

1. A
2. B
3. D
4. E

# Analogies

The directions for this question type look like this:

> **This question consists of a pair of words or phrases that are separated by a colon and followed by five answer choices. Choose the pair of words or phrases in the answer choices that best expresses a relationship similar to that expressed in the original pair.**

On the GRE, the more questions you get right, the harder the analogies you will see.

## The Four Basic Principles of Analogies

*1. Every Analogy Question Consists of Two Words, Called the Stem Pair, That Are Separated by a Colon*

Below the stem pair are five answer choices. That means analogy questions look like this:

MAP : ATLAS ::

- (A) key : lock
- (B) street : sign
- (C) ingredient : cookbook
- (D) word : dictionary
- (E) theory : hypothesis

*2. There Will Always Be a Direct and Necessary Relationship Between the Words in the Stem Pair*

You express this relationship by making a short sentence that we call a *bridge*. A bridge is whatever simple sentence you come up with to relate the two words. Your goals when you build your bridge should be to keep it as short and as clear as possible.

A weak bridge expresses a relationship that isn't necessary or direct. For the sample analogy question above, weak bridges include:

- Some maps are put in atlases.
- A map is usually smaller than an atlas.
- Maps and atlases have to do with geography.
- A page in an atlas is usually a map.

You know you have a weak bridge if it contains such words as *usually, can, might,* or *sometimes.*

A strong bridge expresses a direct and necessary relationship. For the analogy above, strong bridges include:

- Maps are what an atlas contains.
- Maps are the unit of reference in an atlas.
- An atlas collects and organizes maps.

Strong bridges express a definite relationship and can contain an unequivocal word, such as *always, never*, or *must*. The best bridge is a strong bridge that fits exactly one answer choice.

*3. Always Try to Make a Bridge Before Looking at the Answer Choices*
ETS uses certain kinds of bridges over and over on the GRE. Of these we have identified five classic bridges. Exposing yourself to them now will give you a feel for the sort of bridge that will get you the right answer. Try to answer these questions as you go through them.

1. The definition bridge (*is always* or *is never*)

   PLATITUDE : TRITE ::

   - (A) riddle : unsolvable
   - (B) axiom : geometric
   - (C) omen : portentous
   - (D) syllogism : wise
   - (E) circumlocution : concise

2. The function/purpose bridge

   AIRPLANE : HANGAR ::

   - (A) music : orchestra
   - (B) money : vault
   - (C) finger : hand
   - (D) tree : farm
   - (E) insect : ecosystem

3. The lack bridge

   LUCID : OBSCURITY ::

   - (A) ambiguous : doubt
   - (B) provident : planning
   - (C) furtive : legality
   - (D) economical : extravagance
   - (E) secure : violence

**Definition**

Analogy questions consist of two words—the **stem pair**—that are separated by a colon. Stem pairs look like this:

PREPARATION : SUCCESS

**Definition**

A **bridge** is a short sentence that connects the two words in the stem pair. You should always make a bridge before you look at the answer choices.

## Kaplan Tip

What makes a strong
bridge?

You might think that the
words *trumpet* and *jazz*
have a strong bridge.
Don't be fooled. You can
play many things on trum-
pets other than jazz, such
as fanfares and rock music.
You can also play jazz on
things other than trum-
pets. *Trumpet* and *instrument* do have a strong
bridge. A trumpet is a type
of instrument. This is
always true—it's a strong,
definite relationship.

## At a Glance

The five classic bridges:

1. Definition
2. Function/purpose
3. Lack
4. Characteristic action/items
5. Degree

4. The characteristic actions/items bridge

PIROUETTE : DANCER ::

- (A) sonnet : poet
- (B) music : orchestra
- (C) building : architect
- (D) parry : fencer
- (E) dress : seamstress

5. The degree (often going to an extreme) bridge

ATTENTIVE : RAPT ::

- (A) loyal : unscrupulous
- (B) critical : derisive
- (C) inventive : innovative
- (D) jealous : envious
- (E) kind : considerate

So there you have them, the five classic bridges. Keep them in mind as you practice for the GRE.

*4. Don't Fall for "Both Are" Analogies*

Analogies "Both Are" are pairs of words that are not related to each other but only to a third word.

For instance, it may seem as though there is a strong relationship in RING : NECKLACE; they're both types of jewelry. But this type of relationship will never be a correct answer choice on the GRE. If you see an answer choice like this—where the two words are not directly related to one another but only to a third word (like *jewelry*)—you can always eliminate it.

Now that you have a grasp of the Basic Principles of Analogies, let's take a look at the Kaplan method for solving analogy questions.

## The Kaplan Four-Step Method for Analogies

1. Find a strong bridge between the stem words.
2. Plug the answer choices into the bridge. Be flexible: Sometimes it's easier to use the second word first.
3. Adjust the bridge as necessary. You want your bridge to be simple and somewhat general, but if more than one answer choice fits into your bridge, it was too general. Make it a little more specific and try those answer choices again.
4. If stuck, eliminate all answer choices with weak bridges. If two choices have the same bridge—for example, (A) TRUMPET : INSTRUMENT or (B) SCREWDRIVER : TOOL—eliminate them both. Try to work backwards from remaining choices to stem pair and make your best guess.

## Using the Kaplan Four-Step Method
Let's try an example to learn how to use the four-step method.

AIMLESS : DIRECTION ::

(A) enthusiastic : motivation
(B) wary : trust
(C) unhealthy : happiness
(D) lazy : effort
(E) silly : adventure

For this question, a good bridge is: "Someone *aimless* lacks *direction*." Now plug that into the answer choices. Only choice (B) fits. If you were stuck, you should have eliminated choices (A), (C), and (E), because their bridges are weak. Remember: If an answer choice has a weak bridge it cannot be correct, because no stem pair that you'll find on the GRE will ever have a weak bridge. To be correct, an answer choice must have a strong, clear relationship.

If you can't build a good bridge because you don't know the definition of one or both stem words, all is not lost. Even when you can't figure out the bridge for the words in the stem pair, you can guess intelligently by eliminating answer choices. In the following questions, there are no stem words. How are you supposed to do them, you ask? Well, do you remember the scene in *Star Wars* when Obi Wan Kenobi is teaching Luke Skywalker about the Force? He put that helmet on Luke's head so that Luke couldn't see when the little robot tried to zap him. This entire scene was actually just a clever (if subtle) metaphor for what it's like to do an analogy when you don't know what the stem words mean.

### Review

Answers to the five classic bridges drill:

1. C
2. B
3. D
4. D
5. B

## Kaplan Rules

To solve an analogy:

1. Build a bridge between the stem words.
2. Plug in the answer choices.
3. Build a stronger bridge, if necessary.
4. If all else fails, eliminate answer choices with weak bridges.

## Kaplan Tip

Don't waste valuable time reading the directions on test day. Learn them now.

Take a look at the following sets of answer choices and eliminate all choices that have a weak bridge. Also, if two choices in the same problem have the same bridge, you can eliminate them both (because if one of them were correct the other would have to be also).

1. ____ : ____ ::

   Ⓐ  pliant : yield
   Ⓑ  sinister : doubt
   Ⓒ  trivial : defend
   Ⓓ  irksome : annoy
   Ⓔ  noble : admire

2. ____ : ____ ::

   Ⓐ  enlist : draft
   Ⓑ  hire : promote
   Ⓒ  resign : quit
   Ⓓ  pacify : mollify
   Ⓔ  endanger : enlighten

3. ____ : ____ ::

   Ⓐ  congratulate : success
   Ⓑ  amputate : crime
   Ⓒ  annotate : consultation
   Ⓓ  deface : falsehood
   Ⓔ  cogitate : habit

4. ____ : ____ ::

   Ⓐ  tepid : hot
   Ⓑ  lackluster : catatonic
   Ⓒ  unusual : rare
   Ⓓ  pedantic: didactic
   Ⓔ  unique : popular

Now let's turn to the third Verbal question type that you'll be dealing with: Antonyms.

# Antonyms

The directions for this question type will look like this:

> **This question consists of a single word in capital letters followed by five answer choices. Select the answer choice that has the meaning most <u>opposite</u> to the word in capital letters.**

On the GRE, the more questions you get right, the harder the antonym questions you'll see.

## The Seven Basic Principles of Antonyms

*1. Think of a Context in Which You've Heard the Word Before*
For example, you might be able to figure out the meaning of the italicized words in the following phrases from their context: "*travesty* of justice," "crimes and *misdemeanors*," "*mitigating* circumstances," and "*abject* poverty."

*2. Look at Word Roots, Stems, and Suffixes*
Even if you don't know what *benediction* means, its prefix (*bene,* which means good) tells you that its opposite is likely to be something bad. Perhaps the answer will begin with *mal,* as in *malefaction.*

*3. Use Your Knowledge of a Romance Language*
For example, you might guess at the meaning of *credulous* from the Italian, *credere; moratorium* from the French, *morte;* and *lachrimose* from the Spanish, *lagrima.*

*4. Use the Positive or Negative Charges of the Words to Help You*
Use your scratch paper to make little + signs for words with positive connotations, – signs for those with negative connotations, and = signs for neutral words. This strategy can work wonders. For instance:

$$
\begin{array}{cccc}
 & - & - & = \\
\text{PERDITION :} & \text{(A) deterrent} & \text{(B) rearrangement} \\
 & = & + & - \\
 & \text{(C) reflection} & \text{(D) salvation} & \text{(E) rejection}
\end{array}
$$

---

## Teacher Tip

"Some students give up too easily on short verbal questions, especially the analogies and antonyms, because they have no idea what a word means. The Kaplan methods help you eliminate wrong answers even when you don't know definitions."
—Derek Veazey
Fort Worth, Texas

## Kaplan Rules

Strategy for antonyms:

1. Define the root word.
2. Reverse it.
3. Find a similar opposite in the answer choices.
4. If all else fails, eliminate answer choices and guess.

---

## Review

Answers to the answer choice elimination drill:

1. Eliminate A and D because they have the same bridge. Eliminate B and C because they have weak bridges.
2. Eliminate B, D, and E because they have weak bridges.
3. Eliminate B, C, D, and E because they have weak bridges.
4. Eliminate B and C because they have the same bridge. Eliminate E because it has a weak bridge.

*5. Eliminate Any Answer Choices That Do Not Have a Clear Opposite*
For instance, in the sample problem above, neither choice (B) nor choice (C) has a clear and obvious opposite. They are unlikely to be correct.

*6. On Hard Antonym Questions, Watch out for Trick Choices and Eliminate Them*
For instance, if you come across:

CEDE :

(A) make sense of
(B) fail
(C) get ahead of
(D) flow out of
(E) retain

you should eliminate B, C, and D. Why? Because *cede* will remind some people of *succeed*, they will pick B. It will remind others of *recede*, as in *receding hairline* or *receding tide*, so they will pick C or D. ETS never rewards people for goofing up. No one ever "lucks" into the right answer on the GRE by making a mistake.

*7. Choose Answers Strategically*
When in doubt, try to eliminate incorrect answer choices and then guess.

Now that you have a grasp of the basic principles of antonyms, let's look at the Kaplan method for solving antonym questions.

## The Kaplan Four-Step Method for Antonyms
1. Define the root word.
2. Reverse it by thinking about the word's opposite.
3. Now go to the answer choices and find the opposite—that is, the choice that matches your preconceived notion of the choice.
4. If stuck, eliminate any choices you can and guess among those remaining.

**KAPLAN**

## Using Kaplan's Four-Step Method

Now let's put this method to the test. Suppose you encounter *loiter* in an antonym question:

*Step One:* Ask yourself what *loiter* means. Write a definition below:

_____

_____

*Step Two:* Think about *loiter*'s opposite.

The opposite of *loiter* is _____ .

*Step Three:* Choose the answers that best matches your reversal of the original word.

LOITER:

- (A) change direction
- (B) move purposefully
- (C) inch forward
- (D) clean up
- (E) amble

What's the *opposite* of the choice you picked? Does that match the meaning of the original word?

The opposite of *move purposefully* is *stand around*, or *loiter*.

*Step Four:* If you get stuck, eliminate choices and guess. (A) change direction, and (D) clean up, seem to be unlikely choices and can be eliminated.

# Reading Comprehension

Reading comprehension is the only question type that appears on all major standardized tests, and the reason isn't too surprising. No matter what academic area you pursue, you'll have to make sense of some dense, unfamiliar material. The topics for GRE reading comp passages are taken from three areas: social sciences, natural sciences, and humanities.

These passages tend to be wordy and dull, and you may find yourself wondering where the test makers get them (probably from the same source as computer installation manuals). Well, actually, the test makers go out and collect the most boring and confusing essays available, then chop them up beyond all recognition or coherence. The people behind the GRE know that you'll have to read passages like these in graduate school, so they choose test material accordingly. In a way, reading comp is the most realistic of all the question types on the test. And right now is a good time to start shoring up your critical reading skills, both for the test and for future study in your field.

## Format and Directions

The directions for this question type look like this:

> **The questions in this group are based on the content of the passage. After reading the passage, choose the best answer to each question. Answer each question based upon what's <u>stated</u> or <u>implied</u> in the passage.**

On the CAT you will see two to four reading comp passages, each with two to four questions. You will have to tackle the passage and questions as they are given to you.

## The Seven Basic Principles of Reading Comprehension

To improve your reading comp skills, you'll need a lot of practice—and patience. You may not see dramatic improvement after only one drill. But with ongoing practice, the seven basic principles will help to increase your skill and confidence on this section by the day of the test. After reviewing the following principles, you'll find your first opportunity to apply them by working on a sample passage. And later, on the practice test, you'll have an opportunity to master these skills.

*1. Pay Special Attention to the First Third of the Passage*
The first third of a reading comp passage usually introduces its topic and scope, the author's main idea or primary purpose, and the author's tone. It almost always hints at the structure that the passage will follow. Let's take a closer look at these important elements of a reading comp passage.

*Topic and Scope.* *Topic* and *scope* are both objective terms. That means they include no specific reference to the author's point of view. The difference between them is that the topic is broader; the scope narrows the topic. Scope is particularly important because the answer choices (often many) that depart from it will always be wrong. The broad topic of "The Battle of Gettysburg," for example, would be a lot to cover in 450 words. So if you encountered this passage, you should ask yourself, "What aspect of the battle does the author take up?" Because of length limitations, it's likely to be a pretty small chunk. Whatever that chunk is—the prebattle scouting, how the battle was fought—that will be the passage's scope. Answer choices that deal with anything outside of this narrowly defined chunk will be wrong.

*Author's Purpose.* The distinction between topic and scope ties into another important issue: the author's purpose. In writing the passage, the author has deliberately chosen to narrow the scope by including certain aspects of the broader topic and excluding others. Why the author makes those choices gives us an important clue as to why the passage is being written in the first place. From the objective and broadly stated topic (for instance, a passage's topic might be *solving world hunger*) you zoom in on the objective but narrower scope (*a new technology for solving world hunger*), and the scope quickly leads you to the author's subjective purpose (*the author is writing in order to describe a new technology and its promising uses*). The author's purpose is what turns into the author's main idea, which will be discussed at greater length in the next principle.

So don't just "read" the passage; instead, try to do the following three things:

1. Identify the topic.
2. Narrow it down to the precise scope that the author includes.
3. Make a hypothesis about why the author is writing and where he or she is going with it.

*Structure and Tone.* In their efforts to understand what the author says, test takers often ignore the less glamorous but important structural side of the passage—namely, how the 'author says it. One of the keys to success on this section is to understand not only the passage's purpose but also the structure of each passage. Why? Simply because the questions at the end of the passage ask both what the author says *and* how he or she says it. Here's a list of the classic GRE passage structures:

## Kaplan Tip

As you read the first third of the passage, try to zoom in on the main idea of the passage by first getting a sense of the general topic, then pinning down the scope of the passage, and finally zeroing in on the author's purpose in writing the passage.

## Kaplan Rules

Answer choices that deal with matters outside the passage's scope are always wrong.

## Kaplan Rules

As you read a passage:

1. Identify the topic (for example, *solving world hunger*).

2. Narrow its topic down to its precise scope (for example, *a new technology for solving world hunger*).

3. Guess about why the author is writing the passage and where it is leading (for example, *the author is writing in order to describe a new technology for solving world hunger*).

- Passages arguing a position (often a social sciences passage)
- Passages discussing something specific within a field of study (for instance, a passage about Shakespearean sonnets in literature)
- Passages explaining some significant new findings or research (often a science passage)

Most passages that you'll encounter will feature one of these classic structures, or a variation thereof. You've most likely seen these structures at work in passages before, even if unconsciously. Your job is to actively seek them out as you begin to read a passage. Usually, the structure is announced within the first third of the passage. Let these classic structures act as a jump start in your search for the passage's "big picture" and purpose.

As for how the author makes his or her point, try to note the author's position within these structures, usually indicated by the author's tone. For example, in passages that explain some significant new findings or research structure, the author is likely to be clinical in description. In passages that argue a position, the opinion could be the author's, in which case the author's tone may be opinionated or argumentative. On the other hand, the author could simply be describing the strongly held opinions of someone else. In the latter case the author's writing style would be more descriptive, factual, even-handed. His or her method may involve mere storytelling or the simple relaying of information, which is altogether different from the former case.

Notice the difference in tone between the two types of authors (argumentative versus descriptive). Correct answer choices for a question about the main idea would, in the former case, use such verbs as *argue for*, *propose*, or *demonstrate*, whereas correct choices for the same type of question in the latter case would use such verbs as *describe* or *discuss*. Correct answers are always consistent with the author's tone, so noting the author's tone is a good way to understand the passage.

### 2. Focus on the Main Idea

Every passage boils down to one big idea. Your job is to cut through the fancy wording and focus on this big idea. Very often, the main idea will be presented in the first third of the passage, but occasionally the author will build up to it gradually, in which case you may not have a firm idea of it.

In any case, the main idea always appears somewhere in the passage, and when it does, you must take note of it. For one thing, the purpose of everything else in the passage will be to support this idea. Furthermore, many of the questions—not only "main idea" questions but all kinds of questions—are easier to handle when you have the main idea in the forefront of your mind. Always look for choices that sound consistent with the main idea. Wrong choices often sound inconsistent with it.

### 3. Get the Gist of Each Paragraph

It will come as no surprise to you that the paragraph is the main structural unit of any passage. After you've read the first third of the passage carefully, you need to find the gist, or general purpose, of each paragraph and then try to relate each paragraph back to the passage as a whole. To find the gist of each paragraph, ask yourself:

- Why did the author include this paragraph?
- What shift did the author have in mind when moving on to this paragraph?
- What bearing does this paragraph have on the author's main idea?

### 4. Don't Obsess over Details

There are differences between the reading skills required in an academic environment and those that are useful on standardized tests. In school, you probably read to memorize information for an exam. But this isn't the type of reading that's good for racking up points on the GRE reading comprehension section. On the test, you'll need to read for short-term retention. When you finish the questions on a certain passage, that passage is over, gone, done with. Go ahead, forget everything about it!

What's more, there's no need to waste your time memorizing details. The passage will always be right there in front of you. You always have the option to find any details if a particular question requires you to do so. If you have a good sense of a passage's structure and paragraph topics, then you should have no problem navigating back through the text.

### 5. Attack the Passages, Don't Just Read Them

Remember when you took the SAT? Like some of us, did you celebrate when you finally finished the passage and then treat the questions as afterthoughts? If so, we suggest that you readjust your thinking. Remember: you get no points for just getting through the passage.

When we read most materials, a newspaper, for example, we start with the first sentence and read the article straight through.

The words wash over us and are the only things we hear in our minds. This is typical of a passive approach to reading, and this approach won't cut it on the GRE.

To do well on this test you'll need to do more than just read the words on the page. You'll need to read actively. Active reading involves keeping your mind working at all times, while trying to anticipate where the author's points are leading. It means thinking about what you're reading as you read it. It means paraphrasing the complicated-sounding ideas and jargon. It means asking yourself questions as you read:

### Kaplan Tip

You don't have to memorize or understand every little thing as you read the passage. Remember, you can always refer back to the passage to clarify the meaning of any specific detail.

### Kaplan Tip

Read the newspaper daily, either just in the weeks before the test or as part of your permanent routine. You'll have practice overcoming the hurdle of reading unfamiliar or difficult material, and as a bonus you'll sound intelligent and connected during interviews.

## Kaplan Rules

You can be an active reader by:

- Thinking about what you're reading
- Paraphrasing the complicated parts
- Asking yourself questions about the passage
- Jotting down notes

## Kaplan Tip

Everything you need to answer reading comp questions is in the passage.

## Kaplan Tip

Use your own knowledge to help you to understand the passages, but remember that questions often begin with: "According to the author . . . "

- What's the author's main point here?
- What's the purpose of this paragraph? Of this sentence?

While reading actively you keep a running commentary in your mind. You may want to jot down notes in the margin or underline. When you read actively, you don't absorb the passage, you attack it!

### 6. Beware of Classic Wrong Answer Choices

Knowing the most common wrong answer types can help you to eliminate wrong choices quickly, which can save you a lot of time. Of course, ideally, you want to have prephrased an answer choice in your mind before looking at the choices. When that technique doesn't work, you'll have to go to the choices and eliminate the bad ones to find the correct one. If this happens, you should always be on the lookout for choices that:

- Contradict the facts or the main idea
- Distort or twist the facts or the main idea
- Mention true points not relevant to the question (often from the wrong paragraph)
- Raise a topic that's never mentioned in the passage
- Are too strongly worded
- Sound off the wall or have the wrong tone

Being sensitive to these classic wrong choices will make it that much easier to zero in on the correct choice quickly and efficiently.

### 7. Use Outside Knowledge Carefully

You can answer all the questions correctly even if you don't know anything about the topics covered in the passages. Everything you'll need to answer every question is included in the passages themselves. However, as always, you have to be able to make basic inferences and extract relevant details from the texts.

Using outside knowledge that you may have about a particular topic can be beneficial to your cause, but watch out! Outside knowledge can also mess up your thinking. If you use your knowledge of a topic to help you understand the author's points, then you're taking advantage of your knowledge in a useful way. However, if you use your own knowledge to answer the questions, then you may run into trouble because the questions test your understanding of the author's points, not your previous understanding or personal point of view on the topic.

So the best approach is to use your own knowledge and experience to help you to comprehend the passages, but be careful not to let it interfere with answering the questions correctly.

## Reading Comprehension Test Run

Here's a chance to familiarize yourself with a short reading comp passage and questions. You'll have more opportunities to practice later, under timed conditions. For now, we want you to take the time to read actively, to give the seven principles a test run.

> **The questions in this group are based on the content of the passage. After reading the passage, choose the best answer to each question. Answer each question based upon what's <u>stated</u> or <u>implied</u> in the passage.**

Migration of animal populations from one region to another is called faunal interchange. Concentrations of species across regional boundaries vary, however, prompting zoologists to classify routes along which
(5) penetrations of new regions occur.

A corridor, like the vast stretch of land from Alaska to the southeastern United States, is equivalent to a path of least resistance. Relative ease of migration often results in the presence of related species along the entire length of
(10) a corridor; bear populations, unknown in South America, occur throughout the North American corridor. A desert or other barrier creates a filter route, allowing only a segment of a faunal group to pass. A sweepstakes route presents so formidable a barrier that penetration is
(15) unlikely. It differs from other routes, which may be crossed by species with sufficient adaptive capability. As the name suggests, negotiation of a sweepstakes route depends almost exclusively on chance, rather than on physical attributes and adaptability.

1. It can be inferred from the passage that studies of faunal interchange would probably
   - (A) fail to explain how similar species can inhabit widely separated areas
   - (B) be unreliable because of the difficulty of observing long-range migrations
   - (C) focus most directly on the seasonal movements of a species within in a specific geographic region
   - (D) concentrate on correlating the migratory patterns of species that are biologically dissimilar
   - (E) help to explain how present-day distributions of animal populations might have arisen

The seven basic principles of reading comprehension:

1. Read the first third of the passage very carefully.
2. Focus on the main idea.
3. Get the gist of each paragraph.
4. Don't obsess over details.
5. Attack the passages, don't just read them.
6. Beware of classic wrong answer choices.
7. Use outside knowledge carefully.

2. The author's primary purpose is to show that the classification of migratory routes

   Ⓐ is based on the probability that migration will occur along a given route

   Ⓑ reflects the important role played by chance in the distribution of most species

   Ⓒ is unreliable because further study is needed

   Ⓓ is too arbitrary, because the regional boundaries cited by zoologists frequently change

   Ⓔ is based primarily on geographic and climactic differences between adjoining regions

3. The author's description of the distribution of bear populations (lines 10–11) suggests which of the following conclusions?

   I. The distribution patterns of most other North American faunal species populations are probably identical to those of bears.

   II. There are relatively few barriers to faunal interchange in North America.

   III. The geographic area that links North America to South America would probably be classified as either a filter or a sweepstakes route.

   Ⓐ I only

   Ⓑ II only

   Ⓒ III only

   Ⓓ I and II only

   Ⓔ II and III only

4. According to the passage, in order to negotiate a sweepstakes route an animal species

   Ⓐ has to spend at least part of the year in a desert environment

   Ⓑ is obliged to move long distances in short periods of time

   Ⓒ must sacrifice many of its young to wandering pastures

   Ⓓ must have the capacity to adapt to a very wide variety of climates

   Ⓔ does not need to possess any special physical capabilities

*How Did You Do?*

Were you able to zoom in from the broad topic (migration) to the scope (classification of migration routes)? Did the author's tone and purpose become clear, then, as explanatory rather than argumentative? And were you able to focus on the correct answers and not get distracted by outside knowledge or misleading details? You'll be able to assess your performance and skills as you review the next section, where we'll explore the strategies for dealing with the three question types and how these strategies apply to the above questions.

## The Three Common Reading Comp Question Types

We find it useful to break the reading comp section down into the three main question types that accompany each passage: global, explicit detail, and inference. Most test takers find explicit detail questions to be the easiest type in the reading comp section, because they're the most concrete. Unlike inferences, which hide somewhere between the lines, explicit details sit out in the open—in the lines themselves. That's good news for you, because when you see an explicit detail question you'll know that the correct answer requires only recall, and not analysis. Let's look at each of these question types more closely, using the sample questions you just dealt with for illustration.

### 1. Global Questions

*Description.* A global question will ask you to sum up the author's overall intentions, ideas, or passage structure. It's basically a question whose scope is the entire passage. Global questions account for 25 to 30 percent of all reading comp questions. Question 2 in the preceding sample is a global question because it asks you to identify the author's primary purpose.

*Strategy.* In general, any global question choice that grabs onto a small detail—or zeroes in on the content of only one paragraph—will be wrong. Often, scanning the verbs in the global question choices is a good way to take a first cut at the question. The verbs must agree with the author's tone and the way in which he or she structures the passage, so scanning the verbs and adjectives can narrow down the options quickly. The correct answer must be consistent with the overall tone and structure of the passage, whereas common wrong-answer choices associated with this type of question are those that are too broad or narrow in scope and those that are inconsistent with the author's tone. You'll often find global questions at the beginning of question sets, and often one of the wrong choices will play on some side issue discussed at the tail end of the passage.

## Review

Answers to reading comp questions:

1. E
2. A
3. E
4. E

## At a Glance

Global questions:

- Represent 25 to 30 percent of reading comp questions
- Sum up author's overall intentions or passage structure
- Nouns and verbs must be consistent with the author's tone and the passage's scope
- Main idea and primary purpose, title, structure, and tone questions are related

## Kaplan Tip

Key phrases in the global question stem include:

- Which of the following best expresses the main idea . . .
- The author's primary purpose is . . .
- Which of the following best describes the content as a whole . . .
- Which of the following best describes the organization . . .
- The author's tone can best be described as . . .

*Strategy Applied.* Take a closer look at the global question, number 2 in the sample. You've already articulated the passage's topic (migration), scope (the classification of migration routes), and tone (explanatory). The author mentions three different classifications of migration routes—corridors, filter routes, and sweepstakes routes. And what distinguishes one kind of route from another? The likelihood of migration, from the most likely (corridors, with no barriers to migration) to least likely (sweepstakes routes, with barriers that species can cross only by chance). So the author's primary purpose here is to show how the classifications are defined according to how likely migration is along each type of route. That should have led you directly to choice (A).

A scan of verbs and adjectives is enough to eliminate choices (C) and (D); both imply that the author is making judgments about the classification, but the tone of the passage is objective and explanatory. Meanwhile, (B) focuses too much on one part of the passage—the explanation of sweepstakes routes—where the role of chance is mentioned only in relation to that one classification. And (E) is a distortion, because the author nowhere mentions climatic and geographic differences between adjoining regions.

*Main Idea and Primary Purpose Questions.* The two main types of global questions are main idea and primary purpose questions. We discussed these types a little earlier, noting that main idea and purpose are inextricably linked, because the author's purpose is to convey his or her main idea. The formats for these question types are pretty self-evident:

> Which one of the following best expresses the main idea of the passage?

> *or*

> The author's primary purpose is to . . .

*Title Questions.* A very similar form of global question is one that's looking for a title that best fits the passage. A title, in effect, is the main idea summed up in a brief, catchy way. This question may look like this:

> Which of the following titles best describes the content of the passage as a whole?

Be sure not to go with a choice that aptly describes only the latter half of the passage. A valid title, much like a main idea and primary purpose, must cover the entire passage.

*Structure Questions.* Another type of global question is one that asks you to recognize a passage's overall structure. Here's what this type of question might sound like:

> Which of the following best describes the organization
> of the passage?

Answer choices to this kind of global question are usually worded very generally; they force you to recognize the broad layout of the passage as opposed to the specific content. For example, here are a few possible ways that a passage could be organized:

> A hypothesis is stated and then analyzed.
> A proposal is evaluated and alternatives are explored.
> A viewpoint is set forth and then subsequently defended.

When picking among these choices, literally ask yourself, "Was there a hypothesis here? Was there an evaluation of a proposal or a defense of a viewpoint?" These terms may all sound similar but, in fact, they're very different things. Learn to recognize the difference between a proposal, a viewpoint, and so on. Try to keep a constant eye on what the author is doing as well as what the author is saying, and you'll have an easier time with this type of question.

*Tone Questions.* Finally, one last type of global question is the tone question, which asks you to evaluate the style of the writing or how the author sounds. Is the author passionate, fiery, neutral, angry, hostile, opinionated, low-key? Here's an example:

> The author's tone in the passage can best be
> characterized as . . .

Make sure not to confuse the nature of the content with the tone in which the author presents the ideas: a social science passage based on trends in this century's grisliest murders may be presented in a cool, detached, strictly informative way. Once again, it's up to you to separate what the author says from how he or she says it.

## 2. Explicit Detail Questions

*Description.* The second major category of reading comprehension questions is the explicit detail question. As the name implies, an explicit detail question is one whose answer can be directly pinpointed and found in the text. This type makes up roughly 20 to 30 percent of the reading comp questions. Question 4 in the sample above is an explicit detail question because it asks you to go back to the passage and examine the description of a sweepstakes route.

*Strategy.* Often, these questions provide very direct clues as to where an answer may be found, such as a line reference or some text that links up with the passage structure. (Just be careful with line references; they'll bring you to the right area, but usually the actual answer will be found in the lines immediately before or after the referenced line.) Detail questions are usually related to the main idea, and correct choices tend to be related to major points.

Now, you may recall that we advised you to skim over details in reading comp passages in favor of focusing on the big idea, topic, and scope. But now here's a question type that's specifically concerned with details, so what's the deal? The fact is, most of the details that appear in a typical passage aren't tested in the questions. Of the few that are, you'll either:

- Remember them from your reading
- Be given a line reference to bring you right to them
- Simply have to find them on your own in order to track down the answer

In the third case, if your understanding of the purpose of each paragraph is in the forefront of your mind, it shouldn't take long at all to locate the details in question and then choose an answer. And if even that fails, as a last resort you have the option of putting that question aside and returning to it if and when you have the time later to search through the passage. The point is, even with the existence of this question type, the winning strategy is still to note the purpose of details in each paragraph's argument but not to attempt to memorize the details themselves.

*Strategy Applied.* Take a closer look at the explicit detail question in the sample, Question 4. When an explicit detail question directs you to a specific place in the passage, as Question 4 does to the discussion of sweepstakes routes, your first job is to go right to that spot in the passage and reread it. And if you do that here, you read that negotiation of a sweepstakes route depends "almost entirely on chance, rather than on physical attributes and adaptability." The discounting of physical attributes here should have led you directly to choice (E).

Choice (A)'s mention of a desert environment sinks that choice, because the desert was mentioned by the author in the discussion of filter routes. As for the other choices, "short periods of time," "wandering pastures," and "a wide variety of climates" aren't mentioned in the passage with regard to sweepstakes routes.

## At a Glance

Explicit detail questions:

- Represent 20 to 30 percent of reading comp questions
- Answers can be found in the text
- Sometimes includes line references to help you locate the relevant material
- Are concrete and, therefore, the easiest reading comp question type for most people

## Kaplan Tip

Key phrases in the explicit detail question stem include:

- According to the passage/author . . .
- The author states that . . .
- The author mentions which one of the following as . . .

### 3. Inference Questions

*Description.* An inference is something that is almost certainly true, based on the passage. Inferences require you to "read between the lines." Questions 1 and 3 in the preceding sample are Inference questions. Question 1 specifically asks you what can be "inferred from the passage" and Question 3 asks you to glean possible conclusions based on what is presented.

*Strategy.* The answer to an inference question is something that the author strongly implies or hints at but does not state directly. Furthermore, the right answer, if denied, will contradict or significantly weaken the passage.

Extracting valid inferences from reading comp passages requires the ability to recognize that information in the passage can be expressed in different ways. The ability to bridge the gap between the way information is presented in the passage and the way it's presented in the correct answer choice is vital. In fact, inference questions often boil down to an exercise in translation.

*Strategy Applied.* Take a closer look at the sample inference questions, numbers 1 and 3. Question 1 asks you to select a possible application of the migration study, based only on what you know from the passage. Because the different concentrations of animals prompted the zoologists to classify the migration routes in the first place (line 5), it would make sense that the migration study would help explain how these different concentrations, or distributions, would have arisen. So choice (E) is correct.

Choice (A) contradicts the purpose of the passage, which we discussed for question 2, and unless we're told in the passage that the study was a failure (which we are not), we can't guess that it would be one. Choice (B) is outside of the passage's scope because the passage never touches on the reliability of the study or on any difficulties in observing long-range migrations. The answer must be based on the passage. Choices (C) and (D) are misleading distortions. The study does focus on movements of species, but there's no mention of a seasonal influence, and the study does focus on route comparisons but not on species comparisons.

Question 3 asks you to look back to the passage for the example of the bears and decide what conclusion(s) could be drawn based on this example. We read that bear populations occur throughout North America because North America is a "path of least resistance," meaning there are relatively few barriers. The bears did not continue to migrate further south, however, because they're "unknown in South America." This sug-

## At a Glance

Inference questions:

- Involve ability to read between the lines
- Often boil down to paraphrasing the author's points
- Question stem usually provides a clue as to where in the passage the answer will be found
- Will either ask for something that can be inferred from a specific part of the passage, or else for something the author would agree with

## Kaplan Tip

A good inference:

- Stays in line with the gist of the passage
- Stays in line with the author's tone
- Stays in line with the author's point of view
- Stays within the scope of the passage and its main idea
- Is neither denied by, nor irrelevant to, the ideas stated in the passage
- Always makes more sense than its opposite

gests that South America is either a filter or a sweepstakes route. Nowhere are the bears compared with other species, because the focus isn't the bears but the routes. So option I can be eliminated, and options II and III are accurate. This should have led you, then, to choice (E).

## The Kaplan Four-Step Method for Reading Comprehension

Now that you've got the basics of GRE reading comp under your belt, you'll want to learn our four-step method that allows you to put it all together into a single aggressive and energetic *modus operandi*.

*1. Attack the first third of the passage.*

As outlined in the basic principles section, read the first third of the passage with care, thinking about what you're reading, paraphrasing the complicated parts, and identifying the main idea and author's purpose in writing the passage. Two caveats, however: First, in some passages, the author's main idea won't become clear until the end of the passage. Second, some passages don't contain a main idea, being purely descriptive, with an even-handed tone and no strong opinions. Bottom line: Don't panic if you can't immediately pin down the author's main idea and purpose. Read on.

*2. Create a mental roadmap.*

As you quickly read through the rest of the passage, take note of each paragraph, reading for the gist and not the details. Try to get a sense of what's covered in each paragraph and how it fits into the overall structure of the passage. This will help you get a fix on the passage as a whole, and will help you locate specific details later on.

*3. Stop to sum up.*

Before answering the questions, take a few seconds to summarize your mental road map and re-phrase the main idea of the passage in your own words.

*4. Attack the questions.*

Answer the questions based upon your mental roadmap. As necessary, go back into the passage to locate answers to specific questions. Eliminate wrong answers aggressively, and select the choice that best paraphrases the answer you've found.

## Using the Kaplan Four-Step Method
Now let's apply the Four-Step Method to an actual GRE-strength reading comp passage.

**The questions in this group are based on the content of the passage. After reading the passage, choose the best answer to each question. Answer each question based upon what's <u>stated</u> or <u>implied</u> in the passage.**

The search for an explanation of the frequency, as well as the weakness, of U.S. third party movements is illuminated by examining the conditions that have favored the growth of a strong two-party system. Different interests and voting blocs
(5)    predominate in different regions, so that the electorate is geographically fragmented. This heterogeneity is complemented by a federal political structure that forces the major parties to find voter support at state and local levels in separate regions. Historically, for example, the Democratic Party drew support
(10)   simultaneously from northern Black urban voters and segregationists. Such pressures encourage the major parties to avoid political programs that are too narrowly or sharply defined. Instead, they seek broad appeal, supported by sometimes competing promises made to sectional interests. The non-doctrinal
(15)   character of U.S. politics means that important new issues and voting blocs tend to be initially ignored by the major parties. Such issues—opposition to immigration and the abolition of slavery are two historic examples—tend to gain political prominence through third parties.
(20)      Ironically, the same factors that lead to the emergence of third parties contribute to the explanation of their failure to gain national political power. Parties based on narrow or ephemeral issues remain isolated or fade rapidly. At the same time, those that raise increasingly urgent social issues also face
(25)   inherent limits to growth. Long before a third party can begin to substantially broaden its base of voter support, the major parties are able to move to attract the minority of voters that it represents. The Democratic Party, for instance, appropriated the agrarian platform of the Populist Party in 1896, and
(30)   enacted Socialist welfare proposals in the 1930s, in both cases winning much of the popular bases of these parties. Except for the Republican Party, which gained national prominence as the Whigs were declining in the 1850s, no third party has ever

achieved national major party status. Only at state and local
(35) levels have a handful of third parties been sustained by a stable voting bloc that remains unrepresented by a major party.

1. The main concern of the author of this passage is to

   (A) examine the appeal of U.S. third parties at state and local levels
   (B) trace the historical rise and decline of third party movements in the U.S.
   (C) explain why most U.S. third party movements have failed to gain major party status
   (D) demonstrate the non-ideological character of U.S. politics
   (E) suggest a model to explain why certain U.S. third party movements have succeeded while others have failed

2. According to the author, the major factor responsible for the rise of third parties in the U.S. has been the

   (A) domination of major parties by powerful economic interests
   (B) inability of major parties to bring about broad consensus among a variety of voters and interest groups
   (C) slow response of major parties to new issues and voting groups
   (D) exclusion of immigrants and minorities from the mainstream of U.S. politics
   (E) variety of motivations held by voting blocs in different regions

3. It can be inferred that which of the following contributed to the "nondoctrinal character of U.S. politics" (lines 14–15)

   I. The regional diversity of the country
   II. The national political structure
   III. The avoidance of divisive ideological programs by the major parties

   (A) I only
   (B) III only
   (C) I and II only
   (D) II and III only
   (E) I, II, and III

4. Which of the following does the author suggest was an important factor in the establishment of the Republican Party as a major national party?

    (A) the polarization of national opinion at the time of a major social crisis

    (B) the unique appeal of its program to significant sectional interests

    (C) the acceptance of its program by a large bloc of voters unrepresented by a major party

    (D) the simultaneous decline of an established major party

    (E) the inability of the major parties of the era to appeal to all sectional interests

Here's how the Kaplan method works with this passage.

*1. Attack the first third of the passage.*
The very first sentence introduces the topic—third-party movements—as well as the scope and author's purpose—understanding the factors hindering their success and favoring the two-party system. The author then quickly proceeds to enumerate these factors. So just from reading this first part of the passage closely, you have a strong sense of its overall structure and purpose.

*2. Create a road map.*
Notice how paragraph two also opens with a topic sentence that neatly announces what will be covered therein. Make note of the author's point-by-point examination, but don't try to memorize details. You can always refer to the passage to answer questions.

*3. Stop to sum up.*
Now it's time to sum up your road map—from the paragraph gists you should be able to quickly paraphrase the main idea of the entire passage. After that, it's time to dance. As long as you have a sense of where the various details can be found, you should be able to find them when you need them.

    You might have paraphrased the main idea like this: "Factors that lead to the emergence of third parties also lead to their eventual downfall, at least on the national level."

    Armed with this recap, you should be able to move confidently through the questions. You may not be able to answer every question on sight, but you'll know where to locate the details for those questions, which means quick, correct answers.

> **Teacher Tip**
>
> "If you don't have a method that breaks the passage down and reveals its structure, then the passage is just 'oatmeal'—a big, undifferentiated, boring mess."
> —Kurt Keefner
> Bethesda, Maryland and Washington, DC

*4. Attack the questions.*
Work the questions as they appear. Most of the questions should be easy to crack after checking the details, an easy matter with your roadmap.

*Answers and Explanations*

1. **(C)** is the only choice that fits the topic (third-party movements), scope (how they fare on the national level) and the author's purpose (explaining why they have failed to gain national power). Choices (A) and (D) clearly misrepresent all of these, and (E) is out because no model is suggested, particularly one explaining why some third-party movements have succeeded. (B) might seem tempting at first, but beware of verbs such as *trace*, which are too ambitious for a GRE-length passage—there's certainly no attempt made to *trace* these movements throughout U.S. history.

2. **(C)** This detail question asks for a factor responsible for the *rise* of third parties, so you'll probably want to research the passage for the answer. You'll find the relevant discussion at the end of paragraph one, which is neatly paraphrased in choice (C).

3. **(E)** Again, you'll probably want to research the relevant part of the passage, a task which in this case is facilitated by the line reference, although here you'll need to read most of paragraph one for the answer. You'll find that item I is confirmed on line 6, item II on line 8, and item III on line 15. The lesson to be learned here is that even on so-called "inference" questions, the answers are very often paraphrases of information found in the passage.

4. **(D)** Once again, this detail question seems to ask for an inference, but if you look for the relevant discussion of the Republican Party (which is easily found by scanning for the word *Republican*), you'll find (on lines 31–33) that choice (D) directly paraphrases what you find there.

## Review Exercises

Because reading comp primarily tests your ability to read actively, paraphrasing as you go and paying attention to purpose and structure, let's spend some time practicing those critical reading skills.

### Big Ideas and Details

It's important that you're able to pull out the main idea and supporting details quickly and easily on the day of the test. Covering up the sidebars, read the following three minipassages, jotting down their big ideas in the margin and underlining details. Then compare your answers with ours.

Few historians would contest the idea that Gutenberg's invention of the printing press revolutionized the production of literature. Before the press became widely available in the late 1400s, every book published had to be individually copied by a scribe working from a master manuscript. With Gutenberg's system of moveable type, however, books could be reproduced in almost limitless quantities once the laborious process of typesetting was complete. . . .

> **Big Idea:** Gutenberg revolutionized book publishing.
>
> **Details:** late 1400s, moveable type, limitless quantities, typesetting

Plate tectonics, the study of the interaction of the earth's plates, is generally accepted as the best framework for understanding how the continents formed. New research suggests, however, that the eruption of mantle plumes from beneath the plate layer may be responsible for the formation of specific phenomena in areas distant from plate boundaries. A model of mantle plumes appears to explain a wide range of observations relating to both ocean island chains and flood basalt provinces, for example. . . .

> **Big Idea:** Mantle plume eruptions, not plate tectonics, may explain certain phenomena.
>
> **Details:** ocean island chains, flood basalt provinces

Most of the developed countries are now agreed on the need to take international measures to reduce the emission of carbons into the atmosphere. Despite this consensus, a wide disagreement among economists as to how much emission reduction will actually cost continues to forestall policy making. Analysts who believe the energy market is efficient predict that countries that reduce carbon emission by as little as 20 percent will experience a significant depreciation in their national product. Those that hold that the market is inefficient, however, estimate much greater long-term savings in conservation and arrive at lower costs for reducing emissions. . . .

> **Big Idea:** Economists disagree on the cost of emission reduction.
>
> **Details:** international measures, carbon emission, greater savings, conservation

*Paraphrasing: The Key Skill in Reading Comp*

Many people have a hard time paraphrasing passages. Taking dense, academic prose and turning it into everyday English isn't easy under the pressure of time constraints. Yet, this is the most important skill in reading comp. If you are having trouble with paraphrasing, spend some time with the following exercise.

> For centuries, the Roman Empire ruled large parts of Europe, Asia, and Africa. Rome had two assets that made continued domination possible. First, its highly trained army was superior to those of its potential adversaries. Second, and more important, Rome built a sophisticated transportation network linking together all of the provinces of its far flung empire. When necessary, it could deploy powerful military forces to any part of the empire with unmatched speed.

Summarize these lines in your own words:

_____

_____

_____

Now find the best paraphrase:

(A) Rome's army defeated its opponents because it could move quickly along the empire's excellent transportation network.

(B) Rome had a big empire, a powerful army, and a good transportation system.

(C) Rome was able to maintain a large empire because it had an excellent transportation system that allowed its efficient army to move quickly from place to place.

(D) Rome ruled large parts of Europe, Asia, and Africa for centuries because its army was always better than those of its adversaries.

(E) Because it built a sophisticated transportation system, Rome was able to build a big empire in parts of Europe, Asia, and Africa.

## Teacher Tip

"Ordinary reading is too slow to find things and too fast to analyze text. Good test takers scan quickly to find what they need and then analyze intensely. Structural keywords and references from the stem are crucial. Looking for a conclusion? Scan for keywords and for words with heavy emotional content. If the stem asks for an assumption made by a researcher, scan for the word 'research' or 'researcher.' Then read up and down from that spot."
—Eirik Johnson
Chicago, Illinois

Despite overwhelming evidence to the contrary, many people think that flying is more dangerous than driving. Different standards of media coverage account for this erroneous belief. Although extremely rare, aircraft accidents receive a lot of media attention because they are very destructive. Hundreds of people have been killed in extreme cases. Automobile accidents, on the other hand, occur with alarming frequency, but attract little media coverage because few, if any, people are killed or seriously injured in any particular mishap.

Summarize these lines in your own words:

_____

_____

_____

Now find the best paraphrase:

(A) Compared to rare but destructive aircraft accidents, car accidents are frequent but relatively minor.

(B) Because aircraft accidents get a lot of media attention, while car accidents get much less, many people wrongly believe that flying is more dangerous than driving.

(C) Driving is more dangerous than flying because different standards of media coverage have forced airlines to improve their safety standards.

(D) Many people believe that flying is more dangerous than driving, even though overwhelming evidence points to the opposite conclusion.

(E) Media coverage is responsible for the belief that flying is more dangerous than driving, even though every year more people are killed on the roads than in the air.

## Review

Paraphrase answers:

Roman Empire: (C)
Flying: (B)

## Keywords

Remember these? Kaplan keywords are words in reading comprehension passages that link the text together structurally and thematically. Paying attention to keywords will help you understand the passage better, and will also help you get some easy points. Here are some keywords that you should look for when reading a passage:

CONTRADICTION:
However
But
Yet
On the other hand
Rather
Instead

SUPPORT:
For example
One reason that
In addition
Also
Moreover
Consequently

EMPHASIS:
Of primary importance
Especially important
Of particular interest
Crucial
Critical
Remarkable

Take a moment and circle the structural signal words in this short reading comprehension passage:

> Gettysburg is considered by most historians to be a turning point in the American Civil War. Before Gettysburg, Confederate forces under General Robert E. Lee had defeated their Union counterparts—sometimes by
> (5) considerable margins—in a string of major battles. In this engagement, however, the Confederate army was defeated and driven back. Even more important than their material losses, though, was the Confederacy's loss of momentum. Union forces took the initiative, finally

(10) defeating the Confederacy less than two years later. By invading Union territory, the Confederate leadership had sought to shatter the Union's will to continue the war and to convince European nations to recognize the Confederacy as an independent nation. Instead, the Union's
(15) willingness to fight was strengthened and the Confederacy squandered its last chance for foreign support.

Words of emphasis, though rare, are the most important category of Kaplan keywords. Why? Because if you see an emphasis keyword in a sentence, you will always get a question about that sentence. Think about it—if the author thinks something is "of primary importance," it would be pretty silly for the test maker not to ask you about it.

In the Gettysburg passage, did you circle *even more important* (line 7)? You should have. You were bound to get a question about it.

You can also get the gist of this paragraph by paying close attention to the contrast words, beginning on line 6: "In the engagement, *however*, the Confederate army was defeated and driven back." Ah, so they weren't doing so well anymore. Contrast words signal a change in direction, and for this reason they often introduce thematically important information. In fact, if a paragraph contains a contrast word, the topic sentence will almost always be that sentence or the next. And the next sentence, which is indeed the topic sentence, contains another contrast word: "Even more important than their material losses, *though*, was the Confederacy's loss of momentum." Finally, the last sentence contains one more contrast word and introduces one more important idea: "*Instead*, the Union's willingness to fight was strengthened and the Confederacy squandered its last chance of foreign support."

The moral of this story is that by paying attention to keywords, you can be sure that you won't lose sight of the most important information that the author is trying to convey.

By using all of the techniques discussed above, you will be able to tackle the most difficult reading comprehension questions. And now that you have the tools to handle the Verbal sections of the GRE, take a swing at the set of practice questions that follow. Then we'll move on and take a look at the Quantitative sections of the test.

# Verbal Practice Set

## Question 1

Victorien Sardou's play *La Tosca* was originally written as a _____ for Sarah Bernhardt and later _____ into the famous Puccini opera.

- Ⓐ role . . . reincarnated
- Ⓑ biography . . . changed
- Ⓒ metaphor . . . edited
- Ⓓ present . . . fictionalized
- Ⓔ vehicle . . . adapted

## Question 2

Because the law and custom require that a definite determination be made, the judge is forced to behave as if the verdict is _____, when in fact the evidence may not be _____.

- Ⓐ negotiable . . . persuasive
- Ⓑ justified . . . accessible
- Ⓒ unassailable . . . insubstantial
- Ⓓ incontrovertible . . . admissible
- Ⓔ self-evident . . . conclusive

## Question 3

The author presumably believes that all businessmen are _____, for her main characters, whatever qualities they may lack, are virtual paragons of _____.

- Ⓐ clever . . . ingenuity
- Ⓑ covetous . . . greed
- Ⓒ virtuous . . . deceit
- Ⓓ successful . . . ambition
- Ⓔ cautious . . . achievement

## Question 4

Satire is a marvelous reflection of the spirit of an age; the subtle _____ of Swift's epistles mirrored the eighteenth century delight in elegant _____.

- Ⓐ profundity . . . ditties
- Ⓑ poignancy . . . pejoratives
- Ⓒ contempt . . . anachronisms
- Ⓓ provinciality . . . rusticity
- Ⓔ vitriol . . . disparagement

## Questions 5

Ginnie expects her every submission to be published or selected for performance, and this time her _____ is likely to be _____.

- Ⓐ candor . . . dispelled
- Ⓑ anticipation . . . piqued
- Ⓒ enthusiasm . . . dampened
- Ⓓ optimism . . . vindicated
- Ⓔ awareness . . . clouded

## Question 6

His opponent found it extremely frustrating that the governor's solid support from the voting public was not eroded by his _____ of significant issues.

- Ⓐ exaggeration
- Ⓑ misapprehension
- Ⓒ discussion
- Ⓓ selection
- Ⓔ acknowledgment

## Question 7

VEGETATE : ACTIVE ::

- (A) resist : beaten
- (B) mope : gloomy
- (C) grow : small
- (D) hassle : obnoxious
- (E) accept : questioning

## Question 8

PROPONENT : THEORY ::

- (A) nonbeliever : sin
- (B) traitor : country
- (C) adherent : belief
- (D) attorney : law
- (E) scientist : hypothesis

## Question 9

SPECIES : ORGANISM ::

- (A) specialty : physician
- (B) origin : idea
- (C) language : foreigner
- (D) genre : literature
- (E) family : ancestry

## Question 10

DISCHARGED : SOLDIER ::

- (A) fired : cannon
- (B) graduated : student
- (C) appointed : judge
- (D) transferred : employee
- (E) docked : salary

## Question 11

CUT : LACERATION ::

- (A) park : place
- (B) slit : gap
- (C) knife : separation
- (D) hole : puncture
- (E) boil : blister

## Question 12

OUTFOX : STRATEGY ::

- (A) outdo : trickery
- (B) defeat : stamina
- (C) outlast : force
- (D) victimize : terror
- (E) outrun : speed

## Question 13

COAX : BLANDISHMENTS ::

- (A) amuse : platitudes
- (B) compel : threats
- (C) deter : tidings
- (D) batter : insults
- (E) exercise : antics

## Question 14

TITLED : NOBLE ::

- (A) elected : candidate
- (B) acclaimed : artist
- (C) commissioned : officer
- (D) deposed : ruler
- (E) initiated : argument

**Questions 15–17:**

The four Galilean satellites of Jupiter probably experienced early, intense bombardment. Thus, the very ancient surface of Callisto remains scarred by impact craters. The younger, more varied surface of Ganymede reveals distinct light and dark areas, the light areas featuring networks of intersecting grooves and ridges, probably resulting from later iceflows. The impact sites of Europa have been almost completely erased, apparently by water outflowing from the interior and instantly forming vast, low, frozen seas. Satellite photographs of Io, the closest of the four to Jupiter, were revelatory. They showed a landscape dominated by volcanos, many erupting, making Io the most tectonically active object in the solar system. Since a body as small as Io cannot supply the energy for such activity, the accepted explanation has been that, forced into a highly eccentric orbit, Io is engulfed by tides stemming from a titanic contest between the other three Galilean moons and Jupiter.

## Question 15

According to the passage, which of the following is probably NOT true of the surface of Io?

- (A) It is characterized by intense tectonic activity.
- (B) Its volcanos have resulted from powerful tides.
- (C) It is younger than the surface of Callisto.
- (D) It is distinguished by many impact craters.
- (E) It has apparently not been shaped by internal force.

## Question 16

It can be inferred that the geologic features found in the light areas of Ganymede were probably formed

- (A) subsequent to the features found in the dark areas
- (B) in an earlier period than those in the dark areas
- (C) at roughly the same time as the features found in the dark areas
- (D) primarily by early bombardment
- (E) by the satellite's volcanic activity

## Question 17

It can be inferred that the author regards current knowledge about the satellites of Jupiter as

- (A) insignificant and disappointing
- (B) grossly outdated
- (C) complete and satisfactory
- (D) ambiguous and contradictory
- (E) persuasive though incomplete

## Question 18

ZEAL:

- (A) dissatisfaction
- (B) coarseness
- (C) apathy
- (D) wrath
- (E) impudence

## Question 19

ERRONEOUS:

- (A) careful
- (B) vigorous
- (C) accurate
- (D) convincing
- (E) thoughtful

## Question 20

COGNIZANT:

- (A) obsequious
- (B) oblivious
- (C) vigilant
- (D) intangible
- (E) unwise

**KAPLAN**

## Question 21

TENTATIVE:

- (A) permanent
- (B) finite
- (C) definite
- (D) adjacent
- (E) amiable

## Question 22

BAWDY:

- (A) prudish
- (B) superfluous
- (C) gaunt
- (D) ethereal
- (E) legitimate

## Question 23

ABET:

- (A) exaggerate
- (B) arrange
- (C) refuse
- (D) deter
- (E) confuse

## Question 24

DISPASSIONATE:

- (A) sentient
- (B) conspicuous
- (C) compassionate
- (D) partisan
- (E) heedless

## Question 25

PANEGYRIC:

- (A) defamatory essay
- (B) formal monologue
- (C) binding contract
- (D) witty aside
- (E) closing remark

## Question 26

PROLIX:

- (A) recalcitrant
- (B) unimportant
- (C) obstinate
- (D) diverse
- (E) pithy

**Questions 27–30:**

A pioneering figure in modern sociology, French social theorist Emile Durkheim examined the role of societal cohesion on emotional well-being. Believing that scientific methods should be applied to the study of society, Durkheim studied the level of integration of various social formations and the impact that such cohesion had on individuals within the group. He postulated that social groups with high levels of integration serve to buffer their members from frustrations and tragedies that could otherwise lead to desperation and self-destruction. Integration, in Durkheim's view, generally arises through shared activities and values.

Durkheim distinguished between *mechanical solidarity* and *organic solidarity* in classifying integrated groups. *Mechanical solidarity* dominates in groups in which individual differences are minimized and group devotion to a common aim is high. Durkheim identified *mechanical solidarity* among groups with little division of labor and high rates of cultural similarity, such as among more traditional and geographically isolated groups. *Organic solidarity*, in contrast, prevails in groups with high levels of individual differences, such as those with a highly specialized division of labor. In such groups, individual differences are a powerful source of connection, rather than of division. Because people engage in highly differentiated ways of life, they are by necessity interdependent. In these societies, there is greater freedom from some external controls, but such freedom occurs in concert with the interdependence of individuals, not in conflict with it.

Durkheim realized that societies may take many forms and consequently that group allegiance can manifest itself in a variety of ways. In both types of societies outlined above, however, Durkheim stressed that adherence to a common set of assumptions about the world was a necessary prerequisite for maintaining group integrity and avoiding social decay.

## Question 27

The author is primarily concerned with

Ⓐ supporting a specific approach to the study of the integration of social groups

Ⓑ comparing different ways that group dynamics maintain allegiance among group members

Ⓒ illustrating how a highly specialized division of labor can protect individuals from depression

Ⓓ determining what type of society will best suit an individual's emotional needs

Ⓔ contrasting a traditional view of a social phenomenon with a more recent one

## Question 28

The passage contrasts *mechanical solidarity* with *organic solidarity* along which of the following parameters?

Ⓐ the degree to which each relies on objective measures of group coherence

Ⓑ the manner and degree to which members are linked to the central group

Ⓒ the means by which each allows members to rebel against the group norm

Ⓓ the length of time that each has been used to describe the structure of societies

Ⓔ the effectiveness of each in serving the interests of its members

## Question 29

It can be inferred from the passage that

&#9398; as societies develop, they progress from *organic solidarity* to *mechanical solidarity*

&#9399; group integration enables societies to mask internal differences to the external world

&#9400; Durkheim preferred *organic solidarity* to *mechanical solidarity*

&#9401; individuals from societies with high degrees of *organic solidarity* would be unable to communicate effectively with individuals from societies that rest on *mechanical solidarity*

&#9402; the presence of some type of group integration is more important for group perpetuation than the specific form in which it is manifest

## Question 30

The passage states that *organic solidarity* predominates in societies with relatively high levels of intragroup dissimilarity because

&#9398; it enables individual differences to be minimized

&#9399; it causes societies to become more highly specialized, thus aiding industrialization

&#9400; individuals who engage in highly specialized activities must rely on others to ensure that their basic needs are met

&#9401; these societies are at greater risk of being affected by social stressors

&#9402; these societies are more likely to engage in shared activities and values

## Answer Key

| | | | |
|---|---|---|---|
| 1. E | 9. D | 17. E | 25. A |
| 2. E | 10. B | 18. C | 26. E |
| 3. A | 11. B | 19. C | 27. B |
| 4. E | 12. E | 20. B | 28. B |
| 5. D | 13. B | 21. C | 29. E |
| 6. B | 14. C | 22. A | 30. C |
| 7. E | 15. D | 23. D | |
| 8. C | 16. A | 24. D | |

## Explanations

*Question 1*

Taking a creative work like a play and moving it into another medium is an act of adaptation, so having seen *adapted* among the choices you might have been drawn right away to correct choice (E). And *vehicle* should not have been problematic for you—the sentence refers to *vehicle* not as a means of conveyance but as a means of display or expression. We can infer that *La Tosca* was Bernhardt's vehicle in the sense that it was created for her, to display her particular talents. (The purpose of any "star vehicle" is to showcase that star.)

It is incorrect to say that a play is written as a "role" (A)—written "to provide a role" would be more acceptable grammatically—and a work is not "reincarnated" from one medium into another, that verb being best reserved for the reembodiment or rebirth of living entities. The idea of *La Tosca*'s being a "biography" (B) for Bernhardt doesn't make sense (if the play were about her life, *biography of* would work), so this choice is out even though *changed* isn't bad in the second blank. A *metaphor* (C) is a poetic or figurative representation of something, and though we might call a play a metaphor for some event or idea we would not be likely to do so for a human being; *edited* provides a further complication, in that the process of editing requires pruning and revision, whereas changing a play into a musical drama requires a great deal more firsthand creativity. And while M. Sardou might well have offered *La Tosca* as a "present" to Mme. Bernhardt (D), *fictionalized* won't do; a real-life event can be fictionalized—into a play or an opera—but that verb cannot apply to something that is already fiction.

*Question 2*

If the requirement is that the verdict be a "definite determination," then a judge is pressured to consider a verdict to be definitely determined even when there is some room for doubt. (This analysis is supported by the author's use of the phrases *as if,* meaning something hypothetical, and *when in fact,* meaning that which is actually true.) Thus, if the evidence in a case is not "conclusive" (E), if there is room for doubt as to the guilt of the accused, a verdict based upon it probably will not be "self-evident" but will have to be treated as such by a judge (in the face of law and custom, that is).

Certainly if the evidence in a case is not "persuasive" (A), if the conclusion stemming from the evidence is debatable, it surely does suggest there's room for doubt. But pressure for a definite determination would hardly force a judge to view a verdict as "negotiable," that is, open for debate among the interested parties and possibly subject to revision. On the contrary, the more "negotiable" the verdict, the less "definitely determined" it's likely to be. *Justified* (B) works well—the judge might have to consider this verdict warranted even if the evidence didn't support it—but *accessible* in none of its meanings (easily approached; obtainable; open to influence) fits the context. Similarly the first words of (C) and (D), *unassailable* and *incontrovertible* respectively, give us what we need—a verdict that must be seen as a "definite determination"—but their respective second words shoot the choices down. Evidence that's not "insubstantial" is substantial, and there's no contradiction between an "unassailable" verdict and one based on substantial evidence. *Admissible* plays on your associations with real-life law, but the issue of whether or not something may properly be brought into evidence is far removed from the author's central point.

## Question 3

The author mentioned in this sentence believes that businessmen are models of some quality; *whatever qualities they may lack* implies that whatever bad points they possess, there's this one particular good thing about them. All of this should lead you to (A)—if an author's main characters are businessmen, and if they're all paragons of "ingenuity" (meaning inventively talented), one could easily be led to the presumption that the author thinks all businessmen are "clever."

Several of the wrong answers play off your possible biases about people in the business world, (B) being the most blatant in that regard. That choice is tempting only because an author's use of many "greedy" businessman characters might suggest that that author thinks all businessmen are "covetous." But labeling businessmen as greedy contradicts the sense of "whatever qualities they may lack"—as we noted, we need a positive quality. (Also, *paragons of greed* is awkward.) One who is morally upright or "virtuous" (C) would hardly be a paragon of "deceit" (lying, falseness). Characters possessing great "ambition" (D) wouldn't necessarily make one presume that the author believes all such people are "successful," since ambition and success in a field don't always go hand in hand; and there's even less connection between businessman characters who demonstrate great "achievement" (E) and a conclusion that, in the creator's opinion, all businessmen are "cautious."

## Question 4

The idea being communicated is that satire reflects the spirit of the age in which it's written, and the semicolon suggests that what's coming up is an example. So Swift must be a satirist, and something "subtle" about his work parallels something "elegant" about his work, which in turn parallels something "elegant" about his era. No outside knowledge of the eighteenth century is needed, because the only choice that works is (E). *Vitriol* is sulfuric acid in chemistry but sarcastic criticism in literature; literary vitriol, especially the "subtle" kind, would certainly mirror the spirit of an age that took delight in suave put-downs, or elegant "disparagement."

(A) presents a grave contradiction: An age fond of "ditties," brief and insubstantial songs or poems, would hardly be mirrored by "profound" (weight or deep) literary achievement. Two problems with (B): Not only is *poignancy*—the quality of affecting the emotions in a heartfelt way—not a characteristic usually found in any kind of satire, but poignancy would not "mirror the spirit" of elegant "pejoratives," that is, disparaging remarks. Good, wicked satire might very well display scorn or "contempt" (C), but that would have nothing to do with elegant "anachronisms," obsolete or archaic people or devices. (D) is the only choice providing two words that do, in a sense, mirror each other. *Provinciality* is rough-hewn unsophistication associated with those living in provinces, or a limited point of view—also called *parochial*. And *rusticity,* which is a country lifestyle, can also be boorishness and a lack of couth. But the two words aren't associated with the rest of the sentence, in which references to subtlety and (especially) elegance suggest something quite different from rusticity.

## Question 5

The "submissions" described must be manuscripts: Apparently Ginnie is an author who believes she'll strike gold every time she sends in a story or play. The structural signal *and* suggests that her expectations are going to be taken a step further. Now her "optimism" will be "vindicated" (D) and she'll be published. That structural signal, by the way, is what keeps (C) from being correct: If the signal were *but,* then we'd need a contrast, and Ginnie's "dampened enthusiasm" would contrast strongly with her typical expectations of success. Since Ginnie always figures that her stuff will be accepted, there's no reason for the sentence to point to her "anticipation" being " piqued" (B) on this particular occasion: her anticipation is always piqued (aroused, excited). Nothing in the sentence refers to or even hints at Ginnie's habit of speaking frankly, so it would be improper to conclude with a reference to her "candor" (A), "dispelled" or not. Similarly, Ginnie's perennial optimism about her chances at publication really has nothing to do with her "awareness" (E), but even if you justify it as a reference to "awareness of her chances to be published," a "clouded" awareness would suggest she's going to get shot down this time, and would require a contrast signal like *but* rather than *and*.

## Question 6

No candidate would be pleased at his or her opponent's "solid support from the voting public," but any candidate would become mighty frustrated if such support continued despite overwhelming reasons why it should cease. In this instance, we can infer that the popular governor remains popular despite the fact that he either doesn't understand "significance issues" or has made foolish choices as to what the "significant issues" are. In line with that analysis only (B) works: if the governor "misapprehended," or misunderstood, the issues, how frustrating it would be to his opponent when the public seemed not to care!

You might have been tempted by (C) or (D), and both are wrong for pretty much the same reason—each is too neutral in tone. The other choices are a good deal worse. It's not clear how a candidate would "exaggerate" (A) significant issues, nor why public support would be expected to erode as result of such overstatement; and a candidate's "acknowledgment" (E) of the key issues—recognition of their existence, perhaps even of their significance—would probably have an effect opposite to the erosion of voter support.

## Question 7

One who *vegetates* is inert or not *active*. If this gave you trouble, think of vegetables, which are markedly inactive living things, or perhaps the expression "veg out" meaning to stagnate, not think or do anything.

Similarly, one who *accepts* (E) takes things as they are without doubting, doesn't call things into question; he or she is therefore not *questioning*.

Notice that the stimulus conveys a sense of definition—a vegetator by definition is not active; such a sense is missing from (A), since one who *resists* may or may not be *beaten*, now or at some future time. When one *mopes* (B), it's usually because one feels *gloomy*—a gloomy person is characterized by moping, not a lack thereof. If a plant *grows* (C) from a height of 2 feet and 9 inches to a whopping 3 feet, it has indeed grown but remains *small*. As for (D), someone who *hassles* you is probably *obnoxious*, or at least can't be said to show a lack of obnoxiousness.

## Question 8

A *proponent* is someone who argues in favor of or supports some idea or practice. Someone who supports the civil-rights movement can be said to be a proponent of that cause. So we could say that one who supports a particular *theory* is a *proponent* of that *theory*, just as one who support or argues in favor of a particular *belief* (C) can be called an *adherent* of that *belief*. If *adherent* gave you trouble, think of *adhere* (to sick to) or *adhesive* (something that makes things stick together).

While a *nonbeliever* (A) might be likely to commit a sin in the eyes of others, the term *nonbeliever* is rarely applied to a person who supports a particular *sin*. A *traitor* (B) doesn't support his particular *country*, he betrays it; in betraying one country he may be supporting another, but in that sense he becomes a patriot, not a traitor, so this still doesn't work out. Now an *attorney* (D) does deal with the *law*, and must (or should, anyway) support the law. But we really can't say that an attorney is someone who supports a particular law—attorneys deal with all sorts of laws, and are honor-bound to respect them all, whereas adherents or proponents are so-called because of their devotion to one particular idea. And a *scientist* (E) is just as likely to condemn a given *hypothesis* as support it—and at any rate, his position on hypotheses is not what defines him as a scientist.

## Question 9

*Species* is a category of living things, and living things are known as *organisms*. *Species* refers to the particular type of organism in question, just as *genre* (D) is a term used to classify or categorize types of *literature*. Human beings are the species known as *Homo sapiens*, so that's how we're classified among all organisms. The novels of Agatha Christie are classified as mysteries: *mystery* is the classification of them among books.

*Physicians* (A) are, to an extent, categorized by their *specialty*—the obstetricians are different from the pediatricians, etcetera. But *species* and *genre* are both formal means of classification of their respective worlds, and they specifically break down the various groups for purposes of study. The specialty of a physician, on the other hand, isn't so definitive—it's just the branch of medicine the doctor happens to be most involved with. And no one breaks down the group *physicists* into specialties for the purposes of study. The *origin* (B) of an *idea* is not the idea's category—it's where the idea comes from. And the *language* (C) of a *foreigner* is not a category. Finally, *family* (E) is used in several figurative senses to classify things (for example, the tiger is a member of the cat family), but as it relates to *ancestry* it really carries no meaning other than that of a synonym (your ancestry, or the line of your ancestors, is your family).

## Question 10

*Discharged* is what a *soldier* is said to be when his or her tour of duty is up and he or she is released from commitment to the armed forces, just as *graduated* (B) is what a *student* is said to be when he or she has completed a particular stage of schooling, and is released. *Fired* (A) can be applied to a *cannon* that has made a shot, but it's the cannonball in this case that's released, not the cannon. In states in which *judges* (C) are not elected, they are *appointed* to the bench—that is, an important official such as the governor or the president appoints the judge to a job. But that begins his or her commitment rather than ends it. An *employee* (D) who has been *transferred* has not been released, but had his responsibilities shifted or been relocated. And *docked* (E), as it pertains to *salary*, refers to money withheld from an employee, usually as punishment for poor work. *Docked* does not refer to a salary that has finished its responsibility.

## Question 11

A *laceration* is a large *cut*, especially as it pertains to a wound. Or you could say a cut is an especially small or minor laceration. (A laceration might require stitches—a cut generally requires a Band-Aid.) Similarly, a *slit* (B) is a tiny crack, cut, or separation in something, and can be called a small *gap*.

The precise relationship between *park* (A) and *place* isn't entirely clear—perhaps "the park is a place" or "I can't find a place to park"? (And in Monopoly, there's always Park Place.) At any rate, this isn't what we're after. By cutting, a *knife* (C) can separate, but a knife isn't a small *separation* itself. A *hole* (D) and a *puncture* are really the same thing, and you can't say that the former is a smaller version of the latter. And as for (E), not only are *boils* and *blisters* very different from each other, medically speaking, but even if they were more alike, blisters are often smaller sores than boils.

## Question 12

To *outfox* someone is to defeat or win out over him by means of superior *strategy*, just as to *outrun* (E) someone is to beat him by means of superior *speed*. This is one of those items in which the vocabulary is simple, and you may therefore be prone to overconfidence and careless mistakes. The choices have to be examined carefully here. The most tempting wrong answer was perhaps (A), since it is true that one can *outdo* another by means of *trickery*. But *outfoxing*, *outrunning*, and *outlasting* are all specific kinds of outdoing that have to do with specific method, whereas *outdoing* is very general, and could apply to strategy and speed just as easily as it applies to trickery—there are unlimited ways to outdo someone. The same is true of *defeat* (B)—it's simply too general, and there are many means of defeating someone other than having greater *stamina*. To *outlast* someone (C) is, of course, to defeat him by means of superior endurance, or superior patience, not specifically by means of superior *force*. And *victimizing* someone (D) may indeed require *terror*, but victimizing has nothing to do with winning, and there are means other than terror by which people are victimized.

## Question 13

The stimulus and correct answer are really flip sides of each other, but the actions they describe share a common purpose—to get someone to do what you want him to do. In fact, if the stimulus failed—if you couldn't *coax* (or persuade) someone through a series of flattering and cajoling actions and speeches known as *blandishments*, you might take the next step and attempt to *compel* (B) him by making *threats*.

*Platitudes* (A) are trite, dull remarks, usually trotted out as if they were fresh and new but not usually trotted out for the purpose of *amusing* someone. If your aim was to *deter* (C) someone from a particular course, there are many more effective tools than *tidings*, which are news, information, or data. You might *batter* someone (D) with *insults*—in a figurative sense, at least—but you would not use them to batter someone into doing something. And to *exercise* (E) often amounts to engaging in *antics*, but you don't use antics to exercise someone into doing something—not even in the alternative meaning of the verb *exercise,* that is, to annoy or make uneasy.

## Question 14

Here's one that's easier to work with if we phrase the relationship from right to left. A person is called a *noble* (noun) because he or she is *titled*—that is, he or she has been bestowed with a title, such as Sir, Lord, or Squire. Similarly, an *officer* (C), especially one of the military,

is an officer because he or she's been *commissioned*.

A *candidate* (A) may or may not be *elected*—the first word describes an ambition rather than an existing status. An especially good *artist* may be *acclaimed* (B), or highly praised, but that doesn't make him or her an artist. A *deposed* (D) *ruler* is one who has been kicked out. What initiates an argument cannot be made analogous to the stimulus.

## Question 15

GRE science passages often focus on one big contrast—and the questions will focus on the same contrast, again and again. Thus even detail questions like this one are really "main idea" questions in disguise. In this passage, the big contrast is between moons that have remained unchanged since their "early, intense bombardment" (sentence 1), and those whose surfaces have been altered in more recent epochs. Io is mentioned in the last three sentences. These sentences stress recent, indeed ongoing, changes in the satellite's surface. By inference, most impact craters from the long-ago bombardments have probably been obliterated (D). Continuing tectonic activity (A) is mentioned explicitly; tides (B) are mentioned in the final sentence as the probable cause of the tectonic activity, and hence the active volcanos. Inferably Io's surface is younger than the "very ancient" surface of Callisto, (C). (E) is the only tricky choice. The phrase *tectonically active* may automatically conjure up the idea of internal forces, since these cause tectonic activity on the earth. But it's explicitly stated (last sentence) that Io is too small to supply its own energy for such activity, so (E) is true.

## Question 16

Again, keep your eye on the big contrast. The bombardments, and the craters that record them, were laid down long ago; thus a surface marked by impact craters (the dark areas of Ganymede) is older than one not so marked (the lighter areas). In addition, it's mentioned that some features of the light areas prob-

**KAPLAN**

ably result from later iceflows. Thus, (A) is correct, ruling out (B) and (C). The light areas feature grooves and ridges probably resulting from these iceflows, not from early bombardment (D). Volcanic activity, (E), is not mentioned in relation to Ganymede.

## Question 17

The passage conveys a great deal of information, which the author implicitly accepts, ruling out (A). (The word used for the photographs of Io—*revelatory*—is enough by itself to eliminate this choice.) The fact that information about Io comes from satellite photographs rules out (B). No contradictions are mentioned, and though areas of uncertainty remain, (D)'s *ambiguous and contradictory* will not work as a general characterization. On the other hand, (C) is out because of the cautious language used throughout: *probably* (twice), *apparently,* and *the accepted explanation.* Hence the knowledge is persuasive though incomplete, as specified in (E).

## Question 18

*Zeal* means enthusiasm or fanaticism, so if you predict its opposite you should come up with something like *indifference,* or the actual correct response, (C) *apathy.*

## Question 19

*Erroneous* means incorrect, so a good prediction for its opposite would be *correct.* Of the answer choices, the closest match is (C), *accurate.*

## Question 20

To be *cognizant* is to be aware. Look for a word that means *unaware.* (B), *oblivious,* is a nice match. (A), *obsequious,* means overly flattering or servile. If you get stuck, try making opposites of the answer choices and comparing the opposites with the stem word. This should help you eliminate close seconds such as (E), *unwise.*

## Question 21

*Tentative* means provisional or unsettled, as in "a tentative plan"—one that may or may not be carried out. So its best opposite would be (C), *definite.* If you were familiar with the phrase "a tentative plan" you could have also used this phrase to eliminate answer choices. If you can describe a plan as *tentative,* you should also be able to use the opposite of *tentative* to describe a plan. But a *permanent* plan, a *finite* plan, an *adjacent* plan, and an *amiable* plan all sound a bit funny. Only a *definite* plan makes sense.

## Question 22

*Bawdy* means racy or lewd. A good opposite would be *straitlaced* or *proper.* (A), *prudish,* fits perfectly. Of the wrong answers, *superfluous* means unnecessary, *gaunt* means thin, *ethereal* means heavenly or immaterial, and *legitimate* means legal or authentic.

## Question 23

To *abet* means to aid or assist. The phrase "aiding and abetting" is actually a redundancy, much like the phrase "to cease and desist." A good opposite for abet, therefore, would be *hinder.* Choice (D), *deter,* is a good match.

## Question 24

Someone who's *dispassionate* is unbiased or objective. A good prediction for its opposite would be *biased* or *unfair.* Choice (D), *partisan,* meaning biased in favor of one side, matches beautifully. Of the wrong answer choices, *sentient* means conscious or aware; *stoic* means expressionless or impassive.

## Question 25

A *panegyric* is a tough GRE-friendly word meaning formal or elaborate praise in writing or oration. Therefore the best opposite would be (A), *defamatory essay*. On tough Antonyms, particularly ones with phrases in the answer choices, you can always go to answer choices and try to make opposites of them; not all words or phrases have good opposites, and these can be eliminated. For instance, what's a good opposite for (D), *witty aside*? Likewise, (B), *formal monologue*, and (C), *binding contract*, don't lead to clear-cut opposites. The best rule of thumb when you're dealing with unfamiliar Antonym stems is to make opposites of the answer choices, eliminating any choice that takes you more than five seconds to come up with an opposite, make your best guess, and when stuck between two good guesses, go for the one that's more extreme.

## Question 26

Once again you're given a tough GRE-friendly stem word, *prolix*, so if you knew that *prolix* means wordy you could come up with the correct answer, (E), *pithy*, meaning to the point. Otherwise, once again you'd have to work with the answer choices. For instance, if you had a sense that *prolix* has a somewhat negative word charge, you eliminate choices that have negative word charges, (A), (B), and (C). You could also make opposites of the answer choices; for instance, the opposite of (D), *diverse*, would be similar. If you don't think that *prolix* means similar, you can eliminate that answer choice. A final word about Antonyms: Sometimes you simply won't know the stem word—staring at it for a couple of minutes is not going to get you closer to the correct answer. Using word charge, word roots, and word associations, and making opposites of the answer choices can all help you, but at some point, you just have to make your best guess and move on.

## Question 27

The topic of this passage is Emile Durkheim's study of social cohesion in society and the author's purpose might be summed up as describing two different ways that societies can maintain social integration among their members. A road map of the paragraph structure might look like this: paragraph 1 introduces Durkheim and his study of social groups; paragraph 2 discusses two ways societies can maintain social integration; paragraph 3 offers a broader context for interpreting the evidence in paragraph 2.

The final paragraph gives you the key to answering this global question. The author is describing different ways that societies can function without choosing a side or advocating a specific position. You can rule out (A) immediately for its strong stand. (C) distorts a detail beyond its acceptable scope. While the passage does discuss how social cohesion can function in societies with high degrees of labor specialization, this is not the author's main goal. (D) takes a prescriptive stance, and the author never tells us how to live our lives. Finally, (E) makes a comparison that is not there. Both of the mechanisms for maintaining social solidarity were developed by Durkheim at the same time and are part of the same worldview, namely, his. The comparison between a traditional and a recent view is inapplicable here.

## Question 28

What is the crucial difference between *mechanical solidarity* and *organic solidarity*? The level of homogeneity in the group in which each functions. Neither one relies on any measure, objective or otherwise, of group coherence. Rather, they describe the way societies function naturally, ruling out (A). (C) introduces the notion of rebellion, a concept that is not mentioned in the passage and hence, cannot be correct. (D) is wrong because the two types of solidarity were developed at the same time by Durkheim; we do not have a traditional view and a more recent view of the same phenomenon, but rather two different ways that societies can function within the same worldview. (E) brings into question the effectiveness of each, and the last paragraph makes it clear that either one can serve its members needs equally well.

*Question 29*

In this inference question, you will need to think about the author's opinion as you approach the answer choices. (A) is wrong because the author never discusses the two forms of *solidarity* as being related to each other, nor does she discuss the transformation of societies over time. (B) is outside the scope, as the relationship of individual societies to the world-at-large is not an issue that concerns the author. (C) makes a subjective statement about Durkheim that is never suggested by the passage. (D) makes a comparison between the two types of social groups that is not supported by the passage. (E), however, is basically a close paraphrase of the final paragraph of the passage. The particular type of integration that exists within a given society is less important than that it is present in some form.

*Question 30*

In this detail question, you should research the second paragraph, where *organic solidarity* is discussed. There you'll find Durkheim's reasoning for why it exists in societies with high levels of heterogeneity. *Organic solidarity* prevails in societies with fewer similarities among members because when a society is highly specialized its members rely on each other out of necessity—as a way to ensure that everyone's needs are met. Reading through the answers, (C) should jump out at you as conveying this sentiment.

(A) is the opposite of what we want. In societies in which *organic solidarity* dominates, individual differences are relatively high. (B) implies a causal relationship between *organic solidarity* and the way a society is organized, but *organic solidarity* is simply a term to describe the way a society *is* functioning; it is not an active agent of anything. (D) uses information that was never mentioned in the passage—namely, that some societies are more likely to be affected by social stressors. Finally, (E) misappropriates information from the section on societies in which *mechanical solidarity* dominates. Societies that operate by *organic solidarity*, by contrast, tend not to be comprised of members who lead highly similar lives.

# Test Content: Quantitative

- Learn the Basic Principles and the Kaplan Method for answering QCs, Problem Solving, and Graph questions

- Review the key concepts of percentages, simultaneous equations, symbolism, special triangles, multiple and oddball figures, the three Ms, range, and probability

- Complete the Quantitative Practice Set

**Y**ou'll have 45 minutes to complete 28 questions in the Quantitative section. The GRE tests the same sort of mathematical concepts that the SAT does: arithmetic, algebra, and geometry. There is no trigonometry or calculus tested on the GRE. However, the test does contain some mathematical concepts that you didn't see on the SAT: median, mode, range, standard deviation, and simple probability.

There are three formats of GRE math questions: problem solving, which have five answer choices each; graph questions, which have five answer choices each and which are based on one or more graphs; and quantitative comparisons (QCs), which have only four answer choices each. Because about half of the questions on each math section are QCs, let's look at these first.

## Kaplan Rules

To score high on QCs, learn what the answer choices stand for, and know these cold.

## Quantitative Comparisons

In QCs, instead of solving for a particular value, you need to compare two quantities. At first, QCs may appear really difficult because of their unfamiliar format. However, once you become used to them, they can be quicker and easier than the other types of math questions.

## The Questions

The difficulty of the QCs will depend on how well you are doing in the section. In each question, you'll see two mathematical expressions. One is in Column A, the other in Column B. Your job is to compare them. Some questions include additional information about one or both quantities. This information is centered, and is essential to making the comparison.

## The Answer Choices and Directions

QCs are the only questions type on the GRE with four instead of five answer choices. The answer choices to QCs never change and here's what they look like:

- Ⓐ **The quantity in Column A is greater**
- Ⓑ **The quantity in Column B is greater**
- Ⓒ **The two quantities are equal**
- Ⓓ **The relationship cannot be determined from the information given**

Because the answer choices to QCs never change, from here on in we will omit the answer choices from the QC examples in this book. The directions to QCs look something like this:

> **This question consists of two quantities, one in Column A and another in Column B. You are to compare the two quantities and decide whether**
>
> > **the quantity in Column A is greater;**
> >
> > **the quantity in Column B is greater;**
> >
> > **the two quantities are equal;**
> >
> > **the relationship cannot be determined from the information given**
>
> Common information: **In a question, information concerning one or both of the quantities to be compared is centered above the two columns. A symbol that appears in both columns represents the same thing in Column A as it does in Column B.**

## Basic Principles of Quantitative Comparisons

Choices (A), (B), and (C) all represent definite relationships between the quantities in Column A and Column B. But choice (D) represents a relationship that cannot be determined. Here are two things to remember about choice (D) that will help you decide when to pick it:

- **Choice (D) is never correct if both columns contain only numbers.** The relationship between numbers is unchanging, but choice (D) means more than one relationship is possible.
- **Choice (D) is correct if you can demonstrate two different relationships between the columns.**

Suppose you ran across the following QC:

| Column A | Column B |
|----------|----------|
| $2x$ | $3x$ |

If $x$ is a positive number, Column B is greater than Column A. If $x = 0$, the columns are equal. If $x$ equals any negative number, Column B is less than Column A. Because more than one relationship is possible, the answer is (D). In fact, as soon as you find a second possibility, stop work and pick choice (D).

## The Kaplan Method for Quantitative Comparisons

Here are six Kaplan strategies that will enable you to make quick comparisons. In the rest of this chapter you'll learn how they work and you'll try them on practice problems.

1. *Compare piece by piece.*
   This works on QCs that compare two sums or two products.

2. *Make one column look like the other.*
   This is a great approach when the columns look so different that you can't compare them directly.

3. *Do the same thing to both columns.*
   Change both columns by adding, subtracting, multiplying, or dividing by the same amount on both sides in order to make the comparison more apparent.

4. *Pick numbers.*
   Use this to get a handle on abstract algebra QCs.

5. *Redraw the diagram.*
   Redrawing a diagram can clarify the relationships between measurements.

6. *Avoid QC traps.*
   Stay alert for questions designed to fool you by leading you to the obvious, wrong answer.

### Note

No calculators are allowed during the GRE. The test center will provide you with scratch paper on which you can work out your calculations.

Now let's look at how these strategies work.

*1. Compare Piece by Piece*

| Column A | Column B |
|----------|----------|

$$w > x > 0 > y > z$$

| Column A | Column B |
|----------|----------|
| $w + y$ | $x + z$ |

In this problem, there are four variables—$w$, $x$, $y$, and $z$. Compare the value of each "piece" in each column. If every "piece" in one column is greater than a corresponding "piece" in the other column and the only operation involved is addition, the column with the greater individual values will have the greater total value.

From the given information we know that $w > x$ and $y > z$. Therefore, the first term in Column A, $w$, is greater than the first term in Column B, $x$. Similarly, the second term in Column A, $y$, is greater than the second term in Column B, $z$. Because each piece in Column A is greater than the corresponding piece in Column B, Column A must be greater; the answer is (A).

*2. Make One Column Look Like the Other*
When the quantities in Columns A and B are expressed differently, you can often make the comparison easier by changing one column to look like the other. For example, if one column is a percent, and the other a fraction, try converting the percent to a fraction.

| Column A | Column B |
|----------|----------|
| $x(x - 1)$ | $x^2 - x$ |

Here Column A has parentheses, and Column B doesn't. So make Column A look more like Column B: get rid of those parentheses. You then end up with $x^2 - x$ in both columns, which means they are equal and the answer is (C).

Try another example, this time involving geometry.

| Column A | Column B |
|----------|----------|

The diameter of circle $O$ is $d$ and the area is $a$.

| Column A | Column B |
|----------|----------|
| $\dfrac{\pi d^2}{2}$ | $a$ |

**KAPLAN**

Make Column B look more like Column A by rewriting $a$, the area of the circle, in terms of the diameter, $d$. The area of any circle equals $\pi r^2$, where $r$ is the radius.

Since the radius is half the diameter, we can plug in $\frac{d}{2}$ for $r$ in the area formula to get $\pi\left(\frac{d}{2}\right)^2$ in Column B. Simplifying we get $\frac{\pi d^2}{4}$. Since both columns contain $\pi$, we can simply compare $\frac{d^2}{2}$ with $\frac{d^2}{4}$. $\frac{d^2}{4}$ is half as much as $\frac{d^2}{2}$, and since $d^2$ must be positive, Column A is greater and choice (A) is correct.

### 3. Do the Same Thing to Both Columns

Some QC questions become much clearer if you change not just the appearances but also the values of both columns. Treat them like two sides of an inequality, with the sign temporarily hidden.

You can add or subtract the same amount from both columns, and multiply or divide by the same positive amount without altering the relationship. You can also square both columns if you're sure they're both positive. But watch out: Multiplying or dividing an inequality by a negative number reverses the direction of the inequality sign. Since it alters the relationship between the columns, avoid multiplying or dividing by a negative number.

In the QC below, what could you do to both columns?

| Column A | Column B |
|----------|----------|
| | $4a + 3 = 7b$ |
| $20a + 10$ | $35b - 5$ |

## Kaplan Tip

Don't multiply or divide both QC columns by a negative number.

All the terms in the two columns are multiples of 5, so divide both columns by 5 to simplify. You're left with $4a + 2$ in Column A and $7b - 1$ in Column B. This resembles the equation given in the centered information. In fact, if you add 1 to both columns, you have $4a + 3$ in Column A and $7b$ in Column B. The centered equation tells us they are equal. Thus choice (C) is correct.

In the next QC, what could you do to both columns?

| Column A | Column B |
|---|---|

$$y > 0$$

| Column A | Column B |
|---|---|
| $1 + \dfrac{y}{1 + y}$ | $1 + \dfrac{1}{1 + y}$ |

Solution: First subtract 1 from both sides. That gives you $\frac{y}{1+y}$ in Column A, and $\frac{1}{1+y}$ in Column B. Then multiply both sides by $1 + y$, which must be positive since $y$ is positive. You're left comparing $y$ with 1.

You know $y$ is greater than 0, but it could be a fraction less than 1, so it could be greater or less than 1. Since you can't say for sure which column is greater, the answer is (D).

*4. Pick Numbers*
If a QC involves variables, try picking numbers to make the relationship clearer. Here's what you do:

- Pick numbers that are easy to work with.
- Plug in the numbers and calculate the values. Note the relationship between the columns.
- Pick another number for each variable and calculate the values again.

| Column A | Column B |
|---|---|

$$r > s > t > w > 0$$

| Column A | Column B |
|---|---|
| $\dfrac{r}{t}$ | $\dfrac{s}{w}$ |

Try $r = 4$, $s = 3$, $t = 2$, and $w = 1$. Then Column A $= \frac{r}{t} = \frac{4}{2} = 2$. And Column B $= \frac{s}{w} = \frac{3}{1} = 3$. So in this case Column B is greater than Column A.

*Always Pick More Than One Number and Calculate Again.* In the example above, we first found Column B was bigger. But that doesn't mean Column B is always bigger and that the answer is (B). It does mean the answer is not (A) or (C). But the answer could still be (D)—not enough information to decide.

If time is short, guess between (B) and (D). But whenever you can, pick another set of numbers and calculate again.

As best you can, make a special effort to find a second set of numbers that will alter the relationship. Here for example, try making $r$ a lot larger. Pick $r = 30$ and keep the other variables as they were. Now Column A $= \frac{30}{2} = 15$. This time, Column A is greater than Column B, so answer choice (D) is correct.

*Pick Different Kinds of Numbers.* Don't assume all variables represent positive integers. Unless you're told otherwise, variables can represent zero, negative numbers, or fractions. Since different kinds of numbers behave differently, always pick a different kind of number the second time around. In the example above, we plugged in a small positive number the first time and a larger number the second.

In the next three examples, we pick different numbers and get different results. Since we can't find constant relationships between Columns A and B, in all these cases the answer is (D).

| Column A | Column B |
| --- | --- |
| $w$ | $-w$ |

If $w = 5$, Column A = 5 and Column B = $-5$, so Column A is greater.
If $w = -5$, Column A = $-5$ and Column B = 5, so Column B is greater.

| Column A | Column B |
| --- | --- |
| $x \neq 0$ | |
| $x$ | $\frac{1}{x}$ |

If $x = 3$, Column A = 3 and Column B = $\frac{1}{3}$, so Column A is greater.

If $x = \frac{1}{3}$, Column A = $\frac{1}{3}$ and Column B = $\frac{1}{\frac{1}{3}}$ = 3, so Column B is greater.

## Kaplan Tip

If the relationship between Columns A and B changes when you pick other numbers, (D) must be the answer.

| Column A | Column B |
|----------|----------|
| $x$ | $x^2$ |

If $x = \frac{1}{2}$, Column A = $\frac{1}{2}$ and Column B = $\frac{1}{4}$, so Column A is greater.

If $x = 2$, Column A = 2 and Column B = 4, so Column B is greater.

### 5. Redraw the Diagram
- Redraw a diagram if the one that's given confuses you.
- Redraw scale diagrams to exaggerate crucial differences.

Some geometry diagrams may be misleading. Two angles or lengths may look equal as drawn in the diagram, but the given information tells you that there is a slight difference in their measures. The best strategy is to redraw the diagram so that their relationship can be clearly seen.

| Column A | Column B |
|----------|----------|

ABCD is a rectangle.

|   |   |
|---|---|
| $a$ | $b$ |

Redraw this diagram to exaggerate the difference between the 89° degree angle and the 91° angle. In other words, make the larger angle much larger, and the smaller angle much smaller. The new rectangle that results is much wider than it is tall.

In the new diagram, where the crucial difference jumps out, $a$ is clearly greater than $b$.

## 6. *Avoid QC Traps*

To avoid QC traps, always be alert. Don't assume anything. Be especially cautious near the end of the question set.

*Don't Be Tricked by Misleading Information.*

| Column A | Column B |
|----------|----------|
| John is taller than Bob. | |
| John's weight in pounds | Bob's weight in pounds |

The test makers hope you think, "If John is taller, he must weigh more." But there's no guaranteed relationship between height and weight, so you don't have enough information. The answer is (D). Fortunately, problems like this are easy to spot if you stay alert.

*Don't Assume.* A common QC mistake is to assume that variables represent positive integers. As we saw in using the picking numbers strategy, fractions or negative numbers often show another relationship between the columns.

| Column A | Column B |
|----------|----------|
| When 1 is added to the square of $x$ the result is 37. | |
| $x$ | 6 |

It is easy to assume that $x$ must be 6, since the square of $x$ is 36. That would make choice (C) correct. However, it is possible that $x = -6$. Since $x$ could be either 6 or $-6$, the answer is (D).

*Don't Forget to Consider Other Possibilities.*

| Column A | Column B |
|----------|----------|

$$\begin{array}{r} R \\ S \\ +T \\ \hline 1\,W \end{array}$$

In the addition problem above, $R$, $S$, and $T$ are different digits that are multiples of 3, and $W$ is a digit.

| Column A | Column B |
|----------|----------|
| $W$ | 8 |

Because you're told that $R$, $S$, and $T$ are digits and different multiples of 3, most people will think of 3, 6, and 9, which add up to 18. That makes $W$ equal to 8, and Columns A and B equal. But that's too obvious for a QC at the end of the section.

There's another possibility. 0 is also a multiple of 3. So the three digits could be 0, 3, and 9, or 0, 6, and 9, which give totals of 12 and 15, respectively. That means $W$ could be 8, 2, or 5. Since the columns could be equal, or Column B could be greater, answer choice (D) must be correct.

*Don't Fall for Look-Alikes.*

| Column A | Column B |
|:---:|:---:|
| $\sqrt{5} + \sqrt{5}$ | $\sqrt{10}$ |

At first glance, forgetting the rules of radicals, you might think these quantities are equal and that the answer is (C). But use some common sense to see this isn't the case. Each $\sqrt{5}$ in Column A is bigger than $\sqrt{4}$, so Column A is more than 4. The $\sqrt{10}$ in Column B is less than another familiar number, $\sqrt{16}$, so Column B is less than 4. The answer is (A).

Now use Kaplan's six strategies to solve nine typical QC questions. Then check your work against our solutions.

*Practice Problems*

| | Column A | Column B |
|---|:---:|:---:|
| 1. | $x^2 + 2x - 2$ | $x^2 + 2x - 1$ |

$$x = 2y$$
$$y > 0$$

| | Column A | Column B |
|---|:---:|:---:|
| 2. | $4^{2y}$ | $2^x$ |

$$\frac{x}{y} = \frac{z}{4}$$

$x$, $y$, and $z$ are positive.

| | Column A | Column B |
|---|:---:|:---:|
| 3. | $6x$ | $2yz$ |

Column A                                    Column B

*q*, *r*, and *s* are positive integers.

$qrs > 12$

4.          $\dfrac{qr}{5}$                                    $\dfrac{3}{s}$

---

$x > 1$

$y > 0$

5.          $y^x$                                    $y^{(x+1)}$

---

$7p + 3 = r$

$3p + 7 = s$

6.          *r*                                    *s*

---

In triangle *XYZ*, the measure of angle *X* equals the measure of angle *Y*.

7.    The degree measure                The degree measure
      of angle Z                        of angle X plus the
                                        degree measure of
                                        angle Y

---

$h > 1$

8.    The number of                     $\dfrac{60}{h}$
      minutes in *h*
      hours

---

Square *A*          Square *B*

9.    Perimeter of square *A*           Length of *WY*
      Perimeter of square *B*           Length of *PR*

*Answer Key*

**1. (B)** Comparing the respective pieces of the two columns, the only difference is the third piece: $-2$ in Column A and $-1$ in Column B. We don't know the value of $x$, but whatever it is, $x^2$ in Column A must have the same value as $x^2$ in Column B, and $2x$ in Column A must have the same value as $2x$ in Column B. Since any quantity minus 2 must be less than that quantity minus 1, Column B is greater than Column A.

**2. (A)** Replacing the $x$ exponent in Column B with the equivalent value given in the problem, we're comparing $4^{2y}$ to $2^{2y}$. Since $y$ is greater than zero, raising 4 to the $2y$ power will result in a greater value than raising 2 to the $2y$ power.

**3. (B)** Do the same thing to both columns until they resemble the centered information. When we divide both columns by $6y$ we get $\frac{6x}{6y}$ or $\frac{x}{y}$ in Column A, and $\frac{2yz}{6y}$, or $\frac{z}{3}$ in Column B. Since $\frac{x}{y} = \frac{z}{4}$, and $\frac{z}{3} > \frac{z}{4}$ (because $z$ is positive), $\frac{z}{3} > \frac{x}{y}$.

**4. (D)** Do the same thing to both columns to make them look like the centered information. When we multiply both columns by $5s$ we get $qrs$ in Column A and 15 in Column B. Since $qrs$ could be any integer greater than 12, it could be greater than, equal to, or less than 15.

**5. (D)** Try $x = y = 2$. Then Column A $= y^x = 2^2 = 4$. Column B $= y^{x+1} = 2^3 = 8$, making Column B greater. But if $x = 2$ and $y = \frac{1}{2}$, Column A $= \left(\frac{1}{2}\right)^2 = \frac{1}{4}$ and Column B $= \left(\frac{1}{2}\right)^3 = \frac{1}{8}$. In this case, Column A is greater than Column B, so the answer is (D).

**6. (D)** Pick a value for $p$, and see what effect this has on $r$ and $s$. If $p = 1$, $r = (7 \times 1) + 3 = 10$, and $s = (3 \times 1) + 7 = 10$, and the two columns are equal. But if $p = 0$, $r = (7 \times 0) + 3 = 3$, and $s = (3 \times 0) + 7 = 7$, and Column A is smaller than Column B. Since there are at least two different possible relationships, the answer is choice (D).

**7. (D)** Since angle $X$ = angle $Y$, this is an isosceles triangle. We can draw two diagrams with $X$ and $Y$ as the base angles of an isosceles triangle. In one diagram, make the triangle tall and narrow, so that angle $X$ and angle $Y$ are very large, and angle $Z$ is very small. In this case, column B is greater. In the second diagram, make the triangle short and wide, so that angle $Z$ is much larger than angle $X$ and angle $Y$. In this case, Column A is greater. Since more than one relationship between the columns is possible, the correct answer is choice (D).

**8. (A)** The "obvious" answer here is choice (C), because there are 60 minutes in an hour, and 60 appears in Column B. But the number of minutes in $h$ hours would equal 60 times $h$, not 60 divided by $h$. Since $h$ is greater than 1, the number in Column B will be less than the actual number of minutes in $h$ hours, so Column A is greater. (A) is correct.

**9. (C)** We don't know the exact relationship between Square $A$ and Square $B$, but it doesn't matter. The problem is actually just comparing the ratios of corresponding parts of two squares. Whatever the relationship between them is for one specific length in both squares, the same relationship will exist between them for any other corresponding length. If a side of one square is twice the length of a side of the second square, the diagonal will also be twice as long. The ratio of the perimeters of the two squares is the same as the ratio of the diagonals. Therefore, the columns are equal. (C) is correct.

## Teacher Tip

"Many of my GRE students are afraid because they haven't taken math in a long time. I explain to them that the math is easier than the math on the SAT, and that we will help them to brush up on the basics. Just like getting back on a bicycle after having not ridden for a while, the knowledge is still there—we just need to bring it back out."
—Jaelithe Russ
Akron, Ohio

## Kaplan Tip

You will save time on Test Day if you can translate common percents into their fraction and decimal equivalents.

$\frac{1}{5} = 20\% = .20$

$\frac{1}{4} = 25\% = .25$

$\frac{1}{3} = 33\frac{1}{3}\% = .\overline{3}$

$\frac{1}{2} = 50\% = .5$

$\frac{2}{3} = 66\frac{2}{3}\% = .\overline{6}$

$\frac{3}{4} = 75\% = .75$

# Problem Solving

In problem solving, you will have to solve problems that test a variety of mathematical concepts. Problem solving questions typically deal with percentages, simultaneous equations, symbolism, special triangles, multiple and oddball figures, mean, median, mode, range, and probability.

## The Format

### The Questions
You can expect about 10 problem solving questions. As with other question types, the more questions you get right, the harder the problem solving questions you will see.

### The Directions
The directions that you'll see will look something like this:

**Each of Questions 16–20 has five answer choices. For each of these questions, select the best answer choice given.**

## The Kaplan Approach to Percentages

> Last year Julie's annual salary was $20,000. This year's raise brings her to an annual salary of $25,000. If she gets the same percent raise every year, what will her salary be next year?
>
> (A) $27,500
> (B) $30,000
> (C) $31,250
> (D) $32,500
> (E) $35,000

In percent problems, you're usually given two pieces of information and asked to find the third. When you see a percent problem, remember:

- If you are solving for a percent:

$$\text{Percent} = \frac{\text{Part}}{\text{Whole}}$$

- If you need to solve for a part:

$$\text{Percent} \times \text{Whole} = \text{Part}$$

This problem asks for Julie's projected salary for next year—that is, her current salary plus her next raise.

You know last year's salary ($20,000), and you know this year's salary ($25,000), so you can find the difference between the two salaries:

$$\$25,000 - \$20,000 = \$5,000 = \text{her raise}$$

Now find the percent of her raise, by using the formula

$$\text{Percent} = \frac{\text{Part}}{\text{Whole}}$$

Since Julie's raise was calculated on last year's salary, divide by $20,000.

$$\text{Percent raise} = \frac{\$5,000}{\$20,000} = \frac{1}{4} = 25\%$$

You know she will get the same percent raise next year, so solve for the part. Use the formula: Percent × Whole = Part. Her raise next year will be $25\% \times \$25,000 = \frac{1}{4} \times 25,000 = \$6,250$. Add that amount to this year's salary and you have her projected salary:

$$\$25,000 + \$6,250 = \$31,250 \text{ or answer choice (C)}.$$

Make sure that you change the percent to either a fraction or a decimal before beginning calculations.

*Practice Problems*

| Column A | Column B |
| --- | --- |
| 1.     5% of 3% of 45 | 6.75 |

2. If a sweater sells for $48 after a 25 percent markdown, what was its original price?

    (A) $56
    (B) $60
    (C) $64
    (D) $68
    (E) $72

## Kaplan Tip

Be sure you know which whole to plug in. Here you're looking for a percent of $20,000, not $25,000.

## Review

$x$ percent of $y$ = $y$ percent of $x$

20% of 50 = 50% of 20

$$\frac{1}{5} \times 50 = \frac{1}{2} \times 20$$

$$10 = 10$$

*Solutions*

**1. (B)** Percent × Whole = Part. 5% of (3% of 45) = .05 × (.03 × 45) = .05 × 1.35 = .0675, which is less than 6.75 in Column B.

**2. (C)** We want to solve for the original price, the Whole. The percent markdown is 25%, so $48 is 75% of the whole: Percent × Whole = Part.

$$75\% \times \text{Original Price} = \$48$$
$$\text{Original Price} = \frac{\$48}{0.75} = \$64$$

## The Kaplan Approach to Simultaneous Equations

If $p + 2q = 14$ and $3p + q = 12$, then $p =$

- (A) −2
- (B) −1
- (C) 1
- (D) 2
- (E) 3

### Kaplan Tip

Combine the equations—by adding or subtracting them—to cancel out all but one of the variables.

In order to get a numerical value for each variable, you need as many different equations as there are variables to solve for. So, if you have two variables, you need two independent equations.

You could tackle this problem by solving for one variable in terms of the other, and then plugging this expression into the other equation. But the simultaneous equations that appear on the GRE can usually be handled in an easier way.

You can't eliminate $p$ or $q$ by adding or subtracting the equations in their present form. But look what happens if you multiply both sides of the second equation by 2:

$$2(3p + q) = 2(12)$$
$$6p + 2q = 24$$

Now when you subtract the first equation from the second, the $q$s will cancel out so you can solve for $p$:

$$6p + 2q = 24$$
$$-[p + 2q = 14]$$
$$\overline{5p + 0 = 10}$$

If $5p = 10$, $p = 2$.

**KAPLAN**

*Practice Problems*

1. If $x + y = 8$ and $y - x = -2$, then $y =$

   (A)  −2
   (B)  3
   (C)  5
   (D)  8
   (E)  10

2. If $m - n = 5$ and $2m + 3n = 15$, then $m + n =$

   (A)  1
   (B)  6
   (C)  7
   (D)  10
   (E)  15

*Solutions*

**1. (B)** When you add the two equations, the $x$'s cancel out and you find that $2y = 6$, so $y = 3$.

**2. (C)** Multiply the first equation by 2, then subtract the first equation from the second to eliminate the $m$'s and find that $5n = 5$, or $n = 1$. Plugging this value for $n$ into the first equation shows that $m = 6$, so $m + n = 7$, choice (C).

$$2m + 3n = 15 \qquad m - n = 5 \qquad m + n = 6 + 1 = 7$$
$$-2m + 2n = -10 \qquad m - 1 = 5$$
$$5n = 5 \qquad m = 6$$
$$n = 1$$

## The Kaplan Approach to Symbolism

If $a \star b = \sqrt{a + b}$ for all nonnegative numbers, what is the value of $10 \star 6$?

(A)  0

(B)  2

(C)  4

(D)  8

(E)  16

## Kaplan Tip

When a symbolism problem includes parentheses, do the operations inside the parentheses first.

You should be quite familiar with the arithmetic symbols $+$, $-$, $\times$, $\div$, and %. Finding the value of $10 + 2$, $18 - 4$, $4 \times 9$, or $96 \div 16$ is easy.

However, on the GRE, you may come across bizarre symbols. You may even be asked to find the value of $10 \star 2$, $5 \circledast 7$, $10 \circledast 6$, or $65 \heartsuit 2$.

The GRE test makers put strange symbols in questions to confuse or unnerve you. Don't let them. The question stem always tells you what the strange symbol means. Although this type of question may look difficult, it is really an exercise in plugging in.

To solve, just plug in 10 for $a$ and 6 for $b$ into the expression $\sqrt{a + b}$. That equals $\sqrt{10 + 6}$ or $\sqrt{16}$ or 4, choice (C).

How about a more involved symbolism question?

## Kaplan Tip

When two questions include the same symbol, expect the second question to be more difficult and be extra careful.

If $a \blacktriangle$ means to multiply $a$ by 3 and $a \circledast$ means to divide $a$ by $-2$, what is the value of $((8 \circledast) \blacktriangle) \circledast$ ?

(A)  $-6$

(B)  0

(C)  2

(D)  3

(E)  6

First find $8 \circledast$. This means to divide 8 by $-2$, which is $-4$. Working out to the next set of parentheses, we have $(-4)\blacktriangle$, which means to multiply $-4$ by 3, which is $-12$. Lastly, we find $(-12)\circledast$, which means to divide $-12$ by $-2$, which is 6, choice (E).

*Practice Problems*

Column A                                    Column B

If $x \neq 0$, let $\spadesuit\, x$ be defined by $\spadesuit\, x = x - \dfrac{1}{x}$

1.          –3                               $\spadesuit\,(-3)$

---

2. If $r \heartsuit s = r(r - s)$ for all integers $r$ and $s$, then $4 \heartsuit (3 \heartsuit 5)$ equals

    Ⓐ  –8

    Ⓑ  –2

    Ⓒ   2

    Ⓓ  20

    Ⓔ  40

---

Questions 3–4 refer to the following definition:

$$c \star d = \frac{c - d}{c}, \text{ where } c \neq 0$$

3. $12 \star 3 =$

    Ⓐ  –3

    Ⓑ  $\dfrac{1}{4}$

    Ⓒ  $\dfrac{2}{3}$

    Ⓓ  $\dfrac{3}{4}$

    Ⓔ   3

4. If $9 \star 4 = 15 \star k$, then $k =$

    Ⓐ  3

    Ⓑ  6

    Ⓒ  $\dfrac{20}{3}$

    Ⓓ  $\dfrac{25}{3}$

    Ⓔ  9

*Solutions*

**1. (B)** Plug in –3 for *x:* ♠ $x = -3 - \frac{1}{-3} = -3 + \frac{1}{3} = -2\frac{2}{3}$, which is greater than –3 in Column A.

**2. (E)** Start in the parentheses and work out: $(3 \heartsuit 5) = 3(3-5) = 3(-2) = -6$; $4 \heartsuit (-6) = 4[4 - (-6)] = 4(10) = 40$.

**3. (D)** Plug in 12 for *c* and 3 for *d:* $12\star3 = \frac{12-3}{12} = \frac{9}{12} = \frac{3}{4}$.

**4. (C)** Plug in on both sides of the equation:

$$\frac{9-4}{9} = \frac{15-k}{15}$$

$$\frac{5}{9} = \frac{15-k}{15}$$

Cross-multiply and solve for *k:*

$$75 = 135 - 9k$$

$$-60 = -9k$$

$$\frac{-60}{-9} = k$$

$$\frac{20}{3} = k$$

## The Kaplan Approach to Special Triangles

In the triangle above, what is the length of side *BC* ?

- (A)  4
- (B)  5
- (C)  4 √2
- (D)  6
- (E)  5 √2

### Kaplan Tip

Look for the special triangles in geometry problems.

Special triangles contain a lot of information. For instance, if you know the length of one side of a 30-60-90 triangle, you can easily work out the lengths of the others. Special triangles allow you to transfer one piece of information around the whole figure.

The following are the special triangles you should look for on the GRE.

*Equilateral Triangles*
All interior angles are 60° and all sides are of the same length.

*Isosceles Triangles*
Two sides are of the same length and the angles facing these sides are equal.

*Right Triangles*
Contain a 90° angle. The sides are related by the Pythagorean theorem. $a^2 + b^2 = c^2$ where $a$ and $b$ are the legs and $c$ is the hypotenuse.

*The "Special" Right Triangles*
Many triangle problems contain "special" right triangles, whose side lengths always come in predictable ratios. If you recognize them, you won't have to use the Pythagorean theorem to find the value of a missing side length.

*The 3-4-5 Right Triangle*
(Be on the lookout for multiples of 3-4-5 as well.)

*The Isosceles Right Triangle*
(Note the side ratio: 1 to 1 to $\sqrt{2}$.)

*The 30-60-90 Right Triangle*
(Note the side ratio: 1 to $\sqrt{3}$ to 2, and which side is opposite which angle.)

Getting back to our example, you can drop a vertical line from *B* to line *AC*. This divides the triangle into two right triangles.

That means you know two of the angles in the triangle on the left: 90° and 45°. So this is an isosceles right triangle, with sides in the ratio of 1 to 1 to $\sqrt{2}$. The hypotenuse here is $4\sqrt{2}$, so both legs have length 4. Filling this in, you have:

Now you can see that the legs of the smaller triangle on the right must be 4 and 3, making this a 3-4-5 right triangle, and the length of hypotenuse BC is 5.

*Practice Problems*

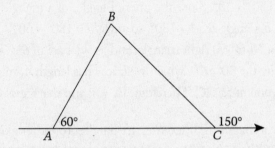

1. In triangle *ABC*, if *AB* = 4, then *AC* =

   Ⓐ  10
   Ⓑ  9
   Ⓒ  8
   Ⓓ  7
   Ⓔ  6

---

Column A                                          Column B

In the coordinate plane, point *R* has coordinates (0,0) and point *S* has coordinates (9,12).

2. The distance from *R* to *S*                    16

---

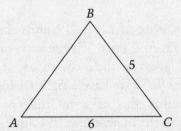

3. If the perimeter of triangle *ABC* above is 16, what is its area?

   Ⓐ  8
   Ⓑ  9
   Ⓒ  10
   Ⓓ  12
   Ⓔ  15

*Solutions*

**1. (C)** Angle *BCA* is supplementary to the angle marked 150°, so angle *BCA* = 180° – 150° = 30°. Since the interior angles of a triangle sum to 180°, angle *A* + angle *B* + angle *BCA* = 180°, so angle *B* = 180° – 60° – 30° = 90°. So triangle *ABC* is a 30-60-90 right triangle, and its sides are in the ratio $1: \sqrt{3}: 2$. The side opposite the 30°, *AB*, which we know has length 4, must be half the length of the hypotenuse, *AC*. Therefore *AC* = 8, and that's answer choice (C).

**2. (B)** Draw a diagram. Since *RS* isn't parallel to either axis, the way to compute its length is to create a right triangle with legs that are parallel to the axes, so their lengths are easy to find. We can then use the Pythagorean theorem to find the length of *RS*.

Since *S* has a *y*-coordinate of 12, it's 12 units above the *x*-axis, so the length of *ST* must be 12. And since *T* is the same number of units to the right of the *y*-axis as *S*, given by the *x*-coordinate of 9, the distance from the origin to *T* must be 9. So we have a right triangle with legs of 9 and 12. You should recognize this as a multiple of the 3-4-5 triangle. 9 = 3 × 3; 12 = 3 × 4; so the hypotenuse *RS* must be 3 × 5, or 15. That's the value of Column A, so Column B is greater.

**3. (D)** To find the area you need to know the base and height. If the perimeter is 16, then *AB* + *BC* + *AC* = 16; that is, *AB* = 16 – 5 – 6 = 5. Since *AB* = *BC*, this is an isosceles triangle. If you drop a line from vertex *B* perpendicular to *AC*, it will divide the base in half. This divides the triangle up into two smaller right triangles:

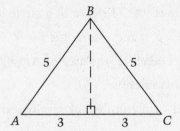

These right triangles each have one leg of 3 and a hypotenuse of 5; therefore they are 3-4-5 right triangles. So the missing leg (which is also the height of triangle *ABC*) must have length 4. We now know that the base of *ABC* is 6 and the height is 4, so the area is $\frac{1}{2} \times 6 \times 4$, or 12, answer choice (D).

## The Kaplan Approach to Multiple and Oddball Figures

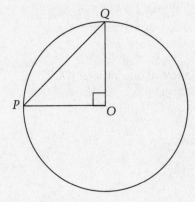

### Kaplan Tip

Look for pieces the figures have in common.

In the figure above, if the area of the circle with center *O* is 9π, what is the area of triangle *POQ* ?

   (A) 4.5

   (B) 6

   (C) 3.5π

   (D) 4.5π

   (E) 9

In a problem that combines figures, you have to look for the relationship between the figures. For instance, if two figures share a side, information about that side will probably be the key.

In this case the figures don't share a side, but the triangle's legs are important features of the circle—they are radii. You can see that *OP* = *OQ* = the radius of circle *O*.

The area of the circle is $9\pi$. The area of a circle is $\pi r^2$, where $r$ is the radius. So $9\pi = \pi r^2$, $9 = r^2$, and the radius $r$ is 3. The area of a triangle is $\frac{1}{2}$ base times height. Therefore, the area of $\Delta POQ$ is $\frac{1}{2}$ (leg$_1$ $\times$ leg$_2$) = $\frac{1}{2}$ (3 $\times$ 3) = $\frac{9}{2}$ = 4.5, answer choice (A).

But what if, instead of a number of familiar shapes, you are given something like this?

What is the perimeter of quadrilateral *WXYZ*?

    (A)    680

    (B)    760

    (C)    840

    (D)    920

    (E)  1,000

Try breaking the unfamiliar shape into familiar ones. Once this is done, you can use the same techniques that you would for multiple figures. Perimeter is the sum of the lengths of the sides of a figure, so you need to find the length of *WZ*. Drawing a perpendicular line from point *X* to side *YZ* will divide the figure into a right triangle and a rectangle. Call the point of intersection *A*.

Opposite sides of a rectangle have equal length, so *WZ* = *XA* and *WX* = *ZA*. *WX* is labeled as 180, so *ZA* = 180. Since *YZ* measures 300, *AY* is 300 − 180 = 120. In right triangle *XYA*, hypotenuse *XY* = 200 and leg *AY* = 120; you should recognize this as a multiple of a 3-4-5 right triangle. The hypotenuse is 5 × 40, one leg is 3 × 40, so *XA* must be 4 × 40 or 160. (If you didn't recognize this special right triangle you could have used the Pythagorean theorem to find the length of *XA*.) Since *WZ* = *XA* = 160, the perimeter of the figure is 180 + 200 + 300 + 160 = 840, answer choice (C).

*Practice Problems*

1. What is the value of *x* in the figure above?

    (A) 4
    (B) $3\sqrt{3}$
    (C) $3\sqrt{5}$
    (D) $5\sqrt{3}$
    (E) 9

2. In the figure above, square *PQRS* is inscribed in a circle. If the area of square *PQRS* is 4, what is the radius of the circle?

  (A) 1

  (B) $\sqrt{2}$

  (C) 2

  (D) $2\sqrt{2}$

  (E) $4\sqrt{2}$

3. In the figure above, the quarter circle with center *D* has a radius of 4 and rectangle *ABCD* has a perimeter of 20. What is the perimeter of the shaded region?

  (A) $20 - 8\pi$

  (B) $10 + 2\pi$

  (C) $12 + 2\pi$

  (D) $12 + 4\pi$

  (E) $\;\;4 + 8\pi$

*Solutions*

**1. (D)** Draw a straight line from point $H$ to point $F$, to divide the figure into two right triangles.

$\Delta EFH$ is a 3-4-5 right triangle with a hypotenuse of length 10. Use the Pythagorean theorem in $\Delta FGH$ to find $x$:

$$x^2 + 5^2 = 10^2$$
$$x^2 + 5^2 = 100$$
$$x^2 = 75$$
$$x = \sqrt{75}$$
$$x = \sqrt{25}\sqrt{3}$$
$$x = 5\sqrt{3}$$

**2. (B)** Draw in diagonal $QS$ and you will notice that it is also a diameter of the circle. Since the area of the square is 4 its sides must each be 2. The diagonal of a square is always the length of a side times $\sqrt{2}$.

Think of the diagonal as dividing the square into two isosceles right triangles. Therefore, the diagonal $= 2\sqrt{2} =$ the diameter; the radius is half this amount or $\sqrt{2}$.

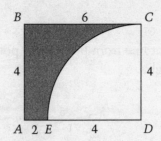

**3. (C)** The perimeter of the shaded region is *BC* + *AB* + *AE* + arc *EC*. The quarter circle has its center at *D,* and point *C* lies on the circle, so side *DC* is a radius of the circle and equals 4. Opposite sides of a rectangle are equal so *AB* is also 4. The perimeter of the rectangle is 20, and since the two short sides account for 8, the two longer sides must account for 12, making *BC* and *AD* each 6. To find *AE,* subtract the length of *ED,* another radius of length 4, from the length of *AD,* which is 6; *AE* = 2. Since arc *EC* is a quarter circle, the length of the arc *EC* is $\frac{1}{4}$ of the circumference of a whole circle with radius 4: $\frac{1}{4} \times 2\pi r = \frac{1}{4} \times 8\pi = 2\pi$. So the perimeter of the shaded region is $6 + 4 + 2 + 2\pi = 12 + 2\pi$.

## Mean, Median, Mode, and Range

The GRE has always tested the concept of a mean, which is also called the arithmetic mean, for no good reason. The mean of several numbers is simply their average. Whenever you see *arithmetic mean* on the GRE, it's not a trick—it just means *average.*

The median of several terms is the number that evenly divides the terms into two groups; half of the terms are larger than the median and half of the terms are smaller than the median. If there is an odd number of terms, the median will be the same as the middle number (not necessarily the average or the mode). If there are an even number of terms, the median will be halfway between the two terms closest to the middle.

For the set {4, 5, 7, 23, 5, 67, 10}, the median is 7, since this divides the set into two smaller sets of three terms each, {4, 5, 5} and {10, 23, 67}.

The mode is even simpler. It's just the term with the most occurrences in a set of numbers. If two or more numbers are tied for the most occurrences, then each is considered a mode.

For the set {4, 5, 7, 23, 5, 67, 10}, the mode is 5, because it occurs the greatest number of times of any of the terms.

### Definition

**Mean** is the average of a set of numbers.

**Median** is the "middle" value in a set of numbers that have been arranged from smallest to greatest. In an odd-numbered set, it's simply the middle term; in an even-numbered set, it's the value halfway between the two terms closest to the middle.

**Mode** is the term that occurs the most in a set of numbers.

The range is the simplest of these four concepts. It's just the difference between the largest term and the smallest term in a set of numbers. Just subtract the smallest from the biggest and you will have the range.

For the set {4, 5, 7, 23, 5, 67, 10}, the range is 63, because the greatest number, 67, minus the smallest, 4, equals 63.

*Practice Problems*

| Column A | Column B |
| --- | --- |
| 1. The median of the integers from 1 through 31, inclusive. | 16 |

| | |
| --- | --- |
| 2.  $2^6$ | The range of the series {8, 9, 9, 15, 71} |

3. The only test scores for the students in a certain class are 44, 30, 42, 30, *x*, 44, and 30. If *x* equals one of the other scores and is a multiple of 5, what is the mode for the class?

   (A)  5
   (B)  6
   (C)  15
   (D)  30
   (E)  44

4. If half the range of the increasing series {11, *A*, 23, *B*, *C*, 68, 73} is equal to its median, what is the median of the series?

   (A)  23
   (B)  31
   (C)  33
   (D)  41
   (E)  62

*Solutions*

**1. (C)** *Inclusive* just means you should include the numbers on the ends—in this case, 1 and 31. The number right in the middle of this series is 16. There are 15 numbers smaller than it and 15 numbers greater than it.

**2. (A)** $2^6$ equals 64. The range of the series in Column B equals $71 - 8$, which equals 63.

**3. (D)** Since *x* equals one of the other scores, it must equal either 30, 42, or 44. And since it must also be a multiple of 5, we can conclude that *x* equals 30. That means that four of the students—more than earned any other score—earned a score of 30, which makes 30 the mode.

**4. (B)** Don't get confused by all the variables; just concentrate on what you know. The range must be the difference of the smallest term and the largest term. Since this is an increasing series, the smallest term must be 11 and the largest must be 73. The difference between them is 62, so that's the range. Half of the range, then, is 31, so 31 must equal the median of the series.

## Probability

A probability is the fractional likelihood of an event occurring. It can be represented by a fraction ("the probability of it raining today is $\frac{1}{2}$"), a ratio ("the odds of it raining today are 50:50"), or a percent ("the probability of rain today is 50 percent"). You can translate probabilities easily into everyday language: $\frac{1}{100}$ = "one chance in a hundred" or "the odds are one in a hundred."

To find probabilities, count the number of desired outcomes and divide by the number of possible outcomes.

Probability = (Number of Desired Outcomes/Number of Possible Outcomes)

For example, what is the probability of throwing a 5 on a six-sided die? There is one desired outcome—throwing a 5. There are six possible outcomes—one for each side of the die. So the probability = $\frac{1}{6}$.

### Definition

A **probability** is the fractional likelihood that a given event will occur. To get a probability, divide the number of desired events by the number of possible events.

All probabilities are between 0 and 1 inclusive. A 0 probability means there is zero chance of an event occurring (i.e., it can't happen). A 1 probability means that an event has a 100 percent chance of occurring (i.e., it must occur). The higher the probability, the greater chance that an event will occur. You can often eliminate answer choices by having some idea where the probability of an event occurring falls within this range.

The odds of throwing a 5 on a die are $\frac{1}{6}$, so the odds of not throwing a 5 are $\frac{5}{6}$. Therefore, you have a much greater probability of not throwing a 5 on a die than of throwing a 5.

*Practice Problems*

| Column A | Column B |
|---|---|

The probability of rain on Thursday is 50 percent. The probability that it will not rain on Friday is $\frac{1}{4}$.

| 1. The probability of rain on Thursday | The probability of rain on Friday |
|---|---|

A hat contains an equal number of red, blue, and green marbles.

| 2. The probability of picking a red marble out of the hat | The probability of picking a green marble out of the hat |
|---|---|

3. If there are 14 women and 10 men employed in a certain office, what is the probability that one employee picked at random will be a woman?

(A) $\frac{1}{6}$

(B) $\frac{1}{14}$

(C) $\frac{7}{12}$

(D) 1

(E) $\frac{7}{5}$

4. If Tom flips a fair coin twice, what is the probability that at least one head will be thrown?

(A) $\frac{1}{4}$

(B) $\frac{1}{3}$

(C) $\frac{1}{2}$

(D) $\frac{2}{3}$

(E) $\frac{3}{4}$

*Solutions*

**1. (B)** The probability of rain on Thursday is $\frac{1}{2}$ and the probability of rain on Friday is $\frac{3}{4}$.

**2. (C)** The number of desired outcomes is the same in each case, since there are an equal number of red and green marbles. The number of possible outcomes in each case is also the same, since the marbles are all being pulled from the same hat. Therefore the probabilities are the same.

**3. (C)** Probability = (Number of Desired Outcomes/Number of Possible Outcomes) = (Number of Women/Number of People) = $\frac{14}{24} = \frac{7}{12}$.

**4. (E)** Desired outcomes = HH or HT or TH. Possible outcomes = HH or HT or TH or TT. Probability = $\frac{3}{4}$.

# Graphs

In the GRE math section, you are likely to get four questions that will be based on one or more graphs. Exactly what ETS is trying to test with these questions we have never been able to determine, unless you need to sharpen your clerical skills before you pursue that Ph.D. in electrical engineering.

## The Basic Principles of Graphs

*Some Will Be Fairly Basic*
You will have to do something like find a value from the graph(s) or compare values in the graph(s). They will take only a few steps.

*Others Will Be Fairly Difficult*
They always require more than just a few steps. They may fool you into thinking that they're easy, but there will be a trick involved. Never, ever pick the obvious answer without checking it first.

## The Kaplan Method for Graphs
We recommend the following method for graph problems:

*1. Familiarize Yourself with the Graph(s)*
Graphs often come in pairs, so get to know the graphs before you tackle the questions.

- Read the title(s).
- Check the scales to see how the information is measured.
- Read any accompanying notes.
- If there are multiple bars or lines on the graph, make sure to refer to the key that explains the distinctions between them.

*2. Answer the Questions That Follow*
Graph questions require a strong understanding of fractions and percents and good attention to detail, but little else.

Graph questions come in sets consisting of one or more graphs accompanied by several questions. You are likely to see either two sets, each accompanied by two questions, or one such set accompanied by four questions. In either case, it's helpful to realize that late questions tend to be trickier than early questions. For instance, when the set contains two graphs, the first question is likely to refer to just one graph, whereas a late question will require you to take data from both graphs and combine this information to answer the question. If you haven't used both graphs for this late question, you're almost certain to get it wrong.

## Kaplan Rules

The Kaplan method for graph problems:

1. Familiarize yourself with the graph(s).
2. Answer the questions that follow.
3. Approximate wherever possible.

### 3. Approximate Wherever Possible

No matter how hard they may appear at first glance, graph questions can usually be made easier if you take advantage of the large spread that is typically found among the quantities in the answer choices—by approximating rather than calculating wherever possible. Since graph questions generally take more time to solve than other GRE math questions, if you are not gunning for a super high quantitative score you may want to consider, if you are running into time trouble, guessing and moving on when you encounter a hard graph question.

### Practice Problems

Questions 1–5 are based on the following graphs.

## MEGACORP, INC.
## REVENUE AND PROFIT DISTRIBUTION FOR FOOD- AND NONFOOD-RELATED OPERATIONS, 1984–1989

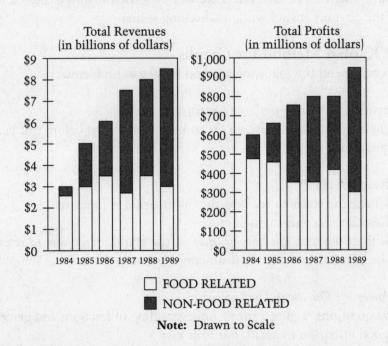

**Note:** Drawn to Scale

## Kaplan Tip

The most common trick in graph questions is to confuse you with the difference between an actual value (a fixed number) and a relative value (a fraction or percent). Make sure you always know which one you're working with.

## PERCENT OF REVENUES FROM FOOD-RELATED OPERATIONS IN 1989 BY CATEGORY

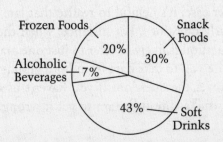

1. Approximately how much did total revenues increase from 1984 to 1987?

   (A) $0.5 billion
   (B) $1.5 billion
   (C) $4.0 billion
   (D) $4.5 billion
   (E) $5.0 billion

2. For the year in which profits from food-related operations increased over the previous year, *total revenues* were approximately

   (A) $3.5 billion
   (B) $4.5 billion
   (C) $5.7 billion
   (D) $6.0 billion
   (E) $8.0 billion

3. In 1988, total profits represented approximately what percent of Megacorp's total revenues?

   (A) 50%
   (B) 20%
   (C) 10%
   (D) 5%
   (E) 1%

4. For the first year in which revenues from nonfood-related operations surpassed $4.5 billion, total profits were approximately

   (A) $250 million
   (B) $450 million
   (C) $550 million
   (D) $650 million
   (E) $800 million

5. In 1989, approximately how many millions of dollars were revenues from frozen food operations?

   (A) 1,700
   (B) 1,100
   (C) 900
   (D) 600
   (E) 450

*Solutions*

**1. (D)** This question asks about total revenues, so you should refer to the left bar graph. The trickiest part is making sure you correctly extract information from the appropriate bars, in this case for 1984 and 1987. Total revenues for 1984 appear to be $3 million and for 1987 they appear to be about $7.5 million (if you're ever having trouble getting a fix on a quantity on a bar graph, place the edge of a piece of paper along the top of the bar to read the scale better). So the increase is roughly $7.5 billion – $3 million = $4.5 billion.

**2. (E)** The wording is somewhat tricky here, and you have to refer to both bar graphs. First you have to refer to the right bar graph to find the lone year in which food-related profits increased over the previous year—the only year in which the unshaded portion of the bar goes up is 1988. Now that you've zeroed in on the year, you must refer to the left bar graph to determine the total *revenues* for that year, which appear to be about $8.0 billion.

**3. (C)** This is percent question, so first you have to extract the information from the bar graphs. From the right bar graph, the total profits for 1988 appear to be $800 million; from the left bar graph, total revenues for that year appear to be $8.0 billion (i.e., $8,000 million). Now you just have to convert the part/whole into a percent: $\frac{800 \text{ million}}{8,000 \text{ million}} = \frac{1}{10} = 10\%$.

**4. (E)** First you have to find the year for which revenues from nonfood-related operations surpassed $4.5 billion, so refer to the left bar graph. Finding the correct bar is made more difficult by the fact that you have to deal with the shaded portion, which is not grounded at $0. So you may want to make a ruler from a sheet of paper, using the scale to mark off the length represented by $4.5 billion, and using this to locate the appropriate bar. You should then be able to see that 1987 is the year in question. The question asks for total *profits*, so once again refer to the right bar graph and you'll see the profits for that year are around $800 million.

**5. (D)** Finally you have a question that refers to the pie chart. You are asked about revenues from frozen food operations, and the pie chart informs you that frozen foods represent 20 percent of all food-related revenues for 1989. To convert this into an amount you need to locate the amount of food-related revenues for 1989, so once again refer to the left bar graph where you'll find the food-related revenues in 1989 were about $3 billion, or $3,000 million. 20 percent of $3,000 million is $600 million.

By using all of the techniques discussed above, you will be able to tackle the most difficult Quantitative questions. (You can brush up on all of your math by referring to the Math Reference Appendix in the back of this book.) And now that you have the tools to handle the Quantitative section of the GRE, try the following set of practice questions. After that, we'll move on and take a look at the Analytical section of the test.

# Quantitative Practice Set

## Numbers

All numbers are real numbers.

## Figures

The position of points, lines, angles, etcetera, may be assumed to be in the order shown; all lengths and angle measures may be assumed to be positive.

Lines shown as straight may be assumed to be straight.

Figures lie in the plane of the paper unless otherwise stated.

Figures that accompany questions are intended to provide useful information. However, unless a note states that a figure has been drawn to scale, you should solve the problems by using your knowledge of mathematics, and not by estimation or measurement.

## Directions

Each of the Questions 1–15 below consists of two quantities, one in Column A and another in Column B. You are to compare the two quantities and answer

- Ⓐ if the quantity in Column A is greater
- Ⓑ if the quantity in Column B is greater
- Ⓒ if the two quantities are equal
- Ⓓ if the relationship cannot be determined from the information given

## Common Information

In a question, information concerning one or both of the quantities to be compared is centered above the two columns. A symbol that appears in both columns represents the same thing in Column A as it does in Column B. (Answers and explanations can be found at the end of the set of questions.)

|  | Column A | Column B |
|---|---|---|
| 1. | $\dfrac{1}{3} + \dfrac{1}{3}$ | $\dfrac{1}{3} \times \dfrac{1}{3}$ |

| 2. | $x + y$ | 180 |
|---|---|---|

| 3. | 16 percent of 30 | 15 percent of 31 |
|---|---|---|

$$x^5 = -32$$

| 4. | $x^3$ | $2x^2$ |
|---|---|---|

$$x < y < z$$
$$0 < z$$

| 5. | $x$ | 0 |
|---|---|---|

$$6(10)^n > 60{,}006$$

| 6. | $n$ | 6 |
|---|---|---|

In a three-digit positive integer $y$, the hundreds' digit is three times the units' digit.

| 7. | The units' digit of $y$ | 4 |
|---|---|---|

| 8. | The perimeter of a square with side 4 | The circumference of a circle with diameter 5 |
|---|---|---|

| Column A | Column B |
|---|---|

$\ell_1 \parallel \ell_2$

9.     $2(x + y)$            $x + a + y + b$

$$\frac{2x}{3} = \frac{2y}{5} = \frac{2z}{7}$$

$z$ is positive.

10.     $x + y$                  $z$

The product of two integers is 10.

11. The average (arithmetic          3
     mean) of the two integers

The remainder when $n$ is divided by 3 is 1, and
the remainder when $n + 1$ is divided by 2 is 1.

12. The remainder when $n - 1$        3
     is divided by 6

The average (arithmetic mean) bowling score of $n$
bowlers is 160. The average of these $n$ scores
together with a score of 170 is 161.

13.     $n$                       10

14.     $7^5 + 7^6$             $8 \times 7^5$

| Column A | Column B |
|---|---|

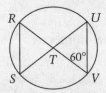

The circle has center $T$. The measure of angle $TVU$ is 60°.

15.     $RT$                     $RS$

After five adults leave a party, there are three times as many
children as adults. After a further 25 children leave the party,
there are twice as many adults as children.

16. The original number          14
     of adults

There are at least 200 apples in a grocery store. The ratio of
the number of oranges to the number of apples is 9 to 10.

17. The number of oranges        200
     in the store

18. How many odd integers are between $\dfrac{10}{3}$ and $\dfrac{62}{3}$ ?

   (A)  19
   (B)  18
   (C)  10
   (D)  9
   (E)  8

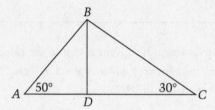

19. In the figure above, if $BD$ bisects $\angle ABC$, then the measure of $\angle BDC$ is

   (A)  50°
   (B)  90°
   (C)  100°
   (D)  110°
   (E)  120°

20. If $d = \dfrac{c-b}{a-b}$, then $b =$

   (A)  $\dfrac{c-d}{a-d}$

   (B)  $\dfrac{c+d}{a+d}$

   (C)  $\dfrac{ca-d}{ca+d}$

   (D)  $\dfrac{c-ad}{1-d}$

   (E)  $\dfrac{c+ad}{d-1}$

21. If $x > 0$, then $(4^x)(8^x) =$

   (A)  $2^{9x}$
   (B)  $2^{8x}$
   (C)  $2^{6x}$
   (D)  $2^{5x}$
   (E)  $2^{4x}$

22. In one class in a school, 30 percent of the students are boys. In a second class that is half the size of the first, 40 percent of the students are boys. What percent of both classes are boys?

   (A)  20%
   (B)  25%
   (C)  28%
   (D)  30%
   (E)  $33\dfrac{1}{3}$%

23. In a circle $O$ above, if $\triangle POQ$ is a right triangle and radius $OP$ is 2, what is the area of the shaded region?

   (A)  $4\pi - 2$
   (B)  $4\pi - 4$
   (C)  $2\pi - 2$
   (D)  $2\pi - 4$
   (E)  $\pi - 2$

24. If $n = 14 \times 22 \times 39$, which of the following is NOT an integer?

   Ⓐ $\dfrac{n}{21}$

   Ⓑ $\dfrac{n}{24}$

   Ⓒ $\dfrac{n}{26}$

   Ⓓ $\dfrac{n}{42}$

   Ⓔ $\dfrac{n}{77}$

**Question 25–28 refer to the following graphs:**

### Team Revenues for 1997

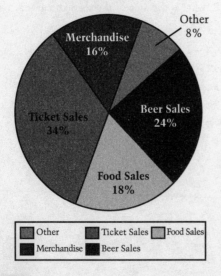

**Percentages of Venue Revenues for Team X, 1997**

25. For the team with the median amount of venue revenue for 1997, media revenue represented approximately what percent of that team's total revenue for that year?

   Ⓐ  25%

   Ⓑ  30%

   Ⓒ  40%

   Ⓓ  55%

   Ⓔ  60%

26. Of the following, which is the closest to the amount of revenues, in millions of dollars, earned by Team X through food sales in 1997?

   Ⓐ  7

   Ⓑ  10

   Ⓒ  14

   Ⓓ  18

   Ⓔ  22

27. Ticket sales represented approximately what percent of total revenue for Team X in 1997?

   Ⓐ   4%

   Ⓑ   8%

   Ⓒ  13%

   Ⓓ  34%

   Ⓔ  54%

28. If Team Y earned a total revenue of $150 million in 1998, Team Y's total revenue increased by approximately what percent from 1997 to 1998?

   Ⓐ  20%

   Ⓑ  25%

   Ⓒ  30%

   Ⓓ  35%

   Ⓔ  40%

# Answer Key

| | | | |
|---|---|---|---|
| 1. A | 8. A | 15. C | 22. E |
| 2. B | 9. C | 16. A | 23. E |
| 3. A | 10. A | 17. D | 24. B |
| 4. B | 11. D | 18. E | 25. C |
| 5. D | 12. C | 19. C | 26. A |
| 6. D | 13. B | 20. D | 27. B |
| 7. B | 14. C | 21. D | 28. B |

# Explanations

## Question 1

$\frac{1}{3} + \frac{1}{3}$ is $\frac{2}{3}$. $\frac{1}{3} \times \frac{1}{3} = \frac{1}{9}$. Since $\frac{2}{3} > \frac{1}{9}$, column A is larger.

## Question 2

The sum of the three interior angles of a triangle is 180°. Since $x$ and $y$ are only two of the angles, their sum must be less than 180 degrees. Column B is greater.

## Question 3

Sixteen percent of 30 is $\frac{16}{100}(30)$ or $\frac{(16)(30)}{100}$. Similarly, 15 percent of 31 is $\frac{15}{100}(31)$ or $\frac{(15)(31)}{100}$. We can ignore the denominator of 100 in both columns, and just compare $(16)(30)$ in Column A to $(15)(31)$ in column B. Divide both columns by 15; we're left with 31 in Column B and $(16)(2)$ or 32 in column A. Since $32 > 31$, Column A is larger.

## Question 4

Start by working with the sign of $x$, and hope that you won't have to go any further than that. If $x^5$ is negative, then what is the sign of $x$? It must be negative—if $x$ were positive, then any power of $x$ would also be positive. Since $x$ is negative, Column A, $x^3$, which is a negative number raised to an odd exponent, must also be negative. But what about column B? Whatever $x$ is, $x^2$ must be positive (or zero, but we know that $x$ can't be zero); therefore, the quantity in Column B must be positive. We have a positive number in column B and a negative number is column A; Column B must be greater.

## Question 5

We could pick numbers here, or else just use logic. We know that $z$ is positive, and that $x$ and $y$ are less than $z$. But does that mean that $x$ or $y$ must be negative? Not at all—they could be, but they could also be positive. For instance, suppose $x = 1$, $y = 2$, and $z = 3$. Then Column A would be larger. However, if $x = -1$, $y = 0$, and $z = 1$, then Column B would be larger. We need more information to determine the relationship between the columns.

## Question 6

Divide both sides of the inequality by 6. We're left with $(10)^n > 10,001$. 10,001 can also be written at $10^4 + 1$, so we know that $(10)^n > 10^4 + 1$. Therefore, the quantity in Column A, $n$, must be 5 or greater. Column B is 6; since $n$ could be less than, equal to, or greater than 6, we need more information.

*Question 7*

Try to set the columns equal. Could be units' digit of $y$ be 4? If it is, and the hundreds' digit is three times the units' digit, then the hundreds' digit must be . . . 12? That can't be right. A digit must be one of the integers 0 through 9; 12 isn't a digit. Therefore, 4 is too big to be the units' digit of $y$. We don't know what the units' digit of $y$ is (and we don't care either), but we know that it must be less than 4. Column B is greater than Column A.

*Question 8*

The perimeter of a square with side 4 is 4(4) or 16. The circumference of a circle is the product of $\pi$ and the diameter, so the circumference in Column B is $5\pi$. Since $\pi$ is approximately 3.14, $5(\pi)$ is approximately 5(3.14) or 15.70, which is less than 16. Column A is greater.

*Question 9*

$\ell_1 \parallel \ell_2$

Column B is the sum of all the angles in the quadrilateral. The sum of the angles in any quadrilateral is 360 degrees. Column B is 360. In Column A, angle $x$ and angle $y$ are angles made when a transversal cuts a pair of parallel lines, in this case, $\ell_1$ and $\ell_2$. Such angles are either equal or supplementary. Angles $x$ and $y$ obviously aren't equal, so they must be supplementary, and their sum is 180. Then Column A is $2(x + y) = 2 \times 180$ or 360. The columns are equal.

*Question 10*

One way to work here is to pick numbers. Just make sure that anything you pick satisfies the requirements of the problem. How about picking $x = 3$, $y = 5$, and $z = 7$, since in the equation these numbers would cancel with their denominators, thus leaving us with the equation $2 = 2 = 2$. Therefore, we know that these values satisfy the equation. In addition, if $z = 7$, then $z$ is positive, so we have satisfied the other requirement as well. Then the sum of $x$ and $y$, in Column A, is $3 + 5$ or 8. This is larger than $z$, so in this case, Column A is larger. That's just one example though; we should really try another one. In fact, any other example we pick that fits the initial information will have Column A larger. To see why, we have to do a little messy work with the initial equations; on the test, you should just pick a couple of sample values, then go on to the next questions.

Start by dividing all of the equations through by 2, and multiply all of the terms through by $3 \times 5 \times 7$, to eliminate all the fractions. This leaves us with:

$$35x = 21y = 15z$$

Now let's put everything in terms of $x$.

$$x = x \qquad y = \frac{35}{21}x = \frac{5}{3}x \qquad x = \frac{35}{15}x = \frac{7}{3}x$$

Then in Column A, the sum of $x$ and $y$ is $x + \frac{5}{3}x = \frac{8}{3}x$. In column B, the value of $z$ is $\frac{7}{3}x$. Now since $z$ is positive, $x$ and $y$ must also be positive. (If one of them is negative, that would make all of them negative.) Since $x$ is positive, $\frac{8}{3}x > \frac{7}{3}x$. Column A is greater.

The moral here is that proving that one column must be bigger can involve an awful lot of time on some GRE QC questions—more time than you can afford on the test. Try to come up with a good answer, but don't spend a lot of time proving it. Even if you end up showing that your original suspicion was wrong, it's not worth it if it took five minutes away from the rest of the problems.

## Question 11

The best place to start here is with some pairs of integers that have a product of 10. The numbers 5 and 2 have a product of 10, as do 10 and 1, and the average of each of these pairs is greater than 3, so you may have thought that (A) was the correct answer. If so, you should have stopped yourself, saying, "That seems a little too easy for such a late QC question. They're usually trickier than that." In fact, this one was. There's nothing in the problem that limits the integers to positive numbers: they can just as easily be negative. The numbers −10 and −1 also have a product of 10, but their average is a negative number—in other words, less than Column B. We need more information here; the answer is (D).

## Question 12

The best way to do this question is to pick numbers. First we have to figure out what kind of number we want. Since $n + 1$ leaves a remainder of 1 when it's divided by 2, we know that $n + 1$ must be an odd number. Then $n$ itself is an even number. We're told that $n$ leaves a remainder of 1 when it's divided by 3. Therefore, $n$ must be 1 more than a multiple of 3, or $n - 1$ is a multiple of 3. So what are we looking for? We've figured out that $n$ should be an even number, that's one more than a multiple of 3. So let's pick a number now. How about 10 ? That's even, and it's one more than a multiple of 3. Then what's the remainder when we divide $n - 1$, or $10 - 1 = 9$, by 6? We're left with a remainder of 3: 6 divides into 9 one time, with 3 left over. In this case, the columns are equal.

Now since this a QC question and there's always a possibility that we'll get a different result if we pick a different number, we should either pick another case, or else use logic to convince ourselves that the columns will always be equal. Let's do the latter here. Since $n$ is even, $n - 1$ must be odd. We saw before that $n - 1$ is a multiple of 3, so we now know that it is an odd multiple of 3. Does this tell us anything about $n - 1$'s relation to 6? Yes, it does: $n - 1$ is 3 multiplied by an odd number $m$, which can be written as $2p + 1$ where $p$ is an integer. So $n - 1 = 3(2p + 1) = 6p + 3$. $6p$ is a multiple of 6, so the remainder when $n - 1$ is divided by 6 must be 3. The answer is (C).

## Question 13

A quick way to analyze a problem such as this one is to realize that the additional bowler with a score of 170 is raising everyone else's average by one point from 160 to 161. Her score is $161 + 9$, so she has 9 extra points that she can distribute to the remaining bowlers by which to raise their scores. Therefore, she can raise the average score of exactly 9 other bowlers from 160 to 161, so $n = 9$ and Column B is greater.

## Question 14

Remember, compare, don't calculate! But in order to compare, you need to put both columns into a similar form. Factoring $7^5$ out of both terms in Column A will help you to do just that: $7^5 + 7^6 = 7^5(1 + 7) = 7^5 \times 8 = 8 \times 7^5$. So the two quantities are equal.

*Question 15*

There are many steps involved with this problem, but none of them is too complicated. The circle has its center at point *T*. To start with the triangle at the right, its vertices are at *T* and two points on the circumference of the circle. This makes two of its sides radii of the circle. Since all radii must have equal length, this makes the triangle an isosceles triangle. In addition, we're told one of the base angles of this triangle has measure 60°. Then the other base angle must also have measure 60° (since the base angles in an isosceles triangle have equal measure). Then the sum of the two base angles is 120°, leaving 180 – 120 or 60° for the other angle, the one at point *T*.

Now, ∠*RTS* is opposite this 60° angle; therefore, its measure must also be 60°. Δ*RST* is another isosceles triangle; since ∠*RTS* has measure 60°, the other two angles in the triangle must also measure 60°. So what we have in the diagram is two equilateral triangles. *RT* and *RS* are two sides in one of these triangles; therefore, they must be of equal length, and the two columns are equal.

*Question 16*

Start by setting the columns equal. Suppose there were originally 14 adults at the party. Then after five of them leave, there are 14 – 5 or nine adults left. There are three times as many children as adults, so there are 3 × 9 or 27 children. Then 25 children leave the party, so there are 27 – 25 or two children left. So nine adults and two children remain at this party. Is that twice as many adults as children? No, it is more than four times as many, So this clearly indicates that the columns can't be equal—but does it mean that Column A is bigger or Column B is

bigger? Probably the simplest way to decide is to pick another number for the original number of adults, and see whether the ratio gets better or worse. Suppose we start with 13 adults. After five adults leave, there are 13 – 5 or eight adults. Multiplying 3 times 8 gives 24 children. Now if 25 children leave, we're left with 24 – 25 or –1 children. But that's no good; how can you have a negative number of children? This means we've gone the wrong way; our ratio has gotten worse instead of better. So 14 isn't right for the number of adults, and 13 is even worse, so the correct number must be something more than 14, and Column A is larger.

*Question 17*

We know that the ratio of oranges to apples is 9 to 10, and that there are "at least" 200 apples. The ratio tells us that there are more apples than oranges. How does that help us? Good question. It helps us because it tells us that there could be fewer than 200 oranges in the store. Could there be more than 200? Sure. If there were a lot more than 200 apples, say 600 apples, then there would be a lot more than 200 oranges. So we have one situation in which Column A is larger, and another case in which Column B is larger. We need more information to decide.

*Question 18*

Here we're asked for the odd integers between $\frac{10}{3}$ and $\frac{62}{3}$. First let's be clearer about this range. $\frac{10}{3}$ is the same as $3\frac{1}{3}$, and $\frac{62}{3}$ is the same as $20\frac{2}{3}$. So we need to count the odd integers between $3\frac{1}{3}$ and $20\frac{2}{3}$. We can't include 3, since 3 is less than $3\frac{1}{3}$. Similarly, we can't include 21, since it's larger than $20\frac{2}{3}$. So the odd integers in the appropriate range are 5, 7, 9, 11, 13, 15, 17, and 19. That's a total of 8.

## Question 19

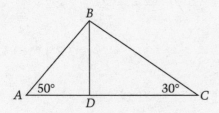

Notice that we're given the measures of two interior angles in $\triangle ABC$: $\angle BAC$ measures 50° and $\angle BCA$ measures 30°. Therefore, $\angle ABC$, the third interior angle in $\triangle ABC$, measures $180 - (50 + 30)$, or $180 - 80$, or 100°. Since $BD$ bisects $\angle ABC$, $BD$ splits up $\angle ABC$ into two smaller angles equal in measure, $\angle ABD$ and $\angle DBC$. Therefore, the measure of $\angle DBC$ is half the measure of $\angle ABC$, so $\angle DBC$ measures $\frac{1}{2}(100)$, or 50°. Now we can use this information along with the fact that $\angle BCD$ measures 30° to find $\angle BDC$. Since these three angles are interior angles of $\triangle BDC$, their measures sum to 180°. So $\angle BDC$ measures $180 - (50 + 30)$, or 100°.

## Question 20

Solve for $b$ in terms of $a$, $c$, and $d$.

$$d = \frac{c - b}{a - b}$$

Clear the denominator by multiplying both sides by $a - b$.　　$d(a - b) = c - b$
Multiply out parentheses.　　$da - db = c - b$

Gather all $b$s on one side.　　$b - db = c - da$

Factor out the $b$s on the left hand side.　　$b(1 - d) = c - da$

Divide both sides by $1 - d$ to isolate $b$.　　$b = \frac{c - ad}{1 - d}$

## Question 21

Remember the rules for operations with exponents. First you have to get both powers in terms of the same base so you can combine the exponents. Note that the answer choices all have base 2. Start by expressing 4 and 8 as powers of 2.

$$(4^x)(8^x) = (2^2)^x \times (2^3)^x$$

To raise a power to an exponent, multiply the exponents:

$$(2^2)^x = 2^{2x}$$
$$(2^3)^x = 2^{3x}$$

To multiply powers with the same base, add the exponents:

$$2^{2x} \times 2^{3x} = 2^{(2x + 3x)}$$
$$= 2^{5x}$$

## Question 22

Pick a sample value for the size of one of the classes. The first class might have 100 students. That means there are 30 percent of 100 or 30 boys in the class. The second class is half the size of the first, so it has 50 students, of which 40 percent of 50 = 20 are boys. This gives us $100 + 50 = 150$ students total, of whom

$30 + 20 = 50$ are boys. So $\frac{50}{150} = \frac{1}{3}$ of both classes are boys. Now convert $\frac{1}{3}$ to a percent. $\frac{1}{3} = \frac{1}{3} \times 100\% = 33\frac{1}{3}\%$.

## Question 23

The area of the shaded region is the area of the quarter-circle (sector $OPQ$) minus the area of right triangle $OPQ$. The radius of circle $O$ is 2, so the area of the quarter-circle is

$$\frac{1}{4}\pi r^2 = \frac{1}{4} \times \pi(2)^2 = \frac{1}{4} \times 4\pi = \pi$$

Each leg of the triangle is a radius of circle $O$, so the area of the triangle is

$$\frac{1}{2}bh = \frac{1}{2} \times 2 \times 2 = 2$$

Therefore, the area of the shaded region is $\pi - 2$.

## Question 24

The easiest way to handle this type of question is to break $n$ even further down into prime factors. Thus $n = 2 \times 7 \times 2 \times 11 \times 3 \times 13$. Now check out the answer choices:

(A) $\frac{n}{21} = \frac{2 \times 7 \times 2 \times 11 \times 3 \times 13}{3 \times 7} = 2 \times 2 \times 11 \times 13$

(B) $\frac{n}{24} = \frac{2 \times 7 \times 2 \times 11 \times 3 \times 13}{2 \times 2 \times 2 \times 3} = \frac{7 \times 11 \times 13}{2}$

(C) $\frac{n}{26} = \frac{2 \times 7 \times 2 \times 11 \times 3 \times 13}{2 \times 13} = 7 \times 2 \times 11 \times 3$

(D) $\frac{n}{42} = \frac{2 \times 7 \times 2 \times 11 \times 3 \times 13}{7 \times 3 \times 2} = 2 \times 11 \times 13$

(E) $\frac{n}{77} = \frac{2 \times 7 \times 2 \times 11 \times 3 \times 13}{7 \times 11} = 2 \times 2 \times 3 \times 13$

Only (B) is not an integer.

## Question 25

Before you get started answering any graph question, begin by examining the graphs. Here you have two graphs, a segmented bar graph representing team revenue breakdowns for 5 teams, and a pie chart showing the distribution of venue revenues for Team X. You're now ready to attack the question, which asks you to find the team with the median revenue for 1997 and to determine what percent of that team's revenues are media revenue. This question must refer to the first graph, and the first part of question—finding the team with the "median" revenue—is a simple matter. "Median" refers to the number in the middle, and since here the bar graphs are arranged in ascending order, the question clearly refers to Team Z, the bar in the middle of the graph. The fastest approach to the answer here (and throughout graph questions generally) is to approximate. The downside to bar graphs is that it's often very hard to get a read on the values. The upside is that if you approximate, often you don't have to read the values. Here we need to determine what percent of the bar is represented by media revenue (the segment in the middle—always be especially careful to isolate the correct piece of data). By approximating, you should be able to see that the middle segment is more than a third and less than a half of the entire bar. Thus the correct answer has to be between 33% and 50%. The only answer that works is (C), 40%.

*Question 26*

The trick to this question is that it involves *both* graphs. The question asks for the amount Team X earned through food sales, which takes us first to the pie chart, where we see that food sales accounted for 18% of the venue revenues for Team X. But to convert that to a dollar amount, we need a figure for the amount earned in venue revenues by Team X. According to the bar graph, this is somewhere around $40 million. Now we just have to take 18% of $40 million: .18 × 40 = 7.2, so the closest answer is (A) 7.

*Question 27*

This question also involves both graphs, since you have to determine the percent of *total* team revenues represented by ticket sales. Beginning at the pie chart, you see that ticket sales represent 34% of the venue revenue for Team X. But venue revenue represents only one portion of the total team revenue, so (D), 34%, is out, as well as (E), since the answer must be less than 34%. Next, examine the bar graph. We've already seen that venue revenue is approximately $40 million, it looks like total team revenue is approximately $160 million, so venue revenue represents about one quarter of the total team revenue. The easiest approach to the answer is to approximate by dividing 34% by 4, since ticket sales represent around 34% of one-quarter of the total team revenue. One-fourth of 34% is 8.5%, so the closest answer choice is choice (B), 8%.

*Question 28*

Percent change problems are extremely popular graph questions, and as long as you know how to set them up they're generally no problem. This question asks for the approximate percent increase in Team Y's total revenue from 1997 to 1998, so we need to figure out (roughly) the amount of increase, place that over the original (or smaller) amount, and then convert the fraction into a percent. We are given the total revenue for 1998 as $150 million, so we just need to locate the total revenue for 1997 from the bar graph. It looks to be approximately $120 million, so the amount of increase is $30 million, and the original (or smaller) amount is $120 million. Now let's apply our formula:

$$\text{Percent increase} = \frac{\$30\,\text{million}}{\$120\,\text{million}} \times 100\% = \frac{1}{4} \times 100\% = 25\%$$

So (B) is the answer.

# CHAPTER FOUR

# Test Content: Analytical

- Learn the Basic Principles and the Kaplan Method for answering Logic Games and Logical Reasoning questions
- Examine the most common types of Logic Games and the strategies for attacking each type
- Familiarize yourself with the five common Logical Reasoning question types
- Complete the Analytical Practice Set

Y ou'll have 60 minutes to complete 35 questions in the Analytical section, which has two question types: logic games and logical reasoning. (ETS once planned to introduce a third type: pattern identification. However, they withdrew that question type after Kaplan developed a strategy so devastating that a test taker could get any pattern identification question correct right away!)

We're going to tackle logic games first, because they are the most difficult Analytical question type for many students.

## Logic Games

> This question or set of questions is based on a passage or a set of conditions. You may wish to draw a diagram to answer some of the questions. Choose the best answer for each question.

### Kaplan Tip

If you're the type of test taker who loves the challenge of Logic Games and Logical Reasoning questions, be sure to take the GRE exam before October 1, 2002! See page vii for more info on the upcoming test changes.

### Teacher Tip

"Knowing what makes an answer wrong is just as important as knowing what makes an answer right. They're two sides of the same coin."
—Marilyn Engle
Encino, California

Nothing inspires more fear in the hearts of GRE test takers than logic games. Why? Partly because the skills tested on the section seem so unfamiliar. You need to turn a game's information to your advantage by organizing your thinking and spotting key deductions, and that's not easy to do.

Games tend to give the most trouble to students who don't have a clearly defined method of attack. And that's where Kaplan's basic principles, game-specific strategies, and five-step method for logic games will help most, streamlining your work so you can rack up points quickly and confidently.

## The Four Basic Principles of Logic Games

The rallying cry of the logic games-impaired is, "I could do these, if only I had more time!" Well, that's true of everybody. You can spend as much time on a game as you like when you're sitting in your own kitchen, but once the clock starts running on your CAT, that's it—you've got to finish the section before time runs out.

Logic games are perhaps the most speed-sensitive questions on the test. The test makers know that if you could spend hours methodically trying out every choice in every question, you'd probably get the right one. But it's all about efficiency, both on the test and in your future studies.

And that brings us to the first (and somewhat paradoxical-sounding) logic games principle.

### 1. To Go Faster, You Need to Slow Down

To gain time in logic games, you must spend more time thinking through and analyzing the setup and the rules. This is not only the most important principle for logic games success, it's also the one that's most often ignored, probably because it just doesn't seem intuitively right; people who have timing difficulties tend to speed up, not slow down. But take our word for it: by spending a little extra time up front thinking through the setup, the "action," and the rules, you'll be able to recognize the game's key issues and make important deductions that will actually save you time in the long run.

Games are structured so that, in order to answer the questions quickly and correctly, you need to search out relevant pieces of information that combine to form valid new statements, called deductions. Now, you can either do this once, up front, and then utilize the same deductions throughout the game, OR you can choose to piece together the same basic deductions—essentially repeating the same work—for every single question.

For instance, let's say that two of the rules for a logic game go as follows:

If Bob is chosen for the team, then Eric is also chosen.
If Eric is chosen for the team, then Pat will not be chosen.

You can, as you read through the rules of the game, just treat those rules as two separate pieces of independent information. But there's a deduction to be made from them. Do you see it? If Bob is chosen, Eric is too. If Eric is chosen, Pat is not. That means that, if Bob is chosen, Pat is not chosen. That's an important deduction—one that will undoubtedly be required from question to question. If you don't take the time to make it up front, when you're first considering the game, you'll have to make it over and over again, every time it's necessary to answer a question. But if you do take the time to make it up front and build it into your entire conception of the game, you'll save that time later.

So, always try to take the game scenario and the rules as far as you can before moving on to the questions. Look for common elements among the rules (like Eric in the previous rules); this will help you combine them and weed out major deductions. The stimulus creates a situation, and the rules place restrictions on what can and cannot happen within that situation. If you investigate the possible scenarios and look for and find major deductions up front, you'll then be able to rack up points quickly and confidently.

### 2. Understand What a Rule Means, Not Just What It Says

If you're interested in demonstrating how well you can read a statement and then spit it back verbatim, you'd be better off training to be a clerk instead of a scholar. That's why you'll never see this on the GRE:

> Rule: Arlene is not fifth in line.
> Question: Which one of the following people is not fifth in line?
> Answer: Arlene.

Some LG questions are easy, but not that easy. The GRE, after all, measures critical thinking, and virtually every sentence in logic games has to be filtered through some sort of analytical process before it will be of any use. You may have to use the information about Arlene to help you eliminate a choice or lead you to the right answer, but even in the simplest of cases, this will involve the application, as opposed to the mere parroting, of the rule.

So, getting back to the principle, it's not enough to just copy a rule off the page (or shorthand it, as we'll discuss momentarily); it's imperative that you think through its exact meaning, including any implications that it might have. And *don't* limit this behavior to the indented rules; statements in the games' introductions are very often rules in themselves and warrant the same meticulous consideration.

For instance, let's say a game's introduction sets up a scenario in which you have three boxes, each containing at least two of the following three types of candy—chocolates, gumdrops, and mints. Then you get the following rule:

> Box 2 does not contain any gumdrops.

### Kaplan Tip

To fully grasp a rule in logic games, you must know more than just what it says. You've got to know what the rule means in the context of the game and in combination with other rules.

### Kaplan Tip

Always try to turn negative rules—Box 2 does not contain any gumdrops—into a positive statement —Box 2 must contain chocolates and mints.

### Kaplan Tip

You must know the rules of a logic game cold— what they mean, how they impact on other rules, what implications they have in the context of the game scenario.

What does that rule say? That there aren't any gumdrops in box 2. But what does that rule mean, when you think about it in the context of the game? That Box 2 does contain chocolates and mints. Each box contains at least two of three things, remember. So, once you eliminate one of the three things for any particular box, you know that the other two things *must* be in that box.

Part of understanding what a rule means, moreover, is grasping what the rule doesn't mean. For example, take the rule we mentioned earlier:

> RULE: If Bob is chosen for the team, then Eric is also chosen.
> MEANS: Whenever Bob is chosen, Eric is, too.
> DOESN'T MEAN: Whenever Eric is chosen, Bob is, too.

### 3. Use Scratchwork and Shorthand

The proper use of scratchwork can help you do your best on logic games. As you may recall, the directions state, "You may wish to draw a rough sketch to help answer some of the questions." Notice that they use the wording *rough sketch*, not *masterpiece, work of art,* or *classic portrait for the ages*. The GRE is not a drawing contest; you get no points for creating beautiful visual imagery on your scratch paper.

Although some recent games aren't even amenable to scratchwork, for most games you'll find that it is helpful to create a master sketch, one that encapsulates all of the game's information in one easy-to-reference picture. Doing so will not only give your eyes a place to gravitate toward when you need information, but it will also help to solidify in your mind the action of the game, the rules, and whatever deductions you come to up front.

Remember to keep your scratchwork simple; the less time you spend drawing, the more time you'll have for thinking and answering questions. Pay careful attention to the scratchwork suggestions in the explanations to the four games on the Practice Test in this book.

The part of your scratchwork where you jot down on your scratch paper a quick and shortened form of each rule is called shorthand. Shorthand is a visual representation of a mental thought process and is useful only if it reminds you at a glance of the rule's meaning. Whether you shorthand a rule or commit it to memory, you should never have to look back at the game itself once you get to the questions. The goal of the entire scratchwork process is to condense a lot of information into manageable, user-friendly visual cues. It's much easier to remember rules written like so:

B → E
No G in 3

## Kaplan Tip

You're applying to grad school, not art school. Don't worry about making elaborate diagrams in logic games. There is no "right diagram" for any game. But there is good scratchwork that will help you get points quicker and more accurately.

## Definition

**Shorthand** is a visual representation of a mental thought process. Use shorthand to remind yourself of the meaning of a rule in a logic games problem.

than rules written like this:

> If Bob is chosen for the team, then Eric is also chosen.
> Box 3 does not contain any gumdrops.

Just remember what your shorthand means—for instance, what the arrow from B to E means—and be consistent in using it. If you can develop a personal shorthand that is instantly understandable to you, you will have a decided advantage come the day of the test.

### 4. Try to Set off Chains of Deduction

When hypothetical information is offered in a question stem, try to use it to set off a chain of deductions. Consider the following question. (Because this question is excerpted without the accompanying introduction and rules, ignore the specific logic of the discussion; it's just presented to make a point.)

> If the speedboat is yellow, which one of the following must be true?
>
> (A) The car is green.
> (B) The airplane is red.
> (C) The train is black.
> (D) The car is yellow.
> (E) The train is red.

The question stem contains a hypothetical, which is an if-clause offering information pertaining only to that particular question. The wrong approach is acknowledging that the speedboat is yellow and then proceeding to test out all of the choices. The muddled mental thought process accompanying this tragic approach might sound something like this:

"All right, the speedboat's yellow, does the car have to be green? Well, let's see, if the speedboat's yellow, *and* the car is green, then the train would have to be yellow, but I can't tell what color the airplane is, and I guess this is okay, I don't know, I better try the next choice. Let's see what happens if the speedboat's yellow and the airplane is red. . . ."

Don't do this kind of dithering! Notice that the question doesn't ask, "What happens, if in addition to this, the car is green?" or "What happens if this is true and the airplane is red?" So why is the confused test taker above intent on answering all of these irrelevant questions? Our second point is that you should never begin a question by trying out answer choices; that's going about it backwards. Only if you're entirely stuck or are faced with a question stem that leaves you no choice, should you resort to trial and error.

### Kaplan Rules

Trial and error with the answer choices should be your last resort, not your first. It's much quicker to follow a chain of deduction until it leads you to the answer. In some cases, trial and error is necessary, but don't turn to it unless you're really stuck.

### Teacher Tip

"Logic games require a systematic approach. Kaplan shows you how to let one piece of information lead you to another. Deductions fall as predictably as dominoes."
—Julie DeMarco
Washington, DC

Most logic games questions are amenable to another, more efficient and systematic methodology. The correct approach is to incorporate the new piece of information into your view of the game, creating one quick sketch if you wish. How do you do this? Apply the rules and any previous deductions to the new information in order to set off a new chain of deductions. Then follow through until you've taken the new information as far as it can go. Just as you must take the game and rules as far as you can before moving on to the questions, you must carry the information in a question stem out as far as you can before moving on to the choices.

So be sure to stay out of answer-choice land until you have sufficiently mined the hypothetical. If the question stem contains a hypothetical, then your job is to get as much out of that piece of information as you can before even looking at the choices. This way, *you* dictate to the test, not the other way around. You'll then be able to determine the answer and simply pick it off the page.

You'll have the chance to see these major logic games principles in action when you review the explanations to the games in the Practice Test in the back of this book.

## Common Logic Game Types

Although the logic games section can contain a wide variety of situations and scenarios, certain game types appear again and again. These are the most common:

### 1. Sequencing Games

Logic games that require sequencing skills have long been a favorite of the test makers. No matter what the scenario in games of this type, the common denominator is that in some way, shape, or form, they all involve putting entities in order. In a typical sequence game, you may be asked to arrange the cast of characters numerically from left to right, from top to bottom, during days of the week, in a circle, and so on. The sequence may be a sequence of degree; ranking the eight smartest test takers from 1 to 8 falls into this category. On the other hand, the sequence may be based on time, such as one that involves the finishing times of runners in a race. In some cases, there are two or even three orderings to keep track of in a single game.

*Typical Issues.* The following is a list of the key issues that underlie sequencing games. Each key issue is followed by a corresponding rule—in some cases, with several alternative ways of expressing the same rule. At the end, we'll use these rules to build a miniature logic game, so that you can see how rules work together to define and limit a game's "action." These rules all refer to a scenario in which eight events are to be sequenced from first to eighth.

## At a Glance

Sequencing games:

- Are historically the most common game type
- Involve putting entities in order
- Involve orderings, which can be in time (runners finishing a race), space (people standing next to one another in line), or degree (shortest to tallest, worst to best, etcetera)

- Which entities are concretely placed in the ordering?

  X is third.

- Which entities are excluded from a specific position in the ordering?

  Y is not fourth.

- Which entities are next to, adjacent to, or are immediately preceding or following one another?

  X and Y are consecutive.
  X is next to Y.
  No event comes between X and Y.
  X and Y are consecutive in the ordering.

- Which entities CANNOT BE next to, adjacent to, or immediately preceding or following one another?

  X does not immediately precede or follow Z.
  X is not immediately before or after Z.
  At least one event comes between X and Z.
  X and Z are not consecutive in the sequence.

- How far apart in the ordering are two particular entities?

  Exactly two events come between X and Q.
  At least two events come between X and Q.

- What is the relative position of two entities in the ordering?

  Q comes before T in the sequence.
  T comes after Q in the sequence.

*How a Sequence Game Works.* Let's see how rules like those above might combine to create a simple logic game.

Eight events—Q, R, S, T, W, X, Y, and Z—are being sequenced from first to eighth.

  X is third.
  Y is not fourth.
  X and Y are consecutive in the sequence.
  Exactly two events come between X and Q.
  Q comes before T in the sequence.

How would you approach this simplified game? Remember our fourth basic principle: Use scratchwork and shorthand. With eight events to sequence from first to eighth, you'd probably want to draw eight dashes on your scratch paper, maybe in two groups of four (so you can easily determine which dash is which). Then take the rules in order of concreteness, starting with the most concrete of all—Rule 1—which tells you that X is third. Fill that into your sketch:

$$ \underline{\phantom{X}} \; \underline{\phantom{X}} \; \underline{X} \; \underline{\phantom{X}} \quad \underline{\phantom{X}} \; \underline{\phantom{X}} \; \underline{\phantom{X}} \; \underline{\phantom{X}} $$

Jump to the next most concrete rule—Rule 4, which tells you that exactly two events come between X and Q. Well, Q must be sixth, then:

$$ \underline{\phantom{X}} \; \underline{\phantom{X}} \; \underline{X} \; \underline{\phantom{X}} \quad \underline{\phantom{X}} \; \underline{Q} \; \underline{\phantom{X}} \; \underline{\phantom{X}} $$

Rule 5 says that Q comes before T. Because Q is sixth, T must be either seventh or eighth. To indicate this, under the sketch, write T with two arrows pointing to the seventh and eighth dashes.

Rule 3 says that X and Y are consecutive. X is third, so Y will be either second or fourth. Rule 2 clears up that matter. Y can't be fourth, says Rule 2, so it will have to be second:

This is how the rules work together to build a sequence game.

The questions might then present hypothetical information that would set off the chain of deduction we mentioned in the basic principles section.

### 2. Grouping Games

A grouping game, much like every other type of game, begins with a set of entities. What sets grouping apart is the "action" of the game, or specifically, what you're asked to do with the entities. In a pure grouping game, unlike sequencing, there's no call for putting the entities in order. Instead, you'll usually be required to select a smaller group from the initial group or distribute the entities in some fashion into more than one subgroup. As a distinct skill, grouping differs from sequencing in that you're not really concerned with what order the entities are in, but rather how they're grouped—who's in, who's out, and who can and cannot be with whom in various subgroups.

## At a Glance

Grouping games:

- Are a very common game type
- Come in two varieties—"selection" and "distribution"
- Contain number elements that are often crucial (how many chosen, how many in each group, etcetera)
- Action involves deciding if each entity is in or out; if in, may then need to determine where (in distribution games)

*Grouping Games of Selection and of Distribution.* The two varieties of grouping games are really very similar under the skin. In "distribution" types of grouping games, we are told every entity has to go somewhere—as in a game where we have to distribute eight marbles into two jars with four marbles each.

In "selection" types of grouping games, we're primarily concerned with which entities go into one subgroup—as in a game where we have eight marbles and we have to select five marbles to go into a jar (and nothing is said about what happens to the other three marbles). What makes these games just two variants on a theme is the fact that you can think of selection games as distribution games. For example, in the second game you can think of the task as that of dividing the marbles into two groups, the group in the jar and the group outside. Grouping games can get quite complicated, involving different sorts of entities (marbles and rocks) and many different groups (three jars and two pockets).

Like sequencing games, grouping games have a language all their own, and it's up to you to speak that language fluently when you come across games that require this particular skill on your test.

*Typical Issues—Grouping Games of Selection.* The following is a list of the key issues that underlie grouping games. Each key issue is followed by a corresponding rule—in some cases, with several alternative ways of expressing the same rule. At the end, again, we'll use these rules to build a miniature logic game.

First, grouping games of selection. These rules all refer to a scenario in which you are to select a subgroup of four from a group of eight entities—Q, R, S, T, W, X, Y, and Z:

- Which entities are definitely chosen?

    Q is selected.

- Which entities rely on a different entity's selection in order to be chosen?

    If X is selected, then Y is selected.
    X will be selected only if Y is selected.
    X will not be selected unless Y is selected.

Note: A common misconception surrounds the rule "If X is selected, then Y is selected." The rule works only in one direction; if X is chosen, Y must be, but if Y is chosen, X *may or may not be.* Remember the discussion of Basic Principle Number 2 above—understand not only what a rule means, but also what it doesn't mean!

- Which entities must be chosen together, or not at all?

> If Y is selected, Z is selected, and vice versa.
> Y will not be selected unless Z is selected, and vice versa.

- Which entities cannot both be chosen?

> If R is selected, Z is not selected.
> If Z is selected, R is not selected.
> R and Z can't both be selected.

*How Grouping Games of Selection Work.* We can combine these rules to create a rudimentary grouping game of selection:

> A professor must choose a group of four books for her next seminar. She must choose from a pool of eight books—Q, R, S, T, W, X, Y, and Z.
> Q is selected.
> If X is selected then Y is selected.
> If Y is selected, Z is selected, and vice versa.
> If R is selected, Z is not selected.

A good way of dealing with this kind of game might be to write out the eight letters—four on top, four on the bottom—and then circle the ones that are definitely selected while crossing out the ones that are definitely not selected. Thus, Rule 1 would allow you to circle the Q:

The other rules can't be built into the sketch just yet, because they describe eventualities (what happens if something else happens). Here's where you would want to use shorthand:

> Rule 2 translates as: "If X, then Y" or "X —> Y"
> Rule 3 might be rendered as: "Y <—> Z" (because the requirement is vice versa).
> Rule 4 could be written in shorthand as "R ≠ Z" (because R and Z are mutually exclusive).

The rules would then be poised to take effect whenever a question would add new hypothetical information, setting off a chain of deduction. For instance, let's say a question reads like so:

If R is selected, which of the following must be true?

This new information would put the rules into motion. R's inclusion would set off Rule 4, "R ≠ Z," so we'd have to circle R and cross out Z:

This would in turn set off Rule 3, "Y <—> Z." Because Z is out, Y is out, since they are chosen together or not at all:

Now Rule 2 comes into play. "X —> Y" means that if Y is not chosen, X can't be either (since X's inclusion would require Y's). So we can take the chain of deduction one step further:

A correct answer to this question, then, might be "X is not included." And that, in a nutshell, is how a (simplified) grouping game of selection works.

*Typical Issues—Grouping Games of Distribution.* Here are the issues involved in the other kind of grouping games—grouping games of distribution—along with the rules that govern them. These rules, by the way, refer to a scenario in which our old favorite group of eight entities—Q, R, S, T, W, X, Y, Z—have to be distributed into three different classes:

• Which entities are concretely placed in a particular subgroup?

X is placed in class 3.

- Which entities are barred from a particular subgroup?

> Y is not placed in class 2.

- Which entities must be placed in the same subgroup?

> X is placed in the same class as Z.
> Z is placed in the same class as X.
> X and Z are placed in the same class.

- Which entities cannot be placed in the same subgroup?

> X is not placed in the same class as Y.
> Y is not placed in the same class as X.
> X and Y are not placed in the same class.

- Which entity's placement depends on the placement of a different entity?

> If Y is placed in class 1, then Q is placed in class 2.

*How Grouping Games of Distribution Work.* The above rules, neatly enough, also can combine to form a miniature grouping game of distribution:

> Eight students—Q, R, S, T, W, X, Y, and Z—must be subdivided into three different classes—Classes 1, 2, and 3.

> X is placed in Class 3.
> Y is not placed in Class 2.
> X is placed in the same class as Z.
> X is not placed in the same class as Y.
> If Y is placed in Class 1, then Q is placed in Class 2.

A good scratchwork scheme for games of this type would be to draw three circles in your booklet, one for each of the three classes. Then put the eight entities in the appropriate circles as that information becomes known.

Here again, start with the most concrete rule first, which is Rule 1, which definitively places X in Class 3. Rule 2 just as definitively precludes Y from Class 2, so build that into the scratchwork, too:

Rule 3 requires Z to join X in Class 3:

Rule 4, prohibiting Y from being in the same class as X, means that Y can't be in Class 3. But we already know that Y can't be in Class 2. We can deduce, therefore, that Y must go in Class 1. That in turn puts Rule 5 into play: if Y is in Class 1 (as it is here), Q is in Class 2:

And that is the dynamic of most grouping games of distribution (though, again, in much simplified form).

### 3. Mapping Games

Mapping games are significantly less common than either sequencing games or grouping games, but you may well see one on the test. We hope you do, because once you know how to set up a mapping game, you will probably find them to be the easiest type on the test.

*Typical Issues.* The key to identifying a mapping game is to see whether the game asks you to make connections between entities in which each entity connects to one or more others. For example, the rules may tell you how rooms in a house are connected to other rooms, or the rules may tell you how bus or rail stops are connected to each other in a transit system.

We call them mapping games because the best way to handle them is to draw a quick-and-dirty map of the connections between entities. Once you've drawn the map, all the answers to the game's questions should fall into your lap.

There are two things to pay special attention to when you've drawn your map. Note the entities that are especially well or poorly connected to others (some will serve as "hubs" while others are "dead ends"). Also note if the connections from one entity to another don't go both ways (for example, you may be able to get from A to B, but you can't go back from B to A). The best way to do this is to draw a one-way arrow in the direction of such connections.

*How Mapping Games Work.*   Now let's see a typical mapping game in action:

> Exactly three public transportation routes serve a municipal airport. The vehicles on each route go in both directions and only pick up or deposit passengers at the designated stops.
>
> Bus Line A stops at the main terminal, the airport hotel, the convention center, the downtown bus depot, and the train station.
>
> Bus Line B stops at the main terminal, Dykman Avenue, Charles Street, 32nd Street, 25th Street, 16th Street, the downtown bus depot, and 4th Street.
>
> The express bus line stops at the main terminal and the train station.

The scratchwork for this game should incorporate all three rules into one easy-to-read diagram. Make it as simple as possible. Start by treating Line A in Rule 1 as a straight line, and symbolize each stop with a letter.

$$M - H - C - D - T$$

Now add Rule 2. Make the stops that are the same for Lines A and B the same on the map (if it helps, also distinguish Lines A and B by using a dotted or a squiggly line for the connections on Line B, and using lowercase letters for the stops).

For Rule 3, we could either add a new line from M to T, or simply circle these stops to indicate that the express bus stops there.

$$\begin{array}{c} 4 \\ | \\ \textcircled{M}-H-C-D-\textcircled{T} \\ | \qquad\quad | \\ d \qquad\quad 17 \\ \backslash \\ c-32-25 \end{array}$$

Now we have all we need to answer any question you're likely to face about the game. Note that M and D are the only places where a transfer is possible between the lines, and there will certainly be questions about making transfers. Likewise, notice that the 4th Street stop and the train station stop are dead ends. There will almost certainly be one or more questions testing your awareness of this in some way.

For example, a question would probably ask where any bus on this transit system must stop before arriving at the 4th Street stop. Hopefully, by now the answer will jump out at you: the bus must stop at the downtown bus depot first.

## General Logic Games Tips

*Hybrid Games*
Some games are what you might call hybrid games, requiring you to combine sequencing and grouping. Keep in mind that while we try to recognize games as a particular type, it's not necessary to attach a strict name to every game you encounter. For example, it really doesn't matter if you categorize a game as a sequencing game with a grouping element or as a grouping game with a sequencing element, as long as you're comfortable with both sets of skills.

*No "Best" Choice*
Unlike the answer choices in logical reasoning, in which the correct answer is the "best" choice, the answers in logic games are objectively correct or incorrect. Therefore, when you find an answer that's definitely right, have the confidence to choose it and move on, without wasting time to check the other choices. This is one way to improve your timing on the section.

**Kaplan Rules**

Like math questions, logic game questions have definite right and wrong answers. Once you find the answer that works, pick it and move on. There's no need to check out the other choices.

## Kaplan Tip

Rules that deal with one or more of the same entities can often be combined to make important deductions.

## Kaplan Tip

If you find that you can't make a single important deduction by combining rules, you're probably missing something. Check the game introduction and rules again to make sure that you're not misinterpreting something.

## Kaplan Rules

The Kaplan Five-Step Method for Logic Games:

1. Get an overview.
2. Visualize and map out the game.
3. Consider the rules individually.
4. Combine the rules.
5. Work on the questions systematically.

*Common Elements and Deductions*

Rules that contain common elements are often the ones that lead to deductions. Consider the following three rules:

> If Sybil goes to the party, then Edna will go to the party.
> If Jacqui goes to the party, then Sherry will not go to the party.
> If Edna goes to the party, then Dale will go to the party.

Rules 1 and 2 have no entities in common, which is a good sign that we can't deduce anything from combining them. The same goes for Rules 2 and 3. But because Rules 1 and 3 have Edna in common, a deduction is likely (although not guaranteed). In this case, combining Rules 1 and 3 would allow us to deduce another rule: If Sybil goes to the party, then Dale will go also.

*Focus on the Important Rules*

Not all rules are created equal—some are inherently more important than others. Try to focus first on the ones that have the greatest impact on the situation, specifically the ones that involve the greatest number of the entities. These are also the rules to turn to first whenever you're stuck on a question and don't know how to set off the chain of deductions.

## The Kaplan Five-Step Method for Logic Games

Now that you have some logic games background, it's time to see how you can marshal that knowledge into a systematic approach to games.

*1. Get an Overview*

Read carefully the game's introduction and rules, to establish the "cast of characters," the "action," and the number limits governing the game.

*2. Visualize and Map out the Game*

Make a mental picture of the situation and let it guide you as you create a sketch, or some other kind of scratchwork, if need be, to help you keep track of the rules and handle new information.

*3. Consider the Rules Individually*

After you've thought through the meaning and implications of each rule, you have three choices. You can:

- Build it directly into your sketch of the game situation
- Jot down the rule in shorthand form to help you remember it
- Underline or circle rules that don't lend themselves to the first two techniques

*4. Combine the Rules*
Look for common elements among the rules; that's what will lead you to make deductions. Treat these deductions as additional rules, good for the whole game.

*5. Work on the Questions Systematically*
Read the question stem carefully! Take special notice of such words as *must, could, cannot, not, impossible,* and *except.* As always, use the hypothetical information offered in *if*-clauses to set off a chain of deductions.

## Using the Kaplan Five-Step Method
Here's how the approach can work with an actual logic game:

> Five repair people—Mona, Patrick, Renatta, Saffie, and Will—are assigned shifts to repair appliances on five days of a single week, Monday to Friday. There are exactly three shifts available to each repair person each day—a morning shift, an afternoon shift, and an evening shift. No more than one repair person works on any given shift. Each repair person works exactly two shifts during the week, but no repair person works more than one shift in a single day.

> Exactly two repair people work on each day of the week.
> Mona and Will work a shift on the same days of the week.
> Patrick doesn't work on any afternoon or evening shifts during the week.
> Will doesn't work on any morning or afternoon shifts during the week.
> Mona works shifts on two consecutive days of the week.
> Saffie's second shift of the week is on an earlier day of the week than Mona's first shift.

> 1. Which one of the following must be true?
>
>    (A) Saffie works a shift on Tuesday afternoon.
>    (B) Patrick works a shift on Monday morning.
>    (C) Will works a shift on Thursday evening.
>    (D) Renatta works a shift on Friday afternoon.
>    (E) Mona works a shift on Tuesday morning.

2. If Will does not work a shift on Friday, which one of the following could be false?

   (A) Renatta works a shift on Friday.
   (B) Saffie works a shift on Tuesday.
   (C) Mona works a shift on Wednesday.
   (D) Saffie works a shift on Monday.
   (E) Patrick works a shift on Tuesday.

(Note that there are only two questions accompanying this game; a typical logic game will have three to six questions. This game is as complicated as any you're likely to see on the GRE.)

*1. Get an Overview*
We need to schedule five repair people, abbreviated M, P, R, S, and W, in a particular order during a five-day calendar week, Monday to Friday. The ordering element tells us we're dealing with a sequencing game, though there is a slight grouping element involved in that a couple of rules deal with grouping issues—namely, which people can or cannot work on the same day of the week as each other.

Be very careful about the numbers governing this game; they go a long way in defining how the game works. There are to be exactly two repair people per day (never working on the same shift). Each repair person must work exactly two shifts, and because repair people are forbidden to take two shifts in the same day, this means that each repair person will work on exactly two days. So, in effect, 10 out of the 15 available shifts will be taken, and five will be left untouched.

*2. Visualize and Map out the Game*
Go with whatever you feel is the most efficient way to keep track of the situation. Most people would settle on a sketch of the five days, each broken up into three shifts, like so:

|       | M | Tu | W | Th | F |
|-------|---|----|---|----|---|
| Morn. |   |    |   |    |   |
| Aft.  |   |    |   |    |   |
| Eve.  |   |    |   |    |   |

Into this sketch—one letter per box—each entity will have to go twice (each repair person does two shifts, remember). So your pool of entities to place would be: MMPPRRSSWW. You might want to include five Xs (or Os) for the five shifts that won't be taken by any of the repair people.

### 3. Consider the Rules Individually

We've already dealt with some of the number-related rules hidden in the game's introduction. Now let's consider this statement from the intro:

> No more than one repair person works in any given shift.

Make sure you interpret rules like this correctly. You may have to paraphrase, in your own words, its exact meaning. In this case: two repair people per shift is no good, three is out of the question, etcetera. But it doesn't mean that any given shift *must* have a repair person. If the test makers meant to imply that, they would have written, "Exactly one repair person works on every given shift." Notice the difference in wording. It's subtle, but it has a huge impact on the game.

Let's consider the other rules. We've already handled Rule 1. You may wish to jot down "2 a day," or something like that, to remind you of this important information.

Rule 2: Mona and Will work on the same days, and that holds for both of the days these repair people work. Write this in any shorthand that seems fitting (one suggestion is to draw MW with a circle around it on your page).

Rules 3 and 4: We can handle these two rules together because they're so similar. You can write shorthand for these rules as they are, but you'd be doing yourself a great disservice. Instead, first work out their implications, which is actually a pretty simple matter: if Patrick doesn't work afternoons or evenings, he must work mornings. If Will doesn't work mornings or afternoons, he must work evenings. Always take the rules as far as you can, and then jot their implications down on your page for reference.

Rule 5: This one is pretty self-explanatory; Mona's shifts must be on consecutive days, such as Thursday and Friday. M = M might be a good way to write this in shorthand.

Rule 6: Here's another sequencing rule—you must place both Ss for Saffie on earlier days of the week than the two Ms for Mona. That means that Saffie and Mona can't work on the same day (although we already knew that from Rule 2), and that Mona's shifts can't come before Saffie's. Try writing this in shorthand as S . . . S . . . M . . . M.

### 4. Combine the Rules

This is the crucial stage for most games. Here, notice that Mona appears in three of the six indented rules; that's a good indication that combining these rules should lead somewhere useful. Combining Rule 2 and Rule 5 gives us two Mona/Will days in a row:

$$\frac{M}{W} = \frac{M}{W}$$

Will must be scheduled for evening shifts (remember, we turned Rule 4 into this positive statement). That means that Mona would take the morning or afternoon shift on these consecutive days.

Rule 6 concerns Mona as well: two Saffies before two Monas. How is this possible? We need two Ss on different days to come before the two consecutive Ms. If Saffie's shifts are as early in the week as possible, she'll work on Monday and Tuesday. That means that the earliest day that Mona can work (and Will as well, thanks to Rule 2) is Wednesday. There's our first really key deduction:

> Mona and Will cannot work on Monday and Tuesday; they must work Wednesday, Thursday, or Friday.

Do we stop there? No, of course not. The difference between the logic games expert and the logic games novice is that the expert knows how to press on when further useful deductive possibilities exist. If you relate this deduction back to Rule 5, it becomes clear that Mona and Will must work on Wednesday and Thursday *or* on Thursday and Friday. This brings us to another big deduction:

> Either way, Mona and Will must work on Thursday. Thanks to Rule 4, we can slot Will in for Thursday evening. Mona will then take Thursday morning OR afternoon. The other Mona/Will day must be either Wednesday or Friday, to remain consecutive.

Here's what your completed sketch may look like, with as many of the rules built into it as possible:

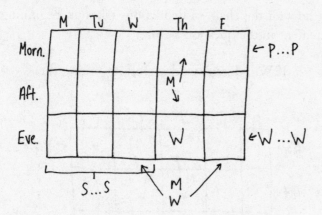

Now that we've combined the rules, and have even uncovered a few big deductions, it's time to move on to the questions.

### 5. Work on the Questions Systematically

Now you'll see how all the work we did up front pays off. Question 1 offers no hypothetical information; it simply asks what must be true. And because we've already deduced a few things that must be true, we can scan the choices for one that matches any one of our newly discovered pieces of information. It doesn't take long to spot choice (C)—it's our big deduction staring us right in the face. You shouldn't even waste time checking the other choices. Instead, have the confidence that you've done the right work the right way, and choose (C) and move on. (Just for the record, for those of you who are curious, (A), (B), and (D) *could* be true, but don't have to be, whereas (E), as we discovered earlier, is an impossibility.)

Question 2 contains a hypothetical: no Will on Friday. One glance at our sketch tells us that the second Mona/Will cluster must therefore be placed on Wednesday, next to the Thursday Mona/Will group. Saffie must then work on Monday and Tuesday, in order to satisfy Rule 6 (although we don't yet know the exact shifts she takes during those days).

That brings us to the two questions that test takers ask all too infrequently, "Who's left?" and more importantly, "Where can they go?" Two Ps and two Rs are left to place, with one spot on Monday, one spot on Tuesday, and two spots on Friday open to place them. How can this be done? Friday can't get both Ps or both Rs (from the last sentence in the introduction), so it will have to get one of each, with P in the morning and R in either the afternoon or evening. The other P and the other R will join S on Monday or Tuesday, in either order. Of course, whichever day P is on, he must be in the morning, whereas the exact shifts for R and S are ambiguous.

Look at how far the chain of deductions takes us, beginning with the simple statement in the question stem:

If Will doesn't work a shift on Friday, then . . .

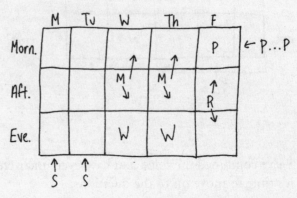

With all of this information at our disposal, there's not a question in the world that we can't answer correctly. This one asks for a statement that could be false—which means that the four wrong choices will all be things that must be true. And in fact, choices (A) through (D) match the situation in this question perfectly, while (E) merely *could* be true: Patrick's first shift of the week could be on Tuesday, but it just as easily could be on Monday as well. (His second shift must be on Friday, of course.) (E) is therefore the only choice that could be false.

## Logical Reasoning

**This question or set of questions is based on a passage or a set of conditions. You may wish to draw a diagram to answer some of the questions. Choose the best answer for each question.**

Most people find GRE logical reasoning to be much easier than logic games. In fact, many people don't do any preparation for this question type at all. It's ironic, then, that this is also one of the most stubborn item types on the test—that is, it's one of the toughest to improve at. That's because there aren't really any quick fixes in logical reasoning. You can only get better by understanding arguments better.

On the GRE CAT, you will probably see one to three logical reasoning questions at the start of the section, followed by a logic game, then one to three more logical reasoning questions. After that, each logical reasoning question is usually followed by a logic game. That is, you will see a total of about eight logical reasoning questions.

### Kaplan Tip

There's nothing bizarre or esoteric about the skills you need for logical reasoning. You've just got to learn how to adapt those skills to the peculiar requirements of a timed, standardized test.

## The Five Basic Principles of Logical Reasoning

*1. Know the Structure of the Argument*
Success on this section hinges on your ability to identify the evidence and conclusion parts of the argument. There is no general rule about where conclusion and evidence appear in the argument: The conclusion could be the first sentence, followed by the evidence, or else it could be the last sentence, with the evidence preceding it. Consider the following short stimulus:

> The Brookdale Public Library will require extensive physical rehabilitation to meet the new building codes just passed by the town council. For one thing, the electrical system is inadequate, causing the lights to flicker sporadically. Furthermore, there are too few emergency exits, and even those are poorly marked and sometimes locked.

Let's suppose that the author of the argument above were only allowed one sentence to convey her point. Do you think that she would waste her lone opportunity on the statement, "The electrical system at the Brookdale Public Library is inadequate, causing the lights to flicker sporadically"? Would she walk away satisfied that she got her main point across? Probably not. Given a single opportunity, she would have to state the first sentence: "The Brookdale Public Library will require extensive physical rehabilitation, etcetera." This is her conclusion. If you pressed her for her *reasons* for making this statement, she would then cite the electrical and structural problems with the building. This is the evidence for her conclusion.

*2. Preview the Question Stem*
Looking over the question stem before you read the stimulus will alert you in advance of what to focus on in your initial reading of the stimulus. In effect, it gives you a jump on the questions. For example, let's say the question attached to the original library argument above asked the following:

> The author supports her point about the need for rehabilitation at the Brookdale Library by citing which of the following?

If you were to preview this question stem before reading the stimulus, you would know what to look for in advance—namely, evidence, the "support" provided for the conclusion. Similarly, if the question asked you to find an assumption that the author is relying on, this would tell you in advance that there was a crucial piece of the argument missing, and you could begin to think about it right off the bat.

### 3. Paraphrase the Author's Point

After you read the stimulus, you'll want to paraphrase the author's main argument, that is, restate the author's ideas in your own words. Frequently, the authors in logical reasoning say pretty simple things in complex ways. But if you mentally translate the verbiage into a simpler form, you'll find the whole thing more manageable.

In the library argument, for instance, you probably don't want to deal with the full complexity of the author's stated conclusion:

> The Brookdale Public Library will require extensive physical rehabilitation to meet the new building codes just passed by the town council.

Instead, you probably want to carry a much simpler form of the point in your mind, something like:

> The library will need fixing up to meet new codes.

Often, by the time you begin reading through answer choices, you run the risk of losing sight of the gist of the stimulus. After all, you can only concentrate on a certain amount of information at one time. Restating the argument in your own words will not only help you get the author's point in the first place, but it'll also help you hold on to it until you've found the correct answer.

### 4. Try to Prephrase an Answer

You must try to approach the answer choices with at least a faint idea of what the answer should look like. This is not to say that you should ponder the question for minutes until you're able to write out your own answer; it's still a multiple-choice test, so the right answer is on the computer screen. Just try to get in the habit of instinctively thinking through the question and framing an answer in your own mind.

For instance, let's say a question for the library argument went like this:

> The author's argument depends on which of the following assumptions about the new building codes?

Having thought about the stimulus argument, an answer to this question may have sprung immediately to mind: namely, the assumption that the new codes are tougher than the old codes. After all, the library will have to be rehabilitated to meet the new codes, according to the author. Clearly, the assumption is that the new codes are more stringent than the old. And that's the kind of statement you would look for among the choices.

## 5. *Keep in Mind the Scope of the Argument*

One of the most important logical reasoning skills, particularly when you're at the point of actually selecting one of the five choices, is the ability to focus in on the scope of the argument. The majority of wrong choices on this section are wrong because they are "outside the scope." In everyday language, that simply means that these choices contain elements that don't match the author's ideas or that simply go beyond the context of the stimulus.

Some common examples of scope problems are choices that are too narrow, or too broad, or literally have nothing to do with the author's points. Also, watch for and eliminate choices that are too extreme to match the argument's scope; they're usually signaled by words such as *all, always, never, none,* and so on. Choices that are more qualified are often correct for arguments that are moderate in tone and contain such words as *usually, sometimes, probably,* etcetera. To illustrate the scope principle, let's look again at the question mentioned above:

> The author's argument depends on which of the following assumptions about the new building codes?

Let's say one of the choices read as follows:

> (A) The new building codes are far too stringent.

Knowing the scope of the argument would help you to eliminate this choice very quickly. You know that this argument is just a claim about what the new codes will require—that the library be rehabilitated. It's not an argument about whether the requirements of the new codes are good, or justifiable, or ridiculously strict. That kind of value judgment is outside the scope of this argument. Recognizing scope problems is a great way of eliminating dozens of wrong answers quickly.

## The Five Common Logical Reasoning Question Types

Now that you're familiar with the basic principles of logical reasoning, let's look at the most common types of questions that you'll be asked. As we said earlier, certain question types crop up again and again on the GRE, and it pays to be familiar with them. Of the types discussed below, the first three predominate, but try to become familiar with the others as well.

### 1. *Assumption Questions*

An assumption bridges the gap between an argument's evidence and conclusion. It's a piece of support that isn't explicitly stated but that is required for the conclusion to remain valid. When a question asks you to

### Kaplan Tip

A remarkable number of wrong answers in Logical Reasoning have scope problems. Always be on the lookout for choices that are too extreme, that contain value judgments that are not relevant to the argument, or that don't match the stimulus in tone or subject matter.

### Teacher Tip

"An assumption is that which an author takes for granted as true in proceeding to his conclusion. Assumptions are neither bad nor good. They're simply risky, as the author is depending on them on faith. If an assumption is proven to be false, then a wedge has been created between evidence and conclusion, and the argument has been weakened."
—Bob Verini
Los Angeles, California

## Definition

Some arguments lack an important bridge between their evidence and their conclusion. That bridge is the necessary **assumption**—a key part of many arguments that remains unspoken.

## At a Glance

Assumption Questions:

- Represent one of the most popular LR question types
- Assumptions unstated in the stimulus
- Bridge the gap between evidence and conclusion
- Must be true in order for the conclusion to remain valid
- Can be checked by applying the denial test

find an author's assumption, it's asking you to find the statement without which the argument falls apart.

In order to test whether a statement is necessarily assumed by an author, therefore, we can employ the denial test. Here's how it works: simply deny or negate the statement and see if the argument falls apart. If it does, that choice is the correct assumption. If, on the other hand, the argument is unaffected, the choice is wrong. Consider, as an example, this simple stimulus:

Allyson plays volleyball for Central High School.
Therefore, Allyson must be over 6 feet tall.

You should recognize the second sentence as the conclusion, and the first sentence as the support, or evidence, for it. But is the argument complete? Obviously not. The piece that's missing—the unstated link between the evidence and conclusion—is the assumption, and you could probably prephrase this one pretty easily:

All volleyball players for Central High School are over 6 feet tall.

To test whether this really is a necessary assumption of the argument, let's apply the "denial test" to it, by negating it. What if it's not true that all volleyball players for Central High School are over 6 feet tall? Can we still logically conclude that Allyson must be taller than 6 feet? No, we can't. Sure, it's possible that she is, but just as possible that she's not. By denying the statement, then, the argument falls to pieces; it's simply no longer valid. And that's our conclusive proof that the statement above is a necessary assumption that the author of this stimulus is relying on.

As we've just seen, you can often prephrase the answer to an assumption question. By previewing the question stem, you'll know what to look for. And stimuli for assumption questions just "feel" like they're missing something. Often, the answer will jump right out at you, as in this case. In more difficult assumption questions, the answers may not be as obvious. But in either case, you can use the denial test to check whichever choice seems correct.

Here are some of the ways in which assumption questions are worded:

- Which one of the following is assumed by the author?
- The argument depends on the assumption that . . .
- The validity of the argument above depends on which one of the following?

## 2. Strengthen/Weaken the Argument

Determining an argument's necessary assumption, as we've just seen, is required to answer assumption questions. But it also is required for another common question type, strengthen-and-weaken-the-argument questions.

One way to weaken an argument is to break down a central piece of evidence. Another way is to attack the validity of any assumptions that the author may be making. The answer to many weaken-the-argument questions is the one that reveals an author's assumption to be unreasonable; conversely, the answer to many strengthen-the-argument questions provides additional support by affirming the truth of an assumption or by presenting more persuasive evidence.

Weakening questions tend to be more common on the GRE than strengthening questions. But here are a few concepts that apply to both question types:

- Weakening an argument is not the same thing as disproving it, whereas strengthening is not the same as proving the conclusion to be true. A strengthener tips the scale toward believing in the validity of the conclusion, whereas a weakener tips the scale in the other direction, toward doubting the conclusion.
- Don't be careless. Wrong answer choices in these question types often have exactly the opposite of the desired effect. That is, if you're asked to strengthen a stimulus argument, it's quite likely that one or more of the wrong choices will contain information that actually weakens the argument. By the same token, weaken questions may contain a choice that strengthens the argument. So once again, pay close attention to what the question stem asks.

The stems associated with these two question types are usually self-explanatory. Here's a list of what you can expect to see on the test:

Weaken:

- Which one of the following, if true, would most weaken the argument above?
- Which one of the following, if true, would most seriously undermine the argument above?

Strengthen:

- Which one of the following, if true, would most strengthen the argument?
- Which one of the following, if true, would provide the most support for the conclusion in the argument above?

## At a Glance

Weaken questions are very popular; strengthen questions less so. Strengthen/weaken questions are:

- Related to assumption: strengthener often shores up central assumption; weakener often shows central assumption to be unreasonable
- You must evaluate each choice as to the effect it would have on the argument if true
- Correct choices don't prove or disprove argument, but simply tip the scale the most in the desired direction

• The argument above would be more persuasive if which one of the following were found to be true?

### 3. Inference Questions

Another of the most common question types you'll encounter on the logical reasoning section is the inference question. The process of inferring is a matter of considering one or more statements as evidence and then drawing a conclusion from them.

Sometimes the inference is very close to the author's overall main point. Other times, it deals with a less central point. In logical reasoning, the difference between an inference and an assumption is that the conclusion's validity doesn't logically depend on an inference, as it does on a necessary assumption. A valid inference is merely something that must be true if the statements in the passage are true—an extension of the argument rather than a necessary part of it.

Be careful. Unlike an assumption, an inference need not have anything to do with the author's conclusion; it may simply be a piece of information derived from one or more pieces of evidence. However, the denial test works for inferences as well as for assumptions: a valid inference always makes more sense than its opposite. If you deny or negate an answer choice, and it has little or no effect on the argument, then chances are that the choice is not inferable from the passage.

Here are some tips for making proper inferences (useful for reading comprehension, as well!). A good inference:

• Stays in line with the gist of the passage
• Stays in line with the author's tone
• Stays in line with the author's point of view
• Stays within the scope of the argument or the main idea
• Is neither denied by, nor irrelevant to, the argument or discussion
• Always makes more sense than its opposite

Here's a quick rundown of the various forms that inference questions are likely to take on your test:

• Which one of the following is implied by the argument above?
• The author suggests that . . .
• If all the statements above are true, which one of the following must also be true?
• The author of the passage would most likely agree with which one of the following?

---

### 4. *Parallel Reasoning Questions*

Parallel Reasoning questions require you to identify the answer choice that contains the argument most similar, or parallel, to that in the stimulus in terms of the reasoning employed. Your task is to abstract the stimulus argument's form, with as little content as possible, and then locate the answer choice that has the form most similar to that of the stimulus. Do not let yourself be drawn to a choice based on its subject matter. A stimulus about music may have an answer choice that also involves music, but that doesn't mean that the reasoning in the two arguments are similar.

A good approach to these questions is to see first if the argument can be symbolized algebraically, using X's and Y's. Take the following example:

> All cows eat grass. This animal eats grass. Therefore, it must be a cow.

This (flawed) argument can be symbolized in the following way:

> All X do Y. This does Y. Therefore, this must be an X.

If the stimulus can be symbolized this way, your job will be to search for the choice that can be symbolized in the same way. Your answer might look something like this:

> Every politician (all X) tells lies (does Y). Jones is lying (this does Y). So he must be a politician (therefore, this must be an X).

Notice how the exact wording doesn't have to match ("all X" means "every X"), and notice that the subject matter doesn't have to match in the least. What's important is the parallel structure.

If the argument's reasoning isn't amenable to symbolization, see if you can put a label on the type of argument being used, such as "arguing from a part to a whole," or "circular reasoning" (evidence and conclusion are identical). Naming the argument will often help eliminate two or three choices that don't even come close to this general form.

But whatever way you choose, as long as you can summarize the argument's form without including content, you're well on your way to finding the parallel argument among the choices.

## At a Glance

Parallel Reasoning:

- Must mimic structure or form, not content, of stimulus
- Sometimes are amenable to algebraic symbolization
- Key is to summarize argument's overall form and match it to that of the correct choice

## Teacher Tip

"Parallel reasoning questions may be among the toughest for some examinees, partly because of a lack a proper definition. Two arguments are 'parallel' when they use the same kind of evidence to draw the same kind of conclusion. Compare the five choices to the original in terms of kind; one and only one will match up."
—Bob Verini
Los Angeles, California

Here are a few more parallel reasoning tips:

- *All* elements of the original argument must be present in its parallel. For example, if the original argument made a generalization to a specific case, a second argument, no matter how similar in structure otherwise, cannot be parallel unless it makes a comparable generalization.
- Stay away from answer choices written about the same subject matter as the original. This is an old trick of the test makers, intended to catch those who mistakenly try to mimic the content rather than the structure of the stimulus.
- Statements that are logically parallel don't have to have all logical elements in the same sequence. If all elements of the first argument exist in the second, even in a different order, the two arguments are parallel.

## At a Glance

Paradox Questions:

- Correct choice will resolve apparent discrepancy or contradiction
- Correct choice should have an intuitive click
- Correct choice will often involve realizing that two groups presented as identical are actually not

*5. Paradox Questions*

A paradox exists when an argument contains two or more seemingly inconsistent statements. You'll know you're dealing with a paradoxical situation if the argument ends with what seems to be a bizarre contradiction. Another sure sign of a paradox is when the argument builds to a certain point, and then the exact opposite of what you would expect to happen happens.

In a typical paradox question, you'll be asked either to find the choice that "explains the paradoxical result" or "resolves the apparent discrepancy." Basically, this will be the choice that reconciles the seemingly inconsistent statements that make up the argument while allowing them all to still be true.

Take the following question:

Fifty-seven percent of the registered voters in this district claimed to support the Democratic candidate, and yet the Republican candidate won the election with 55 percent of the vote.

Which of the following would resolve the apparent discrepancy above?

The stimulus seems paradoxical since the Republican won the election, even though more registered voters preferred the Democrat. But do all registered voters vote? No. So a correct answer for this question might read something like this:

Because of an intensive get-out-the-vote effort in traditionally Republican neighborhoods, a disproportionate number of registered Republicans actually voted in the election.

This statement reconciles the seemingly contradictory elements of the argument by showing that the group of registered voters is not identical to the group of people who actually voted in the election.

A few more tips for handling paradox questions:

- Before attempting to resolve a paradox, make sure you have a good grasp of what the paradox is. If it doesn't hit you right off the bat, look hard for an unexpected result, or what seems to be a blatant contradiction between the author's evidence and conclusion.
- Resolving paradoxes is often a matter of recognizing that two things that are being compared aren't really the same thing. Read critically to note these subtle distinctions.
- In paradox questions, avoid choices that merely amplify points already raised in the argument.

## The Kaplan Four-Step Method for Logical Reasoning

Now that you've learned the basic logical reasoning principles and have been exposed to the full range of question types, it's time to learn how to use all of that knowledge to formulate a systematic approach to logical reasoning. We've developed a four-step method that you can use to attack every question on the section.

*1. Preview the Question Stem*
As we mentioned in the discussion of basic principles, previewing the stem is a great way to focus your reading of the stimulus, so that you know exactly what you're looking for.

*2. Read the Stimulus for Structure*
With the question stem in mind, read the stimulus, paraphrasing as you go. Remember to read actively and critically, pinpointing evidence and conclusion. Also get a sense for how strong or weak the argument is.

*3. Try to Prephrase an Answer*
Sometimes, if you've read the stimulus critically enough, you'll know the answer without even looking at the choices. It will be much easier to find it if you have a sense of what you're looking for among the choices.

**Kaplan Rules**

The Kaplan Four-Step Method for Logical Reasoning:

1. Preview the question stem.
2. Read the stimulus for structure.
3. Try to prephrase an answer.
4. Choose an answer.

*4. Choose an Answer*

Yes, this is obvious, but it matters how you do it. If you were able to prephrase an answer, skim the choices looking for something that sounds like what you have in mind. If you couldn't think of anything, read and evaluate each choice, throwing out the ones that are outside the scope of the argument. After settling on an answer, you may wish to briefly double-check the question stem to make sure that you're indeed answering the question that was asked.

## Using the Kaplan Four-Step Method

Now let's try this method on a genuine logical reasoning item:

A study of 20 overweight men revealed that each man experienced significant weight loss after adding SlimDown, an artificial food supplement, to his daily diet. For three months, each man consumed one SlimDown portion every morning after exercising, and then followed his normal diet for the rest of the day. Clearly, anyone who consumes one portion of SlimDown every day for at least three months will lose weight and will look and feel their best.

Which one of the following is an assumption on which the argument depends?

&#9398; The men in the study will gain back the weight if they discontinue the SlimDown program.

&#9399; No other dietary supplement will have the same effect on overweight men.

&#9400; The daily exercise regimen was not responsible for the effects noted in the study.

&#9401; Women won't experience similar weight reductions if they adhere to the SlimDown program for three months.

&#9402; Overweight men will achieve only partial weight loss if they don't remain on the SlimDown program for a full three months.

*1. Preview the Question Stem*

We see, quite clearly, that we're dealing with an assumption question. Good. We can immediately adopt an "assumption mindset," which basically means that, before even reading the first word of the stimulus, we know that the conclusion will be lacking an important piece of supporting evidence. We now turn to the stimulus, already on the lookout for this missing link.

## Kaplan Tip

The Kaplan four-step method is designed to give structure to your work on the logic reasoning section. But be flexible in using it. These are guidelines, not commandments.

## 2. Read the Stimulus for Structure

The first sentence introduces a study of 20 men using a food supplement product, resulting in weight loss for all 20 of them. The second sentence describes how they used it: once a day, for three months, after morning exercise. So far so good; it feels as if we're building up to something. The structural signal usually indicates that some sort of conclusion follows, and in fact it does: The author concludes in the third sentence that anyone who has one portion of the product daily for three months will lose weight, too.

You must read critically! Notice that the conclusion doesn't say that anyone who follows the same routine as the 20 men will have the same results; it says that anyone who simply consumes the product in the same way will have the same results. You should have begun to sense the inevitable lack of crucial information at this point. The evidence in the second sentence describes a routine that includes taking the supplement after daily exercise, whereas the conclusion focuses primarily on the supplement and entirely ignores the part about the exercise. The conclusion, therefore, doesn't stem logically from the evidence in the first two sentences. This blends seamlessly into the third step.

## 3. Prephrase an Answer

As expected, the argument is beginning to look as if it has a serious shortcoming. Of course, we expected this because we previewed the question stem before reading the stimulus.

In really simplistic terms, the argument proceeds like so: "A bunch of guys did A and B for three months and had X result. If anyone does A for three months, that person will experience X result, too." Sound a little fishy? You bet. The author must be assuming that A (the product), not B (exercise), must be the crucial thing that leads to the result. If not (the denial test), the conclusion makes no sense.

So, you might prephrase the answer like this, "Something about the exercise thing needs to be cleared up." That's it. Did you think your prephrasing had to be something fancy and glamorous? Well, it doesn't. All you need is an inkling of what the question is looking for, and in this case, it just seems that if we don't shore up the exercise issue, the argument will remain invalid and incomplete. So, with our vague idea of a possible assumption, we can turn to the fourth step.

## 4. Choose an Answer

Because we were able to prephrase something, it's best to skim the choices looking for it. And, lo and behold, there's our idea, stated in choice (C). (C) clears up the exercise issue. Yes, this author must assume (C) to make the conclusion that eating SlimDown alone will cause the men to lose weight.

### Teacher Tip

"If you can help it, you should not look at the answer choices without a prediction that you can match to the correct one. You do not want to get caught up in the wiles of the wrong answers. The answer choices are not your friends."
—Kurt Keefner
Bethesda, Maryland and Washington, DC

### Kaplan Tip

Your prephrasing of an answer need not be elaborate or terribly specific. Your goal is just to get an idea of what you're looking for, so the correct answer will jump out at you.

At this point, if you're stuck for time, you simply choose (C) and move on. If you have more time, you may as well quickly check the remaining choices, to find (we hope) that none of them fits the bill.

Of course, once you grasp the structure of the argument and have located the author's central assumption, you should be able to answer any question they throw at you. This one takes the form of an assumption question. But it could have just as easily been phrased as a weaken-the-argument-question.

# Analytical Practice Set

**Directions:** Each question or group of questions is based on a passage or a set of conditions. You may wish to draw a diagram to answer some of the questions. Choose the *best* answer for each question and fill in the corresponding space on your answer sheet. (Answers and explanations can be found at the end of the set of questions.)

**Questions 1–5:** The creative director of an ad agency wants to select four employees to work on different aspects of a new campaign. The seven employees available are Alan, Beatrice, Cindy, Dalen, Enid, Felicity, and Godfrey.

Alan and Beatrice will not work together.
Enid and Beatrice will not work together.
Felicity will not work on the new campaign unless Dalen does, and vice versa.

## Question 1

Which of the following is an acceptable group of four employees?

- (A) Alan, Cindy, Enid, Dalen
- (B) Beatrice, Dalen, Cindy, Godfrey
- (C) Beatrice, Dalen, Enid, Felicity
- (D) Beatrice, Dalen, Alan, Felicity
- (E) Beatrice, Dalen, Felicity, Godfrey

## Question 2

If Beatrice is selected, which of the following must also be selected?

- (A) Godfrey
- (B) Dalen
- (C) Enid
- (D) Cindy
- (E) Alan

## Question 3

Which of the following must be true?

- (A) If Alan is not selected, Felicity must be selected.
- (B) If Godfrey is not selected, Cindy must be selected.
- (C) If Beatrice is not selected, Cindy must be selected.
- (D) If Enid is selected, Cindy must not be selected.
- (E) If Enid is not selected, Beatrice is not selected.

## Question 4

If Cindy and Enid are to be selected as two of the employees, which of the following pairs could be the other two employees?

- (A) Alan and Dalen
- (B) Felicity and Alan
- (C) Alan and Beatrice
- (D) Alan and Godfrey
- (E) Felicity and Godfrey

## Question 5

If Dalen is not chosen, all of the following must be chosen EXCEPT

- (A) Enid
- (B) Cindy
- (C) Alan
- (D) Beatrice
- (E) Godfrey

## Question 6

A recent study has concluded that, contrary to the claims of those trying to ban cigarette advertisements altogether, cigarette ads placed on billboards and in magazines have little to no effect on the smoking habits of the smokers who view the ads. The study, which surveyed more than 20,000 smokers and solicited their reasons for continuing to smoke, found that practically no one in the survey felt that these advertisements influenced their decision to smoke.

The study's conclusion is based upon which of the following assumptions?

   (A) People do not switch cigarette brands based on their exposure to cigarette ads on billboards and in magazines.

   (B) Cigarette ads on billboards and in magazines do not encourage nonsmokers to take up the habit.

   (C) Banning cigarette ads altogether will encourage people to give up smoking.

   (D) People are consciously aware of all the reasons they choose to smoke.

   (E) People who decide to smoke do so for rational reasons.

## Question 7

**The kitchen manager's proposal to prohibit overtime pay for dishwashers is short-sighted.** The new plan calls for scheduling an extra dishwasher at regular pay to work busy shifts, thereby enabling the work to get done without accruing the extra cost. However, business at the restaurant is notoriously unpredictable and the need for overtime does not conform to any set pattern. **The cost of scheduling enough dishwashers to negate the possible need for overtime pay is likely to exceed the cost the overtime pay.**

Which of the following best expresses the relationship between the two bolded statements?

   (A) The first statement provides support for an argument; the second statement is the position the author seeks to establish.

   (B) The second statement provides evidence for a conclusion drawn in the first statement.

   (C) The first statement describes a premise with which the author agrees and the second statement offers conflicting evidence.

   (D) The first statement describes a condition which, if true, undermines the second statement.

   (E) The second statement must be true for the first statement to be true.

## Question 8

Over the past several years, Running River Water Park has experienced a serious decline in attendance and sales despite the addition of several state-of-the-art water slides. This year, the Board of Directors lowered the park's weekday admission prices in order to attract more customers. Attendance during the first two months of this year's season has been thirty percent higher than the attendance during the same two months last year. Clearly, the price cut has had the desired effect.

Each of the following, if true, weakens the conclusion above EXCEPT:

- (A) Nationwide, the number of people attending amusement parks has increased by thirty percent this year over last year.
- (B) Grand Excursions Amusement Park, located 10 miles from Running River, has been closed during most of this year's season due to unexpected equipment problems.
- (C) The most popular movie released this summer, "The Big Chase," features a long action sequence that was filmed at Running River.
- (D) Several large businesses relocated near Running River during the past year bringing with them many employees and their families.
- (E) Most amusement park visitors are aware of the admission prices before they arrive at an amusement park.

**Questions 9–12:** Individual members from eight animal species are to be chosen for a special exhibit habitat. The eight species are P, Q, R, S, T, U, V, and W. Because of the way these animals interact, certain guidelines must be followed.

Animals that will fight cannot be placed in the habitat together.

Members of species V will fight with members of species S, T, and U.

A member of species R will fight with a member of species Q, but only if a member of species V is present.

If a member of species W is present, a member of species P will not fight with any animal.

If a member of species W is not present, a member of species P will fight with members of species Q and R.

No fights other than those described above will occur.

## Question 9

If V is chosen for the habitat, which of the following CANNOT also be chosen?

- (A) P
- (B) Q
- (C) T
- (D) R
- (E) W

## Question 10

If two other animals are to be added to a habitat containing a member of species Q and a member of species V in the habitat, which of the following could be those two animals?

&#9398;   members of species W and P
&#9399;   members of species R and P
&#9400;   members of species S and W
&#9401;   members of species W and R
&#9402;   members of species U and R

## Question 11

If two habitats are set up, one containing members of species P, Q, W, and V, and the other containing members of species S, U, R, and T, which animals could be switched one for the other without provoking any fights?

&#9398;   species W and U
&#9399;   species Q and R
&#9400;   species P and R
&#9401;   species V and S
&#9402;   species W and T

## Question 12

If S, P, and R are chosen for the habitat, which of the following must also be chosen?

&#9398;   W
&#9399;   V
&#9400;   U
&#9401;   T
&#9402;   Q

## Question 13

Those who believe that the stars are influential in shaping our personalities fail to see that astrologers, alleged experts on the heavens, often present widely disparate interpretations of the same individual's astrological chart. If astrology were indeed a science, individuals would be able to present the same information—their birth date, place, and time—to many astrologers and receive the same evaluation and description of their personalities from each one. Since this is never the case, astrology cannot be considered a true science.

A believer in astrology can most effectively counter the author's objection by contending that

&#9398;   most astrologers are not expert enough to recognize the one correct interpretation of a chart.
&#9399;   the definition of astrology implies that it is a true science.
&#9400;   even if astrologers' interpretations aren't exactly the same, they usually contain similarities.
&#9401;   believers in astrology actually like the element of variability inherent in astrological interpretations.
&#9402;   some people do not know exactly what time they were born, and therefore present inaccurate and misleading information to the astrologist.

# Question 14

Plant Y thrives in environments of great sunlight and very little moisture. Desert X is an environment with constant, powerful sunlight, and next-to-no moisture. Although Plant Y thrives in the areas surrounding Desert X, it does not exist naturally in the desert, nor does it survive long when introduced there.

Which of the following would be most useful in explaining the apparent discrepancy above?

(A) Desert X's climate is far too harsh for the animals that normally feed on Plant Y.

(B) For one week in the fall, Desert X gets consistent rainfall.

(C) The environment around Desert X is ideally suited to the needs of Plant Y.

(D) Due to the lack of sufficient moisture, Desert X can support almost no plant life.

(E) Plant Y cannot survive in temperatures as high as those normally found in Desert X.

# Question 15

Although air pollution was previously thought to exist almost exclusively in our nation's cities, the recent increase in the number of persons suffering from illnesses attributed to excessive air pollution leaves us no choice but to conclude that other, nonurban areas are now affected.

Which of the following, if true, would most seriously weaken the conclusion of the argument above?

(A) The nation's cities have seen a marked decrease in their levels of air pollution.

(B) The nation has experienced a sharp decrease in the number of people moving out of its cities.

(C) Illnesses due to air pollution are among the least common causes of death to urban dwellers.

(D) Many illnesses previously thought unrelated to air pollution are now considered to be caused by it.

(E) As a result of the problems in urban areas, non-urban areas have passed strict pollution control measures.

**Questions 16–21:** An assistant principal must assign seven classes—K, L, M, N, O, P, and Q—to the seven classrooms lining the north corridor of her high school. The rooms are numbered 1 through 7, from west to east. There is a broom closet between Rooms 4 and 5. Only Rooms 1 and 7 have taping facilities.

L and M may not be in adjacent rooms.

N and O must be in adjacent rooms.

L must be in Room 3.

Language classes must be in a room with taping facilities.

## Question 16

If M and N are both language classes, and if O and L are in adjacent rooms, it must be true that M is in

(A) Room 1
(B) Room 7
(C) a room adjacent to Q's room
(D) a room adjacent to O's room
(E) a room adjacent to K's room

## Question 17

If K and O are both language classes, and if M is not in a room adjacent to the broom closet, all of the following must be true EXCEPT:

(A) O is in room 1.
(B) N is in room 2.
(C) M is in room 6.
(D) P and L are in adjacent rooms.
(E) Q is in a room adjacent to the broom closet.

## Question 18

If O is a language class, and if K and Q are in the two rooms adjacent to the broom closet, in which room could M be?

(A) Room 1
(B) Room 2
(C) Room 3
(D) Room 4
(E) Room 5

## Question 19

If K and M are in the two rooms adjacent to the broom closet, and if O is in Room 2, which of the following must be true?

(A) N is in Room 7.
(B) P and M are in adjacent rooms.
(C) Q and P are in adjacent rooms.
(D) N and K are in adjacent rooms.
(E) P is in a room with taping facilities.

## Question 20

If O is a language class, and if N and L are not in adjacent rooms, all of the following are possible EXCEPT:

(A) M is in Room 1.
(B) M and N are in adjacent rooms.
(C) M and O are in adjacent rooms.
(D) M and K are in adjacent rooms.
(E) M is in a room adjacent to the broom closet.

## Question 21

If O and P are language classes, and M is in a room adjacent to N, which of the following could be true?

- Ⓐ P is in Room 7.
- Ⓑ N is in Room 5.
- Ⓒ K is in Room 5.
- Ⓓ Q is in Room 2.
- Ⓔ O is in Room 1.

**Questions 22–25:** Four teams of tennis players, A, B, C, and D, have to be redistributed into three new teams. The players on team A are L, M, and N. The players on team B are O, P, Q, and R. The players on team C are S and T. And the players on team D are U, V, and W.

Each of the three new teams must contain at least one member from three of the original four teams (teams A, B, C, and D).
No new team can contain all the members of any of the original teams (teams A, B, C, and D).
V and W cannot be on the same new team.

## Question 22

If one new team is made up of L, N, O, and V only, which of the following groups CANNOT completely represent one of the other new teams?

- Ⓐ M, P, T
- Ⓑ P, S, U, W
- Ⓒ M, R, W
- Ⓓ Q, R, M, S
- Ⓔ R, T, W

## Question 23

If one new team is made up of N, O, P, Q, and U only, which of the following groups CANNOT completely represent one of the other new teams?

- Ⓐ R, T, W
- Ⓑ L, M, T
- Ⓒ M, S, V
- Ⓓ M, R, T, W
- Ⓔ L, R, S, W

## Question 24

What is the maximum number of people who can be on the same new team?

- Ⓐ five
- Ⓑ six
- Ⓒ seven
- Ⓓ eight
- Ⓔ nine

## Question 25

If one group is made up of L, O, and U only, which of the following could be the complete roster of another new team?

- Ⓐ M, N, S, P
- Ⓑ M, N, P, Q
- Ⓒ S, V, W, R
- Ⓓ T, S, V, M
- Ⓔ T, W, M, R

## Question 26

**Consultant:** Every election, the City Council candidate who is endorsed by the Moose Lodge wins the election. My client is a member of the Moose Lodge. I predict that after this year's election, my client will be the newest member of the City Council.

Which of the following must be true for the consultant's prediction to logically follow from the evidence presented?

Ⓐ No other candidate has sought the Moose Lodge endorsement.

Ⓑ The consultant's client is the most popular candidate in the race.

Ⓒ The consultant has guided numerous candidates to electoral success.

Ⓓ Any member of the Moose Lodge who runs for office gets the Moose Lodge endorsement.

Ⓔ Many powerful members of the community belong to the Moose Lodge.

## Question 27

A study found that last year roughly 6,000 homeless people in the United States were admitted to hospitals due to malnutrition. In the same year, a little more than 10,000 non-homeless people were admitted to hospitals for the same reason. These findings clearly show that the non-homeless are more likely to suffer from malnutrition than are the homeless.

The answer to which of the following questions would be most likely to point out the illogical nature of the conclusion drawn above?

Ⓐ What is the relative level of severity of the malnutrition suffered by each group cited in the study?

Ⓑ To what extent, on average, are the non-homeless better off financially than are the homeless?

Ⓒ What percentage of each group cited in the study suffered from malnutrition last year?

Ⓓ To what extent are the causes of malnutrition in the non-homeless related to ignorance of proper dietary habits?

Ⓔ What effect would a large increase in the number of homeless shelters have on the incidence of malnutrition among the homeless?

## Question 28

University systems that use graduation rates to determine which campuses are allotted additional funds are acting counter to their stated goals. The universities say they are trying to raise academic standards, yet they are actually encouraging campuses to graduate students regardless of achievement.

Which of the following statements, if true, would help to validate the approach taken by the university systems mentioned above?

- Ⓐ Graduation rates for university systems with this policy are among the highest in the nation, but the graduates from these systems score poorly on tests of basic skills.
- Ⓑ The campuses that need the additional funds the most are the ones that have the lowest graduation rates.
- Ⓒ The new funds will be allotted for facility upgrades, not new faculty positions or staff pay increases.
- Ⓓ Graduation examinations currently exist that require every graduate at each university to demonstrate a minimum level of achievement.
- Ⓔ An opposing plan focuses on providing extra funding based not on graduation rates, but on the percent of students that pass basic skills tests.

## Question 29

The average cost of transatlantic airfare has nearly doubled over the past five years, yet airlines today are flying at near capacity and are earning nice profits. Since inflation overall has been very low for the past five years, this suggests that people today have relatively more money to spend on vacations than they did five years ago.

The author's argument would NOT be weakened if it were true that

- Ⓐ most people buying transatlantic tickets today use them for business trips and thus do not pay for the tickets themselves.
- Ⓑ due to bankruptcies in the last five years, there are fewer airlines in existence today than five years ago.
- Ⓒ people are taking shorter vacations and staying in cheaper hotels than they did five years ago.
- Ⓓ the only area of passenger growth for airlines has been in transpacific flights.
- Ⓔ domestic airline flights have seen a steady increase in passengers in the past five years.

**Questions 30–35:** Exactly four pieces of pottery stand in line in a window display, numbered 1 through 4 from left to right. Two pieces are glazed and the other two are unglazed. There are two serving bowls, one teacup, and one jug. Exactly one of the pieces has a decorated base. The pieces are arranged according to the following conditions:

The piece of pottery that has a decorated base is either piece 1 or piece 4.
Piece 2 is a serving bowl.
At least one glazed piece stands in line between the two unglazed pieces.
One of the serving bowls has a decorated base.

## Question 30

Which one of the following must be true of piece 3?

Ⓐ It is unglazed piece.
Ⓑ It is a glazed piece.
Ⓒ It is a teacup.
Ⓓ It does not have a decorated base.
Ⓔ It has a decorated base.

## Question 31

If piece 4 is a glazed and has a decorated base, then all of the following must be true EXCEPT:

Ⓐ Piece 1 is an unglazed piece.
Ⓑ Piece 2 is a glazed piece.
Ⓒ Piece 3 is the jug.
Ⓓ Piece 4 is a serving bowl.
Ⓔ Exactly one piece stands in line between the two serving bowls.

## Question 32

If the two glazed pieces stand in line immediately adjacent to each other, then which one of the following must be false?

Ⓐ An unglazed piece of pottery has a decorated base.
Ⓑ The jug has an unglazed piece.
Ⓒ Piece 3 is a glazed piece.
Ⓓ Both serving bowls are glazed.
Ⓔ The teacup is unglazed.

## Question 33

If the serving bowls stand immediately adjacent to each other, and if piece 2 is glazed, then which one of the following correctly describes piece 1?

Ⓐ It is an unglazed serving bowl and has a decorated base.
Ⓑ It is a glazed serving bowl and has a decorated base.
Ⓒ It is an unglazed jug and does not have a decorated base.
Ⓓ It is a glazed jug and does not have a decorated base.
Ⓔ It is a glazed teacup and does not have a decorated base.

## Question 34

If piece 1 is unglazed, then all of the following could be true EXCEPT:

- (A) Piece 1 is a teacup.
- (B) Piece 4 is a jug
- (C) The serving bowls are both glazed.
- (D) The jug and the teacup are both glazed
- (E) The teacup is immediately adjacent to the jug.

## Question 35

If piece 3 is an unglazed teacup, then all of the following must be true EXCEPT:

- (A) If piece 1 is the jug, then piece 4 has a decorated base.
- (B) If the piece that has a decorated base is unglazed, then the jug is glazed.
- (C) If piece 1 has a decorated base, then only one serving bowl is glazed.
- (D) If the jug is unglazed, then both serving bowls are glazed.
- (E) If piece 2 is glazed, then piece 4 has a decorated base.

## Answer Key

| | | | | |
|---|---|---|---|---|
| 1. E | 8. E | 15. D | 22. C | 29. E |
| 2. B | 9. C | 16. B | 23. B | 30. D |
| 3. A | 10. A | 17. D | 24. B | 31. C |
| 4. D | 11. B | 18. A | 25. E | 32. D |
| 5. D | 12. A | 19. C | 26. D | 33. A |
| 6. D | 13. A | 20. C | 27. C | 34. D |
| 7. B | 14. E | 21. D | 28. D | 35. E |

## Explanations

**Questions 1–5:** In this game we're to select groups of exactly four employees from a field of seven, now known as A, B, C, D, E, F, and G. The rules are only three in number, and amount to the facts that one cannot include both A and B, nor can once include both E and B. Furthermore, if either F or D is included in the group, then so is the other, and if either F or D isn't included, then neither is the other.

### Question 1

For Question 1 we can just eliminate the four incorrect groups. Rule 1 says A and B can't both be selected. That eliminates choice (D). Rule 2 says that E and B can't both be selected. That eliminates choice (C). And rule 3 says that F and D must both be in or both be out; that eliminates choices (A) and (B), leaving the only correct choice, (E).

### Question 2

Question 2 asks who must be selected if B is selected. It can't be A; the first rule prohibits that. And it can't be E; the second rule prohibits that. So choices (C) and (E) are out. That leaves, C, D, F, and G, from which we must pull three others. If we were to leave out the F and D pair, we'd have only three employees selected. Clearly, then, F and D must both be

selected. D is listed as choice (B), which is correct. G and C, choices (A) and (D) could go, either one or the other, but neither must go.

### Question 3

We're asked to find something that must be true. The best approach is to deny the answer choices, and see what happens. The one that can't be denied must be true. (A) turns out to be correct here. If A is not selected F must be selected. To not select F would require also not selecting D. With A, D, and F out, we'd have only four employees left. That would require that they all be selected. E and B, however, would be two of those employees, and the second rule says that they can't both go. (B) need not be true because we could have a group of A, E, D, and F. (C) need not be true because E, D, F, and G make an acceptable group. (D) can be eliminated with E, C, D, and F. And (E) can be denied with B, C, D, and F.

### Question 4

Question 4 says that C and E are selected, and asks which of the answer choices lists an acceptable pair to be selected with them. Well, with E chosen, we know B can't be chosen. So choice (C) is immediately out. Furthermore, any pair that lists either D or F must also include the other one. That eliminates (A), (B), and (E). Thus choice (D) is correct. And indeed, there were only two possible pairs to go with C and E: A and G, as (D) says, or D and F, which wasn't listed.

### Question 5

Question 5 says D is not selected, and asks which of the listed answer choices need not be chosen. If D isn't chosen, then F isn't, either. That leaves five employees (A, B, C, E, and G) from which we can get four. Now suppose B were one of those selected. That would mean neither A nor E could be selected, leaving only three employees, which isn't allowed. So B cannot be selected and A, C, E, and G must be selected. That means that choice (D) is correct for question 5.

## Question 6

(D) identifies the key assumption here. If people aren't consciously aware of all of the reasons they choose to smoke, then the fact that those surveyed don't feel that the advertisements influence their decision to smoke does not in fact prove that these ads don't affect their smoking habits.

Now let's look at the other choices: (A) is outside the scope of the argument. The argument concerns smokers' decision to smoke, not which brands they choose once they've decided to smoke. (B) is also outside the scope of the argument. We're concerned with the smoking habits of smokers who view the ads. How nonsmokers react to the ads is of no concern to us. (C) contradicts the argument, which is the opposite of what we're looking for. An assumption should support conclusion. (E) goes way too far. There's nothing in the argument that implies that people who decide to smoke do so for "rational" reasons.

## Question 7

The question stem tells you that you'll need to identify the functions performed by each of the bolded statements. This kind of question essentially tests your ability to identify evidence and conclusion. So which is which? The first bolded statement claims that the plan is no good. The second bolded statement explains why. So the first statement is the conclusion, and the second statement is evidence for that conclusion. (B) has it right.

## Question 8

The only answer that doesn't do any damage to the argument is (E), which strengthens the argument by pointing out that consumers are aware of pricing. The other choices suggest other potential reasons for the increase in attendance, so they weaken the claim that the price cut is responsible. Any time you can find an alternative that the author has neglected, you've found a potential weakener.

**Questions 9–12:** This is a rather odd grouping game of selection, a type that has, however, appeared on the GRE. The key to this game is realizing that "Members of species V will fight with members of species S, T, and U" is another way of saying: "V and S cannot be included in the same habitat, V and T cannot be included in the same habitat . . ." and so forth—because the first rule of the game tells you that fighting species cannot share a habitat. Although there's no "right" way of shorthanding all this, we've chosen an old familiar method for "cannot be together" rules:

$V \neq S$    $V \neq T$    $V \neq U$
$RV \neq Q$
$P \neq Q$    $P \neq R$
$PW = P$ no fighting

## Question 9

Question 9 is a gift to you, as long as you understand that each rule's references to fighting are a backhand way of saying, "This species cannot share the habitat with that species." A quick check of the rules gives you the answer: V cannot share a habitat with S, T, or U, and one of those three—T—is correct choice (C). The remaining choices are all possible roommates for V; their inclusion or exclusion in this habitat depends on their interactions with other species.

## Question 10

Question 10 is a standard grouping-game question—two members of the group have been chosen for you, and your job is to choose two more acceptable members. You're given species V and Q. The first step is to check your rules to eliminate known quarrelsome species. With V in, S, T, and U are definitely out, leaving you with P, R, and W. (You can eliminate answer choices (C) and (E) at this point.) Now you must find an acceptable pair from the remaining three contenders. Can P and R be chosen? No, because the pairing of R and V will cause fighting with Q, and that eliminates choice (B). Can R and W be chosen? No, for the same reason, and now you've eliminated choice (D). That leaves (A), which must be correct—and it is, since W's presence prevents P from fighting with Q and makes a happy habitat.

## Question 11

Question 11 is the odd duck in this game. You're asked about switching between two habitats without causing fighting. The correct choice is (B). Switching species Q and R creates no problems, since V is still separated from the species it fights with and the P-W pair keeps P under control. (A) doesn't work because without the calming influence of W, P is going to fight with Q. (C) unwisely puts both R and V in the habitat with Q—guaranteeing that R and Q will fight. (D) places V in a group with two of its archenemies, T and U, so fighting is certain to result, and (E) creates chaos—V is grouped with U and S, and without W's calming presence, P will certainly fight with Q.

## Question 12

Another must-be situation appears in Question 12. This time the question stem supplies three species and asks you for a fourth, so go to the rules for guidance. You begin with species S, P, and R—wait a minute! P and R should not be in a habitat together, since the fifth rule specifically stated that P fights with R. But there's another rule about P. The fourth rule says that P will not fight if W is present—and there's your must be. W, correct choice (A), must be included in this habitat to make the given group of S, P, and R acceptable.

## Question 13

The argument in Question 13 is an attack on astrology. The author says that since different astrologers, using the same data, arrive at different evaluations of a person, astrology cannot be considered a hard science. This is because if astrology were a hard science (the author implies), identical data would lead to identical interpretations, and therefore someone's astrological chart would have only one scientific interpretation.

We're asked to weaken the argument. Choice (A) does so by pointing out that not every astrologer is an expert. It could be that expert astrologers do agree on the one correct interpretation, and only the inexpert ones differ. (B) is no good because, quite simply, the definition of astrology may be completely wrong. A cardinal rule of thinking says don't confuse the name of a thing with the thing itself. You can call a rose a fish, but it's still not a fish. (C) is too weak, in that being "similar" isn't enough. If a science must provide a single answer, then multiple similar answers still don't cut it. (D) claims that the variability is appealing. So what? Astrology may be appealing even though it's not a science, so (D) is out. And finally, (E) says that inaccurate information is used in constructing the charts. Yet if all the astrologers are given the same inaccurate information then they should still give the same interpretation. The author said astrology wasn't a science because the interpretations differ, not because the data are inaccurate.

## Question 14

Question 14 is a type of question that appears increasingly on the GRE. We have to explain an apparent discrepancy; the key is to find the explanation that is consonant with all of the stimulus information. We're told enough to expect that Plant Y would thrive in Desert X. Yet it doesn't. Why doesn't it? For this we go to what we're told. X is a desert, which means it's dry and sunny. Y likes dry and sunny regions—but we're told nothing about its temperature preferences. So the best explanation is, as choice (E) says, that it's the high temperatures in Desert X that Y can't handle. If the information in (E) were true, you would actually expect Y not to grow in Desert X. (A) won't work because a plant usually doesn't need animals to feed on it in order to survive. One would expect quite the opposite. (B)'s out because one week of consistent rainfall hardly explains why Y isn't in Desert X at other times. The fact that it can easily grow elsewhere isn't relevant to the question of why it doesn't grow in Desert X, so (C) is out. And the ability of other plants to survive in Desert X by itself has nothing to do with Plant Y, so (D) also fails.

*Question 15*

In Question 15 the author gives you an in-your-face signal of what the conclusion is when she says, "leaves us no choice but to conclude that. . . ." Her conclusion then is that nonurban areas are now affected by air pollution. She makes this conclusion based on evidence that there has recently been an increase in the number of persons suffering from illnesses attributable to air pollution. Now we hope you see that this argument has a few holes in it. We're asked to weaken it, and since there are several holes, there are many ways to weaken it. So our best bet may be to go through the answer choices and see what effect they each have.

(A) says that air pollution in the cities is decreasing. Well, that certainly won't weaken an argument that air pollution is rising elsewhere, especially when the number of people suffering from it is on the increase. (B) says that fewer people are moving out of the cities. Well, that won't have an effect. The argument draws a link between those suffering from air pollution–related illnesses and the movement of air pollution out to nonurban areas. The fact that fewer people are leaving the cities doesn't make a difference one way or the other. (C) says that air pollution doesn't kill very many city dwellers. Happy thought, but it would seem that

the new sufferers from air pollution (not necessarily death victims) that the author speaks of would-be noncity dwellers. So the fact that not many urban dwellers die from air pollution has no effect, or a very weakly strengthening effect.

As for (D), ah ha! Here we go. (D) is going to weaken the argument by providing another explanation for the increase in air pollution sufferers. The number of sufferers from air pollution–related illnesses has risen, not because pollution is spreading out to nonurban areas, but because a lot more illnesses are now considered to be caused by air pollution. If that's true, then nothing at all need have changed. It could be the same pollution in the same place, with the same victims, only now, more of them have been identified. So (D) is our answer. (E) is incorrect. Whether or not antipollution measures have been passed is irrelevant. There could still be plenty of pollution in nonurban areas. For example, they could have passed the measures only yesterday.

**Questions 16–21:** The scenario and rules to this sequencing game don't start you off with much in the way of concrete information, and they leave one big mystery: Which are the language classes? A quick overview of the question stems clears this up. The classes designated as "language" change from question to question, so there's no point in worrying about them unduly during your work with the stimulus. As for the rest of it, this is about as concrete as we can get:

$$— \quad — \quad L \quad — \quad / \quad — \quad — \quad —$$

tape                                    tape

L ≠ M

N = O

Note that half the challenge of this game is keeping track of special conditions (broom closet, taping rooms) as well as characters. Most of the characters are still in the realm of "could be true" at this point, so let's go on to the questions.

## Question 16

Since Room 1 and 7 are taping rooms, the first if-clause in the stem of Question 16 means that either M is first and N seventh or vice versa. However, you should see that "vice versa" is in fact what it must be: N seventh would require that O be sixth, yet doing so does not allow O to be adjacent to L, which the question stem specifies. The only possible combination is

$$\boxed{N} \quad O \quad L \quad — \quad / \quad — \quad — \quad \boxed{M}$$

—and notice that these are the only placements that must be true, thus making (B) the correct answer. Notice that (C) and (E) are only possible, while (A) and (D) are impossible.

## Question 17

Question 17 starts off in much the same way as Question 16: the stem tells us that K and O are either first and seventh or seventh and first, respectively. Wherever O is, N must be next to it, so we can set up two options:

$$\boxed{K} \quad — \quad L \quad — \quad / \quad — \quad N \quad \boxed{O}$$
$$\boxed{O} \quad N \quad L \quad — \quad / \quad — \quad — \quad \boxed{K}$$

But the first option must be discarded: if M is prohibited from being next to the broom closet, M can't be fifth; and M can't be second or fourth, either, since L ≠ M. Option 2 is the only prospect, and in it M must be sixth for the reasons we just discussed. P and Q, then, will occupy the positions next to the broom closet, though we don't know in which order. The answer choice that need not be true is (D): P could very well be in Room 5, far from L in Room 3.

## Question 18

The stem of Question 18 doesn't exactly start you off with truly concrete information, but that doesn't

matter; to get this one, you need not know precisely where each class is as long as you know which rooms are in use and which are not. The quickest approach to this question is to first note that the answers do not include Rooms 6 and 7; you're to worry about the first five rooms only. Second, you can eliminate answer choices before dealing with the information in the question stem. L always occupies Room 3, so choice (C) is out; since L ≠ M, M cannot be in Rooms 2 or 4, and choices (B) and (D) are out. This leaves only Rooms 1 and 5 as possibilities; what does the question stem tell you about them? It tells you that Room 5 is definitely occupied, by either K or Q—Room 5 is to the left of the broom closet, so either K or Q will be there. This leaves only one alternative, choice (A).

## Question 19

The stem of Question 19 coyly hints that K and M can be interchangeable between the fourth and fifth spots, but we know better: M can't be fourth, because it would be right next to L in Room 3, which is forbidden. So M is fifth and K fourth. O is second, which means N must be first (again, O = N), leaving only the last two spots to be filled by P and Q in either order. The only answer choice, then, that must be true is (C). Note that (B) and (E) could be true, while (A) and (D) cannot be true.

## Question 20

If, as in Question 20, O is a language course but N is not adjacent to L, we should see that O must be seventh: since O = N, O first would mean N second and that would violate the question stem. So we're left with:

$$\boxed{\phantom{} } \quad — \quad L \quad — \quad / \quad — \quad N \quad \boxed{O}$$

—and a lot of possible locations for the other four classes, though the five answer choices are mainly concerned with where M can possibly go. In point of fact, M can't be next to O, since N is there, so (C) is the correct answer.

*Question 21*

Answering Question 21 is a matter of putting the two pieces of information in the question stem together. O and P will be first and seventh, or vice versa, so we know that N will be either second (if O is 1st) or sixth (if O is seventh). And M will be adjacent to N, so M will be either third (if N is second) or fifth (if N is sixth). But putting O first, N second, and M third won't work, since 3 is permanently occupied by L. So this is the only option:

$$\boxed{P} - L - / M \ N \ \boxed{O}$$

That's what must be true; this question asks for what could be true. The only options left open are for K and Q; they could be either second and fourth or vice versa. Look among the choices for mentions of K and Q: choice (C) mentions K but places K in Room 5, which is already occupied by M. Choice (D), however, states that Q could be in Room 2, which is what we just deduced, and so is the correct answer.

**Questions 22–25:** The last game is a grouping game of distribution. Four teams are being broken up to form three new ones. The first two rules are the type it's best to just remember, or circle and refer to. One of them says that each of the new teams must contain a member from three of the old teams. That tells us each of the three new teams will contain at least three players. The other says that all the members of one of the old teams can't be on the same new team. So, in the case of team C, players S and T cannot be on the same new team. As if that weren't enough to juggle, we're also told in the last rule V and W can't be on the same team.

*Question 22*

Question 22 asks which answer choice can't be one of the new teams, when another of the new teams is L, N, O,

and V. Now the key here and throughout the game is to realize that there must always be three new teams, each of which must conform to the rules. So here it's not merely a matter of checking the listed teams for discrepancies; you must also check the third, unmentioned team, which is composed of the remaining players.

Well, we know the first team is L, N, O, and V. That means M, P, Q, R, S, T, U, and W are left to be distributed into the other two teams. Choice (A) would have M, P, and T on one of the other teams. That would leave Q, R, S, U, and W for the third new team. We have to check both because if the remaining players cannot be from the third team, then the second listed new team is illegitimate. In looking, we see that S and T are split; V and W are split; and the other requirements are met. (B) lists P, S, U, and W. That means the third team would be composed of M, Q, R, T. Again, no problem with this distribution. (C), however, cannot be the new distribution. If M, R, and W are on the second new team, then S and T would be among the members of the third team. That's a no-no because S and T are all the members of one of the original teams, and rule 2 prohibits this kind of distribution.

*Question 23*

Question 23 is exactly the same type of question that we just saw. We use the same procedure and find that the new teams listed in choices (A), (C), (D), and (E) are all acceptable, as the remaining players also form an acceptable team. Choice (B), on the other hand, is unacceptable. With N, O, P, Q, and U on one of the teams, and L, M, and T on another, we would have S, R, V, and W on the third. Since V and W cannot be on the same team, this arrangement is unacceptable.

*Question 24*

Question 24 asks for the maximum number of players that can be put on one of the new teams. The thing to see here is that we don't just want to divvy them up in any old order, so that at the end we have rules telling us where we can and can't put the last players. (If you did this, you may have wound up with incorrect choice (A).) We want to satisfy the rules with as few distributions as possible, so that we're free to throw the remaining players all on on team.

Let's start with V and W, and S and T. We know these pairs must be split. We don't want to put S and T on the same two teams as V and W. That would be maximizing the number of two teams and minimizing the number on one team. We want just the opposite. So, let's say we've got S on Team 1, T and V on Team 2, and W on Team 3. That takes care of original team C, and leaves only U from team D. Since V and W are already split, U will go anywhere we like. We need to get one member from three of the original teams on each of the new teams. Team A has three members—L, M, and N—and we can just put one on each of the new teams: L and S on Team 1, M, T, and V on Team 2, and N and W on Team 3. Original Team A is now exhausted. That leaves all of Team B, and U from Team D. If we look at our new teams, Team 2 has three members from three different original teams. Teams 1 and 3, however, have only two members from two different original teams. Let's fill them out: Put O on Team 1 and P on Team 3. We've now satisfied all the rules, and can place Q, R, and U anywhere we like. Since we're to maximize the players on one team, we'll add all three players to one of the three teams. That'll mean, regardless of which team we add them to, six players maximum—choice (B). If you had trouble with this one, you could eliminate choices by noting that Rule 1 alone requires at least three players per new team, and that in itself makes seven-, eight-, or nine-player teams impossible.

## Question 25

Question 25 tells us that L, O, and U comprise one new team, and then asks which answer choice could comprise another complete team. That leaves M, N, P, Q, R, S, T, V, and W to distribute into the other teams. We know S and T will have to be on separate teams, and that means that any acceptable team must have either S or T listed, and not both. This criterion tells us that (B) and (D) are out. If (B) were a second new team, S and T would both be on Team 3, breaking Rule 2. And (D) blatantly puts them on the same team. The same applies to V and W. Each acceptable second team must have V or W, but not both. That eliminates (A) and (C). (C) puts them on the same team, which isn't allowed, and (A) omits both from the second team, thus forcing them together on the third. That leaves correct answer (E), which is acceptable, and which puts N, P, Q, S, and V on the third team, which is also acceptable.

## Question 26

The question stem tells you that are looking for something that must be true to connect the consultant's evidence to the consultant's prediction. In other words, you are looking for an assumption—the necessary bridge between the evidence and conclusion. *Conclusion*: The consultant's client will be elected to the City Council. *Evidence*: The consultant's client is a member of the Moose Lodge and the candidate endorsed by the Moose Lodge always wins.

The author still needs to make a connection between the candidate's Moose Lodge membership and her prediction about her client's electoral success. (D) provides this link. If the Moose Lodge members who run always get the Moose Lodge endorsement and the candidate who gets the Moose Lodge endorsement always wins the election, it logically follows that the consultant's client—a Moose Lodge member—will be elected.

As to the other choices: (A) Whether the consultant's client was in competition for the endorsement is irrelevant. The argument addresses what follows after a candidate obtains the endorsement. (B) may seem logical but is beyond the scope of the argument. According to the argument, the Moose Lodge endorsement determines who wins the election. You do not know what effect general popularity has. (C) is irrelevant. The consultant's past success—or lack thereof—does not link the candidate's Moose Lodge membership with electoral success. Apply the denial test here. Even if the consultant was brand new, the client could still win. (E) may seem logical, but only provides one possible explanation for the importance of the endorsement. You do not need to know why the endorsement guarantees victory, only that it does.

## Question 27

The question stem reveals that the argument in the stimulus is fatally flawed. As you read the passage, identify the evidence and conclusion, and watch for a questionable assumption or some other flaw along the way. The argument is based on numbers: Since only 6,000 homeless people suffering from malnutrition were admitted to U.S. hospitals last year, compared to 10,000 non-homeless people, the non-homeless must be more likely to suffer from malnutrition. But total numbers mean nothing! We cannot figure the odds of suffering from malnutrition solely from the number of malnourished people in each group. We need to know the percentage of homeless people suffering from malnutrition versus the percentage of non-homeless people suffering from malnutrition. Clearly there are far more non-homeless people than homeless people in the U.S., so the argument contains a ludicrous assumption—that the two groups are comparably sized. The correct answer to this question will somehow point this out, thus making the flaw in the reasoning (using raw numbers as the basis for a conclusion about likelihood) plain to see.

(C) provides the question whose answer would provide the information we need to correctly understand the odds. Since the U.S. has far fewer homeless people than it has people with homes, the 6,000 figure would form a far higher percentage of homeless people who suffer from malnutrition than the percentage of non-homeless people based on the 10,000 cases of malnutrition among this group. (C) allows us to see how the

raw numbers cited do not support the author's counter-intuitive conclusion that the non-homeless are more susceptible to malnutrition than are the homeless.

## Question 28

The question stem asks you to help "validate" the position of the university systems, which means you are going to try to strengthen it. The argument is actually attacking the position of the university systems, so by finding a strengthener for it, you will be weakening the author's argument. The position you want to support is that the Universities' use of graduation rates for funding is not acting counter to their stated goal of raising academic standards.

This may be hard to prephrase. If nothing occurs to you as you read the passage and think about it for a moment, then just move right on to the choices. (A) supports the author's argument, not the universities' position. (B) is unclear, since it is not stated what makes a campus "need" funds the most, nor is it claimed that simply by increasing graduation rates will students' levels of educational achievement improve. (C) doesn't help, since we aren't told the relative effect from where the money is distributed, although taking money from the teachers and putting it into buildings doesn't sound like a promising way of raising educational achievement levels. (D) is what we've been waiting for: not only are the universities paying money based on graduation rates, but these same universities are only graduating students who can pass comprehensive exams. The ability of the schools to bring students to high enough levels of achievement to graduate is being rewarded.

## Question 29

This is sort of a "reverse" weaken question. You have to find the one choice that doesn't weaken the argument, which means it either strengthens it or leaves it alone. There will probably be more than one unstated assumption that is attacked in the answer choices. The evidence is that airlines are doing fine while charging high fares to cross the Atlantic. The conclusion is that the passengers have got more money to spend on their vacations. The evidence only mentions "transatlantic" airfare increasing in price, not transpacific or domestic airfare, while the other bit of evidence concerns the industry as a whole operating at capacity and earning decent profits.

(A) weakens the argument by saying that most people don't pay for tickets themselves, nor are tickets for vacations. This breaks the connection between what people pay and vacation money by denying that the evidence applies to either. As to (B), Airlines today can do a booming business even if the business as a whole is down (i.e. if fewer people are buying tickets, suggesting LESS vacation money), just so long as there are fewer airlines around. (C) says people are skimping elsewhere, which shows that even if they are paying a lot for their airfare, they need not have more vacation money. (D) says that flights across the Pacific are the only flights that have increased in number, which attacks the assumption that people are flying more on transatlantic routes despite high costs. (E), however, won't weaken the argument because it doesn't tell us whether the increase in domestic volume is accompanied by higher, lower, or the same fares. It's correct because it doesn't sever the connection between booming business and vacation money—it just shows more booming business, this time on domestic flights. Since this doesn't imply fewer vacation dollars, it doesn't weaken the argument.

**Questions 30–35:** This hybrid game involves the skills of grouping and sequencing. In addition to their order, we have to keep track of three things about four different pieces of pottery—what the pieces represent, whether they're glazed or unglazed, and whether or not they have a decorated base. There are 2 S's, 1 T, and 1 J; there are also 2 G's and 2 U's; and there is 1 d. You'll have to keep track of a lot of information in the diagram, and in general the

best way to do it for hybrid games is to draw dashes for the order of the entities, and then within each slot use symbols to take care of the grouping elements, as is shown below.

As usual, enter as many of the rules as you can directly into the diagram. Rule 1 can by symbolized by writing "d?" above slots 1 and 4. Rule 2 is nice and concrete; place "S" in slot 2. Rule 3 can be made more concrete by noting that there are only four slots, so to separate the U's by at least one G, there are only three options "U G U G" or "G U G U" or "U G G U." These can be written below the slots of your master diagram. Finally, putting rule 4 into the diagram means that we combine it with rule 1: that one d piece of pottery is also an S, so you can write "Sd" above piece 1 and piece 4, and now we know something about both serving bowls.

In this game, it made sense to engage in steps 3 and 4 pretty much simultaneously. One final deduction you could make is that piece of pottery piece 3 must be either T or J. Your setup may look something like this:

| Sd? | S | — | Sd? | groups |
|-----|---|---|-----|--------|
| U | G | U | G | SSTJ |
| U | G | G | U | GGUU |
| G | U | G | U | D |

*Question 30*

If the decorated piece is piece 1 or 4, then it cannot be piece 3, so (D) is correct. As for the other choices, piece 3 could be G or U, and it could be T or J.

*Question 31*

If piece 4 has a decorated base, then it must be a serving bowl (Rule 4). Since piece 4 is also glazed, in this question at least, then the only way to satisfy Rule 3 is if the other glazed is piece 2, surrounded by unglazed pieces in spaces 1 and 3. The only thing left unresolved is whether the teacup is first and the jug third, or the other way around. The question is looking for something that *need not be true*, and since the teacup/jug issue is the only unresolved point, it's a good bet that the answer will concern one of them. And indeed it does. (C) states that piece 3 must be a jug, but we know better—it could also be a teacup.

## Question 32

There's only one way for the glazed pieces of pottery to stand next to each other and still obey rule 3, and that's if they are pieces 2 and 3, leaving the U's as pieces 1 and 4. (A) and (C) must be true—the decorated piece, whether it's at 1 or 4, must be unglazed and piece 3 is glazed. The statement that must be false is (D). Piece 2 must be a glazed serving bowl, but the other serving bowl is at either 1 or 4, and in this both of these positions are unglazed. Since we found the right answer, we don't have to check (B) or (E) to confirm that they could be true.

## Question 33

This time the serving bowls are standing next to each other, and since one of them is piece 2, obviously the other one must be piece 1. Furthermore, if piece 2 is glazed, as stated in the stem, then piece 1 must be unglazed (Rule 3). The first piece of pottery in line must therefore be an unglazed serving bowl with decorated base, choice (A).

## Question 34

Don't let the phrasing of the question fool you; you're looking for the one answer choice that *must* be false. If piece 1 is glazed, it follows from Rule 3 that the order is either UGGU or UGUG. Aside from that the only thing you know for sure is that piece 2 is a serving bowl; consequently it must be a glazed serving bowl. Everything else is up for grabs, but (D) must be false; if at least one of the two serving bowls is glazed, then the jug and the teacup cannot both be glazed.

## Question 35

This one looks to be a horror show, but it's manageable if you use your pencil and your head, in either order. If piece 3 is UT, then the other U must be piece 1 in order to satisfy rule 3. That means piece 2 and piece 4 are G. Make your diagram, and then note what is left over: the Sd and the J.

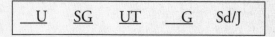

| U | SG | UT | G | Sd/J |
| --- | --- | --- | --- | --- |

Unfortunately, each answer choice begins with an "if-then" clause, so we have to check each one until we find the answer.

(A): If piece 1 is J, then the only place for Sd is piece 4, so this statement is true and we can cross it out.

(B): If Sd is U, then it must be piece 1, which means J is piece 4 and that makes it G, so this statement must be true.

(C): If Sd is piece 1, then indeed it's true that only one S is glazed, since piece 1 is U and piece 2 is G.

(D): If J is U, then it's piece 1, which means Sd is piece 4. That makes S in piece 2 G and S in piece 4 G as the choice says.

(E): If piece 2 is G—well, we already knew that, so let's just see if the "then" clause must be true. Must piece 4 be Sd? We've already seen that Sd could be piece 1. (E) is correct because it could be false.

# CHAPTER FIVE

# Test Mechanics

## HIGHLIGHTS

- Understand how the GRE CAT works and how it affects YOU
- Learn how to easily navigate through the test on your computer
- Study Kaplan's exclusive CAT-specific test-taking strategies

The first year of graduate school is a frenzied experience for many students. It's no surprise, then, that the GRE, the test specifically designed to predict success in the first year of graduate school, is a speed-intensive test that demands good time-management skills.

So when you're comfortable with the content of the test, namely, the type of material discussed in the previous chapters, your next challenge will be to take it to the next level—test mechanics—which will enable you to manage an entire section at a time.

On most of the tests you take in school, you wouldn't dream of not making at least a try at every single one of the questions. If a question seems particularly difficult, you spend significantly more time on it, because you'll probably be given more points for answering a hard question correctly. Not so on the GRE.

You've got to develop a way of handling the test sections to make sure you get as many points as you can as quickly and easily as you can. The following principles will help you do just that.

## Teacher Tip

"One worry many students have is the fact that you can't skip questions on the CAT. I tell them the difference between a good score and a great score is recognizing the tougher questions, using Kaplan's methods for making an educated guess, and moving on to questions where they can focus their strengths. A great score is nothing but a good score topped with smart guesses."
—Jason Anderson
Chicago, Illinois

## Mechanics of the GRE CAT

The CAT is in some ways quite different from the traditional paper-and-pencil tests you've probably taken in the past. In fact, it's pretty weird at first. Here's how it works. You will only see one question at a time. Instead of having a predetermined mixture of basic, medium, and hard questions, the computer will select questions for you based on how well you are doing. The first question will be of medium difficulty. If you get it right, the second question will be a little harder; if you get the first question wrong, the second will be a little more basic.

If you keep getting questions right, the test will get harder and harder; if you slip and make some mistakes, the test will adjust and start giving you easier problems, but if you answer them correctly, it will go back to the hard ones. Ideally, the test gives you enough questions to ensure that scores are not based on luck. If you get one hard question right you might just have been lucky, but if you get 10 hard questions right, then luck has little to do with it. So the test is self-adjusting and self-correcting.

Because of this format, the CAT is very different structurally from a paper-and-pencil test. After the first problem, every problem that you see is based on how you answered the prior problem. That means you cannot return to a question once you've answered it, because that would throw off the sequence. Once you answer a question, it's part of your score, for better or worse. That means you can't skip around within a section and do questions in the order that you like.

Another major consequence is that hard problems count more than easy ones. It has to be this way, because the very purpose of this adaptive format is to find out at what level you reliably get about *half* the questions right; that's your scoring level. It actually makes a lot of sense. Imagine two students—one who does 10 basic questions, half of which she gets right and half of which she gets wrong, and one who does 10 very difficult questions, half of which she gets right and half of which she gets wrong. The same number of questions have been answered correctly in each case, but this does not reflect an equal ability on the part of the two students.

In fact, the student who answered five out of ten very difficult questions incorrectly could still get a very high score on the CAT GRE. But in order to get to these hard questions, she first had to get medium-difficulty questions right. So, no matter how much more comfortable you might be sticking to the basic questions, you definitely want to get to the hard questions if you can, because that's where the points are.

## First Impressions Count

One of the most important things to know is that the early questions are vital for a good score on the CAT. As in life, first impressions make a big difference.

Why? Because the computer doesn't have information about you at the start of the test, and its goal is to get an accurate estimate of your score as quickly as possible. In order to do that, the computer has to make large jumps in the estimation of your score for each of the first few questions.

It's a lot like how you would act if you were trying to guess which number a person had picked from one to 10, and the only thing you could be told was whether the number was higher, lower, or the same as what you guessed. To do this most efficiently, you'd guess five first, since if the right number were higher or lower you could eliminate about half the choices. If you were told the actual number was lower than five, you'd guess three next, since that cuts the possibilities down the most. If the number were higher than three, it would have to be four. If it were lower, it would have to be one or two. Using this method, at most you would have to take three guesses before you knew the answer, whereas if you just started guessing randomly, or started from one and worked your way up, you could guess as many as 10 times before getting the right answer.

Like the efficient guesser, the computer doesn't use intuition to find the right answer, but uses the most effective method. Instead of using numbers to "guess" your score, though, the computer gives you questions that have a precise difficulty level assigned to them. In effect, you tell it whether your score is higher or lower than this difficulty level by getting the question right or wrong.

What's the upshot of all this? Simple: *Pay extra attention to the first few questions, and do all that you can to get them right!* Feel free to spend a little extra time double-checking the first five problems or so, and make sure you try every elimination technique you know before guessing on one of these problems if you don't know the answer.

## Three More Section Management Techniques

First, if you get a lot of mileage from the strategy of eliminating answer choices based on difficulty level, you can apply it on the CAT, though in a different and limited way. It won't be spelled out for you as it would be on a paper-and-pencil test, but as you progress through the questions, you should have a good idea of how you're doing. If you've practiced a lot on real questions, it's fairly easy to maintain a pretty clear sense of the difficulty level of your questions and to eliminate answer choices accordingly. For instance, if you're confident that you've been answering most of the questions correctly, then you should be seeing harder and harder questions. If that seems to be the case, you can safely eliminate answer choices that look too obvious or basic for a difficult question.

### Kaplan Tip

It's difficult for some of us to give up on a tough, time-consuming question, but it must be done occasionally. Remember, there's no point of honor at stake here, but there are GRE points at stake.

### Kaplan Tip

Use your one-minute break between sections to replenish your supply of scratch paper, if necessary.

### Kaplan Tip

Use the computer tutorial to your advantage. Spend as much time as you need to make yourself comfortable with the computer *before* you begin the actual test. Once the test is under way, clicking on "Help" to review the directions or a summary of the tutorial will count against your allotted time for that section of the test.

Secondly, if crossing off answer choices on paper tests really helps to clarify your thinking (using a process of elimination), you may want to consider making a grid on your scratch paper before you begin the CAT. Use it to mark off answer choices that you have eliminated, as shown below. That way you can tell at a glance which answer choices are still in the running. If you end up using it often, it will be worth the 10 seconds it takes to draw a simple grid, like this one:

| A | ✕ | ✕ |   | ✕ |   | ✕ |   |   | ✕ |   | ✕ |   |   |
|---|---|---|---|---|---|---|---|---|---|---|---|---|---|
| B |   | ✕ | ✕ | ✕ |   |   | ✕ | ✕ | ✕ | ✕ |   | ✕ |   |
| C |   |   |   |   | ✕ |   |   |   | ✕ |   |   |   | ✕ |
| D | ✕ |   | ✕ |   | ✕ |   |   | ✕ |   | ✕ |   | ✕ |   |
| E | ✕ | ✕ |   | ✕ |   |   | ✕ |   |   | ✕ |   |   |   |

Finally, the timer in the corner can work to your advantage, but if you find yourself looking at it so frequently that it becomes a distraction, you should turn it off for 10 or 15 minutes and try to refocus your attention on the test, even if you lose track of time somewhat. *The CAT rewards focus and accuracy more than it does raw speed.*

## Navigating the CAT: Computer Basics

Let's preview the primary computer functions that you will use to move around on the CAT. ETS calls them "testing tools," but they're basically just boxes that you can click with your mouse. The following screen is typical for an adaptive test.

Here's what the various buttons do.

*The Time Button*
Clicking on this button turns the time display at the top of the screen on and off. When you have five minutes left in a section, the clock flashes and the display changes from Hours/Minutes to Hours/Minutes/Seconds.

**KAPLAN**

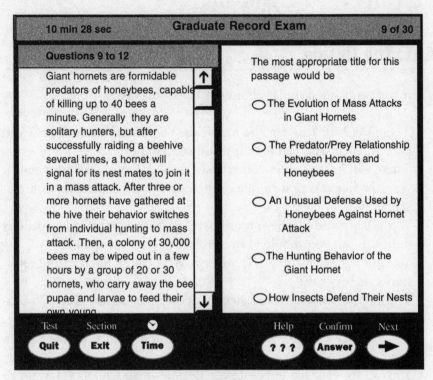

*Typical screen display in the CAT.*

## The Exit Button

This allows you to exit the section before the time is up. If you budget your time wisely you should never have to use this button—time will run out just as you are finishing the section.

## The Help Button

This one leads to directions and other stuff from the tutorial. But beware: The test clock won't pause just because you click on Help.

## The Quit Button

Hitting this button ends the test prematurely. *Do not* use this button unless you want all of your scores canceled and your test invalidated.

## The Next Button

Hit this when you want to move on to the next question. After you press Next, you must hit Confirm.

## The Confirm Button

This button tells the computer you are happy with your answer and are really ready to move to the next question. You cannot proceed until you have hit this button.

## The Scroll Bar

Similar to that on a windows-style computer display, this is a thin, vertical column with up and down arrows at the top and bottom. Clicking on the arrows moves you up or down the page you're reading.

---

### Teacher Tip

"Because you can't skip questions and come back to them, it is essential that you make good judgments about how much time to invest in any one question."
—Tiffany Sanders
Downers Grove, Illinois

---

## CAT: The Upside

There are many good things about the CAT, such as:

- There is a little timer at the top of the computer screen to help you pace yourself (you can hide it if it distracts you).
- There will be only a few other test takers in the room with you—it won't be like taking it in one of those massive lecture halls with distractions everywhere.
- You get a pause of one-minute between each section. The pause is optional, but you should always use it to relax and stretch.
- You can sign up for the CAT just two days before the test, and registration is very easy.
- The CAT is convenient to schedule. It's offered at more than 175 centers three to five days a week (depending on the center) all year long.
- You don't have to take it on the same day as a subject test, which can greatly reduce fatigue.
- You can see your scores before you decide which schools you want to send them to.
- Perhaps the CAT's best feature is that it gives you your scores immediately and will send them to schools just 10 to 15 days later.

## CAT: The Downside

There are also not-so-good things about the CAT.

- You cannot skip around on this test; you must answer the questions one at a time in the order the computer gives them to you.
- If you realize later that you answered a question incorrectly, you can't go back and change your answer.
- You can't cross off an answer choice and never look at it again, so you have to be more disciplined about not reconsidering choices you've already eliminated.
- You have to scroll through reading comprehension passages, graphs, and some games, which means you won't be able to see the whole thing on the screen at once.
- You can't write on your computer screen the way you can on a paper test (though some have tried), so you have to use scratch paper they give you, which will be inconveniently located away from the computer screen.
- Lastly, many people find that computer screens tire them and cause eyestrain—especially after three hours.

> ### Teacher Tip
>
> "When taking a computer adaptive test, you have to overcome your reluctance to guess. Most people don't like to guess, but if you don't guess strategically as you go along, you'll end up having to guess randomly at the end."
> —Kurt Keefner
> Bethesda, Maryland and Washington, DC

# Kaplan CAT Strategies

Using certain CAT-specific strategies can have a direct, positive impact on your score:

❏ At the beginning of the section, each question you get right or wrong will rapidly move the computer's estimate of your score up or down. A key strategy for doing well on the CAT is to get the computer's estimate of your score up to where you are handling the hard questions, because getting a hard question right will help your score a lot, but getting a hard question wrong will hurt your score only slightly. Thus it pays to spend more time on those early questions, double-checking each answer before you confirm it. Getting to the hard questions as quickly as possible can only help your final score.

❏ As you progress through the middle part of the section, try to avoid getting several questions in a row wrong, as this will sink your score on the CAT. If you know that the previous question you answered was a blind guess, spend a little extra time trying to get the next question right.

❏ The CAT will switch from one question type to another within a section (going from Reading Comp to Antonyms, for example) WITHOUT automatically showing the directions for each new question type. Knowing the format and directions of each GRE question type beforehand will save you a lot of time and avoid possible confusion during the exam.

❏ The CAT does not begin with really easy questions that gradually get harder, as do many paper-based tests. Because the order of difficulty will not be predictable, always be on the lookout for answer-choice traps.

❏ Because each right or wrong answer directly affects the next question you get, the CAT does not allow you to go back to questions you've already answered to double-check your work. So be as certain as possible that you have answered a question correctly before moving on.

❏ The CAT does not allow you to skip questions. So if you are given a question you cannot answer, you'll have to guess. Guess intelligently and strategically—eliminating any wrong answer choices that you can spot and guessing among those remaining.

❑ Don't get rattled if you keep seeing really, really difficult questions. It just means you're doing very well on that section. Keep it up!

❑ At the end of the section, you are penalized more heavily for not getting to a question at all than for answering it wrong. So if you only have a minute or two left and several questions remaining, you should guess at random rather than leave anything unanswered. And if you're down to the very last question and have almost no time left, make sure to click on a response first and then attempt to answer the question. You can always change your answer, and you're allowed to confirm whatever answer you've clicked after the time has run out.

**KAPLAN**

# CHAPTER SIX

# Test Mentality

- Learn Kaplan's Four Basic Principles of Good Test Mentality
- Find out how to handle stress leading up to and during the exam
- Know when and how you should cancel your scores

In this test prep section, we first looked at the content that makes up each specific section of the GRE, focusing on the strategies and techniques that you'll need to tackle individual questions, games, and passages. Then we discussed the mechanics involved in taking a computer-adaptive test. Now we're ready to turn our attention to the often overlooked attitudinal aspects of the test. We'll then combine these factors with what we learned in the chapters on test content and test mechanics to put the finishing touches on your comprehensive GRE approach.

## The Four Basic Principles of Good Test Mentality

We've already armed you with the weapons that you need to do well on the GRE. But you must wield those weapons with the right frame of mind and in the right spirit. This involves taking a certain stance toward the entire test. Here's what's involved.

**Kaplan Tip**

The basic principles of good test mentality:

- Test awareness
- Stamina
- Confidence
- The right attitude

## Kaplan Tip

Remember that the GRE isn't like most tests you've taken. You can get a lot of questions wrong and still get a great score. So don't get rattled if you miss a few questions.

## Kaplan Tip

Losing a few extra points here and there won't do serious damage to your score but losing your head will. Keeping your composure is an important test-taking skill.

## Test Awareness

To do your best on the GRE, you must always keep in mind that the test is like no other test you've taken before, both in terms of its content and in terms of its scoring system. If you took a test in high school or college and got a quarter of the questions wrong, you'd probably receive a pretty lousy grade. Not so with the GRE CAT. The test is geared so that only the very best test takers are able to finish every section with time to spare. But even these people rarely get every question right.

What does this mean for you? Well, just as you shouldn't let one tough reading comp passage ruin an entire section, you shouldn't let what you consider to be a subpar performance on one section ruin your performance on the entire test. A lousy performance on one single section will not by itself spoil your score—unless you literally miss almost every question. If you allow that subpar section to rattle you, however, it can have a cumulative negative effect that sets in motion a downward spiral. It's that kind of thing that could potentially do serious damage to your score. Losing a few extra points won't do you in, but losing your head will.

Remember, if you feel that you've done poorly on a section, don't sweat it. It could be the experimental one. And even if it's not, you must remain calm and collected. Simply do your best on each section, and once a section is over, forget about it and move on.

## Stamina

You must work on your test taking stamina. Overall, the GRE is a fairly grueling experience, and some test takers simply run out of gas on the final few sections. To avoid this, you must prepare by taking as many full-length practice tests as possible in the week or two before the test, so that on the test, five sections will seem like a breeze (well, maybe not a breeze, but at least not a hurricane).

One option is to buy *Practicing to Take the GRE General Test,* which is a book of released tests from ETS. There are six real GREs in this book, and they can be great practice for all the strategies that you're learning in this book. Since that book was published, ETS has revised the Analytical and Quantitative sections, adding more logical reasoning questions and questions on probability, median, mode, and range in Quantitative.

Another option, if you have some time and need a really great score, would be to take the full Kaplan course. We'll give you access to every released test plus loads of additional material, so you can really build up your GRE stamina. But most importantly, you'll also have the benefit of our expert live instruction. In fact, you could even set up special one-on-one tutoring sessions with Kaplan experts. If you decide to go this route, call (800) KAP-TEST for a Kaplan center location near you.

## Confidence

Confidence feeds on itself, and unfortunately, so does the opposite of confidence—self-doubt. Confidence in your ability leads to quick, sure answers and an ease of concentration that translates into more points. If you lack concentration, you end up reading sentences and answer choices two, three, or four times. This leads to timing difficulties, which only continue the downward spiral, causing anxiety and a tendency to rush.

If you subscribe to the GRE mindset that we've described, however, you'll be ready and able to take control of the test. Learn our techniques and then practice them on real test material, such as that found in *Practicing to Take the GRE*. That's the way to score your best on the test.

## Attitude

Those who approach the GRE as an obstacle and who rail against the necessity of taking it usually don't fare as well as those who see the GRE as an opportunity to show off the reading and reasoning skills that graduate schools are looking for. Those who look forward to doing battle with the GRE—or, at least, who enjoy the opportunity to distinguish themselves from the rest of the applicant pack—tend to score better than do those who resent or dread it.

It may sound a little dubious, but take our word for it: attitude adjustment is proven to raise points. Here are a few steps you can take to make sure you develop the right GRE attitude:

- Look at the GRE as a challenge, but try not to obsess over it; you certainly don't want to psyche yourself out of the game.
- Remember that, yes, the GRE is obviously important, but, contrary to what some people think, this one test will not single-handedly determine the outcome of your life. In many cases, it's not even the most important piece of your graduate application.
- Try to have fun with the test. Learning how to match your wits against the test makers can be a very satisfying experience, and the reading and thinking skills you'll acquire will benefit you in graduate school as well as in your future career.
- Remember that you're more prepared than most people. You've trained with Kaplan. You have the tools you need, plus the know-how to use those tools.

### Teacher Tip

"Everybody wants to know the easiest way to a higher score. I say, 'Practice. Practice. Practice problems.'"
—Suzanne Riskin
Miami, Florida

### Kaplan Tip

Your attitude towards the test does affect your performance. You don't have to "think nice thoughts" about the GRE, but you should take a good mental stance toward the test.

# The Kaplan Advantage™ Stress Management System

Is it starting to feel as if your whole life is a buildup to the GRE? You've known about it for years, worried about it for months, and now spent at least a few weeks in solid preparation for it. As the test gets closer, you may find that your anxiety is on the rise. You shouldn't worry. Armed with the preparation strategies that you've learned from this book, you're in good shape for the day of the test.

To calm any pretest jitters that you may have, however, let's go over a few strategies for the couple of days before and after the test.

## Quick Tips for the Days Just Before the Exam

- The best test takers do less and less as the test approaches. Taper off your study schedule and take it easy on yourself. Give yourself time off, especially the evening before the exam. By that time, if you've studied well, everything you need to know is firmly stored in your memory bank.
- Positive self-talk can be extremely liberating and invigorating, especially as the test looms closer. Tell yourself things such as "I will do well," rather than "I hope things go well"; "I can," rather than "I cannot." Replace any negative thoughts with affirming statements that boost your self-esteem.
- Get your act together sooner rather than later. Have everything (including choice of clothing) laid out in advance. Most important, make sure you know where the test will be held and the easiest, quickest way to get there. You'll have great peace of mind by knowing that all the little details—gas in the car, directions, etcetera—are set before the day of the test.
- Go to the test site a few days in advance, particularly if you are especially anxious. Better yet, bring some practice material and do at least a section or two.
- Forego any practice on the day before the test. It's in your best interest to marshal your physical and psychological resources for 24 hours or so. Even race horses are kept in the paddock and treated like princes the day before a race. Keep the upcoming test out of your consciousness; go to a movie, take a pleasant hike, or just relax. Don't eat junk food or tons of sugar. And, of course, get plenty of rest the night before—just don't go to bed too early. It's hard to fall asleep earlier than you're used to, and you don't want to lie there worrying about the test.

### Kaplan Tip

Don't try to cram a lot of studying into the last day before the test. It probably won't do you much good, and it could bring on a case of test burnout.

### Kaplan Tip

Don't study on your bed, especially if you have problems with insomnia. Your mind may start to associate the bed with work, and will make it even harder for you to fall asleep.

## Handling Stress During the Test

The biggest stress monster will be the test itself. Fear not; there are methods of quelling your stress during the test.

- Keep moving forward instead of getting bogged down in a difficult question. You don't have to get everything right to achieve a fine score. So, don't linger out of desperation on a question that is going nowhere even after you've spent considerable time on it.

- Don't be thrown if other test takers seem to be working more busily and furiously than you are. Don't mistake the other people's sheer activity as signs of progress and higher scores.

- Keep breathing! Weak test takers tend to share one major trait: They don't breathe properly as the test proceeds. They might hold their breath without realizing it, or breathe erratically or arrhythmically. Improper breathing hurts confidence and accuracy. Just as important, it interferes with clear thinking.

- Some quick isometrics during the test—especially if concentration is wandering or energy is waning—can help. Try this: Put your palms together and press intensely for a few seconds. Concentrate on the tension you feel through your palms, wrists, forearms, and up into your biceps and shoulders. Then, quickly release the pressure. Feel the difference as you let go. Focus on the warm relaxation that floods through the muscles. Now you're ready to return to the task.

- Here's another isometric that will relieve tension in both your neck and eye muscles: Slowly rotate your head from side to side, turning your head and eyes to look as far back over each shoulder as you can. Feel the muscles stretch on one side of your neck as they contract on the other. Repeat five times in each direction.

# Test Day!

Let's now discuss what you can expect on the day of the test itself. The day should start with a moderate, high energy breakfast. Cereal, fruit, bagels, or eggs are good. Avoid donuts, danishes, or anything else with a lot of sugar in it. Also, unless you are utterly catatonic without it, it's a good idea to stay away from coffee. Yeah, yeah, you drink two cups every morning and don't even notice it. But it's different during the test. Coffee won't make you alert (your adrenaline will do that much more effectively); it will just give you the jitters. Kaplan has done experiments in which test takers go into one exam having drunk various amounts of coffee and another exam without having drunk coffee. The results indicate that even

## Teacher Tip

"Take care of yourself. Sounds simple, no? Sleep well, eat well, be nice to others, and drive safely before you take the test. Sick and injured people don't do well on exams!"
—Tanya Kormeili
Los Angeles, California

## Kaplan Tip

On the night before the test, get together a "GRE survival kit" containing the following items:

- Photo ID card
- Your admission ticket
- A watch
- Bottle of water (but don't drink too much)
- Aspirin or other painkiller, in case you get a headache
- A snack (You must eat a high-energy snack during the break or you'll run out of gas during later parts of the test. Fruit or energy bars are good snacks. Candy bars aren't.)
- Names of schools where you'd like to send your scores

the most caffeine-addicted test takers will lose their focus midway through the second section if they've had coffee, but they report no alertness problems without it.

When you get to the test center, you will be seated at a computer station. Some administrative questions will be asked before the test begins, and once you're done with those . . . it's showtime. While you're taking the test, a small clock will count down the time you have left in each section. The computer will tell you when you're done with each section, and when you're completed the test itself.

Finally, here are some last-minute reminders to help guide your work on the test:

- Give all five answer choices a fair shot in Verbal (especially reading comp) and in logical reasoning, time permitting. For Quantitative and logic games, go with the objectively correct answer as soon as you find it and blow off the rest.
- Don't bother trying to figure out which section is unscored. It can't help you, and you might very well be wrong. Instead, just determine to do your best on every section.
- Pay no attention to people who are chattering on their break. Just concentrate on how well prepared you are.
- Dress in layers for maximum comfort. This way, you can adjust to the room's temperature accordingly.
- Take a few minutes now to look back over your preparation and give yourself credit for how far you've come. Confidence is key. Accentuate the positives and don't dwell on the negatives! Your attitude and outlook are crucial to your performance on the test.
- During the exam, try not to think about how you're scoring. It's like a baseball player who's thinking about the crowd's cheers, the sportswriters, and his contract as he steps up to the plate. It's a great way to strike out. Instead, focus on the question-by-question task of picking the correct answer choice. After all, the correct answer is there. You don't have to come up with it; it's sitting right there in front of you! Concentrate on each question, each passage, each game—on the mechanics, in other words—and you'll be much more likely to hit a home run.

## Cancellation and Multiple Scores Policy

Unlike many things in life, the GRE allows you a second chance. If, at the end of the test, you feel that you've definitely not done as well as you can, you have the option to cancel your score. The trick is, you must decide whether you want to keep your scores before the computer shows them to you. If you cancel, your scores will be disregarded. (You also won't get to see them.) Canceling a test means that it won't be scored. It will just appear on your score report as a canceled test. No one will know how well or poorly you really did—not even you.

Two legitimate reasons to cancel your test are illness and personal circumstances that cause you to perform unusually poorly on that particular day. Also, if you feel that you didn't prepare sufficiently, then it may be acceptable to cancel your score and approach your test preparation a little more seriously the next time.

But keep in mind that test takers historically underestimate their performance, especially immediately following the test. This underestimation is especially true on the CAT, which is designed to give you questions at the limits of your abilities. They tend to forget about all of the things that went right and focus on everything that went wrong. So unless your performance is terribly marred by unforeseen circumstances, don't cancel your test.

If you do cancel, your future score reports will indicate that you've canceled a previous score. But since the canceled test was never scored, you don't have to worry about bad numbers showing up on any subsequent score report. If you take more than one test without canceling, then all the scores will show up on each score report, so the graduate schools will see them all. Most grad schools average GRE scores, although there are a few exceptions. Check with individual schools for their policies on multiple scores.

## Post-GRE Festivities

After all the hard work that you've put in preparing for and taking the GRE, make sure you take time to celebrate afterwards. Plan to get together with friends the evening after the test. Relax, have fun, let loose. After all, you've got a lot to celebrate. You prepared for the test ahead of time. You did your best. You're going to get a great score.

### Kaplan Tip

The key question to ask yourself when deciding whether to cancel is this: "Will I really do significantly better next time?"

### Teacher Tip

"Students become so involved in the exam that they forget they must produce a flawless, professional application document in addition to jumping through the other hoops. I help students to balance their focus, so that they can meet effectively both the challenge of the test and the rigors of the application process.
—Chris Skinner
Santa Barbara, California

# CHAPTER SEVEN

# The Subject Tests

## HIGHLIGHTS

- Learn about the various GRE Subject Tests and how they differ from the GRE General Test

**S**ubject Tests are designed to test the fundamental knowledge most important for successful graduate study in a particular subject area. In order to do well on a Subject Test, you basically need to have an extensive background in the particular subject area—the sort of background you would be expected to have if you majored in the subject. In this section, we'll answer the most common questions about Subject Tests.

## Do You Have to Take a Subject Test?

Not every graduate school or program requires Subject Tests, so check admissions requirements at those schools in which you're interested.

## What's the Purpose of Subject Tests?

Unlike the GRE General Test, which assesses skills that have been developed over a long period of time and are not related to a particular subject area, Subject Tests assess knowledge of a particular field of study. They enable admissions officers to compare students from different colleges with different standards and curricula.

**Note**

Online registration is available for Subject Tests (but not for the GRE General Test). Go to www.gre.org to fill out and submit your registration form electronically.

## What Are Subject Tests Like?

All Subject Tests are administered in paper-and-pencil format. Except for the Revised Music test, Subject Tests consist exclusively of multiple-choice questions that are designed to assess knowledge of the areas of the subject that are included in the typical undergraduate curriculum.

On Subject Tests, you'll earn one point for each multiple choice question that you answer correctly but lose one-quarter point for each incorrectly answered question. Unanswered questions aren't counted in the scoring. Your raw score is the number of correctly answered questions minus one-quarter of the incorrectly answered questions. This raw score is then converted into a scaled score, which can range from 200 to 900. The range varies from test to test.

Some Subject Tests also contain subtests, which provide more specific information about your strengths and weaknesses. The same questions that contribute to your subtest scores also contribute to your overall score. Subtest scores, which range from 20 to 99, are reported along with the overall score. For further information on scoring, you should consult the relevant Subject Test Descriptive Booklet, available from ETS.

### Note

On a Subject Test, you gain one point for each correct answer—but lose one-quarter point for each wrong answer.

## Are There Any Different Test-Taking Strategies for the Subject Tests?

Because the multiple-choice questions on Subject Tests have a wrong-answer penalty of one-quarter point, you should adopt a different test-taking strategy for your Subject Test than the one you're going to use for the GRE General Test. On the Subject Tests, you shouldn't attempt to fill in an answer for every question on the test, nor do you have to guess at every question you see if you want to get another question (like on the CAT). On Subject Tests, you should guess only if you can eliminate one or more of the answer choices.

## When Should You Take the Subject Test?

Subject Tests are offered three times a year: in November, December, and April. Note that not all of the Subject Tests are offered on every test date; consult the relevant Subject Test Descriptive Booklet, available from ETS, for upcoming test dates and registration deadlines.

# How Many Subject Tests Are There and What Fields Do They Cover?

At present, ETS is in the process of eliminating several of the GRE Subject Tests. As of April 2001, only eight Subject Tests will be offered. A list of them follows, along with a brief description of each.

## Biochemistry, Cell, and Molecular Biology

This test consists of 180 questions and is divided among three subscore areas: biochemistry, cell biology, and molecular biology and genetics.

## Biology

This test consists of about 200 questions divided among three subscore areas: cellular and molecular biology, organismal biology, and ecology and evolution.

## Chemistry

This test consists of about 136 questions. There are no subscores, and the questions cover the following topics: analytical chemistry, inorganic chemistry, organic chemistry, and physical chemistry.

## Computer Science

This test consists of approximately 70 questions. There are no subscores, and the questions cover the following topics: software systems and methodology, computer organization and architecture, theory, mathematical background, and other, more advanced topics, such as modeling, simulation, and artificial intelligence.

## Literature in English

This test consists of 230 questions on literature in the English language. There are two basic types of questions: factual questions that test the student's knowledge of writers typically covered in the undergraduate curriculum, and interpretive questions that test the student's ability to read various types of literature critically.

## Mathematics

This test consists of 66 questions on the content of various undergraduate courses in mathematics. Most of the test assesses the student's knowledge of calculus, abstract algebra, linear algebra, and real analysis. About a quarter of the test, however, requires knowledge in other areas of math.

## Note

"Testing aids" are not allowed to be used, including calculators, rulers, translators, highlighters, etcetera.

## Physics

This test consists of 100 questions covering mostly material covered in the first three years of undergraduate physics. Topics include classical mechanics, electromagnetism, atomic physics, optics and wave phenomena, quantum mechanics, thermodynamics and statistical mechanics, special relativity, and laboratory methods. About 9 percent of the test covers advanced topics, such as nuclear and particle physics, condensed matter physics, and astrophysics.

## Psychology

This test consists of 220 questions drawn from courses most commonly included in the undergraduate curriculum. Questions fall into three categories. The experimental or natural science-oriented category includes questions in learning, cognitive psychology, sensation and perception, ethology and comparative psychology, and physiological psychology. The social or social science-oriented category includes questions in abnormal psychology, developmental psychology, social psychology, and personality. Together, these make up about 85 percent of the test, and each of the two categories provides its own subscore. The other 15 percent or so of the questions fall under the "general" category, which includes the history of psychology, tests and measurements, research design and statistics, and applied psychology.

For more information, you should consult the relevant Subject Test Descriptive Booklet, available from ETS. You can also visit the Kaplan Website (kaptest.com) for a more detailed description of each subject test and some free sample questions.

# CHAPTER EIGHT

# The GRE Writing Assessment

- Learn the Basic Principles and the Kaplan Method for GRE writing

- Practice writing and evaluating Issue and Argument essays

- Familiarize yourself with the holistic scoring system

The ability to write clearly about complex subjects and make fine distinctions is an important part of graduate school. In October 1999, ETS introduced a standardized way for schools to evaluate a student's academic writing ability: a separate test called the **Analytical Writing Assessment** (AWA). Because the Writing Assessment has been so successful, ETS has decided to incorporate it into the GRE General Test. Starting on October 1, 2002, the Writing Assessment (retitled the **Analytical Writing Measure**) will become a mandatory part of the GRE General Test, replacing the multiple-choice Analytical section. You will still be able to take the Writing Assessment as a separate test until December 31, 2002; after that time, the separate test will be discontinued.

The new mandatory Analytical Writing Measure is identical to the stand-alone Writing Assessment: They contain the same tasks and are evaluated in the same way. So you can use this chapter to polish your skills for either GRE writing test.

## What to Expect

The writing tests consist of two timed essay sections. The first is what ETS calls an "Analysis of Issue" essay: You'll be shown two essay topics— each a sentence or paragraph that expresses an opinion on an issue of

### Kaplan Tip

If you take the GRE General Test on or after October 1, 2002, you'll be required to write two essays. Study the GRE writing strategies in this chapter to help maximize your writing score.

## Kaplan Tip

Effective GRE writing style is:
- Concise
- Forceful
- Correct

## Kaplan Tip

Write your essay in a clear, straightforward manner. Keep word choice, sentence structure, and your argument simple (but not simplistic).

general interest. You must choose one of the two topics. You then have 45 minutes to plan and write an essay that communicates your own view on the issue. Whether your agree or disagree with the opinion on the screen is irrelevant: What matters is that you support your view with relevant examples and statements.

The second of the two writing tasks is the "Analysis of Argument" essay. This time, you will be shown a paragraph that argues a certain point. You will then be given 30 minutes to assess that argument's logic. As with the "Issue" essay, it won't matter whether you agree with what you see on the screen. The test makers want you to critique the reasoning behind the argument, and not the argument itself.

### How the Essays Are Administered

The stand-alone Writing Assessment is a computer-based exam. At the start of the Writing Assessment, you will be given a brief tutorial on how to use the word processor. The program you'll use on the GRE is quite simple, as the only functions you'll use are: inserting text, deleting text, cut and paste, and undo. If you wish to handwrite your essays, you must register to take the Writing Assessment on a test date that allows you this option.

For the Analytical Writing Measure section of the new GRE General Test, the essay tasks will be delivered on the computer, but you can freely choose whether to word-process or handwrite your essays. (If you choose to handwrite your responses, score reporting may take up to six weeks.)

## The Four Basic Principles of GRE Writing

GRE writing is a simple, two-stage process: First you decide what you want to say about a topic, and then you figure out how to say it. If your writing style isn't clear, your ideas won't come across, no matter how brilliant they are. Good GRE English is not only grammatical but also clear and concise, and by using some basic principles, you'll be able to express your ideas clearly and effectively in both of your essays.

### 1. Your Control of Language Is Important

Writing that is grammatical, concise, direct, and persuasive displays the "superior control of language" (as the test makers term it) that earns top GRE scores. To achieve effective GRE style in your essays, you should pay attention to the following points.

*Grammar*

Your writing must follow the rules of standard written English. If you're not confident of your mastery of grammar, brush up before the test.

*Diction*

Diction means word choice. For example, do you use the words *affect* and *effect* correctly? Be careful with such commonly confused words as *precede/proceed, principal/principle, whose/who's,* and *stationary/stationery.*

*Syntax*

Syntax refers to sentence structure. Do you construct your sentences so that your ideas are clear and understandable? Do you vary your sentence structure, sometimes using simple sentences and other times using sentences with clauses and phrases?

## 2. It's Better to Keep Things Simple

Perhaps the single most important thing to bear in mind when writing GRE essays is to keep everything simple. This rule applies to word choice, sentence structure, and organization. If you obsess about how to spell an unusual word, you can lose your flow of thought. The more complicated your sentences are, the more likely it is that they will be plagued by errors. The more complex your organization gets, the more likely it is that your argument will get bogged down in convoluted sentences that obscure your point. But keep in mind that simple does not mean simplistic. A clear, straightforward approach can still be sophisticated and convey perceptive insights.

## 3. Minor Grammatical Flaws Won't Torpedo Your Score

Many test takers mistakenly believe that they'll lose points because of a few mechanical errors such as misplaced commas, misspellings, or other minor glitches. Occasional mistakes of this type will not dramatically affect your GRE essay score. In fact, the test makers' description of a top-scoring essay acknowledges that there may be minor grammatical flaws. The essay graders understand that you are writing first-draft essays. They will not be looking to take points off for minor errors, provided you don't make them consistently. However, if your essays are littered with misspellings and grammar mistakes, then the graders may conclude that you have a serious communication problem.

To write an effective essay, you must be concise, forceful, and correct. An effective essay wastes no words, makes its point in a clear, direct way, and conforms to the generally accepted rules of grammar and form.

## 4. Keep Sight of Your Goal

Remember, your goal isn't to become a prize-winning stylist. It's to write two solid essays that will convince admissions officers you can write well enough to clearly communicate your ideas to a reader—or academic colleague. GRE essay graders don't expect rhetorical flourishes, but they do expect effective expression.

## Kaplan Rules

The basic principles of GRE Writing:

1. Use language effectively.
2. Keep it simple.
3. Don't worry excessively about making minor errors.
4. Keep sight of your goal.

# The Kaplan Five-Step Method for GRE Writing

Here's the deal: You have a limited amount of time to show the graduate school admissions people that you can think logically and express yourself in clearly written English. They don't care how many syllables you can cram into a sentence or how fancy your phrases are. They care that you're making sense. Whatever you do, don't try to hide beneath a lot of hefty words and abstractions. Just make sure that everything you say is clearly written and relevant to the topic. Get in there, state your main points, back them up, and get out.

1.  **Digest the Issue/Argument**
    - Read it through to get a sense of the scope of the matter.
    - Note any terms that are ambiguous and need defining.
    - Frame the issue/argument.

2.  **Select the Points You Will Make**
    - In the "Analysis of Issue" essay, think of the arguments for both sides and make a decision as to which side you will support or the exact extent to which you agree with the stated position.
    - In the "Analysis of Argument" essay, identify all the important gaps between the evidence and the conclusion. Think of remedies for the problems you discover.

3.  **Organize**
    - Outline your essay.
    - Lead with your best arguments.
    - Think about how the essay as a whole will flow.

4.  **Write/Type**
    - Be direct.
    - Use paragraph breaks to make your essay easier to read.
    - Make transitions, link related ideas; it will help your writing flow.
    - Finish strongly.

5.  **Proofread**
    - Save enough time to read through the entire essay.
    - Have a sense of the errors you are liable to make.

As explained before, the two essay types you'll meet on the GRE, the Issue and the Argument, require generally similar tasks. You must analyze a subject, take an informed position, and explain that position in writing. The two essay types, however, require different specific tasks.

# The Issue Essay

The Issue essay requires you to construct your own argument by making claims and providing evidence to support your position on a given issue.

## The Question Stem

The screen directions will ask you to take a position on the issue and instruct you to explain your position convincingly, using reasons or examples to back up your assertions.

The directions for the Issue essay will be similar to this:

**Directions: You will have 45 minutes to plan and write an essay that communicates your perspective on a given topic. Choose one of the two topics provided. No other topics are admissible for this essay.**

**The topic is a short quotation that expresses an issue of general interest. Write an essay that agrees with, refutes, or qualifies the quotation, and support your opinion with relevant information drawn from your academic studies, reading, observation, or other experiences.**

**Feel free to consider the issue for a few minutes before you beginning your writing. Be certain that your ideas are fully developed and organized logically and make sure you have enough time left to review and revise what you've written.**

## The Stimulus

Expect a sentence or two that discuss a broad, general issue, sometimes presenting two competing points of view, sometimes only one. Either way, it will state an argument for which one or more counterarguments could be constructed. While the issue will be one upon which reasonable people could disagree, it will not bring up an emotionally charged religious or social issue. You won't be expected to have prior knowledge of any specific subject matter.

In short, the topic will present a point of view. Your job is to form an opinion on the topic and make a case for that opinion.

The topics you see in the Issue section might be similar to these:

*The invention of gunpowder was the single most destructive achievement in history.*

*The main purpose of public education should be to prepare students for specific jobs.*

*The drawbacks to the use of nuclear power mean that it is not a long-term solution to the problem of meeting ever-increasing energy needs.*

## Applying the Kaplan Five-Step Method to the Issue Essay

Let's use the Kaplan Five-Step method on one of the sample issue topics
we saw before:

*The drawbacks to the use of nuclear power mean that it is not a long-
term solution to the problem of meeting ever-increasing energy needs.*

### 1. Digest the Issue

It's simple enough. The person who wrote this believes that nuclear
power is not a suitable replacement for other forms of energy.

### 2. Select the Points You Will Make

Your job, as stated in the directions, is to decide whether or not you agree
and explain your decision. Some would argue that the use of nuclear
power is too dangerous, while others would say that we can't afford not
to use it. So which side do you take? Remember, this isn't about showing
the admissions people what your deep-seated beliefs about the environment are—it's about showing that you can formulate an argument and
write it down. Quickly think through the pros and cons of each side, and
choose the side for which you have the most relevant things to say. For
this topic, that process might go something like this:

*Arguments for the use of nuclear power:*

- *Inexpensive compared to other forms of energy*
- *Fossil fuels will eventually be depleted*
- *Solar power still too problematic and expensive*

*Arguments against the use of nuclear power:*

- *Radioactive byproducts are deadly*
- *Safer alternatives like nuclear fusion may be viable in the future*
- *Solar power already in use*

Again, it doesn't matter which side you take. Let's say that in this case
you decide to argue against nuclear power. Remember, the question is
asking you to argue *why* the cons of nuclear power outweigh the pros—
the inadequacy of this power source is the end you're arguing toward, so
don't list it as a supporting argument.

### 3. Organize Your Argument

You've already begun to think out your arguments—that's why you picked
the side you did in the first place. Now's the time to write them all out,
including ones that weaken the opposing side.

*Nuclear power is not a viable alternative to other sources of energy because:*

- *Radioactive, spent fuel has leaked from storage sites (too dangerous)*
- *Reactor accidents can be catastrophic—Three Mile Island, Chernobyl (too dangerous)*
- *More research into solar power will bring down its cost (weakens opposing argument)*
- *Solar-powered homes and cars already exist (alternatives proven viable)*
- *No serious effort to research other alternatives like nuclear fusion (better alternatives lie undiscovered)*
- *Energy companies don't spend money on alternatives; no vested interest (better alternatives lie undiscovered)*

### 4. Compose Your Essay

Remember, open up with a general statement and then assert your position. From there, get down your main points. Your essay for this assignment might look like the following:

### Sample Essay 1

At first glance, nuclear energy may seem to be the power source for the future. It's relatively inexpensive, it doesn't produce smoke and its fuel supply is virtually inexhaustible. But a close examination of the issue reveals that nuclear energy is more problematic and dangerous than other forms of energy production.

A main reason that nuclear energy is undesirable is the problem of radioactive waste storage. Highly toxic fuel left over from nuclear fission remains toxic for thousands of years, and the spills and leaks from existing storage sites are hazardous and costly to clean up. Even more appalling is the prospect of accidents at the reactor itself: Incidents at the Three Mile Island and Chernobyl power plants have proven that the consequences of a nuclear meltdown can be catastrophic and have consequences that are felt worldwide.

Environmental and health problems aside, the bottom line for the production of energy is profit. Nuclear power is a business just like any other, and the large companies that produce this country's electricity and gas claim they can't make alternatives like solar power affordable. Yet—largely due to incentives from the federal government—there exist today homes that are heated by solar power, and cars that are fueled by the sun have already hit the streets. If the limited resources that have been devoted to energy alternatives have already produced working models, a more intensive effort is likely to make those alternatives less expensive and problematic.

Options like solar power, hydroelectric power, and nuclear fusion are far better in the long run in terms of cost and safety. The only money required for these alternatives is for the materials required to harvest them: Sunlight, water, and the power of the atom are free. They also don't produce any toxic byproducts for which long-term storage—a hidden cost of nuclear power—must be found. And, with the temporary exception of nuclear fusion, these sources of energy are already being harnessed today.

While there are arguments to be made for both sides, it is clear that the drawbacks to the use of nuclear power are too great. If other alternatives are explored more seriously than they have been in the past, safer and less expensive sources of power will undoubtedly prove to be better alternatives.

*5. Proofread Your Work*
Take that last couple of minutes to catch any glaring errors.

# The Argument Essay

The Argument essay requires you to critique the construction of someone else's argument by assessing its claims and evaluating the evidence provided. Note that you are not being asked to agree or disagree with the author's *position* or *conclusion*; instead, you must analyze the *line of reasoning* used in the argument.

## The Question Stem

The screen directions will instruct you to decide how convincing you find the argument. To make your case, first analyze the argument itself and evaluate its use of evidence; second, explain how a different approach or more information would make the argument itself better (or possibly worse).

The directions for the Argument essay will look something like this:

**Directions: You will have 30 minutes to plan and write a critique of an argument presented in the form of a short passage. You will be asked to consider the logical soundness of the argument. No other topics are admissible for this essay.**

**Your essay will be evaluated in terms of the following:**

- **Identifying and analyzing the argument's important points**
- **Organizing, developing, and expressing your ideas**
- **Supporting your ideas with relevant reasons and/or examples**
- **Demonstrating a knowledge of standard written English**

**Feel free to consider the issue for a few minutes before planning your response and beginning your writing. Be certain that your ideas are fully developed and organized logically, and make sure you have enough time left to review and revise what you've written.**

## The Stimulus

This time you're given an expressed point of view—an "argument"—that contains a conclusion and supporting evidence. Here the writer tries to persuade you of something (her conclusion) by citing some evidence. You should read the "arguments" in Analysis of Argument questions with a critical eye. Be on the lookout for *assumptions* in the way the writer moves from evidence to conclusion.

The topics you see in the Argument section may be similar to these:

*The problem of poorly trained teachers that has plagued the state public school system is bound to become a good deal less serious in the future. The state has initiated comprehensive guidelines that oblige state teachers to complete a number of required credits in education and educational psychology at the graduate level before being certified.*

*The commercial airline industry in the country of Freedonia has experienced impressive growth in the past three years. This trend will surely continue in the years to come, since the airline industry will benefit from recent changes in Freedonian society: Incomes are rising, most employees now receive more vacation time, and interest in travel is rising, as shown by an increase in media attention devoted to foreign cultures and tourist attractions.*

*The Kiddie Candy Company has instituted a new policy of paying factory employees for the number of candies each employee produces, rather than for the time they spend producing the candy. This policy will increase the number and raise the quality of the candies produced, allow the company to reduce their staff size, and enable their factories to operate for fewer hours, resulting in savings on electricity and security costs. These changes will ensure that the best workers keep their jobs and that the company will earn a profit in the coming year.*

## Applying the Kaplan Five-Step Method to an Argument Essay

Let's use the Kaplan Five-Step Method on one of the Analysis of an Argument topics we saw before:

> *The problem of poorly trained teachers that has plagued the state public school system is bound to become a good deal less serious in the future. The state has initiated comprehensive guidelines that oblige state teachers to complete a number of required credits in education and educational psychology at the graduate level before being certified.*

Explain how logically persuasive you find this argument. In discussing your viewpoint, analyze the argument's line of reasoning and its use of evidence. Also explain what, if anything, would make the argument more valid and convincing or help you to better evaluate its conclusion.

### 1. Digest the Argument

First, identify the conclusion—the point the argument's trying to make. Here, the conclusion is:

> *The problem of poorly trained teachers that has plagued the state public school system is bound to become a good deal less serious in the future.*

Next, identify the evidence—the basis for the conclusion. Here, the evidence is:

> *The state has initiated comprehensive guidelines that oblige state teachers to complete a number of required credits in education and educational psychology at the graduate level before being certified.*

Finally, sum up the argument in your own words:
*The problem of badly trained teachers will become less serious because they'll be getting better training.*

Explain how logically persuasive you find this argument. In explaining your viewpoint, analyze the argument's line of reasoning and its use of evidence. Also explain what, if anything, would make the argument more valid and convincing or would help you to better evaluate its conclusion.

- *Credits in education will improve teachers' classroom performance*
- *Present bad teachers haven't already met this standard of training*
- *Current poor teachers will not still be teaching in the future, or will have to be trained, too*

## Kaplan Rules

In attacking the argument, remember to:
- Jot down the conclusion
- Identify the evidence
- Sum up the essential argument in your own words

## 2. Select the Points You Will Make

Analyze the use of evidence in the argument. Determine whether there's anything relevant that's not discussed.

- *Whether the training will actually address the cause of the problems*
- *How to either improve or remove the poor teachers now teaching*

Also determine what types of evidence would make the argument stronger or more logically sound. In this case, we need some new evidence supporting the assumptions.

- *Evidence verifying that this training will make better teachers*
- *Evidence making it clear that present bad teachers haven't already had this training*
- *Evidence suggesting why all or many bad teachers won't still be teaching in the future (or why they'll be better trained)*

## 3. Organize

For an essay on this topic, your opening sentence might look like this:

*The writer concludes that the present problem of poorly trained teachers will become less severe in the future because of required course work in education and psychology.*

Then use your notes as a working outline. Remember to lead with your best arguments. You might also recommend new evidence you'd like to see and explain why.

*The argument says that:*
*The problem of poorly trained teachers will become less serious with better training.*

*It assumes that:*
- *Course work in education will improve teachers' classroom performance*
- *Present bad teachers haven't already met this standard of classroom training*
- *Current poor teachers will not be teaching in the future or will get training, too*

## Kaplan Rules

In writing your essay, cover each point in your outline and employ the four basic principles of analytical writing.

## Kaplan Tip

A two-paragraph essay may be the most natural format for your response. However, consider using a third or fourth if you wish to discuss a number of different features of an argument.

*4. Compose Your Essay*

Begin typing or writing your essay now. Keep in mind the basic principles of writing that we discussed earlier.

Your essay might look something like this:

**Sample Essay 2**

The writer concludes that the present problem of poorly trained teachers will become less severe in the future because of required credits in education and psychology. However, the conclusion relies on assumptions for which there is no clear evidence.

First, the writer assumes that the required courses will make better teachers. In fact, the courses might be entirely irrelevant to the teachers' failings. If, for example, the prevalent problem is cultural and linguistic gaps between teacher and student, graduate level courses that do not address these specific issues probably won't do much good. The argument that the courses will improve teachers would be strengthened if the writer provided evidence that the training will be relevant to the problems.

In addition, the writer assumes that current poor teachers have not already had this training. In fact, the writer doesn't mention whether or not some or all of the poor teachers have had similar training. The argument would be strengthened considerably if the writer provided evidence that current poor teachers have not had training comparable to the new requirements.

Finally, the writer assumes that poor teachers currently working will either stop teaching in the future or will have received training. The writer provides no evidence, though, to indicate that this is the case. As the argument stands, it's highly possible that only brand-new teachers will receive the training, and the bright future to which the writer refers is decades away. Only if the writer provides evidence that all teachers in the system will receive training—and will then change their teaching methods accordingly—does the argument hold.

*5. Proofread*

Save a few minutes to go over your essay and catch any obvious errors.

# Practice Essays

**Directions: Write an essay on each of the topics below. While writing, pay particular attention to making your essay concise, forceful, and grammatically correct. After you've finished with each essay, proofread to catch your errors. Allow yourself 45 minutes to complete the first essay and 30 minutes to complete the second essay.**

## Essay 1: Analysis of Issue

Present your perspective on the issue below, using revelant reasons and/or examples to support your view:

> *Elementary schools should not waste their limited resources by teaching children a second language, especially since so many children are still struggling to master the most basic reading, writing, and arithmetic skills.*

## Essay 2: Analysis of Argument

Discuss how well-reasoned you find the following argument:

> *Many lives might be saved if inoculations against cow flu were routinely administered to all people in areas in which the disease is detected. However, since there is a small possibility that a person will die as a result of the inoculations, we cannot permit inoculations against cow flu to be routinely administered.*

# Holistic Scoring

The GRE writing tests are scored by hand, not by computer. Holistic scoring uses a single letter or a number—on the GRE it's a number from zero to six—to provide an overall evaluation of an essay as a whole. A holistic score emphasizes the interrelation of different thinking and writing qualities in an essay (such as content, organization, or syntax) and tries to denote the unified effect that all of these elements combine to produce. Although the GRE writing tests consist of two different essays, a single combined score is reported, representing the average of your scores for the two essays.

Each of the two essay tasks requires a different type of response and so has a slightly different set of grading criteria. But both kinds of topic require similar essay qualities. The following list, based on information from the Graduate Record Examinations Board, will give you a general idea of the guidelines a GRE grader will have in mind when reading your essays.

## Note

Your official score represents the average of your two essay scores.

## Note

Because your essays need to be read and scored by real-live people, you won't receive your Writing Assessment (or Analytical Writing Measure) score at the test center. Scores will be sent to institutions and test takers within 10 to 15 days.

**6:** **"Outstanding" Essay**
- Insightfully presents and convincingly supports an opinion on the issue or a critique of the argument
- Ideas are very clear, well organized and logically connected
- Shows superior control of language: grammar, stylistic variety, and accepted conventions of writing; minor flaws may occur

**5:** **"Strong" Essay**
- Presents well-chosen examples and strongly supports an opinion on the issue or a critique of the argument
- Ideas are generally clear and well organized; connections are logical
- Shows solid control of language: grammar, stylistic variety, and accepted conventions of writing; minor flaws may occur

**4:** **"Adequate" Essay**
- Presents and adequately supports an opinion on the issue or a critique of the argument
- Ideas are fairly clear and adequately organized; logical connections are satisfactory
- Shows satisfactory control of language: grammar, stylistic variety, and accepted conventions of writing; some flaws may occur

**3:** **"Limited" Essay**
- Succeeds only partially in presenting and supporting an opinion on the issue or a critique of the argument
- Ideas may be unclear and poorly organized
- Shows less than satisfactory control of language: contains significant mistakes in grammar, usage, and sentence structure

**2:** **"Weak" Essay**
- Shows little success in presenting and supporting an opinion on the issue or a critique of the argument
- Ideas lack clarity and organization
- Meaning is impeded by many serious mistakes in grammar, usage, and sentence structure

**1:** **"Fundamentally Deficient" Essay**
- Fails to present a coherent opinion and/or evidence on the issue or a critique of the argument
- Ideas are seriously unclear and disorganized
- Lacks meaning due to widespread severe mistakes in grammar, usage, and sentence structure

**0:** **"Unscorable" Essay**
- Completely ignores topic

## You Be the Evaluator

You've now seen what both types of essays look like, and you know more about the criteria used to evaluate essays. With this information in mind, review your own practice essays and see how you think they measure up.

For this exercise, it's not critical that you assign the "right" grade. It's more important that you understand whether the essays are well written and how well they fulfill the required tasks.

# GRE Writing Style Checklist

## Be Concise

❏ Cut out words, phrases, and sentences that do not add any information or serve a purpose.

❏ Watch out for repetitive phrases such as *refer back* or *serious crisis.*

❏ Don't use conjunctions to join sentences that would be more effective as separate sentences.

## Be Forceful

❏ Avoid jargon and pompous language; it won't impress anybody.

❏ Avoid clichés and overused terms or phrases. (For example, *beyond the shadow of a doubt.*)

❏ Don't be vague. Avoid generalizations and abstractions when more specific words would be clearer. (For example, write *a waste of time and money* instead of *pointless temporal and financial expenditure.*)

❏ Don't use weak sentence openings. Avoid beginning a sentence with "There is" or "There are."

❏ Don't refer to yourself needlessly. Avoid pointless phrases like *in my personal opinion.*

❏ Don't be monotonous: Vary sentence length and style.

❏ Use transitions to connect sentences and make your essay easy to follow. Paragraphs should clarify the different parts of your essay.

## Be Correct

❏ Stick to the rules of standard written English.

# The GRE Practice Test

# How to Take This Practice Test

Since the interactive test experience of a CAT is impossible to reproduce in a book, this is a paper-and-pencil test. Before taking this Practice Test, find a quiet place where you can work uninterrupted for three hours. Make sure you have a comfortable desk and several pencils. Time yourself according to the time limits shown at the beginning of each section. It's okay to take a short break between sections, but for best results you should go through all three sections in one sitting. Use the answer grid on the following page to record your answers.

You'll find the answer key and score converter following the test. Good luck.

If you purchased the edition of this book that is bundled with a CD-ROM, you will find four realistic CATs to practice with in the software. If you purchased the edition that doesn't come with a CD-ROM, you can take a practice CAT on Kaplan's Website (www.kaptest.com), or purchase Kaplan's test-prep software separately at your local software store.

## SECTION ONE: VERBAL
Time—60 minutes   76 questions

Directions: Each of the following questions begins with a sentence that has either one or two blanks. The blanks indicate that a piece of the sentence is missing. Each sentence is followed by five answer choices that consist of words or phrases. Select the answer choice that completes the sentence best.

1. The fundamental _____ between dogs and cats is for the most part a myth; members of these species often coexist _____.

    (A) antipathy . . amiably
    (B) disharmony . . uneasily
    (C) compatibility . . together
    (D) relationship . . peacefully
    (E) difference . . placidly

2. His desire to state his case completely was certainly reasonable; however, his lengthy technical explanations were monotonous and tended to _____ rather than _____ the jury.

    (A) enlighten . . inform
    (B) interest . . persuade
    (C) provoke . . influence
    (D) allay . . pacify
    (E) bore . . convince

3. In some countries, government restrictions are so _____ that businesses operate with near complete impunity.

    (A) traditional
    (B) judicious
    (C) ambiguous
    (D) exacting
    (E) lax

4. The recent Oxford edition of the works of Shakespeare is _____ because it not only departs frequently from the readings of most other modern editions, but also challenges many of the basic _____ of textual criticism.

    (A) controversial . . conventi
    (B) typical . . innovations
    (C) inadequate . . norms
    (D) curious . . projects
    (E) pretentious . . explana

5. The early form of writing known as Linear B was _____ in 1952, but one has yet succeeded in the _____ of the still more ancient Linear A.

    (A) superseded . . explanation
    (B) encoded . . transcription
    (C) obliterated . . ana
    (D) deciphered . . in ation
    (E) discovered . . ob on

N TO THE NEXT PAGE

6. Considering everything she had been through, her reaction was quite normal and even _____ ; I was therefore surprised at the number of _____ comments and raised eyebrows that her response elicited.

    Ⓐ  commendable . . complimentary
    Ⓑ  odious . . insulting
    Ⓒ  apologetic . . conciliatory
    Ⓓ  commonplace . . typical
    Ⓔ  laudable . . derogatory

7. The purpose of the proposed insurance policy is to _____ the burden of medical costs, thereby removing what is for many people a major _____ medical care.

    Ⓐ  augment . . problem with
    Ⓑ  eliminate . . perquisite of
    Ⓒ  ameliorate . . study of
    Ⓓ  assuage . . impediment to
    Ⓔ  clarify . . explanation for

Directions: Each of the following questions consists of a pair of words or phrases that are separated by a colon and followed by five answer choices. Choose the pair of words or phrases in the answer choices that are most similar to the original pair.

8. NOVEL : BOOK ::

   Ⓐ epic : poem
   Ⓑ house : library
   Ⓒ tale : fable
   Ⓓ number : page
   Ⓔ play : theater

9. HUNGRY : RAVENOUS ::

   Ⓐ thirsty : desirous
   Ⓑ large : titanic
   Ⓒ famous : eminent
   Ⓓ dizzy : disoriented
   Ⓔ obese : gluttonous

10. BOUQUET : FLOWER ::

   Ⓐ humidor : tobacco
   Ⓑ mosaic : tile
   Ⓒ tapestry : color
   Ⓓ pile : block
   Ⓔ sacristy : vestment

11. REALIST : QUIXOTIC ::

   Ⓐ scholar : pedantic
   Ⓑ fool : idiotic
   Ⓒ idler : lethargic
   Ⓓ tormentor : sympathetic
   Ⓔ diner : dyspeptic

12. SHARD : GLASS ::

   Ⓐ grain : sand
   Ⓑ morsel : meal
   Ⓒ strand : rope
   Ⓓ scrap : quilt
   Ⓔ splinter : wood

13. FILTER : IMPURITY ::

   Ⓐ expurgate : obscenity
   Ⓑ whitewash : infraction
   Ⓒ testify : perjury
   Ⓓ perform : penance
   Ⓔ vacuum : carpet

14. PARAPHRASE : VERBATIM ::

   Ⓐ approximation : precise
   Ⓑ description : vivid
   Ⓒ quotation : apt
   Ⓓ interpretation : valid
   Ⓔ significance : uncertain

15. ONCOLOGY : TUMOR ::

   Ⓐ chronology : time
   Ⓑ theology : tenet
   Ⓒ oral : sound
   Ⓓ philology : religion
   Ⓔ taxonomy : classification

16. INTRANSIGENT : FLEXIBILITY ::

   Ⓐ transient : mobility
   Ⓑ disinterested : partisanship
   Ⓒ dissimilar : variation
   Ⓓ progressive : transition
   Ⓔ ineluctable : modality

**GO ON TO THE NEXT PAGE**

Directions: After each reading passage you will find a series of questions. Select the best choice for each question. Answers are based on the contents of the passage or what the author implies in the passage.

There can be nothing simpler than an elementary particle: it is an indivisible shard of matter, without internal structure and without detectable shape or size. One might expect
(5) commensurate simplicity in the theories that describe such particles and the forces through which they interact; at the least, one might expect the structure of the world to be explained with a minimum number of
(10) particles and forces. Judged by this criterion of parsimony, a description of nature that has evolved in the past several years can be accounted a reasonable success. Matter is built out of just two classes of elementary particles:
(15) the leptons, such as the electron, and the quarks, which are constituents of the proton, the neutron, and many related particles. Four basic forces act between the elementary particles. Gravitation and electromagnetism have long
(20) been familiar in the macroscopic world; the weak force and the strong force are observed only in subnuclear events. In principle this complement of particles and forces could account for the entire observed hierarchy of material structure,
(25) from the nuclei of atoms to stars and galaxies. An understanding of nature at this level of detail is a remarkable achievement; nevertheless, it is possible to imagine what a still simpler theory might be like. The existence of two disparate
(30) classes of elementary particles is not fully satisfying; ideally, one class would suffice. Similarly, the existence of four forces seems a needless complication; one force might explain all the interactions of elementary particles. An
(35) ambitious new theory now promises at least a partial unification along these lines.

The theory does not embrace gravitation, which is by far the feeblest of the forces and may be fundamentally different from the
(40) others. If gravitation is excluded, however, the theory unifies all elementary particles and forces. The first step in the construction of the unified theory was the demonstration that the weak, the strong,
(45) and the electromagnetic forces could all be described by theories of the same general kind. The three forces remained distinct, but they could be seen to operate through the same mechanism. In the course of this
(50) development a deep connection was discovered between the weak force and electromagnetism, a connection that hinted at a still grander synthesis. The new theory is the leading candidate for accomplishing
(55) the synthesis. It incorporates the leptons and the quarks into a single family and provides a means of transforming one kind of particle into the other. At the same time the weak, the strong, and the electro-
(60) magnetic forces are understood as aspects of a single underlying force. With only one class of particles and one force (plus gravitation), the unified theory is a model of frugality.

17. All of the following are differences between the two theories described by the author EXCEPT

   Ⓐ  the second theory is simpler than the first
   Ⓑ  the first theory encompasses gravitation while the second does not
   Ⓒ  the second theory includes only one class of elementary particles
   Ⓓ  the first theory accounts for only part of the hierarchy of material structure
   Ⓔ  the second theory unifies forces that the first theory regards as distinct

**GO ON TO THE NEXT PAGE**

18. The primary purpose of the passage is to

   Ⓐ correct a misconception in a currently accepted theory of the nature of matter
   Ⓑ describe efforts to arrive at a simplified theory of elementary particles and forces
   Ⓒ predict the success of a new effort to unify gravitation with other basic forces
   Ⓓ explain why scientists prefer simpler explanations over more complex ones
   Ⓔ summarize what is known about the basic components of matter

19. According to the passage, which of the following are true of quarks?

   I. They are the elementary building blocks for neutrons.
   II. Scientists have described them as having no internal structure.
   III. Some scientists group them with leptons in a single class of particles.

   Ⓐ I only
   Ⓑ III only
   Ⓒ I and II only
   Ⓓ II and III only
   Ⓔ I, II, and III

20. The author considers which of the following in judging the usefulness of a theory of elementary particles and forces?

   I. The simplicity of the theory
   II. The ability of the theory to account for the largest possible number of known phenomena
   III. The possibility of proving or disproving the theory by experiment

   Ⓐ I only
   Ⓑ II only
   Ⓒ I and II only
   Ⓓ I and III only
   Ⓔ II and III only

21. It can be inferred that the author considers the failure to unify gravitation with other forces in the theory he describes to be

   Ⓐ a disqualifying defect
   Ⓑ an unjustified deviation
   Ⓒ a needless oversimplification
   Ⓓ an unfortunate oversight
   Ⓔ an unavoidable limitation

22. The author organizes the passage by

   Ⓐ enumerating distinctions among several different kinds of elementary particles
   Ⓑ stating a criterion for judging theories of nature, and using it to evaluate two theories
   Ⓒ explaining three methods of grouping particles and forces
   Ⓓ criticizing an inaccurate view of elemental nature and proposing an alternative approach
   Ⓔ outlining an assumption about scientific verification, then criticizing the assumption

23. It can be inferred that the author would be likely to consider a new theory of nature superior to present theories if it were to

   Ⓐ account for a larger number of macroscopic structures than present theories
   Ⓑ reduce the four basic forces to two more fundamental, incompatible forces
   Ⓒ propose a smaller number of fundamental particles and forces than current theories
   Ⓓ successfully account for the observable behavior of bodies due to gravity
   Ⓔ hypothesize that protons but not neutrons are formed by combinations of more fundamental particles

**GO ON TO THE NEXT PAGE**

The majority of white abolitionists and the majority of suffragists worked hard to convince their compatriots that the changes they advocated were not revolutionary, that far from
(5) undermining the accepted distribution of power they would eliminate deviations from the democratic principle it was supposedly based on. Non-Garrisonian abolitionists repeatedly disavowed miscegenationist or revolutionary
(10) intentions. And as for the suffragists, despite the presence in the movement of socialists, and in the final years of a few blacks, immigrants, and workers, the racism and nativism in the movement's thinking were not an aberration and
(15) did not conflict with the movement's objective of suffrage. Far from saying, as presentist historians do, that the white abolitionists and suffragists compromised the abiding principles of equality and the equal right of all to life, liberty, and the
(20) pursuit of happiness, I suggest just the opposite: the non-Garrisonian majority of white abolitionists and the majority of suffragists showed what those principles meant in their respective generations, because they traced the
(25) farthest acceptable boundaries around them.

24. The author's main point is that

&#9398; the actions of the abolitionist and suffragist movements compromised their stated principles

&#9399; the underlying beliefs of abolitionists and suffragists were closer than is usually believed

&#9400; abolitionists' and suffragists' thinking about equality was limited by the assumptions of their time

&#9401; presentist historians have willfully misrepresented the ideology of abolitionists and suffragists

&#9402; historians should impose their own value systems when evaluating events of the past

25. Which of the following does the author imply about the principle of equality?

I. It does not have a fixed meaning.
II. Suffragists applied it more consistently than abolitionists.
III. Abolitionists and suffragists compromised it to gain their political objectives.

&#9398; I only
&#9399; II only
&#9400; III only
&#9401; I and II only
&#9402; II and III only

26. The author takes exception to the views of presentist historians by

&#9398; charging that they ignore pertinent evidence

&#9399; presenting new information that had not been available before

&#9400; applying a different interpretation to the same set of facts

&#9401; refuting the accuracy of their historical data

&#9402; exposing a logical contradiction in their arguments

27. Which of the following is suggested about the abolitionist movement?

&#9398; Its members disguised their objectives from the public.

&#9399; It contained different groupings characterized by varied philosophies.

&#9400; It undermined its principles by accommodating public concerns.

&#9401; A majority of its members misunderstood its objectives.

&#9402; Its progress was hindered by the actions of radical factions within it.

**GO ON TO THE NEXT PAGE**

Directions: Each of the following questions begins with a single word in capital letters. Five answer choices follow. Select the answer choice that has the most opposite meaning of the word in capital letters.

Since some of the questions require you to distinguish fine shades of meaning, be sure to consider all the choices before deciding which one is best.

28. UNDERMINE:

  (A) appreciate
  (B) donate
  (C) bolster
  (D) decay
  (E) simplify

29. OBSEQUIOUS:

  (A) original
  (B) haughty
  (C) casual
  (D) virtuous
  (E) informative

30. BLANCH:

  (A) stand
  (B) repay
  (C) flush
  (D) relax
  (E) cope

31. DISSIPATED:

  (A) temperate
  (B) pleased
  (C) inundated
  (D) encouraged
  (E) planned

32. FECUNDITY:

  (A) levity
  (B) sanity
  (C) cowardice
  (D) sterility
  (E) ventilation

33. ENCUMBER:

  (A) animate
  (B) inaugurate
  (C) bleach
  (D) disburden
  (E) obliterate

34. DISSEMINATE:

  (A) fertilize
  (B) ordain
  (C) suppress
  (D) explain thoroughly
  (E) make an impression

**GO ON TO THE NEXT PAGE**

35. RESTIVE:

    (A) morose
    (B) intangible
    (C) fatigued
    (D) patient
    (E) curious

36. SYNCOPATED:

    (A) carefully executed
    (B) normally accented
    (C) brightly illuminated
    (D) easily understood
    (E) justly represented

37. VITUPERATIVE:

    (A) lethal
    (B) incapacitated
    (C) laudatory
    (D) insulated
    (E) prominent

38. SATURNINE:

    (A) magnanimous
    (B) ebullient
    (C) finicky
    (D) unnatural
    (E) impoverished

GO ON TO THE NEXT PAGE

**Directions:** Each of the following questions begins with a sentence that has either one or two blanks. The blanks indicate that a piece of the sentence is missing. Each sentence is followed by five answer choices that consist of words or phrases. Select the answer choice that completes the sentence best.

39. Her concern for the earthquake victims _____ her reputation as a callous person.

 (A) restored
 (B) rescinded
 (C) created
 (D) proved
 (E) belied

40. Due to unforeseen circumstances, the original plans were no longer _____ and were therefore _____ .

 (A) relevant . . adaptable
 (B) applicable . . rejected
 (C) expedient . . adopted
 (D) acceptable . . appraised
 (E) capable . . allayed

41. The microscopic cross section of a sandstone generally shows a _____ surface, each tiny layer representing an _____ of deposition that may have taken centuries or even millennia to accumulate.

 (A) ridged . . enlargement
 (B) multifaceted . . angle
 (C) distinctive . . area
 (D) stratified . . interval
 (E) coarse . . episode

42. The convict has always insisted upon his own _____ and now at last there is new evidence to _____ him.

 (A) defensiveness . . incarcerate
 (B) culpability . . exonerate
 (C) blamelessness . . anathematize
 (D) innocence . . vindicate
 (E) contrition . . condemn

43. The theory of plate tectonics was the subject of much _____ when it was first proposed by Alfred Wegener, but now most geophysicists _____ its validity.

 (A) opposition . . grant
 (B) consideration . . see
 (C) acclamation . . boost
 (D) prognostication . . learn
 (E) contention . . bar

44. Despite her professed _____ , the glint in her eyes demonstrated her _____ with the topic.

 (A) intelligence . . obsession
 (B) interest . . concern
 (C) obliviousness . . confusion
 (D) indifference . . fascination
 (E) expertise . . unfamiliarity

45. Lacking sacred scriptures or _____ , Shinto is more properly regarded as a legacy of traditional religious practices and basic values than as a formal system of belief.

 (A) followers
 (B) customs
 (C) dogma
 (D) relics
 (E) faith

**GO ON TO THE NEXT PAGE**

Directions: Each of the following questions consists of a pair of words or phrases that are separated by a colon and followed by five answer choices. Choice the pair of words or phrases in the answer choices that are most similar to the original pair.

46. IMPECCABLE : FLAW ::

    Ⓐ impeachable : crime
    Ⓑ obstreperous : permission
    Ⓒ impetuous : warning
    Ⓓ moribund : living
    Ⓔ absurd : sense

47. SEISMOGRAPH : EARTHQUAKE ::

    Ⓐ stethoscope : health
    Ⓑ speedometer : truck
    Ⓒ telescope : astronomy
    Ⓓ thermometer : temperature
    Ⓔ abacus : arithmetic

48. GUZZLE : DRINK ::

    Ⓐ elucidate : clarify
    Ⓑ ingest : eat
    Ⓒ boast : describe
    Ⓓ stride : walk
    Ⓔ admonish : condemn

49. ORATOR : ARTICULATE ::

    Ⓐ soldier : merciless
    Ⓑ celebrity : talented
    Ⓒ judge : unbiased
    Ⓓ novice : unfamiliar
    Ⓔ dignitary : respectful

50. BADGE : POLICEMAN ::

    Ⓐ placard : demonstrator
    Ⓑ tattoo : sailor
    Ⓒ dog-tag : soldier
    Ⓓ pedigree : dog
    Ⓔ fingerprint : defendant

51. SCRUTINIZE : OBSERVE ::

    Ⓐ excite : pique
    Ⓑ beseech : request
    Ⓒ search : discover
    Ⓓ smile : grin
    Ⓔ dive : jump

52. INDULGE : EPICUREAN ::

    Ⓐ frighten: ugly
    Ⓑ retract : revocable
    Ⓒ hesitate : unproductive
    Ⓓ revenge : vindictive
    Ⓔ understand : comprehensible

53. FLOOD : DILUVIAL ::

    Ⓐ punishment : criminal
    Ⓑ bacteria : biological
    Ⓒ verdict : judicial
    Ⓓ light : candescent
    Ⓔ heart : cardiac

54. SPHINX : PERPLEX ::

    Ⓐ oracle : interpret
    Ⓑ prophet : prepare
    Ⓒ siren : lure
    Ⓓ jester : astound
    Ⓔ minotaur : anger

**GO ON TO THE NEXT PAGE**

<u>Directions:</u> After each reading passage you will find a series of questions. Select the best choice for each question. Answers are based on the contents of the passage or what the author implies in the passage.

Although the schooling of fish is a familiar form of animal social behavior, how the school is formed and maintained is only beginning to be understood in detail. It had been thought that
(5) each fish maintains its position chiefly by means of vision. Our work has shown that, as each fish maintains its position, the lateral line, an organ sensitive to transitory changes in water displacement, is as important as vision. In each
(10) species a fish has a "preferred" distance and angle from its nearest neighbor. The ideal separation and bearing, however, are not maintained rigidly. The result is a probabilistic arrangement that appears like a random aggregation. The
(15) tendency of the fish to remain at the preferred distance and angle, however, serves to maintain the structure. Each fish, having established its position, uses its eyes and its lateral lines simultaneously to measure the speed of all the
(20) other fish in the school. It then adjusts its own speed to match a weighted average that emphasizes the contribution of nearby fish.

55. According to the passage, the structure of a fish school is dependent upon which of the following?

I. rigidly formed random aggregations
II. the tendency of each fish to remain at a preferred distance from neighboring fish
III. measurements of a weighted average by individual fish

Ⓐ II only
Ⓑ III only
Ⓒ I and II only
Ⓓ I and III only
Ⓔ II and III only

56. Which of the following best describes the author's attitude toward the theory that the structure of fish schools is maintained primarily through vision?

Ⓐ heated opposition
Ⓑ careful neutrality
Ⓒ considered dissatisfaction
Ⓓ cautious approval
Ⓔ unqualified enthusiasm

57. The passage suggests that, after establishing its position in the school formation, an individual fish will subsequently

Ⓐ maintain its preferred position primarily by visual and auditory means
Ⓑ rigorously avoid changes that would interfere with the overall structure of the school
Ⓒ make continuous sensory readjustments to its position within the school
Ⓓ make unexpected shifts in position only if threatened by external danger
Ⓔ surrender its ability to make quick, instinctive judgments

**GO ON TO THE NEXT PAGE**

Whether as a result of some mysterious tendency in the national psyche or as a spontaneous reaction to their turbulent historical experience after the breakup of the Mycenaean
(5) world, the Greeks felt that to live with changing, undefined, unmeasured, seemingly random impressions—to live, in short, with what was expressed by the Greek word *chaos*—was to live in a state of constant anxiety.

(10) If the apparent mutability of the physical world and of the human condition was a source of pain and bewilderment to the Greeks, the discovery of a permanent pattern or an unchanging substratum by which apparently chaotic experi-
(15) ence could be measured and explained was a source of satisfaction, even joy, which had something of a religious nature. For the recognition of order and measure in phenomena did more than simply satisfy their intellectual
(20) curiosity or gratify a desire for tidiness; it also served as the basis of a spiritual ideal. "Measure and commensurability are everywhere identified with beauty and excellence," was Plato's way of putting it in a dialogue in which measure is
(25) identified as a primary characteristic of the ultimate good. Rational definability and spirituality were never mutually exclusive categories in Greek thought. If the quest for order and clarity was in essence the search for a kind of spiritual
(30) ideal, it was not an ideal to be perceived in rapturous emotional mysticism but rather one to be arrived at by patient analysis.

We see this process at work especially in Greek philosophy, which in various ways was
(35) aimed at alleviating the anxiety that is inherent in the more spontaneous expression of lyric poetry. The Milesian philosophers of the sixth century were interested above all in discovering a primary substance from which all other phe-
(40) nomena could be explained. Neat, clear, and sub-

limely undisturbed by the social world of humanity, which took shape and dissolved within the natural order of things, it was an austere ideal, an astringent antidote to the appar-
(45) ent senselessness of life. The person who contemplated it deeply could feel a part of a great system that was impersonal but predictable, and, like Lucretius, who revived the Milesian attitude in a later age, he or she could derive a
(50) peculiar peace from it. As time passed and Greek philosophy developed, the urge to find order in experience was shifted from physics to the realm of mathematical abstraction by the Pythagoreans, and to the world of human
(55) behavior by various thinkers of the later fifth century; and, finally, Plato and Aristotle attempted to weave all these foci of interest into comprehensive pictures of the relationship between human life and the world as a whole.
(60) But in all these epochs the basic quest—the search for a "kosmos"—remained the same.

58. The author's primary purpose is to

    (A) evaluate conflicting viewpoints
    (B) challenge an accepted opinion
    (C) question philosophical principles
    (D) enumerate historical facts
    (E) describe a cultural phenomenon

**GO ON TO THE NEXT PAGE**

59. The author indicates that the discovery of "an unchanging substratum" (lines 13–14) served primarily to

   Ⓐ alter the Greeks' perception of the mutability of existence
   Ⓑ help eradicate severe social problems
   Ⓒ alleviate painful memories of national suffering
   Ⓓ calm a restless intellectual curiosity
   Ⓔ foster a more mystical understanding of the physical world

60. It can be inferred from the passage that rational thought and spiritual ideals were categories of experience that were

   Ⓐ unimportant and unfamiliar to most ordinary Greeks
   Ⓑ advocated by the Milesians and rejected by the Pythagoreans
   Ⓒ neglected by most philosophers before Plato and Aristotle
   Ⓓ seen by the Greeks as essentially compatible
   Ⓔ embraced mainly by Greek poets

61. All of the following can be inferred about the Greeks' anxiety over the possibility of "chaos" EXCEPT that it

   Ⓐ had sources in their national consciousness
   Ⓑ was reflected in specific aspects of their religion
   Ⓒ was related to their sense of change in the physical world
   Ⓓ led to a striving for order in their philosophy
   Ⓔ was expressed in their lyric poetry

62. The author implies that the Milesian philosophers of the sixth century sought relief from worldly anxiety by

   Ⓐ focusing narrowly on inherently human questions
   Ⓑ establishing sharp distinctions between spiritual and rational understanding
   Ⓒ focusing primarily on an impersonal natural order
   Ⓓ attempting to integrate rational and mystical worldviews
   Ⓔ withdrawing from the physical world into the realm of mathematical abstraction

63. Which of the following best describes the organization of lines 17–28 of the passage ("For the recognition of order . . . in Greek thought.")?

   Ⓐ The author summarizes two viewpoints, cites historical evidence, and then declines to support either of the viewpoints.
   Ⓐ The author makes an observation, admits to evidence that weakens the viewpoint, and then revises his observation.
   Ⓒ The author specifies two distinct arguments, examines both in detail, then advances a third argument that reconciles the other two.
   Ⓓ The author clarifies a previous statement, offers an example, and then draws a further conclusion based on these ideas.
   Ⓔ The author states a thesis, mentions an opposed thesis, and cites evidence supporting it, and then restates his original thesis.

**GO ON TO THE NEXT PAGE**

64. According to the passage, the Pythagoreans differed from the Milesians primarily in that the Pythagoreans

    (A) focused on mathematical abstractions rather than physical phenomena
    (B) placed a renewed emphasis on understanding human behavior
    (C) focused primarily on a rational means to understanding truth
    (D) attempted to identify a fundamental physical unit of matter
    (E) stressed concrete reality over formal theory

65. In the context of the author's overall argument, which of the following best characterizes the Greeks' "search for a 'kosmos'" (line 61)?

    (A) a mystical quest for a strong national identity
    (B) efforts to replace a sterile philosophical rationalism with revitalized religious values
    (C) attempts to end conflict among key philosophical schools
    (D) a search for order and measure in an unpredictable world
    (E) a search for an alternative to a narrow preoccupation with beauty and excellence

GO ON TO THE NEXT PAGE

Directions: Each of the following questions begins with a single word in capital letters. Five answer choices follow. Select the answer choice that has the most opposite meaning of the word in capital letters.

Since some of the questions require you to distinguish fine shades of meaning, be sure to consider all the choices before deciding which one is best.

66. ENMITY:

    (A) friendship
    (B) reverence
    (C) boredom
    (D) stylishness
    (E) awkwardness

67. DILATE:

    (A) enclose
    (B) shrink
    (C) hurry
    (D) inflate
    (E) erase

68. CHARLATAN:

    (A) genuine expert
    (B) powerful leader
    (C) false idol
    (D) unknown enemy
    (E) hardened villain

69. PERIPHERAL:

    (A) civilized
    (B) partial
    (C) central
    (D) unharmed
    (E) stable

70. MERITORIOUS:

    (A) effulgent
    (B) stationary
    (C) uneven
    (D) narrow-minded
    (E) unpraiseworthy

71. DISCHARGE:

    (A) heal
    (B) advance
    (C) enlist
    (D) penalize
    (E) delay

72. MALEDICTION:

    (A) blessing
    (B) preparation
    (C) good omen
    (D) liberation
    (E) pursuit

**GO ON TO THE NEXT PAGE**

73. MAWKISH:

  (A) unsentimental
  (B) sophisticated
  (C) graceful
  (D) tense
  (E) descriptive

74. TEMERITY:

  (A) blandness
  (B) caution
  (C) severity
  (D) strength
  (E) charm

75. JEJUNE:

  (A) morose
  (B) natural
  (C) mature
  (D) contrived
  (E) accurate

76. VITIATE:

  (A) deaden
  (B) trust
  (C) rectify
  (D) drain
  (E) amuse

# END OF SECTION

## SECTION TWO—QUANTITATIVE
Time—60 minutes   60 questions

Numbers:    The numbers in this section are real numbers.

Figures:    You may assume that the position of points, lines, angles, etcetera are in the order shown and that all lengths and angle measures may be assumed to be positive.

You may assume that lines that look straight are straight.

Figures are in a plane unless otherwise stated.

Figures are not drawn to scale unless otherwise stated.

Directions:   Questions 1–15 provide two quantities, one in Column A and another in Column B. Compare the two quantities and answer

Ⓐ   if the quantity in Column A is greater
Ⓑ   if the quantity in Column B is greater
Ⓒ   if the two quantities are equal
Ⓓ   if the relationship cannot be determined from the information given

Common
Information:   In each question, information relating to one or both of the quantities in Column A and Column B is centered above the two columns. A symbol that appears in both columns represents the same thing in Column A as it does in Column B.

| Column A | Column B | Sample Answers |
|----------|----------|----------------|
| | | |

Example 1:       $3 \times 4$          $3 + 4$          ● Ⓑ Ⓒ Ⓓ

GO ON TO THE NEXT PAGE

| Column A | Column B | Sample Answers |
| --- | --- | --- |

Examples 2–4 refer to the figure below.

Example 2:          $x$          $y$

ⓐ ⓑ ⓒ ⬤

(Because we cannot assume
the angles are equal, even
though they appear that way.)

Example 3:          $x + y$          90

ⓐ ⓑ ⬤ ⓓ

(Because the sum of the angles
is 180°.)

Example 4:          $x$          90

ⓐ ⬤ ⓒ ⓓ

(Since $\triangle ABC$ is a right
triangle, $x$ is less than 90°.)

**GO ON TO THE NEXT PAGE**

| Column A | Column B |
|----------|----------|
| 1.    0.0260 | 0.0256 |

$\triangle ABD$ and $\triangle CDB$ are right triangles.

| Column A | Column B |
|----------|----------|
| 2.    $w^2 + x^2$ | $y^2 + z^2$ |

$$x + 4y = 6$$
$$x = 2y$$

| Column A | Column B |
|----------|----------|
| 3.    $x$ | $y$ |

| Column A | Column B |
|----------|----------|
| 4.    $\sqrt{4^2 + 5^2}$ | $\sqrt{3^2 + 6^2}$ |

---

| Column A | Column B |
|----------|----------|

In a certain accounting firm, there are exactly three types of employees: managerial, technical, and clerical. The firm has 120 employees and 25 percent of the employees are managerial.

| Column A | Column B |
|----------|----------|
| 5.  The number of managerial employees | Two-thirds of the number of clerical employees |

| Column A | Column B |
|----------|----------|
| 6.  $\dfrac{12 \times 1}{12 + 1}$ | $\dfrac{12 + 1}{12 \times 1}$ |

| Column A | Column B |
|----------|----------|
| 7.  $(a + 1)(b + 1)$ | $ab + 1$ |

In the two-digit number $jk$, the value of the digit $j$ is twice the value of the digit $k$.

| Column A | Column B |
|----------|----------|
| 8.  $k$ | 6 |

$P$ is the center of the circle and the area of sector $PQR$ is 4.

| Column A | Column B |
|----------|----------|
| 9.  The area of circle $P$ | $4\pi$ |

**GO ON TO THE NEXT PAGE**

| Column A | Column B |
| --- | --- |

Henry purchased $x$ apples and Jack purchased 10 apples fewer than one-third of the number of apples Henry purchased.

10. The number of apples Jack purchased

$$\frac{x - 30}{3}$$

11. The volume of a rectangular solid with a length of 5 feet, a width of 4 feet, and a height of $x$ feet

The volume of a rectangular solid with a length of 10 feet, a width of 8 feet, and a height of $y$ feet

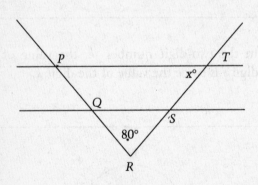

$PQ = ST$
$QR = RS$

12. $x$          50

| Column A | Column B |
| --- | --- |

$$2 \times 16 \times 64 = 2 \times 4n \times 256$$

13. $n$          2

$$y \neq 0$$

$$-\frac{2}{y} + \frac{1}{3} = -\frac{1}{2y}$$

14. $y$          4

The perimeter of isosceles $\triangle ABC$ is 40 and the length of side $BC$ is 12.

15. The length of side $AB$          14

GO ON TO THE NEXT PAGE

KAPLAN

Directions: Questions 16–30 each have five answer choices. For each of these questions, select the best of the answer choices given.

16. If $\dfrac{p-q}{p} = \dfrac{2}{7}$, then $\dfrac{q}{p}=$

  Ⓐ $\dfrac{2}{5}$

  Ⓑ $\dfrac{5}{7}$

  Ⓒ $1$

  Ⓓ $\dfrac{7}{5}$

  Ⓔ $\dfrac{7}{2}$

17. Which of the following numbers is both a multiple of 8 and a factor of 72?

  Ⓐ 4
  Ⓑ 9
  Ⓒ 16
  Ⓓ 24
  Ⓔ 36

18. In the figure above, what is the value of $a + b + c$?

  Ⓐ 110
  Ⓑ 250
  Ⓒ 290
  Ⓓ 330
  Ⓔ 430

19. John has four ties, 12 shirts, and three belts. If each day he wears exactly one tie, one shirt, and one belt, what is the maximum number of days he can go without repeating a particular combination?

  Ⓐ 12
  Ⓑ 21
  Ⓒ 84
  Ⓓ 108
  Ⓔ 144

20. Which of the following is the greatest?

  Ⓐ $\dfrac{0.00003}{0.0007}$

  Ⓑ $\dfrac{0.0008}{0.0005}$

  Ⓒ $\dfrac{0.007}{0.0008}$

  Ⓓ $\dfrac{0.006}{0.0005}$

  Ⓔ $\dfrac{0.01}{0.008}$

GO ON TO THE NEXT PAGE

## Questions 21–25 refer to the charts below.

U.S. PHYSICIANS IN SELECTED SPECIALTIES BY SEX, 1986

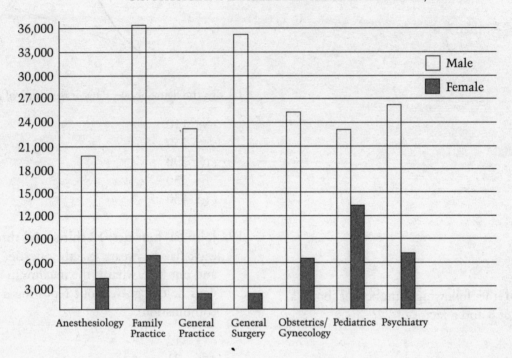

GENERAL SURGERY PHYSICIANS BY AGE, 1986

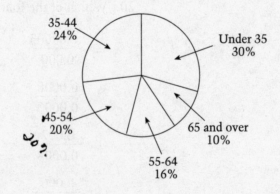

21. Approximately what percent of all general practice physicians in 1986 were male?

    Ⓐ 23%
    Ⓑ 50%
    Ⓒ 75%
    Ⓓ 82%
    Ⓔ 90%

22. Which of the following physician specialties had the lowest ratio of males to females in 1986?

    Ⓐ Family practice
    Ⓑ General surgery
    Ⓒ Obstetrics/gynecology
    Ⓓ Pediatrics
    Ⓔ Psychiatry

23. In 1986, approximately how many general surgery physicians were between the ages of 45 and 54, inclusive?

    Ⓐ 5,440
    Ⓑ 6,300
    Ⓒ 7,350
    Ⓓ 7,800
    Ⓔ 8,900

24. If in 1986 all the family practice physicians represented 7.5 percent of all the physicians in the United States, approximately how many physicians were there total?

    Ⓐ 300,000
    Ⓑ 360,000
    Ⓒ 430,000
    Ⓓ 485,000
    Ⓔ 570,000

25. If the number of female general surgeon physicians in the under-35 category represented 3.5 percent of all the general surgeon physicians, approximately how many male general surgeon physicians were under 35 years?

    Ⓐ 9,200
    Ⓑ 9,800
    Ⓒ 10,750
    Ⓓ 11,260
    Ⓔ 11,980

**GO ON TO THE NEXT PAGE**

26. $|3| + |-4| + |3 - 4| =$

   (A) 14

   (B) 8

   (C) 7

   (D) 2

   (E) 0

27. What is the area of the shaded region in the figure above?

   (A) 0.5

   (B) 0.7

   (C) 0.9

   (D) 2.7

   (E) 4.5

28. A computer can perform 30 identical tasks in six hours. At that rate, what is the minimum number of computers that should be assigned to complete 80 of the tasks within three hours?

   (A) 6

   (B) 7

   (C) 8

   (D) 12

   (E) 16

15 for 3

29. The volume of the cube in the figure above is 8. If point $A$ is the midpoint of an edge of this cube, what is the perimeter of $\triangle ABC$ ?

   (A) 5

   (B) $2 + 2\sqrt{3}$

   (C) $2 + 2\sqrt{5}$

   (D) 7

   (E) $6 + \sqrt{5}$

30. Which of the following is 850 percent greater than $8 \times 10^3$ ?

   (A) $8.5 \times 10^3$

   (B) $6.4 \times 10^4$

   (C) $6.8 \times 10^4$

   (D) $7.6 \times 10^4$

   (E) $1.6 \times 10^5$

**GO ON TO THE NEXT PAGE**

| Column A | Column B |
| --- | --- |

$$y = (x + 3)^2$$

**31.** The value of $y$ when $x = 1$      9

---

**32.** The number of miles traveled by a car that traveled for four hours at an average speed of 40 miles per hour | The number of miles traveled by a train that traveled for two and a half hours at an average speed of 70 miles per hour

---

**33.** The number of cookies in a bag that weighs 3 kilograms | The number of grapes in a bag that weighs 2 kilograms

---

**34.**      $AB$            $BC$

| Column A | Column B |
| --- | --- |

$$8a + 8b = 24$$

**35.** The length of segment $PQ$      2

---

$$x < y$$

**36.**      $y - x$            $x - y$

---

The area of triangular region $ABE$ is 75.

**37.** The area of $\triangle ABC$ | The area of $\triangle ADE$

GO ON TO THE NEXT PAGE

Column A      Column B        Column A      Column B

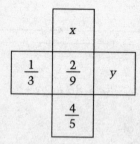

The sum of the numbers in the horizontal row of boxes equals the sum of the numbers in the vertical row of boxes.

38.      $x$              $y$

39.    $\dfrac{\frac{1}{3} \times \frac{1}{4}}{\frac{2}{3} \times \frac{1}{2}}$         $\dfrac{\frac{2}{3} \times \frac{1}{2}}{\frac{1}{3} \times \frac{1}{4}}$

Eileen drives due north from town $A$ to town $B$ for a distance of 60 miles, then drives due east from town $B$ to town $C$ for a distance of 80 miles.

*6400 + 3600*

40. The distance from town     120
     $A$ to town $C$ in miles

*100*

*2.79*        *-.645*

41. $(\sqrt{7} - 2)(\sqrt{7} + 2)$    $(2 - \sqrt{7})(-\sqrt{7} - 2)$

*.645*          *2.99*

42.    $r$             $s$

$x$ is an integer greater than 0.

43.    $1 - \left(\dfrac{1}{4}\right)^{x}$        0.95

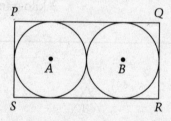

The two circles with centers $A$ and $B$ have the same radius.

44. The sum of the      The perimeter of
     circumferences of    rectangle $PQRS$
     of the two circles

45.    $3^{17} + 3^{18} + 3^{19}$        $3^{20}$

**GO ON TO THE NEXT PAGE**

**KAPLAN**

Directions: Questions 46–60 each have five answer choices. For each of these questions, select the best of the answer choices given.

46. If $4 + y = 14 - 4y$, then $y =$

    (A) $-4$

    (B) $0$

    (C) $\dfrac{5}{8}$

    (D) $\dfrac{4}{5}$

    (E) $2$

47. $\dfrac{4}{5} + \dfrac{5}{4} =$

    (A) $1$

    (B) $\dfrac{9}{8}$

    (C) $\dfrac{6}{5}$

    (D) $\dfrac{41}{20}$

    (E) $\dfrac{23}{10}$

48. If $3^m = 81$, then $m^3 =$

    (A) $9$

    (B) $16$

    (C) $27$

    (D) $54$

    (E) $64$

49. In the figure above, there are three square gardening areas. The area of square $A$ is 81 square meters and the area of square $B$ is 49 square meters. What is the area, in square meters, of square $C$?

    (A) $2$

    (B) $4$

    (C) $9$

    (D) $27$

    (E) $32$

50. In a certain history class, all except 23 students scored under 85 on a test. If 18 students scored over 85 on this test, how many students are there in this history class?

    (A) $33$

    (B) $37$

    (C) $39$

    (D) $41$

    (E) It cannot be determined from the information given.

GO ON TO THE NEXT PAGE

## Questions 51–55 refer to the following graphs

ENERGY USE BY YEAR, COUNTRY Y, 1950–1980
(in millions of kilowatt-hours)

ENERGY USE BY TYPE, COUNTRY Y

Total personal use = population × per-capita personal use

GO ON TO THE NEXT PAGE

KAPLAN

51. In which of the following years was the energy use in country *Y* closest to 650 million kilowatt-hours?

    (A) 1960
    (B) 1965
    (C) 1970
    (D) 1975
    (E) 1980

52. In 1965, how many of the categories shown had energy use greater than 150 million kilowatt-hours?

    (A) none
    (B) one
    (C) two
    (D) three
    (E) four

53. In which of the following years was industrial use of energy greatest in country *Y*?

    (A) 1960
    (B) 1965
    (C) 1970
    (D) 1975
    (E) 1980

54. If the population of country *Y* increased by 20 percent from 1960 to 1965, approximately what was the percent decrease in the per-capita personal use of energy between those two years?

    (A) 0%
    (B) 17%
    (C) 25%
    (D) 40%
    (E) It cannot be determined from the information given.

55. Which of the following can be inferred from the graphs?

    I. Farm use of energy increased between 1960 and 1980.
    II. In 1980, industrial use of energy was greater than industrial use of energy in 1965.
    III. More people were employed by the government of country *Y* in 1980 than in 1960.

    (A) I only
    (B) II only
    (C) I and II only
    (D) II and III only
    (E) I, II, and III

GO ON TO THE NEXT PAGE

56. If the average of two numbers is $3y$ and one of the numbers is $y - z$, what is the other number, in terms of $y$ and $z$?

    (A) $y + z$
    (B) $3y + z$
    (C) $4y - z$
    (D) $5y - z$
    (E) $5y + z$

57. In the figure above, the area of $\triangle ABC$ is 35. What is the length of $DC$?

    (A) 6
    (B) 8
    (C) $6\sqrt{2}$
    (D) 10
    (E) $6\sqrt{3}$

58. In the figure above is a triangular field. What is the minimum distance, in meters, that a person would have to walk to go from point $A$ to a point on side $BC$?

    (A) 60
    (B) 80
    (C) 100
    (D) 140
    (E) 180

59. If the ratio of $2a$ to $b$ is 8 times the ratio of $b$ to $a$, then $\dfrac{b}{a}$ could be

    (A) 4
    (B) 2
    (C) 1
    (D) $\dfrac{1}{2}$
    (E) $\dfrac{1}{4}$

60. A certain dentist earns $n$ dollars for each filling she puts in, plus $x$ dollars for every 15 minutes she works. If in a certain week she works 14 hours and puts in 21 fillings, how much does she earn for the week, in dollars?

    (A) $\dfrac{7}{2}x + 21n$
    (B) $7x + 14n$
    (C) $14x + 21n$
    (D) $56x + 21n$
    (E) $56x + \dfrac{21}{4}n$

## END OF SECTION

## SECTION THREE—ANALYTICAL
Time—60 minutes          50 questions

Directions: Each group of questions is based on a passage or a set of conditions. You may wish to draw a diagram to answer some of the questions. Choose the best answer for each question.

Questions 1–3

A spice farmer must harvest exactly five spices grown on her farm. The spices must be harvested consecutively, the harvest of one being completed before the harvest of the next begins. The five spices to be harvested are allspice, cloves, nutmeg, sage, and thyme.

Nutmeg must be harvested before thyme.
Cloves must be harvested immediately after allspice.
Sage must not be harvested first.

1.  Which of the following is an acceptable order for the harvesting of the five spices?

    (A) nutmeg, sage, allspice, cloves, thyme
    (B) sage, nutmeg, thyme, allspice, cloves
    (C) allspice, sage, thyme, cloves, nutmeg
    (D) cloves, nutmeg, allspice, sage, thyme
    (E) allspice, cloves, thyme, sage, nutmeg

2.  If nutmeg is the fourth spice harvested, which of the following must be false?

    (A) Allspice is the first spice harvested.
    (B) Sage is harvested immediately after cloves.
    (C) Exactly one crop is harvested between sage and thyme.
    (D) Nutmeg is harvested immediately after cloves.
    (E) Thyme is the last spice harvested.

3.  If sage is the second spice harvested, allspice must be which of the following?

    (A) the first or the third spice harvested
    (B) the first or the fourth spice harvested
    (C) the third or the fourth spice harvested
    (D) the third or the fifth spice harvested
    (E) the fourth or the fifth spice harvested

4.  If a judge is appointed for life, she will make courtroom decisions that reflect the accumulated wisdom inherent in this country's judicial history, relying upon the law and reason rather than upon trends in political thinking. If, on the other hand, the judge is appointed or elected for short terms in office, her decisions will be heavily influenced by the prevailing political climate. In sum, the outcome of many court cases will be determined by the method by which the presiding judge has been installed in her post.

    Which one of the following, if true, does NOT support the argument in the passage above?

    (A) Surveys indicate that judges enjoy their work and want to remain in office as long as possible.
    (B) Judges appointed for life are just as informed about political matters as are judges who are elected or appointed for short terms.
    (C) The rulings of judges who must run for re-election are generally approved of by the voters who live in their elective districts.
    (D) Most judges appointed for life hand down identical rulings on similar cases throughout their long careers.
    (E) Only judges who are elected or appointed for short terms of office employ pollsters to read the mood of the electorate.

5. There are those who claim that reductions in the spending on and deployment of weapons systems would result in a so-called "climate of peace," thereby diminishing the likelihood of armed conflict. The facts show otherwise. These self-proclaimed pacifists are either the victims or the propagators of a false argument.

Which of the following is an assumption underlying the conclusion of the passage above?

Ⓐ Military actions involving our forces can be instigated by any number of different factors.

Ⓑ Our buildup of weapons systems and combat personnel has prevented our adversaries from increasing their own spending on defense.

Ⓒ The increased defense spending of the past 10 years has lessened the need for significant military expenditure in future decades.

Ⓓ At the present time, state-of-the-art weapons systems and the augmentation of combat personnel are equally important to a nation's defense.

Ⓔ An established correlation between greater spending on weapons systems and a decreased incidence of conflict will persist.

6. Should present trends continue, within five years it will be cheaper for audio enthusiasts to build their stereo systems around sets of separate, high quality tuners and amplifiers, rather than around integrated tuners and amplifiers, known as receivers. While receivers have been considered the necessary compromise for those with budget restrictions, recent trends in retail pricing seem destined to change that perception. The average retail price of a high-quality tuner has declined at a rate of 20 percent each of the last two years, and the average retail price of a high-quality amplifier has declined at the rate of 35 percent for each of those years. At the same time, the average retail price of integrated receivers has declined only 12 percent.

In evaluating the claim made in the passage above, information about which of the following would be most useful?

Ⓐ the average life expectancy of stereo tuners as compared to the average life expectancy of stereo amplifiers

Ⓑ the number of integrated receivers sold each year and the number of sets of separate tuners and amplifiers sold each year

Ⓒ the present average retail price of an integrated receiver and the present average retail price of a tuner and amplifier set

Ⓓ the number of separate tuner and amplifier sets expected to be purchased over the next five years and the number of integrated receivers expected to be purchased over the next five years

Ⓔ the percentage of audio enthusiasts who prefer separate tuner and amplifier sets to integrated receivers

**GO ON TO THE NEXT PAGE**

## Questions 7–10

An editor must choose five articles to be published in the upcoming issue of an arts review. The only articles available for publication are theater articles *F*, *G*, *H*, and *J*, and dance articles *K*, *L*, *M*, and *O*.

At least three of the five published articles must be dance articles.

If *J* is chosen, then *M* cannot be.

If *F* is chosen, then *J* must also be chosen.

7. If *M* is not chosen for the issue, which of the following must be chosen?

   (A)  *F*
   (B)  *G*
   (C)  *H*
   (D)  *J*
   (E)  *K*

8. How many acceptable groupings of articles include *J*?

   (A)  one
   (B)  two
   (C)  three
   (D)  four
   (E)  five

9. The choice of which article makes only one group of articles acceptable?

   (A)  *F*
   (B)  *G*
   (C)  *J*
   (D)  *L*
   (E)  *M*

10. If *G* is chosen for the issue, which of the following must be true?

   (A)  *J* is not chosen.
   (B)  Exactly three dance articles are chosen.
   (C)  *H* is not chosen.
   (D)  All four of the dance articles are chosen.
   (E)  *F* is not chosen.

GO ON TO THE NEXT PAGE

## Questions 11–14

An obedience school is experimenting with a new training system. To test the system, three trainers (Luis, Molly, and Oprah) and three dogs (Lassie, Mugs, and Onyx) are assigned to three different rooms, one trainer, and one dog per room. The initial assignment is as follows:

Room 1: Luis and Lassie
Room 2: Molly and Mugs
Room 3: Oprah and Onyx

The participants have learned five different commands, each of which they will execute as soon as the command is given.

Command $W$ requires the trainer in Room 1 to move to Room 2, the trainer in Room 2 to move to Room 3, and the trainer in Room 3 to move to Room 1.

Command $X$ requires the dogs in Rooms 1 and 2 to change places.

Command $Y$ requires the dogs in Rooms 2 and 3 to change places.

Command $Z$ requires the dogs in Rooms 3 and 1 to change places.

Command $A$ requires each of the dogs to go to the room containing the trainer it was matched with in the initial assignment.

11. If the participants in the initial assignment are given exactly one command, Command $W$, which of the following will be true in the resulting arrangement?

 &#9398; Oprah and Mugs will be in the same room.
 &#9399; Molly will be in Room 3.
 &#9400; Molly and Lassie will be in the same room.
 &#9401; Luis will be in Room 3.
 &#9402; Luis and Onyx will be in the same room.

12. Which of the following commands or series of commands will yield a final arrangement in which Onyx is in Room 2?

 &#9398; One call of $W$
 &#9399; Two calls of $X$
 &#9400; Two calls of $W$ followed by one call of $A$
 &#9401; Two calls of $W$ followed by one call of $Z$
 &#9402; Two calls of $X$ followed by one call of $Z$

13. Which of the following sequences of commands will yield a final arrangement in which Oprah and Lassie are in Room 2?

 &#9398; $X, Y, W$
 &#9399; $X, W, W$
 &#9400; $Z, W, A$
 &#9401; $X, Y, A, W$
 &#9402; $Z, W, W, X$

14. Which of the following sequences of commands could result in a final arrangement in which Molly and Onyx are in Room 1, Oprah and Mugs are in Room 2, and Luis and Lassie are in Room 3?

 &#9398; $Z, W, X$
 &#9399; $W, Y, Z$
 &#9400; $W, A, Y, W$
 &#9401; $W, Z, W, X$
 &#9402; $X, Z, W, W$

GO ON TO THE NEXT PAGE

**KAPLAN**

## Questions 15–18

There are eight apartments in a two-story building, four on each floor. The top floor is called Level A, the bottom floor is Level B. The rooms on each level are numbered 1 through 4 in order from one end of the building to the other, such that the apartments on Level A are directly above the apartments with the same numbers on Level B. Exactly seven people—P, Q, R, S, T, V, and W—live in the building, one to an apartment. One of the apartments is empty.

W's apartment is directly above S's apartment.

S and Q live on different levels.

P's apartment is adjacent to T's apartment on the same level.

T's apartment is directly between two other apartments on the same level.

W's apartment is adjacent to the empty apartment on the same level.

15. Which of the following must be on Level B?

    Ⓐ  P's apartment
    Ⓑ  Q's apartment
    Ⓒ  R's apartment
    Ⓓ  V's apartment
    Ⓔ  the empty apartment

16. If W lives in Apartment 2 on Level A, which of the following must be true?

    Ⓐ  V lives in Apartment 1 on Level B.
    Ⓑ  The empty apartment is Apartment 3 on Level A.
    Ⓒ  R's apartment is on Level A.
    Ⓓ  P lives in Apartment 4 on Level A.
    Ⓔ  T lives in Apartment 3 on Level B.

17. If R lives in Apartment 3 on Level A, directly above P's apartment, in which apartment must V live?

    Ⓐ  Apartment 1 on Level A
    Ⓑ  Apartment 4 on Level A
    Ⓒ  Apartment 1 on Level B
    Ⓓ  Apartment 2 on Level B
    Ⓔ  Apartment 4 on Level B

18. If Q lives in Apartment 2 on Level A, directly above T's apartment, which of the following could possibly be Apartment 1 on Level A?

    Ⓐ  P's apartment
    Ⓑ  S's apartment
    Ⓒ  V's apartment
    Ⓓ  W's apartment
    Ⓔ  the empty apartment

GO ON TO THE NEXT PAGE

## Questions 19–22

Exactly seven people are present in the game room of a club. Three of those present—*F*, *G*, and *H*—are senior club members, two—*K* and *M*—are junior club members, and two—*P* and *R*—are club applicants. They decide that two of those present will play backgammon, two will play chess, and three will play dominoes.

Each person present can play only one of the three games.
There must be a senior club member playing each game.
*G* cannot play the same game that *R* plays.
*H* and *P* must play the same game.
*M* cannot play dominoes.

19. Which of the following is an acceptable grouping of people playing backgammon, chess, and dominoes, respectively?

    (A) *G, K*; *H, P*; *F, M, R*
    (B) *G, M*; *K, R*; *F, H, P*
    (C) *F, R*; *G, P*; *H, K, M*
    (D) *H, P*; *G, M*; *F, K, R*
    (E) *F, M*; *H, P*; *G, K, R*

20. If *K* and *R* play the same game, which of the following must be true?

    (A) *H* plays dominoes.
    (B) *P* plays chess.
    (C) *G* plays backgammon.
    (D) *F* plays dominoes.
    (E) *M* plays backgammon.

21. If *R* plays backgammon, how many different groupings of people and games are possible?

    (A) one
    (B) two
    (C) three
    (D) four
    (E) six

22. Which of the following pairs CANNOT play the same game?

    (A) *H* and *R*
    (B) *K* and *M*
    (C) *F* and *M*
    (D) *G* and *M*
    (E) *P* and *R*

**GO ON TO THE NEXT PAGE**

23. European nations are starting to decrease the percentage of their foreign aid that is "tied"—that is, given only on the condition that it be spent to obtain goods and materials produced by the country from which the aid originates. By doing so, European nations hope to avoid the ethical criticism that has been recently leveled at some foreign aid donors, notably Japan.

Which of the following can most reasonably be inferred from the passage?

(A) Many non-European nations give foreign aid solely for the purpose of benefiting their domestic economies.

(B) Only ethical considerations, and not those of self-interest, should be considered when foreign aid decisions are made.

(C) Many of the problems faced by underdeveloped countries could be eliminated if a smaller percentage of the foreign aid they obtain were "tied" to specific purchases and uses.

(D) Much of Japan's foreign aid returns to Japan in the form of purchase orders for Japanese products and equipment.

(E) Non-European nations are unwilling to offer foreign aid that is not "tied" to the purchase of their own manufactures.

24. Our environment can stand only so much more "progress." We must take a few steps backward and accept some inconvenience if we want to secure the health and well-being of our planet. This is not merely a matter of using manual mowers instead of power mowers, or foregoing a few outdoor barbecues. Something must be done about the 51.1 percent of total ozone that is contributed by vehicles and fuel. The percentage must be cut regardless of the cost or inconvenience. Such concerns are irrelevant here; what needs to be done must be done.

The author of the passage above makes which of the following arguments?

(A) People will have to go back to living as they did a century ago if they want to save the environment.

(B) If people would be willing to drive their cars less, pollution would be drastically reduced.

(C) People can continue to use power lawn mowers and have barbecues as long as industry cuts down on its use of fuel.

(D) People must accept drastic and costly measures as they are necessary to save the environment.

(E) Lack of concern for the environment leads people to continue their overuse of the automobile.

**GO ON TO THE NEXT PAGE**

25. If you stop in the movie studio's commissary during lunch time, you may be able to meet the actors. Although the actors always eat elsewhere on workdays when the commissary does not serve fish, they always eat there on workdays when the commissary does serve fish.

If all the statements above are true, and it is true that the actors are eating in the commissary, which of the following must also be true?

Ⓐ It is not a workday, or the commissary is serving fish, or both.

Ⓑ It is a workday, or the commissary is serving fish, or both.

Ⓒ It is not a workday and the commissary is not serving fish.

Ⓓ It is not a workday and the commissary is serving fish.

Ⓔ It is a workday and the commissary is serving fish.

Questions 26–29

A new kind of lock is opened by pushing symbols in sequence on a keyboard. The sequence is called a combination. All acceptable combinations must consist of exactly five symbols—four letters and one single-digit number. Acceptable combinations must also conform to the following rules:

The number must be either the second or third symbol in the combination.

The fourth and fifth symbols in the combination must not be the same.

If the third symbol is a number, then the fifth must be either B or D.

If the third symbol is a letter, then there must be no Fs or Gs in the combination.

The first symbol must be a letter closer to the beginning of the alphabet than any other symbol in the combination.

26. Which of the following sequences of symbols is an acceptable combination?

Ⓐ E, R, 2, K, B

Ⓑ F, 6, T, T, Y

Ⓒ B, W, 4, G, G

Ⓓ C, 7, M, Q, D

Ⓔ A, X, L, 3, P

GO ON TO THE NEXT PAGE

27. Which of the following could possibly be the first symbol in an acceptable sequence?

Ⓐ F
Ⓑ 7
Ⓒ Y
Ⓓ 3
Ⓔ E

28. A combination whose first symbol is B and whose fourth symbol is G could have which of the following as its second, third, and fifth symbols, respectively?

Ⓐ J, 6, D
Ⓑ A, 9, T
Ⓒ 9, Z, X
Ⓓ 3, H, G
Ⓔ M, 4, S

29. The combination C, Q, 8, P, F can be made acceptable by doing which of the following?

Ⓐ replacing the F with a B
Ⓑ reversing the C and the P
Ⓒ reversing the Q and the 8
Ⓓ replacing the F with a D
Ⓔ replacing the C with an A

30. Some scientists argue that if fish are as common in unfished areas of the oceans as they are in the areas we now fish, current estimates of the amount of protein that our planet supports are far too low. Thus, even if Earth's population continues to grow at its present rate, we can ensure the availability of protein for even the poorest of countries over the next two decades.

Which of the following, if true, would most weaken the argument above?

Ⓐ Some scientists believe that the unfished areas of the ocean support substantially fewer fish per cubic kilometer than do the areas currently fished.
Ⓑ The technology needed to fish new areas of the oceans is more expensive than that now used in ocean fishing.
Ⓒ Increasing the supply of other sources of protein, such as beef and poultry, would be less expensive than fishing new parts of the oceans.
Ⓓ The rate of increase of Earth's population will slowly decline over the next two decades.
Ⓔ It will take at least 30 years to develop the technology necessary for fishing the unfished areas of the ocean.

GO ON TO THE NEXT PAGE

31. Travelers may enter and remain in the Republic for up to 59 days. If a traveler is to stay for more than seven days, however, a special visa is required.

If the statements above are true, which of the following must also be true?

Ⓐ A traveler who is staying in the Republic for 14 days must have a special visa.

Ⓑ Many travelers who stay in the Republic do not need visas.

Ⓒ Some travelers who stay in the Republic for more than seven days do not have the appropriate visas.

Ⓓ Travelers who stay less than seven days in the Republic do not need visas.

Ⓔ Travelers who merely pass through the Republic while en route to other destinations do not need visas.

32. Despite a steady stream of pessimistic forecasts, our economy continues to grow and prosper. Over the last 15 years the service sector of our economy has greatly expanded. Last year alone, 500,000 Americans found employment in the service sector. In the face of evidence such as this, one cannot argue that our economy is wilting.

Which of the following, if true, would most seriously undermine the conclusion drawn above?

Ⓐ Many Americans who took jobs in the service sector last year were also offered jobs in other sectors of the economy.

Ⓑ Most of the job growth in the service sector can be attributed to people forced out of the declining manufacturing sector.

Ⓒ American society has developed many programs that greatly offset the consequences of a sluggish economy.

Ⓓ Forty years ago the American economy experienced a period of prosperity far greater than that of today.

Ⓔ The importance of the service sector in determining the well-being of the overall American economy has decreased somewhat in the past ten years.

**GO ON TO THE NEXT PAGE**

## Questions 33–37

There are three bells in a clock tower. One of the bells produces a low-pitched ring, one produces a medium-pitched ring, and one produces a high-pitched ring. The bell ringer must decide on a sequence of eight rings to play on special occasions. He decides that, for the sequence, the low bell must be rung exactly three times, the medium bell must be rung exactly three times, and the high bell must be rung exactly twice. The bell ringer's choice of sequence is further limited by the following rules:

The sixth ring must be that of the medium bell.
The low bell must not be rung twice in succession.
The high bell must be rung twice in succession.

33. Which of the following is an acceptable eight-ring sequence?

   Ⓐ medium, low, high, low, high, medium, low, medium
   Ⓑ low, high, high, low, medium, medium, low, medium
   Ⓒ medium, low, high, high, medium, low, medium, low
   Ⓓ medium, high, high, low, low, medium, low, medium
   Ⓔ low, medium, low, low, medium, medium, high, high

34. If the high bell is rung fifth in the sequence, all of the following must be true EXCEPT:

   Ⓐ The low bell is rung first.
   Ⓑ The medium bell is rung second.
   Ⓒ The low bell is rung third.
   Ⓓ The high bell is rung fourth.
   Ⓔ The low bell is rung seventh.

35. If the medium bell is rung fourth, the high bell CANNOT be rung

   Ⓐ first
   Ⓑ second
   Ⓒ third
   Ⓓ fifth
   Ⓔ eighth

36. Which of the following CANNOT be the order of bells rung third, fourth, and fifth, respectively?

   Ⓐ high, medium, low
   Ⓑ low, medium, low
   Ⓒ high, high, low
   Ⓓ high, medium, medium
   Ⓔ high, low, medium

37. Which of the following is IMPOSSIBLE?

   Ⓐ The high bell is rung first.
   Ⓑ The low bell is rung second.
   Ⓒ The medium bell is rung third.
   Ⓓ The high bell is rung fourth.
   Ⓔ The low bell is rung fifth.

## Questions 38–42

A large corporation has branches in the following six cities—Atlanta, Beijing, Caracas, Dakar, Edinburgh, and Fresno. Memos of two types, Priority 1 and Priority 2, are sent from the head office to the branches.

Priority 1 memos are sent directly from the head office to either Atlanta or Dakar.

Priority 2 memos are sent directly from the head office to either Atlanta or Beijing.

Any branch that receives a memo directly from the head office must pass it on to at least one other branch. That other branch can pass it on to yet another branch, though it is not required to do so. The passing of memos from branch to branch must conform to the following rules:

Atlanta can send memos of either type to Caracas only.

Beijing can send Priority 1 memos to Edinburgh only and Priority 2 memos to Fresno only.

Caracas can send memos of either type to either Beijing or Dakar.

Dakar can send Priority 1 memos to Caracas only and Priority 2 memos to Edinburgh only.

Edinburgh can send memos of either type to either Fresno or Atlanta.

Fresno cannot send memos to any other branches.

38. A memo that is sent from the home office to Atlanta must be sent on to which of the following?

     (A) Beijing
     (B) Caracas
     (C) Dakar
     (D) Edinburgh
     (E) Fresno

39. A memo that is sent from Edinburgh to Fresno could NOT be which of the following?

     (A) A Priority 1 memo that was initially sent to Atlanta
     (B) A Priority 1 memo that was sent to Edinburgh from Beijing
     (C) A Priority 1 memo that was initially sent to Dakar
     (D) A Priority 2 memo that was sent to Edinburgh from Dakar
     (E) A Priority 2 memo that was initially sent to Beijing

GO ON TO THE NEXT PAGE

**KAPLAN**

40. A Priority 2 memo that was not originally sent to Atlanta could have been seen by a maximum of how many branches?

   (A) two
   (B) three
   (C) four
   (D) five
   (E) six

41. A memo that reaches Edinburgh without having passed through Atlanta must have been seen in a minimum of how many branches besides Edinburgh?

   (A) one
   (B) two
   (C) three
   (D) four
   (E) five

42. Which of the following cannot be the complete progress of a memo from the head office?

   (A) Atlanta to Caracas to Beijing
   (B) Atlanta to Caracas to Beijing to Edinburgh
   (C) Atlanta to Caracas to Dakar to Edinburgh
   (D) Beijing to Edinburgh to Fresno
   (E) Dakar to Caracas to Beijing

## Questions 43–47

An athlete has six trophies to place on an empty three-shelf display case. The six trophies are bowling trophies *F*, *G*, and *H* and tennis trophies *J*, *K*, and *L*. The three shelves of the display case are labeled 1 to 3 from top to bottom. Any of the shelves can remain empty. The athlete's placement of trophies must conform to the following conditions:

> *J* and *L* cannot be on the same shelf.
> *F* must be on the shelf immediately above the shelf that *L* is on.
> No single shelf can hold all three bowling trophies.
> *K* cannot be on Shelf 2.

43. If *G* and *H* are on Shelf 2, which of the following must be true?

   (A) *K* is on Shelf 1.
   (B) *L* is on Shelf 2.
   (C) *J* is on Shelf 3.
   (D) *G* and *J* are on the same shelf.
   (E) *F* and *K* are on the same shelf.

44. If no tennis trophies are on Shelf 3, which pair of trophies must be on the same shelf?

   (A) *F* and *G*
   (B) *L* and *H*
   (C) *L* and *G*
   (D) *K* and *J*
   (E) *G* and *H*

45. If *J* is on Shelf 2, which of the following must also be on Shelf 2?

   (A) *K*
   (B) *G*
   (C) *F*
   (D) *L*
   (E) *H*

46. If Shelf 1 remains empty, which of the following must be FALSE?

   (A) *H* and *F* are on the same shelf.
   (B) There are exactly three trophies on Shelf 2.
   (C) *G* and *H* are on the same shelf.
   (D) There are exactly two trophies on Shelf 3.
   (E) *G* and *K* are on the same shelf.

47. If *L* and *G* are on the same shelf, and if one of the shelves remains empty, which of the following must be true?

   (A) If *H* is on Shelf 3, then *J* is on Shelf 2.
   (B) *K* and *L* are on the same shelf.
   (C) If *H* is on Shelf 2, then *J* is on Shelf 3.
   (D) *F* and *K* are on the same shelf.
   (E) If *J* is on Shelf 2, then *H* is on Shelf 1.

48. Painting wood furniture requires less time than does finishing the furniture with a stain and polyurethane. On the other hand, a finish of stain and polyurethane lasts much longer than does paint. Yet one further fact in favor of paint is that it costs significantly less than does stain and polyurethane. Therefore, if reducing work time and saving money are more important to people, they will paint their wood furniture rather than finish it with stain and polyurethane.

The argument in the passage above makes which of the following assumptions?

   (A) It is better to paint wood furniture than it is to stain and polyurethane it.
   (B) Most people consider reducing work time and saving money to be more important than the longevity of a finish.
   (C) Most people prefer to paint or to stain and polyurethane wood furniture, rather than to leave the wood unfinished.
   (D) Work time, cost, and longevity are equally important factors in deciding whether to paint wood furniture or stain and polyurethane it.
   (E) Work time, cost, and longevity are the only important differences between painting wood furniture and finishing it with stain and polyurethane.

GO ON TO THE NEXT PAGE

49. Young Cowonga lion cubs in the wild often engage in aggressive play with their siblings. This activity is instigated by the cubs' mother. Cowonga lion cubs born in captivity, however, never engage in this aggressive play. Some zoologists have concluded that this particular form of play teaches the young lions the skills needed for successful hunting in the wild, and that such play is not instigated in captivity because the development of hunting skills is unnecessary in such an environment.

The zoologists' conclusion would be most strengthened if it could be demonstrated that

Ⓐ all Cowonga lion cubs raised in the wild are capable of hunting successfully

Ⓑ other predatory animals also engage in aggressive play at a young age

Ⓒ no Cowonga lion cub that has been raised in captivity is able to hunt successfully in the wild

Ⓓ the skills used in aggressive play are similar to the skills necessary for successful hunting

Ⓔ female lions that were raised in captivity will not instigate aggressive play among their offspring

50. According to a recent school survey, the number of students who regularly attend religious services on campus has increased 50 percent from the figure 10 years ago. It must be an increased religiosity at our college that has massively reduced incidences of cheating on exams during this period.

Which of the following, if true, most significantly weakens the inference above?

Ⓐ Most of the students who now attend campus services do so only for social reasons.

Ⓑ Campus chaplains have time and again spoken about the importance of academic honesty.

Ⓒ Fifteen years ago, the college switched from an honor system to faculty-proctored exams.

Ⓓ Not all students responded to the survey.

Ⓔ Cheating was never a major problem at this school.

# END OF SECTION

# Practice Test
# Answers And
# Explanations

# Practice Test Answer Key

## VERBAL

| | | | | | |
|---|---|---|---|---|---|
| 1. A | 14. A | 27. B | 40. B | 53. E | 66. A |
| 2. E | 15. E | 28. C | 41. D | 54. C | 67. B |
| 3. E | 16. B | 29. B | 42. D | 55. E | 68. A |
| 4. A | 17. D | 30. C | 43. A | 56. C | 69. C |
| 5. D | 18. B | 31. A | 44. D | 57. C | 70. E |
| 6. E | 19. E | 32. D | 45. C | 58. E | 71. C |
| 7. D | 20. C | 33. D | 46. E | 59. A | 72. A |
| 8. A | 21. E | 34. C | 47. D | 60. D | 73. A |
| 9. B | 22. B | 35. D | 48. D | 61. B | 74. B |
| 10. B | 23. C | 36. B | 49. C | 62. C | 75. C |
| 11. D | 24. C | 37. C | 50. C | 63. D | 76. C |
| 12. E | 25. A | 38. B | 51. B | 64. A | |
| 13. A | 26. C | 39. E | 52. D | 65. D | |

## QUANTITATIVE

| | | | | | |
|---|---|---|---|---|---|
| 1. A | 11. D | 21. E | 31. A | 41. C | 51. C |
| 2. C | 12. C | 22. D | 32. B | 42. B | 52. C |
| 3. A | 13. B | 23. C | 33. D | 43. D | 53. D |
| 4. B | 14. A | 24. E | 34. C | 44. A | 54. D |
| 5. D | 15. D | 25. B | 35. A | 45. B | 55. A |
| 6. B | 16. B | 26. B | 36. A | 46. E | 56. E |
| 7. D | 17. D | 27. C | 37. D | 47. D | 57. B |
| 8. B | 18. B | 28. A | 38. B | 48. E | 58. A |
| 9. A | 19. E | 29. C | 39. B | 49. B | 59. D |
| 10. C | 20. D | 30. D | 40. B | 50. E | 60. D |

## ANALYTICAL

| | | | | | |
|---|---|---|---|---|---|
| 1. A | 10. E | 19. D | 28. A | 37. C | 46. D |
| 2. D | 11. B | 20. D | 29. D | 38. B | 47. A |
| 3. C | 12. C | 21. A | 30. E | 39. E | 48. E |
| 4. B | 13. B | 22. B | 31. A | 40. A | 49. C |
| 5. E | 14. C | 23. D | 32. B | 41. C | 50. A |
| 6. C | 15. A | 24. D | 33. B | 42. D | |
| 7. E | 16. E | 25. A | 34. E | 43. B | |
| 8. C | 17. E | 26. D | 35. D | 44. D | |
| 9. A | 18. C | 27. E | 36. D | 45. C | |

# Calculate Your Score

## Step 1

Add together your total number correct for each section: Verbal, Quantitative, and Analytical.
This is your raw score for each measure.

**Verbal**

": 420
38th perc.

Total Correct   $\boxed{38}$   (raw score)

**Quantitative**

600
66th perc.

Total Correct   $\boxed{46}$   (raw score)

**Analytical**

Total Correct   $\boxed{\phantom{00}}$   (raw score)

# Step 2

Find your raw score on the table below and read across to find your scaled score and your percentile.

## Verbal

| Raw Score | Scaled Score | Percentile Rank | Raw Score | Scaled Score | Percentile Rank |
|---|---|---|---|---|---|
| 0 | 200 | 1 | 39 | 420 | 41 |
| 1 | 200 | 1 | 40 | 420 | 41 |
| 2 | 200 | 1 | 41 | 430 | 44 |
| 3 | 200 | 1 | 42 | 440 | 48 |
| 4 | 200 | 1 | 43 | 450 | 51 |
| 5 | 200 | 1 | 44 | 460 | 54 |
| 6 | 200 | 1 | 45 | 470 | 56 |
| 7 | 200 | 1 | 46 | 470 | 59 |
| 8 | 200 | 1 | 47 | 480 | 61 |
| 9 | 200 | 1 | 48 | 490 | 67 |
| 10 | 200 | 1 | 49 | 510 | 69 |
| 11 | 200 | 1 | 50 | 520 | 72 |
| 12 | 200 | 1 | 51 | 530 | 74 |
| 13 | 220 | 1 | 52 | 530 | 76 |
| 14 | 230 | 1 | 53 | 540 | 78 |
| 15 | 240 | 1 | 54 | 550 | 80 |
| 16 | 250 | 1 | 55 | 560 | 82 |
| 17 | 260 | 1 | 56 | 570 | 84 |
| 18 | 270 | 2 | 57 | 580 | 85 |
| 19 | 270 | 3 | 58 | 590 | 87 |
| 20 | 280 | 4 | 59 | 590 | 89 |
| 21 | 290 | 5 | 60 | 600 | 90 |
| 22 | 300 | 6 | 61 | 610 | 92 |
| 23 | 310 | 7 | 62 | 620 | 93 |
| 24 | 320 | 9 | 63 | 630 | 94 |
| 25 | 320 | 10 | 64 | 640 | 95 |
| 26 | 330 | 12 | 65 | 650 | 95 |
| 27 | 330 | 14 | 66 | 660 | 96 |
| 28 | 340 | 16 | 67 | 670 | 97 |
| 29 | 350 | 16 | 68 | 680 | 98 |
| 30 | 360 | 20 | 69 | 690 | 98 |
| 31 | 360 | 22 | 70 | 700 | 99 |
| 32 | 360 | 24 | 71 | 710 | 99 |
| 33 | 370 | 24 | 72 | 720 | 99 |
| 34 | 380 | 26 | 73 | 740 | 99 |
| 35 | 390 | 30 | 74 | 760 | 99 |
| 36 | 400 | 33 | 75 | 780 | 99 |
| 37 | 410 | 36 | 76 | 800 | 99 |
| 38 | 420 | 38 | | | |

## Quantitative

| Raw Score | Scaled Score | Percentile Rank | Raw Score | Scaled Score | Percentile Rank |
|---|---|---|---|---|---|
| 0 | 200 | 1 | 31 | 430 | 24 |
| 1 | 200 | 1 | 32 | 440 | 26 |
| 2 | 200 | 1 | 33 | 460 | 28 |
| 3 | 200 | 1 | 34 | 470 | 32 |
| 4 | 200 | 1 | 35 | 480 | 35 |
| 5 | 200 | 1 | 36 | 490 | 37 |
| 6 | 200 | 1 | 37 | 500 | 40 |
| 7 | 200 | 1 | 38 | 510 | 42 |
| 8 | 200 | 1 | 39 | 520 | 45 |
| 9 | 200 | 1 | 40 | 530 | 48 |
| 10 | 210 | 1 | 41 | 540 | 49 |
| 11 | 220 | 1 | 42 | 540 | 51 |
| 12 | 240 | 1 | 43 | 560 | 57 |
| 13 | 260 | 1 | 44 | 570 | 59 |
| 14 | 270 | 1 | 45 | 580 | 61 |
| 15 | 280 | 2 | 46 | 600 | 66 |
| 16 | 290 | 2 | 47 | 610 | 68 |
| 17 | 300 | 3 | 48 | 630 | 72 |
| 18 | 310 | 4 | 49 | 640 | 74 |
| 19 | 310 | 5 | 50 | 660 | 78 |
| 20 | 320 | 5 | 51 | 670 | 80 |
| 21 | 330 | 6 | 52 | 690 | 84 |
| 22 | 340 | 7 | 53 | 690 | 86 |
| 23 | 360 | 9 | 54 | 700 | 89 |
| 24 | 370 | 10 | 55 | 720 | 92 |
| 25 | 380 | 13 | 56 | 730 | 94 |
| 26 | 390 | 14 | 57 | 750 | 97 |
| 27 | 400 | 16 | 58 | 770 | 97 |
| 28 | 410 | 18 | 59 | 780 | 97 |
| 29 | 420 | 20 | 60 | 800 | 97 |
| 30 | 420 | 22 | | | |

## Analytical

| Raw Score | Scaled Score | Percentile Rank | Raw Score | Scaled Score | Percentile Rank |
|-----------|--------------|-----------------|-----------|--------------|-----------------|
| 0 | 200 | 1 | 26 | 530 | 38 |
| 1 | 210 | 1 | 27 | 550 | 40 |
| 2 | 230 | 1 | 28 | 560 | 46 |
| 3 | 230 | 1 | 29 | 580 | 49 |
| 4 | 250 | 1 | 30 | 580 | 55 |
| 5 | 260 | 1 | 31 | 590 | 58 |
| 6 | 280 | 1 | 32 | 600 | 64 |
| 7 | 300 | 1 | 33 | 620 | 67 |
| 8 | 310 | 1 | 34 | 640 | 72 |
| 9 | 330 | 1 | 35 | 650 | 74 |
| 10 | 330 | 1 | 36 | 660 | 76 |
| 11 | 340 | 1 | 37 | 670 | 81 |
| 12 | 360 | 2 | 38 | 680 | 85 |
| 13 | 370 | 3 | 39 | 690 | 87 |
| 14 | 390 | 4 | 40 | 700 | 88 |
| 15 | 400 | 6 | 41 | 710 | 91 |
| 16 | 420 | 7 | 42 | 720 | 92 |
| 17 | 420 | 10 | 43 | 730 | 95 |
| 18 | 430 | 12 | 44 | 740 | 96 |
| 19 | 450 | 15 | 45 | 750 | 97 |
| 20 | 460 | 17 | 46 | 760 | 98 |
| 21 | 470 | 20 | 47 | 770 | 99 |
| 22 | 490 | 23 | 48 | 780 | 99 |
| 23 | 500 | 27 | 49 | 790 | 99 |
| 24 | 500 | 31 | 50 | 800 | 99 |
| 25 | 520 | 35 | | | |

# Section One Explanations–Verbal

**1** **(A)** We're told that the fundamental (blank) between cats and dogs is a myth, that the species actually coexist quite (blankly). We need a contrast, and we find it in (A)—*antipathy* means aversion or dislike, and *amiably* means agreeably.

In (B), if the members of the species coexisted "uneasily," their "disharmony" wouldn't be a myth. In (C), both *compatibility* and *together* imply that dogs and cats are good friends. In (D), it doesn't make sense to say that the "relationship" between dogs and cats is a myth. In (E), no one could claim that there's no "difference" between dogs and cats.

**2** **(E)** The clue is the signal *rather than*: We need a contrast between what the speaker intended and what he achieved. The word *monotonous* clues you into boredom, and *bore* in (E), followed by *convince* makes the contrast we need. In (A), *enlighten* and *inform* are similar. *Interest* and *persuade,* (B), don't show contrast. In (C), *provoke* and *influence* don't express a contrast. *Allay* in (D) means to relieve, which is similar to *pacify,* which means to calm or to make peace. No contrast here, and again, it's (E) for this question.

**3** **(E)** The blank is part of a cause-and-effect structure as the keyword *that* indicates. Because government restrictions are so something, businesses can operate with nearly complete impunity. There's an absence of restrictions, so we need a word that cancels out restrictions. Would a "traditional" restriction, (A), be canceled out? No. (B), *judicious,* means wise or having sound judgment, but a wise restriction would probably be effective. In (C), *ambiguous* means unclear, but though ambiguity might interfere with the effectiveness of restrictions, it doesn't cancel them out. (D), *exacting,* means very strict, which is the opposite of what we want. (E), *lax,* means loose, careless, or sloppy. This describes restrictions that aren't very strict, and it's correct for this question.

**4** **(A)** The first blank describes a book—the recent Oxford edition of the works of Shakespeare is (blank). The word *because* tells us that what follows is an explanation of why this book is whatever it is. The "not only but also" structure tells us that there are *two* reasons why: it departs from the readings of other editions, and it challenges basic (blanks) of textual criticism. In (A), we could say that challenging conventions could make a book "controversial." Conventions are accepted practices, so challenging conventions would make a book controversial. What else have we got? (B) gives us the book is typical because it challenges innovations. *Typical* doesn't fit in with *departs from other editions.* How about (C)? Challenging norms, which are rules or patterns, wouldn't make something "inadequate." (D)—a book that is different might be called curious, but could you call a book curious for challenging projects? Finally, (E) says the book is pretentious because it challenges explanations—no good. So the best answer is (A).

**5** **(D)** We learn that an early form of writing, Linear B, was (blank) in 1952. The keyword *but* tells us that Linear A, an older form, met with a contrasting fate, so we'll look for a pair of contrasting words. The words *no one has yet succeeded in* precede the second blank, so instead of a word that is contrasted with the first blank, we need a word that means about the same thing. That leads us to pick (D)—the words *deciphered* and *interpretation* are similar since both imply understanding.

The word *superseded* in (A) means replaced by something more up to date—not giving an explanation of something. (B)—in the context of ancient languages, a *transcription* would probably be a decoded version of something. That would be the opposite of *encoding* something. (C)'s *obliterated* and *analysis* imply a contrast—wiping something out is different from figuring it out. In (E) *discovered* and *obfuscation* are more at odds than they are alike. Obfuscation means confusion, while a discovery usually sheds light on a situation.

**6** **(E)** The clue here is the structure "quite normal and even (blank)"—the missing word has a more positive meaning than the word *normal*. Then we get, "I was therefore surprised," which tips us off to look for contrast. *Commendable* and *complimentary* in (A) are both positive. In (B), *odious* means hateful, so *odious* and *insulting* are both negative. *Conciliatory* in (C) means placating or reconciling, which fits in with *apologetic*. *Commonplace* and *typical* in (D) mean the same thing. Only correct choice (E) is left—*laudable* means praiseworthy while *derogatory* means belittling or detracting.

**7** **(D)** Whatever we're doing to the burden of medical costs is causing the removal of the second blank, signaled by *thereby*. In (A), it doesn't make sense to say that to *augment* or add to the burden would remove a problem—it could make the problem worse. In (B), a *perquisite* is a reward over and above one's salary. But would eliminating a burden remove a perquisite? In (C), to *ameliorate* means to improve, but you can't talk about removing a major study of medical care. (D) is perfect. To *assuage* means to make less severe and an *impediment* is an obstacle. Assuaging the burden would remove an impediment to medical care, so (D)'s correct. As for (E), to *clarify* means to explain or make clear, and explaining the burden of medical costs wouldn't remove an explanation.

**8** **(A)** A *novel* is a type of *book*. That's an easy bridge. In (A), is an *epic* a type of *poem*? Yes, an epic is a long narrative poem, so (A) is right. In (B), a *house* isn't a type of *library*. (C) is tempting—*tales* and *fables* are related—but a fable is a kind of tale, not vice versa, so it's not parallel. In (D), a *number* is not a type of *page*, and in (E), a *play* isn't a type of *theater*.

**9** **(B)** *Ravenous* means extremely *hungry*—the second word is an extreme version of the first word. In (A), *desirous* means desiring or wanting something—it's not an extreme form of *thirsty*. (B) is perfect—*titanic* is an amplification of *large*. *Titanic*

means gigantic, so (B) is the answer.

*Eminent* and *famous* in (C) mean the same thing. (D)'s *disoriented* and *dizzy* are close in meaning. To be disoriented means to have lost your bearings, and when you're dizzy, you feel as if you're going to fall down. (E)'s *obese* and *gluttonous* could be related, but don't have to be. *Gluttonous* comes from *gluttony*—it means excessive eating or drinking. Gluttony doesn't have to result in obesity and it's not an extreme form of it.

**10** **(B)** A *bouquet* is an arrangement of *flowers*, so the first word will be an arrangement of the second word. In (A), a *humidor* is a container for *tobacco*—a container for tobacco is not the same as a formal arrangement of it. The next choice, (B), is more like it. A *mosaic* is made of *tiles*, just as a bouquet is made up of flowers. That's a good match. In (C), a *tapestry* is not made of *color*, it's made of threads woven to make a design. You can't argue that a tapestry is an arrangement of colors. (D) also has problems. A *pile* of *blocks* could be an arrangement. But a bouquet isn't just a group of flowers—it's a formal arrangement. In the same way, a mosaic is an orderly arrangement of tiles. A pile isn't a formal arrangement. What about *sacristy* and *vestment* in (E)? A sacristy is a room in a church where priests' clothes or vestments are kept, so vestments are stored in a sacristy. The correct answer is (B).

**11** **(D)** *Quixotic* means impractical, after the hero of *Don Quixote*. A *realist* is a person who is especially realistic. *Realistic* is the opposite of *quixotic,* so a realist is never quixotic. In (A), *pedantic* people show off their learning. Many scholars are pedantic, so this won't work. In (B), a *fool* is foolish—a synonym for *idiotic*. The same relationship holds true for (C)—an *idler* is a *lethargic* person. (D) looks good—a *tormentor* is vicious or cruel. The opposite sort of person would be kinder and more *sympathetic*—a tormentor is never sympathetic. (E) *dyspeptic* means suffering from indigestion. A *diner* is someone who eats—some diners get dyspeptic, some don't, so (D)'s correct.

**12** **(E)** A *shard* is a broken fragment of *glass* or crockery. Glass, when it shatters, creates shards, so a shard is a piece of broken glass. (E) shows the same analogy—a *splinter* is a piece of broken *wood*. As for the wrong choices, in (A), a *grain* is the basic unit that *sand* comes in, but you can't talk about breaking sand. (B)'s *morsel* means a bit of food, but a *meal* doesn't shatter into morsels. In (C), a *rope* is composed of *strands,* and in (D), a *quilt* is made from *scraps.* The correct answer is (E).

**13** **(A)** The word *filter* is used as a verb. When you use a filter, an *impurity* is removed, so you *filter* to remove an *impurity.* The word *expurgate* in (A) means to censor, to remove *obscenities*—you *expurgate* to remove an *obscenity.* To *whitewash,* (B), is to misrepresent a bad thing to make it look better. An *infraction* isn't removed by *whitewashing* it, it's only covered up, so (B) isn't parallel. In (C), *perjury* is the crime of lying under oath. To *testify* doesn't mean to remove a false statement. In (D), *penance* is something you do to atone for a sin, but you don't *perform* to remove *penance.* And in (E), you don't *vacuum* to remove a *carpet.* So (A) is correct.

**14** **(A)** *Paraphrase* means restatement of a text using different words. *Verbatim* means word for word or exact. A paraphrase is not verbatim—the words are near opposites. The only choices opposite in meaning are *approximation* and *precise,* in (A). An approximation is an estimate, while something that's precise is exact, so an approximation is not precise. A description might or might not be vivid in (B). In (C), *apt* means appropriate, so a quotation could be apt. There's no relationship in (D), *interpretation* and *valid,* or in (E), *significance* and *uncertain.* (A) is correct.

**15** **(E)** Even if you didn't know what *oncology* means, you might have guessed the study of something because of the *ology* ending, and judging from the other word it's probably the study of tumors. The choices look like sciences too. (A)'s pairing of *chronology* and *time* looks okay, but not dead on. There's a science called chronology, the science of arranging time into periods. Chronology is not exactly the study of time—it's a science involved with mapping events in time. Likewise, (B) is almost there. The *theo* in *theology* comes from the Greek word for god, and *theology* means the study of gods or religious beliefs. *Tenet,* on the other hand, means a particular belief or principle. It's too narrow to say theology is the study of tenets. We can eliminate (C) because *aural* is not the study of sound—that would be closer to *acoustics.* In (D), *philology* is a field that includes the study of literary history, language history, and systems of writing, not the study of religion. *Taxonomy,* (E), is the study of *classification,* the correct answer. *Taxonomy* is also used to refer specifically to the classification of organisms.

**16** **(B)** *Intransigent* means unyielding—the opposite of *flexible.* Our bridge is "a person who is intransigent is lacking in flexibility." The only pair that looks good is (B), *disinterested* and *partisanship.* One who's disinterested is unbiased—he doesn't have an interest in either side of a dispute. *Partisan* means partial to a particular party or cause. That's the opposite of disinterested. So partisanship, the quality of being biased, is lacking in a person who could be described as disinterested.

In (A), *transient* means transitory, so you wouldn't say that someone transient lacks *mobility.* In (C), *dissimilar* means not similar, along the same lines as *variation.* You can't say that something progressive lacks transition, so (D) is no good. The word *ineluctable* in (E) means inescapable, while *modality* is a longer way of saying mode.

## Reading Passage: Questions 17–23

The longer of the two reading comp passages appears first. The author's main concern, the aim of science to derive a theory which describes particles and their forces as simply as possible, becomes apparent early in the first paragraph. Simplicity is so important that the author sets it up as a criterion for judging the specific theory of nature. Then the author outlines a recently developed theory which he considers to be a remarkable achievement for its frugality and level of detail. He then asserts that an even simpler theory is conceivable and goes on to mention one that promises at least a partial unification of elementary particles and forces. The last half of the second paragraph and the final paragraph describe this theory in greater detail.

**17** **(D)** We need either a choice that describes the similarity between the theories, or one that falsifies information about them. (D) should raise your suspicions. The author acknowledged at the end of the first paragraph that the first theory could account for the entire observed hierarchy of material structure. (D) is right, but let's look at the others.

(A) is a valid difference between the two theories—the second is presented as a simpler alternative to the first. (B) is also a real difference. The first theory encompass gravitation and the second unifies three of the four forces, which makes it a better theory, but it doesn't account for gravitation. The first theory includes leptons and quarks, while the second combines these two classes into just one, so (C) is valid. In a similar way, the second theory unifies three of the four forces outlined in the first theory, so (E) is valid. Again, it's (D).

**18** **(B)** This question asks for the primary purpose, and we know that the author is concerned with theories that describe, simply and precisely, particles and their forces. The author's primary purpose is to describe attempts to develop a simplified theory of nature. Skimming through the choices, (B) looks good. (E) doesn't fit at all. You might say the author summarizes the theories describing matter, but he doesn't summarize all that is known about matter itself. As for (A), the author doesn't cite a misconception in either of the theories he describes. At most, he mentions ways in which the first could be simplified but this doesn't imply that there's a misconception. The author does refer to the second theory as a leading candidate for achieving unification, but predicting its success, (C), is far from his primary purpose. As for (D), although it's implied that scientists in general do prefer simpler theories, their reasons for this preference are never discussed. Again, it's (B) for Question 18.

**19** **(E)** This question is a scattered detail question concerning quarks. In the first paragraph we're told that quarks are constituents of the proton and the neutron. It's reasonable, then, to say that quarks are the elementary building blocks of protons and neutrons, option I. Since option I is correct, we can eliminate choices which exclude it, (B) and (D). The remaining choices are either I only, I and II only, or I, II, and III. You could skip II and go to III. If you're sure III is right, you can assume that II is also and pick (E). It turns out that III can be easily checked at the end of paragraph three, where the author states that a new theory incorporates the leptons and quarks into a single family or class, so option III is correct. For a complete list, let's look at option II. In the very first sentence the author tells us that elementary particles don't have an internal structure and since quarks are elementary particles, option II is indeed correct, and (E) is our answer.

**20** **(C)** It should be clear that the author has some very definite criteria for judging the usefulness or worth of various theories of nature. As for option I, *simplicity* should leap off the page at you—it's what this passage is all about. We can eliminate (B) and (E). The author also takes the theory's completeness into consideration. He commends the first theory he describes because it accounts for the entire observed hierarchy of material structure and therefore option II is correct. We know that (C) must be correct because there is no I, II, and III choice. But let's look at III anyway. Does the author ever mention proving either of those two theories he describes? Proof is of no concern to him—there's no mention in the passage of any experiments, or of wanting to find experimental proof. So III is out and (C) it is.

**21** **(E)** We've mentioned that the second theory doesn't include gravitation in its attempt to unify the four basic forces. We need the author's opinion about this omission. The author introduces the theory in the second paragraph, describing it as an ambitious theory that promises at least a partial unification of elementary particles and forces. The failure to include gravitation and achieve complete unification doesn't dampen the author's enthusiasm and he seems to suggest that gravitation's omission can't be helped, at least at this stage. So, although the omission is a limitation—it prevents total unification—it is also unavoidable. It looks like (E) does the trick.

You could see the limitation as a defect, (A), but the author never gives the impression that the omission of gravitation disqualifies the theory. As for (B), *deviation* is a funny word—deviation from what? More important, we've already seen that the author doesn't consider the omission to be unjustified. For the same reason, (C) can be eliminated. If the omission of gravitation can't be avoided, then it certainly isn't a needless oversimplification. Finally (D) is out because there's no way that gravitation's omission could be an oversight. A scientist just forgot about one of the four basic forces when developing a theory of nature? No, the idea is that, for now at least, gravitation just can't be fit in, and (E) is correct.

**22** **(B)** The passage begins with the author's discussion of the simplicity of elementary particles and the theories which describe them. In the third

sentence, the author sets forth simplicity as a standard for judging theories of nature. In the rest of the passage, the author measures two specific theories against this standard. (B) summarizes this setup nicely and it's our answer. (A) is way off base. Although the author might be said to enumerate distinctions between how the two theories treat elementary particles, he doesn't enumerate distinctions among the particles. (C) is easy to eliminate—the author describes only two methods of grouping particles and forces—not three. As for (D), the author doesn't criticize the first theory he describes or call it inaccurate—he commends it. Finally, (E) goes overboard. As we mentioned in our discussion of option III in Question 20, the author is not interested in scientific verification. Nothing is ever mentioned about proving or verifying either of the theories he describes. Again, (B) is correct.

**23** **(C)** This question shouldn't be difficult. It asks us to put ourselves in the author's shoes and figure out what sort of theory he would find superior to present theories. We already know—a simpler theory. The author's criteria for judging a theory are its simplicity and its ability to account for the largest possible number of known phenomena. Which choice represents a theory with one or both of these characteristics? (A) misrepresents the two theories described in the passage. The author says that the first theory could account for the entire observed hierarchy of material structure. The second does also, even though gravitation must be thrown in as a separate force. A theory that could account for a larger number of structures isn't what's needed.

As for (B), why would the author approve of a theory that reduces the four basic forces to two which are incompatible? (C) is on the right track. The author would prefer a theory that accounts for all matter with the fewest particles and forces and this is offered by (C), the correct answer. (D) is out because it wouldn't represent an improvement on currently existing theories. They account for gravitation, although they haven't yet unified it with the other three forces. Finally, (E) represents a step backwards.

The current theories hypothesize that both protons and neutrons are formed by combinations of elementary particles. Again, it's (C).

## Reading Passage: Questions 24–27

The second passage is short but dense, and the author doesn't arrive at her main point until the last sentence. We see that the author sets herself in opposition to presentist historians, people who believe that white abolitionists and suffragists comprise the abiding principles of equality and the equal right of all to life, liberty, and the pursuit of happiness.

Their evidence is presented in the first three sentences. First, a majority of both groups tried to assure people that the changes they advocated weren't revolutionary and served to support rather than to undermine the status quo. A certain group of abolitionists disclaimed miscegenationist intentions—they were careful to assert that their interest in obtaining freedom for blacks didn't mean they were advocating mixing of races. And finally, suffragists saw no conflict between racism or nativism and their movement's objectives. Presentist historians apparently think that, by denying any revolutionary intentions and miscegenationist intentions, and by justifying nativism and racism, both groups were undermining their own principles. And, because their objectives—the abolition of slavery and voting rights for all—go hand in hand with our present conception of equality, presentist historians think that both groups undermine the principle of equality at the same time. The author uses the same evidence to argue that the actions of both groups served not to show how far these groups deviated from a fixed principle of equality, but to show what the principle meant in their own generations. The author thinks that the principle of equality is not unchanging, but means different things for different generations and that presentist historians err when they judge these movements by our conception of equality.

**24** **(C)** We need the author's main point, which we just formulated—the actions of abolitionists and suffragists demonstrate the meaning that equality had in their time. (C) expresses this, and it's the correct answer. (A) is wrong because it's the presentist historians who believe that the actions of the abolitionists and suffragists compromised their principles. (B) has nothing to do with the author's discussion. A comparison of beliefs never occurs. As for (D), the author charges presentist historians with misinterpreting abolitionist and suffragist ideology, not with willfully misrepresenting it. Finally, (E) constitutes a criticism the author makes about presentist historians—that they impose their own value systems on the past, rather than interpreting actions in the appropriate historical context. Again, it's (C) for this question.

**25** **(A)** We can infer something about the author's concept of the principle of equality—it's clear that the author thinks the principle of equality is not abiding. Rather, she thinks, it encompasses different things for people at different times. We can give the nod to option I, which eliminates (B), (C), and (E). Since the only choices left include option I only or options I and II only, option III can be eliminated. Option II—does the author suggest that the suffragists applied the principle of equality more consistently than abolitionists? No, if anything, she implies that they applied it equally consistently. We're left with (A) as our answer. We know option III can't be true—presentist historians say that abolitionists and suffragists compromised the principle of equality, not the author, who thinks their actions conform to their generation's conception of equality.

**26** **(C)** This question deals with the logical structure of the author's argument, how she argues her case against the presentist historians. She uses the same evidence to support her views that they do, cites the actions of the suffragists and abolitionists, states that the presentist historians knew of these actions, then presents her own interpretation of these same actions. She's applying a different interpretation to the same set of facts, and (C) is our answer. The author doesn't cite any new evidence, so both (A) and (B) can be ruled out. As for (D), the author refutes not the accuracy of the historians' data but the accuracy of their interpretation. Finally, the author doesn't claim that the historians' argument is flawed by a logical contradiction, (E). She claims instead that they erred by assuming that equality is an abiding value and by measuring the actions of past groups against this concept of equality. Again, it's (C) for this question.

**27** **(B)** We need to know what the author suggests about the abolitionist movement. Well, in her references to this movement, the author mentions the non-Garrisonian abolitionists. If there were non-Garrisonian abolitionists, it seems reasonable to assume that Garrisonian abolitionists existed. Also, the author refers to a majority of white abolitionists who made certain denials. This implies that there was a minority of abolitionists who didn't make such denials and also that there were black abolitionists. In other words, the abolitionist movement was subdivided into different groups and these groups didn't always share identical ideologies. This corresponds closely to (B), the correct answer. As for (A), the passage does state that some abolitionists denied that they had revolutionary or miscegenationist intentions, but these denials don't seem to be an attempt to disguise their real intentions. (C) is wrong because the author thinks the abolitionists did live by their principles. As for (D), presentist historians might claim that abolitionists undermined their objectives by making certain disclaimers to the public. But even they wouldn't say that these disclaimers were the result of abolitionists misunderstanding their objectives. Finally, the passage makes no mention of radical factions within the abolitionist movement and the effects of abolitionists' actions on their movement's progress is never discussed, so (E) is out. Again, (B) is correct.

**28** **(C)** Our first word is *undermine,* which means to weaken or cause to collapse, especially by secret means. The opposite would be something like *build up* or make *stronger.* The best choice here is (C), *bolster,* meaning to support. The only other tempting choice was (A), *appreciate,* but a better opposite for appreciate would be *resent.*

**29** **(B)** *Obsequious* means servile or submissive. The opposite of *obsequious* would be something like *snooty* or *arrogant. Haughty,* (B), fits perfectly. A haughty person is overly arrogant while an obsequious person is overly eager to please. None of the other choices comes close.

**30** **(C)** The word *blanch* may be familiar to you if you cook. Foods like broccoli are blanched by plunging them in boiling water so they lose color. In the same way, a person might blanch from fear, shock, or dismay. Since *blanch* means to whiten or turn pale, the opposite would be to redden or blush. (C), *flush* is what we need. None of the other answer choices are particularly colorful.

**31** **(A)** The word *dissipated* can be a pejorative reference to someone devoted to the pursuit of pleasure—the opposite of dissipation is restraint or moderation. (A) is correct because *temperate* means moderate or self-restrained. None of the other answer choices have to do with moderation. *Inundated* means overwhelmed or deluged.

**32** **(D)** *Fecundity* means fertility, the capacity for producing life, whether it be children or vegetation. Clearly the opposite would be (D), *sterility,* which refers to an inability to reproduce. None of the other choices comes close, and the only unusual word is (A)'s *levity,* which means silliness or frivolity.

**33** **(D)** In Question 33, *encumber* means to block or weigh down. A good synonym would be *oppress*. The best opposite is (D), *disburden*, which means to free from oppression. *Animate* (A), means to make alive—its opposite would be something like deaden. To *inaugurate*, (B), is to begin or commence. To *bleach* is to pale or whiten and to *obliterate* means to erase or remove.

**34** **(C)** The word *disseminate* isn't easy to figure out if you don't know it—it means to spread widely. Ideas, theories, and beliefs can all be disseminated. The opposite of spreading an idea is *suppressing* it, (C). None of the other choices work.

**35** **(D)** *Restive* looks like the word rested, but the two don't mean the same thing at all. Restive can mean stubborn or restless. A mule that won't move is restive, as is a fidgety child. We need something like *obedient*, *quiet*, or *settled*, and it's *patient*, (D). *Morose* in (A) means gloomy. *Intangible* means untouchable or elusive. *Fatigued* means tired and the opposite of *curious* would be *indifferent*.

**36** **(B)** If you didn't know what *syncopated* means, you might have guessed it had something to do with rhythm from the expression *out of sync*. That would lead you to (B), *normally accented*. *Syncopation* refers to a pattern or rhythm in which stress is shifted onto normally unaccented beats.

The opposite of (A)'s *carefully executed* would be *haphazard*, and (C)'s *brightly illuminated* is the opposite of *dim*. *Obscure* would be an antonym for (D)'s *easily understood*. *Justly represented*, in (E) isn't easy to match, but even if you couldn't eliminate all the choices, you could have at least narrowed the field.

**37** **(C)** *Vituperative* means verbally abusive. The opposite of defaming someone with vituperative remarks would be praising them—(C)'s *laudatory* means expressing praise. As for the other choices, *lethal* means deadly and *incapacitated* means inca-

pable or unfit. In (D), *insulated* means protected, as in *insulation*, and *prominent*, (E), means famous.

**38** **(B)** *Saturnine* is probably the hardest word in the section. It means heavy, gloomy, sluggish, so its opposite is *cheerful* or *lively*. The answer is (B), *ebullient* which means bubbling with enthusiasm or high spirited. (A)'s *magnanimous* means generous or high minded. *Finicky*, (C), means fussy or picky. The opposite of (D), *unnatural* is natural and (E), *impoverished* means poor.

**39** **(E)** *Callous* means unfeeling, uncaring, but if this person has concern for the earthquake victims, her reputation must be an unfounded one, so the correct choice will mean *contradicted* or *proved false*. This is one of the meanings of *belied*, correct choice (E). (B), *rescinded*, is the second best answer. It means revoked or withdrawn, but you don't say that a reputation is rescinded. (A), (C), and (D) are the opposite of what we're looking for—they don't make sense in this context.

**40** **(B)** *No longer* and *therefore* show strong contrast—something is done with the original plans because they are no longer something else. (B) expresses this contrast, *applicable . . . rejected*, and if we plug in these words, the plans could no longer be applied so they were tossed aside. In (A), there's no contrast between something being *relevant*, or pertinent, and its being *adaptable*, capable of being changed to fit a new situation. In (C), *expedient* means convenient—it makes no sense for something not expedient to be *adopted* or taken up. In (D), *appraised* means judged or rated, which doesn't follow from no longer being *acceptable*. In (E) it doesn't make sense to say that the plans were no longer *capable* or that the plans were *allayed*, or minimized—again, (B) is the best choice.

**41** **(D)** The second half of the sentence is about each tiny layer of the surface of the cross-section of the sandstone. This must explain what the first part alludes to, so the first blank must mean *layered*—otherwise, what tiny layers is the author talking about? On this basis, (D) is the best answer since *stratified* means layered. In (A), a ridge isn't really a layer. In (B), a facet is a face or flat surface, so *multifaceted* can't be right. *Distinctive,* in (C) means distinguishing or individual. And *coarse* in (E) means rough. Looking at the second blank, *enlargement,* in (A), has nothing to do with the formation of the stone. In (B), if the phrase *angle of deposition* means anything at all, it's an obscure geological term and can't be what we want here. The remaining choices could refer to the time or place in which material is deposited. Since (D) has the best answer for the first blank and a possible answer for the second blank, it's correct.

**42** **(D)** The phrase *and now* suggests that the second part of the sentence will say something consistent with the first part. Whatever the convict has always insisted upon, the new evidence must support his claim. (D) gets this connection right—*innocence . . vindicate.* To vindicate means to clear from an accusation, to prove innocent. The convict has always insisted upon his own innocence and now at last there is new evidence to vindicate him—this makes perfect sense and it's the answer. In (A), *defensiveness* means a tendency to defend oneself and *incarcerate* means to put in prison. In (B), *culpability* is guilt, as in the word *culprit,* and *exonerate* means to clear from guilt. In (C), to *anathematize* someone means to curse him or pronounce a strong sentence against him but that doesn't go with *blamelessness.* In (E) *contrition* is a sense of remorse, while to *condemn* someone means to pass judgment against him. This is probably second best, but it doesn't follow as logically as (D), so (D) is correct.

**43** **(A)** The word *but* signals a contrast between the opinion of plate tectonics when the theory was first proposed, and the opinion of it now—either people disbelieved the theory at first and believe it now or vice versa. (A), *opposition . . grant* provides the contrast. If most geophysicists now grant

its validity, they believe in it. That's the opposite of opposing it, so (A) is the answer. In (B), *consideration* is a neutral term—people are thinking about the theory, but it doesn't provide the necessary contrasts with *see,* which implies that physicists now recognize the validity of the theory. In (C), *acclamation* means loud praise and *boost* means to support enthusiastically—no contrast there. In (D), a *prognostication* is a prediction of the future, which doesn't make sense in this context and *learn its validity* doesn't make sense either, so (D) isn't a good choice. In (E), *contention* is argument and to *bar* means to exclude or forbid—there is no contrast with this pair. Again, (A) is the correct answer.

**44** **(D)** *Despite* clues you in to a contrast between something professed, claimed or pretended, and reality, indicated by the glint in her eyes. A glint in someone's eye is a sign of strong interest, so *obsession* and *fascination,* in (A) and (D) are tempting. We want a contrast with strong interest, so the first word is something like *disinterest.* We find *indifference* in (D) and *obliviousness* in (C). Since both words in (D) fit, it must be correct. None of the others offers the kind of contrasts we need. There's no contrast between *intelligence* and *obsession,* in (A), between *interest* and *concern* in (B), or between *obliviousness* and *confusion* in (C). We get a contrast in (E) between *expertise* and *unfamiliarity,* but the words don't make sense—a glint in someone's eye isn't a sign of unfamiliarity.

**45** **(C)** We're looking for something that goes with sacred scriptures and implies a formal system of belief, but something whose absence doesn't rule out a legacy of traditional religious practices and basic values. We can eliminate choices (A), (B), and (E) because if Shinto lacked *followers, customs,* or *faith* it wouldn't be a legacy of traditional religious practices and basic values. *Relics,* (D), are sacred objects but relics don't make something a formal system of beliefs. The best choice is (C)—a *dogma* is a formal religious belief.

**46** **(E)** Something *impeccable* is perfect, it doesn't have a *flaw*. In (A) *impeachable* means subject to accusation, so something impeachable is not necessarily without *crime*. *Obstreperous,* in (B) means loud or unruly, not without *permission*. *Impetuous,* in (C) means rash or without care, rather than without *warning*. In (D), *moribund* means in the process of dying, so it's inappropriate to use *living*. In (E), *absurd* means without *sense*, so this is the correct answer.

**47** **(D)** A *seismograph* is an instrument used to measure an earthquake, so we need another instrument used to measure something. In (A), a *stethoscope* is an instrument used to listen to a patient's chest. Only indirectly can this be used to measure a patient's *health*. In (B), a *speedometer* doesn't measure a *truck*—it measures the speed of any kind of vehicle. In (C), a *telescope* doesn't measure *astronomy*. A telescope is an instrument used to observe far away objects. In (D), a *thermometer* measures *temperature*, so this looks like a promising answer. In (E), an *abacus* is used in *arithmetic* as a calculator but it doesn't measure arithmetic. So (D) is the best answer.

**48** **(D)** To *guzzle* is to *drink* very quickly, taking big gulps, so the relationship is one of speed or degree. In (A), *elucidate* and *clarify* mean to make clearer. One doesn't imply greater speed or volume than the other. Similarly, with (B) to *ingest* is to *eat* or drink—it doesn't mean to eat in big bites. In (C), to *boast* and to *describe* are two unrelated ways of talking. In (D), to *stride* is to *walk* quickly, taking big steps, so this may be the answer. In (E), *condemn* is stronger than the first word *admonish,* meaning to rebuke—the opposite of how the stem pair is presented. So (D) is the best answer.

**49** **(C)** An *orator* is a public speaker and *articulate* means able to express oneself well. You can form the bridge, "A successful orator is one who is articulate." With that in mind, (A) may seem tempting but the profession of *soldier* isn't defined as aspiring towards being *merciless*. In (B) a *celebrity* is a famous person, not by definition a *talented* one. (C) is good—a good *judge* has to be *unbiased*. It's safe to say that a biased judge is a bad judge in the same way that an inarticulate orator is a bad orator. In (D), a *novice* is a beginner—it wouldn't be unusual for a novice to be *unfamiliar* but that's not what makes a good novice. In (E), a *dignitary* is a person of high rank, and such a person doesn't need to be *respectful*. (C) is correct.

**50** **(C)** A *badge* is the identification worn by a *policeman*. In (A), a *placard* is a sign carried by a *demonstrator*. There's a link here but a placard isn't an official ID and a demonstrator doesn't necessarily carry a placard. (B) is wrong because although there is a tradition for a *sailor* to have a *tattoo*, a tattoo isn't an official identification of a sailor. In (C), a *soldier* wears a *dog-tag* on his uniform to identify him, so this is plausible. In (D), the *pedigree* of a *dog* is the dog's lineage or genealogy, not something worn by the dog as identification. In (E), even though a *fingerprint* may be used to identify a *defendant*, everybody has fingerprints. So the best answer is (C).

**51** **(B)** To *scrutinize* means to *observe* intently, so the relationship is one of degree. In (A), to *pique* interest is to *excite* interest. The words mean the same thing. In (B), to *beseech* means to *request* with great fervor—this is more like it. In (C), to *search* is the process you go through to *discover* something. That's different from the stem pair. In (D) to *grin* is to *smile* broadly—this reverses the original pair. And in (E), to *dive* means to *jump* in a certain way or under certain conditions, not to jump intently. The best answer is (B).

**52** **(D)** If you didn't know what *epicurean* means, you might have had trouble here, but you can still eliminate some choices. There must be some relationship between *epicurean* and *indulge*. Could (A) have the same relationship? No, because there really is no relationship between *frightened* and *ugly*. Something ugly doesn't necessarily frighten people.

Same with (C)—there's no relationship between *hesitate* and *unproductive*. There are good relationships for the other choices but let's see if we can eliminate them. In (E), the relationship is that something *comprehensible* can be *understood*. Do you think that something *epicurean* can be *indulged*? That sounds odd—just about everyone and everything can be indulged.

In (B), *revocable* means something can be taken back, so the relationship is, "Something *revocable* can be *retracted*." That's the same relationship that we just saw in (E), another clue that they must be wrong. If (B) and (E) share the same relationship, they can't both be right, so they must both be wrong. That leaves us with (D), and there our relationship is something like, "someone *vindictive* is likely to *revenge* himself," and that sounds better. In fact, an epicurean person is one who is likely to indulge himself, so (D) is correct here.

**53** **(E)** *Diluvial* means having to do with a *flood*. You may have heard the word *antediluvian*, meaning before the flood, Noah's flood, that is—in other words, a long time ago. So our bridge is "having to do with." In (A), *criminal* can mean "having to do with crime" but it doesn't mean having to do with *punishment*. In (B), *biological* means "having to do with living things." *Bacteria* are living things but to define *biological* as "having to do with bacteria" would be too narrow. In (C), *judicial* means "having to do with the administration of justice." A *verdict* is the decision about the guilt or innocence of a defendant, a small part of the judicial process. (D)'s *candescent* means "giving off *light*" rather than "having to do with light." This leaves (E) and *cardiac* means "having to do with the *heart*," so (E) is correct.

**54** **(C)** It is in the nature of a *sphinx* to *perplex*. This comes from Greek mythology—the sphinx was a monster that asked a riddle that no one could answer. *Sphinx* can be used to mean anything that is difficult to understand, so our bridge is: "A sphinx is known for perplexing." In (A), an *oracle* is a soothsayer, someone who predicts the future—an oracle doesn't

*interpret*. In (B), a *prophet* is someone who foretells the future. This may help someone to *prepare* but you don't say that a prophet is known for preparing. In (C), a *siren* can be a beautiful or a seductive woman who *lures* men. So (C) looks good—a siren lures in the same way that a sphinx perplexes. In (D), the role of a *jester* is to amuse, not necessarily to *astound*. In (E), a *minotaur* is a mythological monster—it didn't, by definition, *anger* someone. So (C) is correct.

## Reading Passage: Questions 55–57

This reading comp passage is short and it's followed by three questions—the remaining passage will be long with eight questions. The style of this natural science passage is factual, descriptive and straightforward, although the discussion does get fairly detailed. The topic is clear from the first sentence: our knowledge of how fish schools are formed and how their structure is maintained. The next two sentences get more specific and express the author's main point—that, contrary to the previous theory, the structure of fish schools is not primarily dependent on vision.

The tone is objective, but it's worth noting that since the author is contrasting the new knowledge about lateral lines with older, outdated knowledge, he must be skeptical of the notion that vision is the primary means of forming and maintaining fish schools. The rest of the passage is a more technical report of how the schools are structured, how individual fish actually behave in forming schools—this is detail and the best way to deal with it is to read it attentively but more quickly than the earlier lines.

**55** **(E)** This Roman numeral-format question focuses on detail. The stem is asking what the structure of fish schools depends on, and the options focus on the more technical elements in the last half of the passage. The author states that ideal positions of individual fish aren't maintained rigidly and this contradicts option I right away. The idea of random aggregation appears: the school formation results from a probabilistic arrangement that appears like a random aggregation, so the idea is that fish are positioned probabilistically, but not rigidly. Option II is true, repeating the idea in the next sentence that fish school structure is maintained by the preference of fish to have a certain distance from their neighbors. Option III is true, too. It's a paraphrase of the last two sentences, that each fish uses its vision and lateral line first to measure the speed of the other fish, then to adjust its own speed to conform, based primarily on the position and movements of other fish. So options II and III are true and (E) is the right choice.

**56** (C) You know the primary purpose here is to present new ideas that challenge the emphasis of the old theory. So you're probably safe in assuming that the author's attitude toward the old idea will be at least somewhat negative. You can therefore cross off choices that sound neutral or positive, (B), (D), and (E). The negative choices are (A) and (C). (A) is out because it is much too extreme—the author is not offended or indignant, nor does he or she argue that vision is insignificant—quite the contrary. This leaves (C), the best choice. The author disagrees with the old theory since it overlooks the role of the lateral line, but the disagreement is tempered by an acknowledgment that the old theory did recognize the role of vision. So it's a qualified or measured disagreement—the adjective *considered* works well here. Again, the correct answer is (C).

**57** (C) This question involves inference as the word *suggests* in the stem suggests. It refers to the latter, more detailed half of the passage, and that's where correct answer (C) is. It's logically suggested by the last couple of sentences where you're told that once it establishes its position, each fish uses its eyes and lateral line to measure the movements of nearby fish in order to maintain appropriate speed and position. Since the school is moving, each fish's adjustments must be ongoing and continuous, as (C) states. (A) is wrong because auditory organs aren't mentioned. Lateral lines correspond to a sense of touch,

not hearing. (B) and (D) both have words that should strike you as improbable. Nothing suggests that each fish rigorously avoids any disruptive movements, (B), or that the fish would make sudden unexpected movements only in the presence of danger, (D). The idea in (E) also isn't mentioned. It's never suggested that a fish, once part of a school, completely loses its ability to act on its own. Again, (C) is our answer for this question.

## Reading Passage: Questions 58–65

This passage is divided into three paragraphs. If you figure out what each paragraph covers, you've understood the passage's handful of ideas, plus you've sketched out a rough mental map. In this passage, the first 10 or 15 lines take you through the first paragraph and into the second and if you were careful you picked up the author's broad topic area (ancient Greek social anxiety), the style of the writing (dense and scholarly) and the tone or attitude (expository and neutral).

The second paragraph gives you the central point—what the Greeks apparently succeeded in doing was discovering a way of measuring and explaining chaotic experience so that chaos was no longer so threatening and anxiety producing. This recognition of order in the midst of chaos served as the basis of a spiritual ideal for the Greeks. So by the end of the second paragraph you have the author's central idea plus all the information about style, tone, and topics in the beginning. The first sentence of the last paragraph tells you the search for order and clarity in the midst of chaos is reflected especially in Greek philosophy. The rest of the paragraph is a description of how various philosophers and schools of philosophy offered solutions to the problem of finding order and measure in a disorderly world.

**58** (E) This kind of primary purpose question is common, and here the right answer is (E). In this case, both the noun and the verb are right on the money. The verb is exactly right for this author's expository neutral tone, and a cultural phenomenon, the Greeks' perception of chaos and their solution to the problem, is what the author is describing. The verbs in (B) and (C), *challenge* and *question* eliminate them right away—no opinion is given but the author's own, and philosophy in (C) is discussed only in the last paragraph. The noun phrase in (A), *conflicting viewpoints* is wrong. (D) is the most tempting—the author is looking at history and mentioning certain facts, but this misses the author's purpose, which is not to simply list facts but rather to describe and define something in the form of a thesis. Again, (E) is the correct answer.

**59** **(A)** This is from the first sentence of the second paragraph and it's the central idea that's being focused on, that the discovery of this substratum helped bring a satisfying new sense of order into experience, thus reforming the Greeks' perception of worldly chaos. The choice that paraphrases this point is (A), the perception of constant change was altered by the idea of a permanent principle of order lying underneath it—this is the main point of the passage. (B) is out because severe social problems are never mentioned, at least not in any concrete way. As for (C), it misses the point made in the sentence the question refers to. The passage does refer to pain and bewilderment and to an earlier period of political turbulence, but this choice goes overboard with its notions of painful memories and national humiliation and so on. As for (D), a few lines into the second paragraph the author says directly that the discovery did much more than satisfy intellectual curiosity. And (E) also contradicts the author, distorting a detail at the end of the paragraph. It's not mysticism, but rationality and careful analysis that lead to order and clarity, so it's (A) for this question.

**60** **(D)** The author is arguing in the second, third, and fourth sentences that the Greeks identified rational thought and spiritual ideals as inseparable. Rationality, order, measure, and so forth became equivalent to spiritual ideals for the Greeks.

Toward the end of the second paragraph the author states that rationality and spirituality are not mutually exclusive. The choice that's most clearly consistent with this is (D). As for (A), the passage never suggests that ordinary Greeks were unfamiliar with or uninterested in the concepts of rational thought and spiritual ideals. The passage suggests quite the contrary. (B) and (C) are both inconsistent with the passage as well. All the philosophers mentioned accepted the notion that rationality was the key, amounting to an ideal to understanding the world. (E) picks up on the mention of poetry at the beginning of the last paragraph, but the point there is that Greek poetry manifested the sense of cultural anxiety that philosophy tried to alleviate.

**61** **(B)** This question is looking for the choice that isn't mentioned as reflecting the Greeks' anxieties about chaos. The one that's never mentioned is (B), that it was reflected in aspects of their religion. We don't actually learn anything about Greek religion in the passage—we just don't know and we certainly can't infer anything about specific aspects. Each of the other choices is mentioned specifically. (A) is implied in the long opening sentence of the first paragraph—the national psyche and historical experience both relate to national consciousness. (C), the sense of change in the physical world, is mentioned at the start of paragraph two. (D), the striving for order and philosophy, is discussed throughout the third paragraph. And finally (E), lyric poetry, is mentioned at the start of the paragraph as one place where the sense of anxiety was expressed directly.

**62** **(C)** Your mental map should have taken you straight to the last paragraph—the Milesians are discussed in the first several sentences. (C) encapsulates what the passage says, that Milesians were interested primarily in understanding a fundamental order in nature, outside the disturbing world of human society. (A) gets it backwards—the Milesians apparently ignored questions that were inherently human. (B) and (D) contradict the passage. None of the philosophies mentioned did what these choices suggest, either to sharply distinguish between rationality and spirituality, (B), or to integrate rationality and mysticism, (D). (E), finally, describes the approach of the Pythagoreans who were absorbed by the logic and order of mathematics, rather than by attempts to explain physical phenomena.

**63** **(D)** You're being asked not the actual content, but the logical progression of the contents. Is he or she making a series of disconnected assertions? Making a point and backing it up with factual evidence, or what? What's the author up to logically in the lines referred to? In the preceding sentence the author is talking about the Greeks' discovery of order and measure, and that it helped them get a secure handle on chaotic experience. The discovery was a relief—its impact was almost religious in nature. In the next sentence, the author says that this recognition, discovery, of order and measure was much more than merely intellectually satisfying—it served as a basic part of their spiritual values. The author quotes Plato to support his point, to give an idea of the significance of measure.

In the last of the three sentences the author finishes up with a statement that pulls the strands of the thesis together and puts the basic point into clear cultural perspective. Rational definability or measure was never regarded by the Greeks as inconsistent with spirituality—(D) is the choice that describes things best. The problem with (A) is that the author isn't summarizing two viewpoints but discussing one thesis. As for (B), the author neither mentions evidence that weakens his thesis nor revises it. (C) is out because the author is not discussing two separate arguments that need to be reconciled by a third. It's just one argument that's the topic here. (E), finally, is wrong for the same reason—the author discusses one thesis only and never suggests any other.

**64** **(A)** We know from our rough map of the structure that except for one reference to Plato in the middle of the second paragraph, philosophy is discussed only in the last paragraph, so that's where you'll find out about the Pythagoreans. The main thing about them was that they concentrated on mathematical abstraction. They shifted the focus in philosophy from the physical realm to the mathematical. The Milesians focused on physical phenomena, and that's the idea you see immediately in (A), the correct choice. (B) lists an idea that mentions the Pythagoreans—thinkers who came *after* the Pythagoreans focused on human behavior. (C) won't work because both of these schools and all other philosophies mentioned used rationality as the means to truth. (D) picks up what characterized the Milesians—we want the Pythagorean side of the contrast. (E) gets things backward—the Pythagoreans stressed mathematical theory over physical matter. Again, it's (A).

**65** **(D)** The last sentence is saying that in all these various periods of Greek history and philosophy, the basic preoccupation of the Greeks was with the search for a kosmos. The term *kosmos* hasn't been used before, but because this sentence is at the end of the passage and because it's phrased as a summary, you should realize that the basic quest here must be the same one the author has been talking about all along. So this refers to the central problem for Greek society—how to find order and measure in a seemingly confusing and disorderly world. This search for a kosmos then is the passage's main idea, and correct choice (D) restates it.

(A) is out because the word *mystical* is incorrect, since the author states at the end of paragraph two that the Greeks stressed rationalism over mysticism. (B) and (E) are inconsistent with some major points. In (B), the idea that the Greeks would have regarded rationalism as sterile is completely wrong. And in (E), the ideals of beauty and excellence, as mentioned in paragraph two, are preeminent and fundamental within the Greeks' world view. Finally, (C) talks about ending conflict among important schools of philosophy. This last sentence about the search for kosmos is talking about a quest you find in Greek thought as a whole, a much bigger topic than mere conflicts among philosophers.

**66** **(A)** *Enmity* is the state of being an enemy—the opposite is *friendship*, (A). *Reverence*, (B), is great respect, the opposite of contempt. The opposite of *boredom*, (C), is interest. The opposite of (D), *stylishness*, is a lack of style, and the opposite of (E), *awkwardness*, is skillfulness.

**67** **(B)** *Dilate* means expand and widen. The opposite is the word *contract*, so (B), *shrink*, is what we're looking for. (A), *enclose*, means to confine. The opposite of the word *hurry*, (C), is *delay*. *Inflate*, (D), means to expand or fill with air. The opposite of (E), *erase*, might be *preserve* or *set down*.

**68** **(A)** A *charlatan* is a fraud or a quack. (A), *genuine expert*, is a possible answer. The opposite of a *powerful leader*, (B), is a follower or maybe a weak leader. The opposite of a *false idol*, (C), is a true god or a hero. The opposite of an *unknown enemy*, (D), is a known enemy, an unknown friend or a known friend. The opposite of (E), *hardened villain*, might be an innocent person or first offender. So it's (A).

**69** **(C)** *Peripheral* means having to do with the periphery, the outer edge of something. The opposite of *peripheral* is *central*, (C). The opposite of (A), *civilized*, is *crude* or *savage*. (B), *partial*, means favoring or biased, or incomplete—it has lots of opposites but *peripheral* isn't one of them. *Harmed* is the opposite of *unharmed*, and the opposite of (E), *stable*, is *weak* or *inconstant*. (C) is correct.

**70** **(E)** *Meritorious* means full of merit, deserving reward. Its opposite is *unpraiseworthy*, (E), the best choice. *Effulgent*, (A), means shiny—its opposite is *dull*. (B), *stationary*, means not moving. Neither (C), *uneven*, nor (D), *narrow-minded*, works, so (E) is correct.

**71** **(C)** *Discharge* means to unburden, eject, or exude. However, it has a more specific meaning in military context: to release or remove someone from service. The opposite is to *enlist*, (C). The opposite of (A), *heal*, is *sicken*. The opposite of (B), *advance*, is *retreat*. (D) *penalize*, means to punish. The opposite of *delay*, (E), is *hasten*.

**72** **(A)** A *malediction* is a curse. We want something like *benediction*, and we find *blessing* in (A). The opposite of *preparation*, (B), is *lack of preparation*. (C), *good omen*, has *bad omen* as its opposite. The opposite of (D), *liberation*, is *captivity*. The opposite of *pursuit*, (E), is tough, but it sure isn't *malediction*, so (A) is correct.

**73** **(A)** *Mawkish* means sickeningly sentimental. *Unsentimental*, (A), is the answer here. The opposite of (B), *sophisticated*, is *naive* or *simple*. The opposite of *graceful*, (C), is *clumsy*. The opposite of *tense*, (D), is *relaxed*. There are various antonyms to *descriptive*, (E), but *mawkish* isn't one.

**74** **(B)** *Temerity* is recklessness or foolish daring. Its opposite is *hesitancy* or *carefulness*. *Blandness*, (A), is a lack of character, not a lack of courage. (B), *caution*, fits—one with temerity lacks caution. The opposite of (C), *severity*, is *leniency*. The opposite of (D), *strength*, is *weakness*. *Charm*, (E), is personal appeal. The best answer is (B), caution.

**75** **(C)** *Jejune* can mean immature or sophomoric. The opposite would be *adult* or correct choice (C), *mature*. *Morose*, (A), means sad or moody. The opposite of *natural*, (B), is *artificial*. (D), *contrived*, means deliberately planned. Its opposite is *natural*. *Accurate*, (E), means precise or exact.

**76** **(C)** *Vitiate* means to corrupt, put wrong, spoil, or make worse, and the opposite is *improve* or *correct*. The closest choice is *rectify*, (C). (A), *deaden*, is way off. The opposite of *trust*, (B), is *distrust* or *suspect*. The opposite of *drain*, (D), is *fill*. And the opposite of *amuse*, (E), is *bore* or *upset*.

# Section Two Explanations—Quantitative

**1** **(A)** To compare these two quantities, work column by column starting with the decimal point and working to the right. Both have a 0 in the tenths column, so no difference there. In the hundredths column, both have a 2, so we go to thousandths. Column A has a 6 and Column B has a 5—there are more thousandths in A than in B, so Column A is larger and (A) is the correct answer.

**2** **(C)** Right triangles $ABD$ and $CDB$ share a hypotenuse, segment $DB$. The squared quantities should clue you to use the Pythagorean theorem. See that $w$ and $x$ are lengths of the legs of right triangle $ABD$. Side $AD$ has length $w$, side $AB$ has length $x$. Also, $y$ and $z$ are lengths of the legs of right triangle $CDB$. Side $CD$ has length $z$, side $CB$ has length $y$. Where $a$ and $b$ are lengths of the legs of a right triangle, and $C$ is the length of the hypotenuse, $a^2 + b^2 = c^2$, so $w^2 + x^2 = $ length $BD^2$. $y^2 + z^2$ also equals length $DB^2$, the quantities are equal and the answer is (C).

**3** **(A)** We have $x + 4y = 6$ and $x = 2y$, and we want to compare $x$ and $y$, so substitute $2y$ for $x$ in the first equation. Using that information, solve for the other variable. Substitute $2y$ for $x$ into $x + 4y = 6$ and get $2y + 4y = 6$ or $6y = 6$. Divide both sides by 6 and we get $y = 1$. If $y = 1$ and $x = 2y$ as the second equation tells us, $x$ must equal 2. Since 2 is greater than 1, the quantity in Column A is greater.

**4** **(B)** Question 4 looks hard—but you don't have to simplify to find the relationship. With positive numbers, you can square both without changing the relationship. That leaves you with $4^2 + 5^2$ in Column A and $3^2 + 6^2$ in Column B. $4^2$ is 16, $5^2$ is 25, 16 + 25 is 41. In Column B we have $3^2$, that's $9 + 6^2$, that's 36, 9 + 36 is 45. 45 is greater than 41, Column B is greater than Column A, and the answer is (B).

**5** **(D)** Column A asks for the number of managerial employees—that's easy. There are 120 employees in the firm, and 25 percent of them are managerial. One-fourth of 120 is 30, the value of Column A.

Column B asks for two-thirds of the clerical employees. But we can't figure out how many workers are clerical workers, so we can't find two-thirds of that number. We can't determine a relationship, and the answer is choice (D).

**6** **(B)** We have $12 \times 1$ over $12 + 1$ in Column A: $12 \times 1$ is 12 and $12 + 1$ is 13. So we have $\frac{12}{13}$ in Column A. In Column B we have $12 + 1 = 13$ in the numerator, and $12 \times 1 = 12$ in the denominator. So $\frac{12}{13}$ in Column A versus $\frac{13}{12}$ in Column B. Of course, $\frac{12}{13}$ is less than 1 while $\frac{13}{12}$ is greater than 1, and the answer is (B).

**7** **(D)** You might suspect (D) because there are no variable restrictions. To make the columns look as much alike as you can, multiply out Column A. You'll get $a \times b$ or $ab$, plus $1 \times b$, plus $1 \times a$, plus $1 \times 1$ or 1. So you get $ab + a + b + 1$. Column B has $ab + 1$. We can subtract $ab$ from both sides, and it won't change the relationship and we have $1 + a + b$ in Column A, and 1 in Column B. Subtract 1 from both sides and we have $a + b$ in Column A and 0 in Column B. But consider that $a$ and $b$ could be negative numbers. Since $a + b$ could be positive, negative, or zero, the answer is (D).

**8** **(B)** In the two-digit number $jk$ the value of digit $j$ is twice the value of digit $k$. We have to compare the value of $k$ in Column A with 6 in Column B. If you plug in 6 for $k$, then go back, you see that the value of digit $j$ is twice digit $k$. We know that $j$ isn't just a number—it's a digit, which means it's 0, 1, 2, 3, 4, 5, 6, 7, 8, or 9. So 12, twice the value of 6, can't be $j$. In other words, $k$ has to be something less than 6, so the answer must be (B), the value in Column B is greater.

**9** (A) We have a circle with right angle $QPR$ as a central angle. The area of sector $PQR$ is 4 and we're asked to compare the area of the circle with $4\pi$. There's a shortcut—the right angle defines the sector, and you have the area of that sector. A 90° angle cuts off one-fourth of the circle. If you multiply by four, you have the area of the circle. So in Column A you have $4 \times 4$, and in Column B, you have $4\pi$. $\pi$ is about 3.14, and 4 is bigger than that, so Column A, $4 \times 4$, must be bigger than $4\pi$, and the answer is (A).

**10** (C) Henry purchased $x$ apples and Jack purchased 10 apples less than one-third the number of apples Henry purchased. *One-third of* means the same as *one-third times* and the number of apples Henry purchased is $x$. So this boils down to $j = \frac{1}{3}x - 10$. You can plug this in for Column A. We have $\frac{1}{3}x - 10$ in Column A and in Column B we have $x - \frac{30}{3}$. Now you can clear the fraction in Column B. Let's split Column B to two fractions. $\frac{x}{3} - \frac{30}{3}$. We leave the $\frac{x}{3}$ alone and cancel the factor of 3 from the numerator and denominator of $\frac{30}{3}$ and we're left with $\frac{x}{3} - 10$. What's $\frac{x}{3}$? It's one-third of $x$, so these two quantities are equal. Column A equals $\frac{1}{3}x - 10$, while Column B also equals $\frac{1}{3}x - 10$, so the answer is (C).

**11** (D) You can suspect (D) because there are unrestricted variables. In Column A we have the volume of a rectangular solid with length 5 feet, width 4 feet, and height $x$ feet. The formula is length times width times height, so we have 5 times 4 times $x$, or $20x$. In Column B we need the volume of rectangular solid with length 10 feet, width 8 feet, and height $y$ feet. 10 times 8 times $y$ gives you a volume of $80y$. Now you may think, I've got $20x$, and $80y$, so $80y$ must be bigger because there are more $y$s than $x$s. That would be true if $x$ and $y$ were close together, but the variables are unrestricted, and the answer is (D).

**12** (C) We want to compare 50 with $x$, one of the angles formed by the intersection of $ST$ and $PT$. Now angle $QRS$ is labeled 80. We also know $PQ$ and $ST$ have the same length and $QR$ and $RS$ have the same length. If you add $PQ$ and $QR$, you get $PR$. If you add $ST$ and $RS$, you get $RT$. If you add equals to equals, you get equals, so $PQ + QR$ must be the same as $ST + RS$, which means that $PR$ and $RT$ are the same. You have isoceles triangle $PRT$ and we're given one angle that has measure 80 and the second angle that has measure $x$. The angle measuring $x$ is opposite equal side $PR$. That means the other angle must have the same measure, because it's opposite the other equal side. The sum of the interior angles in a triangle always equals 180°. $x + x + 80$ must equal 180, $2x$ must equal 100, $x = 50$. So $x$ and 50 are equal, and the answer is (C).

**13** (B) First we can cancel factors of 2 from $2 \times 16 \times 64$ on the left, and $2 \times 4n \times 256$ on the right. If we cancel a factor of 2 we have $16 \times 64$ on the left, $4n \times 256$ on the right. 64 goes into 256 four times, so let's cancel a factor of 64. That leaves us 16 on the left and $4n \times 4$ on the right. We can cancel a factor of 4 and we're left with 4 on the left and $4n$ on the right. If $4 = 4n$, $n$ must equal 1, so we have $n = 1$ for Column A. Column B is 2, so the answer is (B).

**14** **(A)** Try to solve the centered equation for $y$. First get all the $y$s on one side by adding $\frac{2}{y}$ to both sides. This gives $\frac{1}{3} = \frac{2}{y} - \frac{1}{2y}$. Multiplying both sides by $y$ gives $\frac{y}{3} = 2 - \frac{1}{2} = 1\frac{1}{2}$. Multiplying both sides by 3 gives $y = 3 \times 1\frac{1}{2} = 4\frac{1}{2}$. So Column A is greater than Column B.

**15** **(D)** The perimeter of $ABC$ is 40 and the length of $BC$ is 12, and we want to compare the length of $AB$ with 14. In an isosceles triangle there are two sides with equal length, but we don't know whether side $BC$ is one of those sides or not. If side $BC$ is the unequal side, we have two unknown sides plus 12 and they have a sum of 40, the perimeter. The two remaining sides have a sum of 28, so each is 14. That would mean that $AB$ and $AC$ would have length 14. Then the answer would be (C). If $BC$ is one of the equal sides, we have two sides length 12 and a third unknown side, and the sum is 40. 12 + 12 is 24, so that the third side has length 16. $AB$ could be one of the sides length 12, or the side length 12. There are three possible lengths for side $AB$—16, 14, and 12—so the answer is (D).

**16** **(B)** Isolate $\frac{q}{p}$. Multiplying both sides of the equation by $p$ gives $p - q = \frac{2p}{7}$. Subtracting $p$ from both sides gives $-q = \frac{2p}{7} - p = \frac{2p}{7} - \frac{7p}{7} = -\frac{5p}{7}$. So $-q = \frac{5p}{7}$, or $q = \frac{5p}{7}$. Dividing both sides by $p$ gives $\frac{q}{p} = \frac{5}{7}$.

**17** **(D)** We need the number that's a multiple of 8 and a factor of 72. Since 4 and 9 aren't multiples of 8, you can eliminate (A) and (B). 16 is, 24 is, but 36, (E), isn't. We're down to just 16 and 24; count by 16s and see if 16 is a factor of 72: 16, 32, 48, 64, 80. Well, that's not a factor of 72, so 24, (D) is correct.

**18** **(B)** We need the value of $a + b + c$. We know that $a$, $b$, and $c$ are exterior angles of our quadrilateral in the diagram and there's a fourth exterior angle which isn't labeled. But the measure of the interior angle next to it is given to us—it's 70°. The sum of the exterior angles of any figure is always 360°. So we can figure out the measure of the missing angle, then subtract it from 360 and get the sum of the other three. The unlabeled angle must be 110°. Now we know $110 + a + b + c = 360$, we subtract to get the sum of $a$, $b$, and $c$ and we get 250, (B) as the correct answer.

**19** **(E)** John has four ties, 12 shirts and three belts, and we need the number of days he can go without repeating. So we multiply the number of ties times the number of shirts times the number of belts. Four ties, 12 shirts—48 combinations. Multiply by three choices of belt, and you get $3 \times 48$ or 144 combinations, (E).

**20** **(D)** Move the decimal points to the right until they disappear—but keep track of how many places you move the decimal. In (A) we have .00003 in the numerator. Move five places to the right to change it to 3. Then we change from .0007 to 70 in the denominator and we end up with $\frac{3}{70}$. In (B) we have .0008 on top, .0005 on the bottom—we get $\frac{8}{5}$. We have $\frac{70}{5}$ for (C). In (D), we end up with $\frac{60}{5}$ and $\frac{10}{8}$ in (E). Clearly (D), 12, is the largest value.

## Graphs: Questions 21–25

**21** **(E)** The bar graph doesn't give us the total number of general practice physicians, but if we add the number of males to the number of females, we get the total number of g.p. physicians. To find the percent who are male, we take the number of males and put it over the total number and that will give us our percent. We have about 2,000 women and about 23,000 men, making the total about 25,000. Well, if there are around 25,000 g.p. physicians altogether and 2,000 to 3,000 of them are female, that's what percent of 25,000? It's around 10 percent. About 22,500 are male, which gives us 90 percent, (E).

**22** **(D)** We're looking for the lowest ratio of males to females so we have to get the smallest number of males and the largest number of females. Skimming the bar graphs, we can see that in pediatrics the female graph and the male graph are closer than any of the others. Pediatrics is (D), the correct answer.

**23** **(C)** To refer to ages of physicians, we need to find the slice of the pie that goes from 45 to 54. It's 20 percent, but 20 percent of what? We're not looking for a percent, we're looking for a number of doctors. For general surgery the male bar goes up to about 35,000 and the female bar goes up to about 2,000—about 37,000 total. So 20 percent of 37,000 is the number of general surgery physicians between ages 45 and 54, inclusive. What's 20 percent of 37,000, or $\frac{1}{5}$ of 37,000? Well, let's see, $\frac{1}{5}$ of 35,000 is 7,000, $\frac{1}{5}$ of 2,000 is 400, making 7,400. (C) is 7,350, the correct answer.

**24** **(E)** We'll have to find the total number of family practice physicians, which represents 7.5 percent of all the physicians in the United States, then we can find 100 percent of that number. The male bar of family practice physicians goes just over 36,000, so we'll say it's 36,000 plus. The number of females goes just over 6,000 so we'll call that 6,000 plus, so we have about 43,000 all together. This is 7.5 percent of all the physicians. 7.5 percent is awkward—it's three-quarters of 10 percent, which is $\frac{3}{4} \times \frac{1}{10}$, or $\frac{3}{40}$. So 43,000 is $\frac{3}{40}$ of the total number of doctors. To change 43,000 into the number of total physicians, we multiply it by $\frac{40}{3}$. Think of it this way: we have an equation now, $\frac{3}{40}$ of the number we're looking for, we'll call it $N$, the number of physicians, equals 43,000. We want to get $N$ by itself, so we have to get rid of that $\frac{3}{40}$. So we multiply by the reciprocal, $\frac{40}{3}$, and that leaves us $N$ by itself on the left. But the hard part is multiplying $\frac{40}{3} \times 43,000$. What's $\frac{40}{3}$? It's $13\frac{1}{3}$ and that's easier to multiply. $13 \times 43$ is 559, so $13 \times 43,000$ is 559,000—you can look at your choices and estimate. Only one is close to 559,000—(E), 570,000, and we're going to add on to that, so (E) is the correct answer.

# 25

**(B)** How many male general surgeon physicians were under 35 years old? The pie chart breaks down general surgery physicians by age, so we'll be working with it. And, since we're looking for a number of general surgery physicians, we know that we're going to have to find the total number of general surgery physicians, then break it down according to the percentages on the pie chart.

We're told the number of female general surgery physicians in the under-35 category represented 3.5 percent of all the general surgery physicians. What this does is break that slice of the pie for under-35 into two smaller slices, one for men under 35 and one for women under 35. Now we know that the whole slice for under-35-year-olds is 30 percent of the total and we've just been told that the number of females under 35 is 3.5 percent of the total. So the difference between 30 percent and 3.5 percent must be the men in the under-35 category, which leaves 26.5 percent, which we have to multiply by the total number of general surgery physicians.

We figured out in Question 23 that there were 37,000 total general surgery physicians, and 26.5 percent of those are men under 35. What's 26.5 percent of 37,000? One-quarter of 37,000 is 9,250 and that's very close to (A), but remember we've still got another 1.5 percent to go. One percent of 37,000 is 370 and half of that, or .5 percent will be 185, so if you add 370 and 185 to 9,250 you end up with a total of 9,805 which is very close to (B), the correct answer.

# 26

**(B)** We want to find the sum of the absolute value of three, the absolute value of −4 and the absolute value of 3 − 4. Well, the absolute value of 3 is 3, the absolute value of −4 is 4. What's the absolute value of 3 − 4? Do the subtraction inside the absolute value sign first, and we get −1. What's the absolute value of −1? It's 1, so we have 3 + 4 + 1 or 8 as our sum for Question 26, (B).

# 27

**(C)** This looks like a right triangle on a coordinate grid, but it's not a normal coordinate grid—the lines on the grid don't represent integer units, they represent units of less than an integer. Going up on the $y$-axis, we have .5, 1.0, 1.5, and 2.0, so the lines each represent half an integer and, going to the left, the lines are labeled −0.4, −0.8, −1.2, so these each represent .4, and yet the diagram's not drawn to scale. Going left to right, the vertical lines are actually farther apart than the horizontal lines, which represent more value on the number line. Now, to find the area of the shaded region, a triangle, we need a base and a height. This is a right triangle because its base lies on the horizontal line on our grid and its height, the side to the right, lies right on a vertical line on the grid. What's the length of the bottom side? The far right end point is at −0.4 and the far left end point is at −1.6, and the difference is 1.2 units, so the base is 1.2. The lower right vertex has value .5 and the upper right vertex has value 2.0—the difference is 1.5, so that's the height. The base is 1.2 and the height is 1.5, and the formula for the area of a right triangle is one half base times height. We have 1.2 as our base, we can call that $\frac{6}{5}$, 1.5 is $\frac{3}{2}$ so the area is $\frac{1}{2} \times \frac{6}{5} \times \frac{3}{2}$—that's $\frac{9}{10}$ or .9, choice (C).

**28** **(A)** You could find the number of tasks per hour from one computer, but that would add extra steps, because you want to find out how many computers you need to do a certain number of tasks in three hours. Well, if it can do 30 tasks in six hours, it can do 15 tasks in three hours. So, if you have two computers, that's 30 tasks, three is 45, four is 60, five is 75, six is 90. You can't get by with five because you have to get 80 tasks done, so you'll need six computers, (A).

**29** **(C)** One side of triangle $ABC$ is an edge of our cube, segment $BC$. But segments $AB$ and $AC$ aren't lengths of the edge of the cube or fractions of a length of an edge of the cube. Well, let's find the length of an edge of the cube. If the cube has volume 8, that's the length of an edge to the third power. Since 2 cubed is 8, the length of an edge of this cube is 2. We need $AB$ and $AC$, and so we have to concentrate on smaller right triangles on the same face of the cube that includes triangle $ABC$.

On the upper left, directly above point $A$ is an unlabeled vertex—let's call that point $Y$—and down below point $A$ is an unlabeled vertex—we'll call that point $X$. Look at triangle $AXC$. It's a right triangle because angle $AXC$ is one of the angles formed by two edges of a cube—and $AC$ is its hypotenuse. $AX$ is half an edge of the cube because point $A$'s the midpoint of edge $XY$. That means that $AX$ has length 1 and $XC$ is an edge of the cube, so it has length 2 . The legs of this right triangle are 1 and 2, so we can use the Pythagorean theorem to find the length of $AC$. $AX^2$ is $1^2$, $XC^2$ is $2^2$, $1^2$ is 1, $2^2$ is 4, the sum of 1 and 4 is 5, $AC^2$ is 5 and $AC$ has length $\sqrt{5}$. $AB$ is identical to $AC$ because triangle $AYB$ is identical to triangle $AXC$, so $AB$ also has length $\sqrt{5}$ and the perimeter of $ABC$ is $2 + 2\sqrt{5}$, choice (C).

**30** **(D)** The catch here is that it's not which of the following is 850 percent *of* $8 \times 10^3$, it's which of the following is 850 percent *greater than* $8 \times 10^3$. Well, what's bigger, 850 percent of 1 or a number that's 850 percent greater than 1? 850 percent of 1 is $8.5 \times 1$ or $8\frac{1}{2}$. But a number that's 850 percent greater than 1 is 1 + 850 percent of 1, it's 1 + 8.5 or 9.5. So the number we want is $9.5 \times 8 \times 10^3$. $9.5 \times 8 = 76$, so the answer is $76 \times 10^3$, or $7.6 \times 10^4$, in scientific notation.

**31** **(A)** We have to plug 1 in for $x$ and solve the equation for $y$. Well, $x + 3$ is 1 + 3— that's what's inside the parentheses and we do that first. We have 1 + 3 = 4 inside the parentheses. $y = 4^2$, $4^2$ is 16, and 16 is greater than 9, so the answer is (A).

**32** **(B)** In both columns we'll use the basic formula: rate × time = distance. In Column A, 40 mph × 4 hours traveled gives you 160 miles. In Column B, 70 mph × $2\frac{1}{2}$ hours, $2 \times 70 = 140$, half of 70 is 35, and 140 + 35 = 175 miles in Column B. 175 is greater than 160, so the answer is (B).

**33** **(D)** This is intended to conjure up a picture of heavy cookies in one bag and light grapes in the other, but you can't assume that because cookies are usually bigger than grapes, these cookies weigh more than these grapes. Since you don't know how much each cookie and each grape weighs, you can't find the number of cookies or grapes, so it's (D).

**34** **(C)** Here we have triangle $ABC$—base $BC$ has been extended on one side so we have an exterior angle drawn in and labeled 120°. We want to compare side lengths $AB$ and $BC$—in any triangle, the largest side will be opposite the largest angle, so we want to see which of these sides is opposite a larger angle. Since angle $A$ is labeled 60°, is angle $C$ less than, equal to, or greater than 60? Notice that the adjacent angle is 120°—the two together form a straight line, so their sum is 180°. 180 − 120 = 60, so angle $C$ is a 60° angle. Since the angles are equal, the sides are equal, and the answer is (C).

**35** (A) Notice the way the diagram is set up—$a + b$ is the same as $PQ$. Our equation is $8a + 8b = 24$. Divide by 8. We end up with $a + b = 3$. $PQ$ is 3 and since 3 is greater than 2, the answer is (A).

**36** (A) All we know is that $x$ is less than $y$ but though we don't know their values, we may know enough to determine a relationship. In Column A we have $y − x$, the larger number minus the smaller number, so you must get a positive difference, even if both numbers are negative. In Column B you have the smaller number minus the larger number—the difference is the same except this time it is negative. So you can determine a relationship—you know the answer is (A), the quantity in Column A is always greater than the quantity in Column B.

**37** (D) Remember, area equals $\frac{1}{2} \times$ base $\times$ height. Both triangles have the same height, because they have the same apex point $A$ and each of them has as its base a part of line $EB$. So the one with the larger base has the larger area. Which is bigger, $CB$ or $DE$? We have no way to figure it out. We are not given any relationships or lengths for any of those segments, so the answer is (D).

**38** (B) There's one box that's in both rows— the one in the middle with value $\frac{2}{9}$. In fact, we have $\frac{1}{3} + \frac{2}{9} + y$ in the horizontal row, $x + \frac{2}{9} + \frac{4}{5}$ in the vertical row, and we are comparing $x$ and $y$. Since $\frac{2}{9}$ is part of both rows, we can throw it out. So we have $\frac{1}{3} + y = \frac{4}{5} + x$. We have $\frac{1}{3} + y$ and that is the same as $\frac{4}{5} + x$. Since $\frac{4}{5}$ is greater than $\frac{1}{3}$, the number we add to $\frac{4}{5}$ has to be less than the number we add to $\frac{1}{3}$ for the sums to be the same. Since $\frac{4}{5}$ is greater than $\frac{1}{3}$, $x$ must be less than $y$. The answer is (B).

**39** (B) Looking at the fraction in Column A we have $\frac{1}{3} \times \frac{1}{4}$ in the numerator, $\frac{2}{3} \times \frac{1}{2}$ in the denominator. We can cancel the factor of $\frac{1}{3}$ from the numerator and denominator, right? Cancel a $\frac{1}{3}$ from each and you end up with $1 \times \frac{1}{4}$ in the numerator, $2 \times \frac{1}{2}$ in the denominator. Using the same approach, we can cancel a factor of $\frac{1}{4}$, so we're left with $1 \times 1$ in the numerator and $2 \times 2$ in the denominator, so the value of Column A is $\frac{1}{4}$. Now take a look at Column B. It's the reciprocal of the value in Column A. You have $\frac{2}{3} \times \frac{1}{2}$ in the numerator and $\frac{1}{3} \times \frac{1}{4}$ in the denominator. So you have $\frac{4}{1}$ as your value for Column B. With 4 in Column B and $\frac{1}{4}$ in Column A, the answer is (B).

**40** (B) Make a map—if you have trouble with geometry, this will make it much easier. Eileen drives due north from town $A$ to town $B$ for 60 miles. Start at a point and draw a line straight up. Label the point you started at $A$ and the point above it, $B$. Label 60 as the length of the distance from $A$ to $B$. Next she drives due east from town $B$ to town $C$ for a distance of

80 miles. Start at point *B*, draw a line straight over to the right, call the right endpoint *C,* and label as 80 the distance *BC.* You have a right angle, angle *ABC.* Well, the distance from town *A* to town *C* is the hypotenuse of a right triangle if you draw line *AC.* The two legs are 60 and 80 and this is one of our Pythagorean ratios. It is a 6-8-10 triangle except this time it is 60-80-100. So the distance from *A* to *C* is 100 miles, the same as our value for Column A, so the answer is (B).

**41** **(C)** Let's see if we can do something to make these look more alike by getting both sets of binomials so the $\sqrt{7}$s are in the front. We have $\sqrt{7} - 2$. Is that a positive or negative quantity? $2^2$ is 4, $3^2$ is 9 so $\sqrt{7}$ is between 2 and 3. We have $\sqrt{7} - 2$, that is positive, times $\sqrt{7} + 2$, that is positive again. Two positives in Column A and the product of two positives is always positive. What do we have in Column B? $2 - \sqrt{7}$, that is a negative number times negative $\sqrt{7} - 2$. $-\sqrt{7}$ is a negative, $-2$ is negative, that quantity is negative. You have the product of two negatives in Column B, but a product of two negatives is positive also, so you can't tell which is greater. Let's see if we can make these quantities look more alike. With the last one on the right, $-\sqrt{7} - 2$, if we divide the whole thing by $-1$, we're left with a positive $\sqrt{7}$ and a positive 2, $\sqrt{7} + 2$. On the right in Column B we have $(2 - \sqrt{7}) \times (-1) \times (\sqrt{7} + 2)$, and $(\sqrt{7} + 2)$ is also in Column A, so we can cancel. Those two factors are the same, right? We have $-1 \times (2 - \sqrt{7})$. Let's distribute again. What is $-1 \times 2$? It's $-2$. What is $-1 \times -\sqrt{7}$? It's $+\sqrt{7}$ so we end up with $+\sqrt{7} + -2$ or $\sqrt{7} - 2$. It's exactly the same as the factor in Column A. So the quantities are equal and the answer is (C).

**42** **(B)** We can see from our diagram that *r* and *s* are the coordinates of a point on our line. We have a line on the graph with one point with coordinates $(\frac{5}{2}, \frac{7}{2})$. The line also goes through the origin (0, 0), so what can we figure out about this line? Well, draw in the line *x* = *y*, a line which makes a 45° angle with the *x*-axis that goes from the lower left to the upper right—you notice that it goes through the point $\left(\frac{5}{2}, \frac{5}{2}\right)$, because any point on line *x* = *y* has the same *x* coordinate and *y* coordinate. Point $\left(\frac{5}{2}, \frac{7}{2}\right)$ falls above point $\left(\frac{5}{2}, \frac{5}{2}\right)$, because the *y* coordinate is greater, it's above the *x* = *y* line. Similarly, point (*r*, *s*) lies above the *x* = *y* line so the *y* coordinate is greater than the *x* coordinate and the *y* coordinate of that point is *s*. Where we have coordinates (*r*, *s*), *r* is the *x* coordinate, *s* is the *y* coordinate; *s* is greater than *r* in this case. The answer is (B), the quantity in Column B is greater.

**43** **(D)** We have $1 - \left(\frac{1}{4}\right)$ to the *x* power in Column A and we have 0.95 in Column B. That's a bizarre comparison, isn't it? Converting Column B, 0.95 into fraction form, $0.95 = \frac{95}{100} = \frac{19}{20}$. What do we have in Column A if *x* = 1? We have $1 - \frac{1}{4}$ or $\frac{3}{4}$. $\frac{19}{20}$ is greater than $\frac{3}{4}$. What happens if we have *x* = 2? Column A becomes $1 - \left(\frac{1}{4}\right)^2$. $\frac{1}{4}^2$ is $\frac{1}{4} \times \frac{1}{4}$ or $1 - \frac{1}{16}$ is $\frac{15}{16}$. So what's bigger, $\frac{15}{16}$ or $\frac{19}{20}$? Still $\frac{19}{20}$, but as *x* gets larger and we multiply $\frac{1}{4}$ times itself more times, the amount that we're taking away from 1 is going to get smaller and we'll be taking less than $\frac{1}{20}$ away from 1 as soon as we get to

$x = 3$. $\frac{1}{4}$ to the third power is $\frac{1}{64}$ and at that point Column A becomes $\frac{63}{64}$. What is bigger, $\frac{19}{20}$ or $\frac{63}{64}$? Well, $\frac{63}{64}$ is bigger, it is closer to 1, and there are two possible relationships here. If $x$ is 1 or 2, Column B is greater. If $x$ is 3 or larger, Column A is greater. The answer is choice (D).

**44** **(A)** If you draw in some diameters in the circles, you will see that $PS$ is equal to one diameter, and $PQ$ is equal to two diameters. Let one diameter be $d$. The perimeter of $PQRS$ is then $PS + PQ + SR + QR = 6d$. The circumference of a circle is $\pi d$, where $d$ is a diameter. Since we have two circles, the combined circumferences is $2 \times \pi d = 2\pi d$. Since $\pi$ is greater than 3 (it's about 3.14), the value in Column A is greater than $6d$ in Column B.

**45** **(B)** I hope you didn't try to figure out the exact values of each of these. Instead, if you look at Column B and Column A, they look sort of alike because they both have 3 in terms of a power. What is $3^{20}$? It's $3 \times 3^{19}$ right? So we can have $3^{19} + 3^{19} + 3^{19}$ in Column B. In Column A we have $3^{17} + 3^{18} + 3^{19}$. We can subtract $3^{19}$ from both sides and we're left with $3^{17} + 3^{18}$ in Column A and $3^{19} + 3^{19}$ in Column B. We know that $3^{19}$ is bigger than $3^{17}$ or $3^{18}$ so we know that $3^{19} + 3^{19}$ is bigger than $3^{17} + 3^{18}$. The answer is (B), the quantity in Column B is greater.

**46** **(E)** We have $4 + y = 14 - 4y$ and we want to solve for $y$. We can isolate the $y$s on one side of the equal sign by adding $4y$ to both sides, giving us $4 + 5y = 14$. Subtracting the 4 from both sides we get $5y = 10$. Divide both sides by 5 and get $y = 2$, (E).

**47** **(D)** Let's go the quickest, most obvious route and use the common denominator method. With $\frac{4}{5}$ and $\frac{5}{4}$, the denominator that we will use is easy to find; just use $5 \times 4$ or 20. $\frac{4}{5}$ is $\frac{16}{20}$ and $\frac{5}{4}$ is $\frac{25}{20}$. $\frac{16}{20} + \frac{25}{20}$ is $\frac{41}{20}$, which is (D).

**48** **(E)** First we need to find $m$. We are told that $3^m$ is 81. Well, 81 is $9 \times 9$. 9 is $3^2$. So we have $3^2 \times 3^2 = 81$ or $3 \times 3 \times 3 \times 3 = 81$. How many factors of 3 are there in 81? There are 4, so $m$ has the value 4. Now what's $4^3$? $4 \times 4$ is 16. $16 \times 4$ is 64. So (E) is correct, 64 is $m^3$.

**49** **(B)** We are looking for the area in square meters of square $C$. Now notice we have one side of square $B$ butted up against one side of square $A$—they're not the same length, but the difference in their lengths is made up by the length of a side of square $C$. One side of square $B$ + one side of square $C$ = one side of square $A$. We can figure out the length of the side of $A$ and length of the side of $B$, which will let us figure out the length of side of $C$. That is what we need to figure out the area of square $C$. The area of a square is its side squared. The area of square $A$ is 81, so it has a side of $\sqrt{81} = 9$. The area of square $B$ is 49, so it has sides of length $\sqrt{49} = 7$. So $9 = 7 + C$, so $C$ must have length 2. So we have 2 as the length of the side of square $C$, $2^2$ is 4, there are 4 square meters in gardening area $C$, and the answer is (B).

**50** **(E)** We can figure out how many students scored exactly 85. Twenty-three scored 85 or over, and 18 scored over 85. So $23 - 18$ or 5 students scored exactly 85 on the exam, but that's no help. How many students scored less than 85? We don't know—we can't answer this question. It's (E), it can't be determined.

**51** **(C)** We're asked in which year the energy use in country *Y* was closest to 650 million kilowatt hours, so we just have to follow the jagged line which represents energy use from left to right until we encounter a vertical line representing a year in which we're close to 650 million. The one year in which this is true is 1970. In no other year are we as close, so (C), 1970, is our answer.

**52** **(C)** In order to find how many categories had energy use greater than 150 million kilowatts, you have to find out how many total kilowatts were used in that year using the line graph. You see that there were 600 million kilowatts used in 1965. What is the relationship of 150 million kilowatts to 600 million kilowatts? It's 25 percent of 600 million kilowatts, so we're looking for categories with more than 25 percent of the energy use for 1965. How many categories exceeded 25 percent? Just two, government and industrial. So our answer is (C).

**53** **(D)** We can estimate quite a bit from our graph. If we look at our line chart, we can see that as time goes on, energy use goes up pretty steadily. It went up sharply between 1960 and 1965, then more gradually from 1965 to 1980. Because in more recent years the overall use was much greater, if the percent of industrial use was about the same over all the years, then as the overall use increases, the amount used for industrial purposes will increase also. Let's take a quick look at the bar graph and see if that is the case. Was the percent being used for industrial use about the same? Well, it didn't fluctuate much from 1960 to 1970, but in 1975 industrial use jumped significantly as a percent of the total, then shrank significantly going to 1980. The most likely answer is 1975, and if you find 40 percent of 690 million, your amount for 1975, you get 276 million kilowatt hours. Then if you find 20 percent of 710 million, your amount for 1980, you only get 142 million kilowatt hours, so (D), 1975, is the correct answer.

**54** **(D)** What we are going to do for 1960 and 1965 is find the per capita personal use, then find the percent decrease from 1960 to 1965. To do that, we have to plug in a value for the population of country *Y* for 1960. Let's use 100 million for the '60s population. The per capita use in 1960 is the total personal use, which is 30 percent of 500 million, that's 150 million. We know that 150 million, the total personal use, equals 100 million, the population × the per capita use. The per capita use is $\frac{3}{2}$ or 1.5. Going on to 1965, we are told the population increased by 20 percent, so in 1965 the population was 120 million people. What was the total personal use of energy? It was a little bit less than 20 percent of our total 600 million so we'll call it 20 percent of 600 million, or 120 million. If total personal use is 120 million and we have 120 million people, that's one kilowatt hour per person. What's the percent decrease? It's a decrease of $\frac{1}{3}$, $33\frac{1}{3}$ percent. But remember, in 1965, they were using a little more energy for personal use than we figured. The correct answer must be a little greater than $33\frac{1}{3}$ percent, so 40 percent, (D), is the correct answer.

**55** **(A)** Statement I says farm use of energy increased between 1960 and 1980. In 1960, 500 million. In 1980, 710 million kilowatt hours were used. What was the percent of farm use in 1960? It was 30 percent of the total in 1960 and a little bit less than 30 percent, around 28 percent, in 1980. The percent is very close together while the whole has become much larger from 1960 to 1980, so 30 percent of 500 million is less than 28 percent of 710 million. Farm use of energy did go up in that 20-year period and Statement I is going to be part of our answer. That eliminates two answer choices, (B) and (D).

How about Statement II? This one is harder. It says that in 1980, industrial use of energy was greater than industrial use of energy in 1965. But what was it in 1965? Industrial use of energy in 1965 was 30 percent of 600 million. We got the percent from the bar graph, the total from the line chart. Okay, 30 percent of 600 million is 180 million. But what about 1980? In 1980 industrial use of energy was 20 percent of a larger whole, 710 million kilowatt hours. Well, 20 percent of 710 is 142 million. That's less than 180 million, isn't it? In fact, industrial use of energy went down from 1965 to 1980, so this can't be inferred from the graph and it's not part of our answer. That cuts out (C) and (E), leaving choice (A), I only. Statement III is another easy one to eliminate because it says more people were employed by the government of country Y in 1980 than in 1960. These graphs deal only with energy use, not with employment, so it's irrelevant and we can eliminate it. Only Statement I can be inferred, and (A) is correct.

**56** (E) The average is $\frac{\text{The sum of terms}}{\text{The number of terms}}$. Here we have $y - z$ and the other number, which we will call $x$. The average of $x$ and $y - z$ is $3y$, so $3y = \frac{x + y - z}{2}$. Multiplying both sides by 2 gives $6y = x + y - z$. Subtracting $y - z$ from both sides gives $5y + z = x$. So the other number, $x$, is $5y + z$, answer choice (E).

**57** (B) We're told that the area of triangle $ABC$ is 35 and in our diagram we're given a height for triangle $ABC$. If we use $BC$ as the base of the triangle, the perpendicular distance from segment $BC$ up to point $A$ is 7, so we can find the length of $BC$. When we find the length $BC$, the base of triangle $ABC$, what do we have? We have the hypotenuse of right triangle

$BDC$. Given the hypotenuse and the length of leg $BD$, which is given in the diagram as 6, we'll be able to find the third leg of the triangle, side $DC$, which is what we're looking for. Okay, going back to triangle $ABC$ where we started, the area is 35 and the height is 7. The area of a triangle is $\frac{1}{2}$base $\times$ height, so $\frac{1}{2}$base $\times$ height is 35, $\frac{1}{2} \times 7 \times$ length $BC$ is 35. That means $7 \times$ length $BC$ is 70, so $BC$ must have length 10. Now we can look at right triangle $BDC$. Here is a right triangle with one leg of length 6, the hypotenuse of length 10 and the third side unknown; what we have is a 6-blank-10 right triangle. That's one of our famous Pythagorean ratios—it's a 6-8-10 triangle. So $DC$ must have length $2 \times 4$, or 8, (B).

**58** (A) We're trying to find the shortest distance in meters a person would have to walk to go from point $A$ to a point on side $BC$ of the triangular field represented in our diagram. In order to get the shortest distance from side $BC$ up to point $A$, we want to draw a perpendicular line from point $A$ down to side $BC$. That will divide up the triangular field into right triangles. Let's draw in the path from point $A$ down to segment $BC$ and call the new vertex we make point $D$. We just created two smaller right triangles, $ADC$ and $ADB$. Now our diagram tells us that length $BC$ is 160 meters and $AB$ is 100 meters—$AC$ is also 100 meters. Now each of these two right triangles has 100 meters as the length of its hypotenuse. What does that tell you about triangle $ABC$? $AB$ and $AC$ have the same lengths, so this is an isosceles triangle. That means that when you drew in the perpendicular distance from $A$ down to $D$, you split that isosceles triangle into two identical right triangles. Length $BD$ is the same as length $BC$. So each of them is half of 160 meters, or 80 meters each. We have right triangles with hypotenuses of length 100 meters each and one leg of each these right triangles is 80 meters. This is a 3-4-5 right triangle, with each member of the ratio multiplied by 80. So $AD$ must have length 60, and the minimum distance is 60 meters, (A).

# 59

**(D)** We're told the ratio of $2a$ to $b$ is eight times the ratio of $b$ to $a$. That's awkward to keep track of in English—it's a little easier to write fractions. The ratio of $2a:b$ equals $2\frac{a}{b}$. So $2\frac{a}{b} = 8\left(\frac{b}{a}\right)$. We're asked to find what $\frac{b}{a}$ could be; that may tell you there's more than one possible value for $\frac{b}{a}$, but let's start with the equation we just put together using translation and isolate $\frac{b}{a}$. To do that, we'll divide both sides of the equation by 8, which is the same as multiplying by $\frac{1}{8}$. So now we have $\frac{1}{8} \times 2\frac{a}{b} = \frac{b}{a}$. Well, what is $\frac{1}{8} \times 2\frac{a}{b}$? It's $\frac{a}{4b}$. So $\frac{a}{4b} = \frac{b}{a}$. We need to multiply both sides of the equation right now on both sides by $\frac{b}{a}$. It'll be more complicated on the right side but simpler on the left because the $a$s and $b$s on the left side will cancel out, and you'll be left with $\frac{1}{4}$. On the right you have $\frac{b}{a} \times \frac{b}{a} = \frac{b^2}{a^2}$. So we have $\frac{1}{4} = \frac{b^2}{a^2}$. So $\frac{b}{a}$ could represent positive or negative $\frac{1}{2}$.

# 60

**(D)** A dentist earns $n$ dollars for each filling plus $x$ dollars for every 15 minutes. So the money is figured in two different ways; dollars for each filling and dollars per hour, represented in terms of 15 minutes. Our result will be a two-part answer choice. If you can figure out one part, it will let you eliminate some choices. She put in 21 fillings. She makes $n$ dollars for each, so she gets $21n$ dollars for fillings. You can eliminate (B) and (E) because (B) has only $14n$ in it, and (E) has $\frac{21}{4}n$ dollars in it. That narrows our choices to (A), (C), and (D).

How about the hourly rate? The dentist works 14 hours in a week. Does that mean she makes $14x$ dollars? No, because the rate is dollars for every 15 minutes. Now if she makes $x$ dollars for every 15 minutes and 15 minutes is $\frac{1}{4}$ of an hour, then we have to multiply that rate by 4 to get the rate per hour, it's $4x$ dollars per hour. Well, $4x$ times 14 hours is $56x$, so (D), $56x + 21n$, is correct.

## Section Three Explanations–Analytical

### Game 1: Questions 1–3

*The Action*
Five spices to arrange: *A, C, N, S,* and *T.*

*The Rules*
1) *N* must be harvested before *T.*

2) Cloves must be harvested immediately after allspice—no other spice can come between them.
3) *S* can't be first.

There are no overlaps here—no spices are mentioned by more than one rule. We know from Rule 1 that *T* isn't first, from Rule 2 we know *C* isn't first and from Rule 3 we know that *S* isn't first, so the first spice is either *N* or *A.*

**1** **(A)** Let's take Rule 3 first and try to throw out answer choices. (B) has sage in the number one spot, so it's out. Rule 2 gives us our *AC* unit—*A* has to be immediately before *C*—choice (C) has *A* first and *C* fourth, and (D) has *C* before *A,* so they're both out. Rule 1 gives us our answer—*N* is before *T,* and choice (E) has *N* coming after *T.* (E)'s out, so it's (A) for this question.

**2** **(D)** If we put *N* fourth, what are the consequences? Rule 1 springs to mind—nutmeg is before thyme. If *N* is fourth, *T* must be fifth. Now we have our *AC* unit, and we have *S.* We know *S* can't be first, and it can't be second either, since we can't separate *A* and *C.* *S* is third, so we've completed our sequence—*A, C, S, N, T.* Choice (D) must be false, since cloves can't be immediately followed by nutmeg. We need cloves, sage, and nutmeg second, third, and fourth. We don't have to go through the others as long as you know that only sequence *A, C, S, N,* and *T* will work, and, again, it's (D) for Question 2.

**3** **(C)** First, put *S* in the second slot and look for a spot for *A*—it's joined with *C,* which limits our options. *A* can't be first since *C* would then be second and the second slot is taken, so eliminate choices (A) and (B). *A* can't be last since *C* comes after *A,* so scratch (D) and (E), leaving (C). So (C), third and fourth, is correct, and that's it for that game, which was short and quite easy.

**4** **(B)** We need a statement that weakens or has no effect on the logic. The conclusion here is that the way a judge came into his job often determines the result of a case. Judges decide differently depending on their term length—short termers think in light of political influences, while lifelong judges rely on a tradition of judicial wisdom. The author provides no supporting evidence, so the wrong choices will likely be evidence that strengthens the argument.

(A) gives support, asserting that if judges want to keep their jobs, they're likely to be swayed by voters, to improve their election chances. (C) shows that short termers rule in ways that the voters approve of. In (E), we find that only short term judges use pollsters—people who track public opinion. So (A), (C) and (E) lend credence to the allegations about the political sensitivity of short-term judges. (D) supports the viewpoint on lifelong judges, saying that appointed judges show consistency, implying that those judges turn a blind eye to politics. We're left with (B). If long termers act on their political knowledge, they're as fickle as the short termers. If they don't act on their political knowledge, it's simply irrelevant. (B) doesn't support the argument, and it's correct for this question.

**5** **(E)** The author believes that a climate of peace has been created by spending on weapons systems and supports this claim by indicating that a decrease in conflicts can be attributed to the robust deployment of weapons systems. The author sees a causal connection between defense readiness maintained by greater spending and the lower number of attacks. (E) is the assumption underlying this connection. The author must assume that had defense spending not gone up, the number of attacks would have increased.

(A), in its reference to the causes of military action, is outside the scope. In (B), the author doesn't tell us that more defense spending has prevented military actions, and it is certainly not a necessary assumption. There's no claim about the future of peace for (C). Finally, (D)'s equation of weapons and personnel is silly—if the author has an opinion on this issue, he's keeping it to himself, so we can't ascribe this view to him. (E)'s the answer for Question 5.

**6** **(C)** Within five years it will be cheaper to buy tuners and amplifiers separately instead of buying an integrated receiver. Previously, a receiver combining both tuner and amp was cheaper than the two purchased separately. What has changed? In other words, what's the basis of the author's claim? It's a recent trend showing that the average retail prices of tuners and amps have declined 20 percent and 35 percent respectively, while the average retail price of an integrated receiver has declined only 12 percent. But percentages often can't be compared unless you know the actual numbers. Try plugging in numbers. If tuners and amps each used to cost $1,000 apiece, while receivers used to cost only $100 apiece, then the 20 percent decline in the tuner and the 35 percent decline in the amp over the past two years wouldn't have brought them near the cost of a receiver. Tuners would cost $800 and amps $650 while a 12 percent decline in the price of a receiver would bring its price to under $90. In five years a receiver will probably still be the better bargain. While the author implies that the price gap has been closing in the past two years, we don't know how much it has closed or the rate at which it will close in the next five years, so (C) is correct.

(A), (B), (D), and (E) don't help you decide the significance of the percent decline in the average prices. The life expectancy of stereo equipment, (A), is outside the scope. As for (B), this doesn't tell you anything about which component costs less—outside the scope. So is (D)—sales projections tell you nothing about the actual cost of the equipment. (E) is even farther out in left field in talking about the consumers rather than the equipment, so it's (C) for this question.

## Game 2: Questions 7–10

*The Action*
Eight articles—five must be selected. Let's put theater articles in capitals and dance articles in lower case: *F, G, H, J, k, l, m, o.*

*The Rules*
1) We need at least three lowercase letters, so we either have three lowercase and two capitals, or four lowercase and one capital. If you're told that one lowercase isn't chosen, you can circle the other three. This kind of unpacking of rules can help you make realizations at the top of the game.

2) If *J* is chosen, *m* can't be. Put this together with Rule 1, and you see that if you cross out *m*, you know you can circle *k*, *l*, and *o*, and if you choose *m*, you have to cross out *J*.

3) If you choose *F*, you must choose *J*. Note: This doesn't mean that if you have *J* you have *F*.

*Rule Overview*
Both Rule 2 and Rule 3 mention *J*, and you can combine them. If you have *J*, you can't have *m* and in order to have *F*, you must have *J*, so this tells us that you can't have *F* and *m* in the same group.

**7** **(E)** Question 7 tells us that *m* isn't chosen, and since *m* is a lowercase letter you have to choose the three remaining ones. So cross out *m*, circle *k*, *l*, and *o* and you need go no further. We're asked which must be chosen—(E) suggests *k*, and it's our answer. (A) through (D) are all capital letters, so they're out and it's (E) for this question.

**8** **(C)** Let's make out a roster, circle *J*, and see what happens. Rule 2 tells us that if *J* is chosen, *m* is not, and if we cross out *m* we circle *k*, *l* and *o*. We have *J, k, l,* and *o* circled. Any of the remaining letters can be fifth—*F, G,* or *H.* There are three possible groupings—*J, k, l, o, F; J, k, l, o, G;* and *J, k, l, o, H.* So (C), three, is correct.

**9** (A) We just know that the choice of one article will make only one group of published articles acceptable, so let's start with the entities that we know the most about. As we saw in Question 8, choosing *J* yields three possible groups, not just one, so we can eliminate (C). *m,* (E), was mentioned in Rule 2 and in our deduced rule about *F* and *m* being incompatible. If you circle *m,* you have to cross out *J* and *F,* but the rest is wide open, so we can eliminate (E). What about *F?* If you circle *F,* Rule 3 says you have to circle *J,* and when you circle *J,* Rule 2 says you have to cross out *m,* and once you cross out *m,* you have to circle *k, l,* and *o,* and those are your five articles, *F, J, k, l, o,* so (A) is correct for this question.

**10** (E) If you circle *G,* what follows? Nothing obvious, so our best bet is to try out the choices by attempting to disprove them. (A)—must it follow if *G* is chosen that *J* is not chosen? Well, what happens if *J* is chosen? If *G* and *J* are circled, we need three lowercase letters to satisfy Rule 1, and *k, l,* and *o* will fit the bill quite nicely, since we know we can't have *m* according to Rule 2, so as a group, *G, J, k, l, o* is perfectly acceptable. We can have *G* and *J,* so we can eliminate (A). (B) looks a little wordy—let's jump to (C), which says *H* is not chosen. If you circle *G* and *H,* you could fill out an acceptable group—you could have *G, H, k, l, m* or *G, H, l, m, o* or *G, H, k, l, o,* etcetera. Let's jump to (E) which says *F* isn't chosen. Well, if we circle *F* along with *G,* we know that we have to circle *J,* since Rule 3 says if *F* is chosen, *J* is chosen. But we have to choose five, and we've got three capitals circled here—there'd be no way to get three lowercase letters. If *G* is chosen, *F* can't be chosen—since we can disprove the statement in (E), choice (E) is correct.

For the record let's look at choices (B) and (D). The grouping *G, J, k, l, o* shows that (D) needn't be true and the grouping *G, k, l, m, o* shows that (B) needn't be true.

## Game 3: Questions 11–14

*The Action*
This oddball game involves matching up dogs and trainers, then moving them around according to different commands. We have three trainers, *L, M,* and *O* for short and three dogs with the same initials—*l, m,* and *o.* We have three rooms, rooms 1, 2, and 3. We start with an initial room assignment for each trainer and each dog: *Ll* in Room 1, *Mm* in Room 2, and *Oo* in Room 3.

*The Rules*
1) Command *W* involves trainers only—the trainer in Room 1 moves to Room 2, the trainer in Room 2 moves to Room 3, and the trainer in Room 3 moves to Room 1.
2) With command *X,* the dogs in Rooms 1 and 2 switch places, and the dog in Room 3 stays put.
3) When command *Y* is called, the dogs in Rooms 2 and 3 switch places.
4) When command *Z* is called, the dogs in Rooms 1 and 3 switch places.
5) Command *A* is trickier—the dogs return to their original trainers. So *l* returns to *L, m* to *M* and *o* to *O.*

**11** (B) Question 11 is basic—*Ll* in Room 1, *Mm* in Room 2, and *Oo* in Room 3. Command *W* is called, and Luis in Room 1 moves to Room 2, Molly in Room 2 moves to Room 3, and Oprah in Room 3 moves to Room 1. So we have in Room 1, *Ol*—the lowercase letters, the dogs, have stayed put—in Room 2 *Lm* and in Room 3 *Mo.* Which choice is true of that arrangement? (B), Molly is in Room 3. Yes, she's there with Onyx.

Looking at the wrong choices, (A) is out because Oprah is with Lassie, not with Mugs. (C) is out because Molly is with Onyx. (D) is out since Luis is in Room 2, and (E) is out because Luis is with Mugs, not with Onyx.

# 12

**(C)** We need to get Onyx to Room 2 from Room 3. One *Y* would do it—the dogs in Rooms 2 and 3 would switch, but that's not a choice. The only single command here is the one call of *W* in choice (A), but that moves trainers, not dogs, so it's out. The two calls of *X* suggested by (B) would leave Onyx where she started in Room 3. What about (C), two *W*s, then one *A*? Well, the *W* command moves only trainers so we'd have Oprah in Room 1, Luis in Room 2, and Molly in Room 3. A second call of *W* would move Molly to Room 1, Oprah to Room 2, and Luis to Room 3. Then if we got a call of *A*, all of the dogs would seek out their original trainers—Mugs with Molly in Room 1, Onyx with Oprah in Room 2 and Lassie with Luis in Room 3—and Onyx would end up in Room 2. That's what we're looking for.

Let's see why choices (D) and (E) are wrong. (D) suggests two *W*s and one *Z*. The two *W*s give us *Ml* in Room 1, *Om* in Room 2, and *Lo* in Room 3. The *Z* would switch the dogs in Rooms 1 and 3, putting Onyx in Room 1, not in Room 2. The same for (E)—it puts Onyx in Room 1 because the two *X* calls cancel each other out and the *Z* would switch Lassie and Onyx—we're trying to get Onyx into Room 2, not Room 1. So (C) is correct for Question 12.

# 13

**(B)** There's a long way and a short way to do Question 13—the long way is to try out each sequence and see which one yields *O* and *l* in Room 2. The short, and smart way, is to think it through—see where *O* and *l* are in the original arrangement and see what commands would move them to Room 2. Thus, to get Oprah from her original position in Room 3 to the desired position in Room 2 you'd have to use *W*, the only one that moves trainers, twice. The first *W* moves Oprah to Room 1, and the second *W* moves her to Room 2. We also want to get Lassie from Room 1 to Room 2, and to do that we need one *X*. Do any of the choices have two *W*s and one *X*? (B) does, and it's correct for Question 13.

Let's look through the wrong choices. (A)'s sequence of *X*, *Y*, and *W* puts Oprah in Room 1 and Lassie in Room 3. (C)'s suggestion of *Z*, *W*, and *A* puts Oprah again in Room 1, but Lassie in Room 2. (D) puts *O* and *l* together but in Room 1 rather than Room 2. (E) puts Oprah in Room 2, but Lassie's in Room 3. Again, it's (B).

# 14

**(C)** We can answer this question the same way we answered Question 13. We want to get Molly and Onyx in Room 1, Oprah and Mugs in Room 2, and Luis and Lassie in Room 3. Let's deal with the trainers first. In order to get from *L*, *M*, *O* to *M*, *O*, *L*, you call *W* twice. Call *W* once, you'll get *O*, *L*, *M* in rooms 1, 2, and 3 respectively—call it again and you'll get *M*, *O*, *L*, which is what we want. Now for the dogs—how to go from *l*, *m*, *o* to *o*, *m*, *l*? One call of *Z* will do it. Command *Z* will make the dogs in Rooms 1 and 3 change places, giving us *o*, *m*, *l* as desired.

But two *W*s and one *Z* isn't a choice, so there must be some other way to get this arrangement. What if we tried calling A between the two calls of *W*? The first *W* would give us Oprah in 1, Luis in 2, and Molly in 3 with the dogs in their original positions. But if you called *A*, the dogs would seek out their original trainers, so you'd have Oprah and Onyx in Room 1, Luis and Lassie in Room 2, and Molly and Mugs in Room 3. Keeping in mind that we'll have a second *W* for the trainers, what will line up the dogs? *Y* will, putting Mugs in Room 2 and Lassie in Room 3 and we'd have our dogs all set. Our second *W* will get the trainers in the proper place, so we've got our answer, *W*, *A*, *Y*, *W*, choice (C).

## Game 4: Questions 15–18

### The Action

Seven people to distribute in eight apartments—one will remain empty. You can think of it as seven people and one nonperson to be distributed in the eight apartments, which are arranged in two levels of four adjacent apartments. The action of the game is taking your people, P, Q, R, S, T, V, W, and E for the empty apartment, and filling them in the eight apartments. We'll make A level the top and B level the bottom.

### The Rules

1) W lives directly above S, which tells us that there has to be another apartment. W is on the A level and S is on the B level.

2) S and Q are on different levels, so Q must be on A level.

3) P and T are adjacent on the same level. Adjacent means it could be either TP or PT.

4) This jibes nicely with Rule 3—it tells us that T is not in one of the end apartments—T is not in Apartment 1 or in apartment 4. We know from Rule 3 that P is in an Apartment on one side of T, and Rule 4 tells us someone else is on the other side of T. So T is in either Apartment 2 or Apartment 3.

5) W is next to the empty apartment on the same level. We know that W is on level A, so the empty apartment is on level A.

**Recap:** So far we have W, the empty apartment, and Q on level A, S on level B—who's still up in the air? P, T, V, and R. But we know that P and T have to be adjacent on the same level, and they can't be on level A, since there are three apartments filled there, so by deduction we know that P and T are on level B. V and R are left—one will be on A, the other on B.

15 **(A)** Who must be on level B? Well, the only definite person on level B among the choices is P, choice (A) the correct answer. As for the others, Q, choice (B), and the empty apartment, (E),

are both on Level A. As for choices (C) and (D), R and V, we know that one's on Level A, the other on B, but we don't know which is which. Again (A) is the correct answer.

16 **(E)** Here we learn about W—W lives in Apartment A-2 (Level A, Apartment 2). With W there, we put S directly underneath in Apartment B-2. We also know that the empty apartment is either A-1 or A-3 so that it's adjacent to W on the same level. T has to be in either B-2 or B-3, because it can't be on the end, so since B-2 is occupied by S, T has to go in B-3 and we can put P in B-4, so (E) is correct.

As for (D), P is in Apartment 4 on B level, not on A level. And with choices (A) and (C), we have no more light on the R and V issue here. We know one's on Level A, the other's on B, but that's all we know. As for (B), we know the empty apartment could be either 1 or 3 on Level A. Again, (E) is correct.

17 **(E)** We're told that R is in A-3 and that R is directly above P. So P is in B-3, and we need a place for V. Once we have P in B-3, we know that since T can't be on the end so it can't be in B-1 or B-4, it has to be next to P in B-2. Now turn to your other large unit, the W, S, empty unit. Either W and S could be in the two Apartment 1s or in the two Apartment 4s. But they can't be in the two Apartment 4s since the empty apartment has to be next to W on the same level. The apartment next to A-4 is A-3 and that's occupied by R. So W and S have to be in A-1 and B-1 respectively, and the empty apartment goes next to W in A-2. Q would go into A-4 and we've got the place for V—only B-4 is left. That's (E), which is the correct answer.

18 **(C)** Put Q in A-2, directly above T, which is in B-2. The question asks about A-1, so we'll keep an eye on it as we make our deductions.

Now we turn to our W, S, empty apartment unit. Since W and the empty apartment have to be adjacent on Level A, there's only one place for them—in A-3 and

4, in either order. So only two people could go in A-1. Q, W and the empty apartment are out of the running, and T, P, and S are out because they're on Level B. It's between V and R—but since we're only looking for possibility here, either one will do. R is not an answer choice but V is—it's (C), which is correct for Question 18.

## Game 5: Questions 19–22

### The Action
Seven people to distribute into three groups. Let's put senior members in capitals, F, G, H, and the junior members and applicants in lowercase letters, k, m and p, r—the only distinction that's significant is senior members from the rest since there has to be one senior member in each game. There are three different groups—backgammon with two people, chess with two, and dominoes with three.

### The Rules
1) Seven people—seven slots.
2) We have three senior members, so we have one capital letter in each group.
3) G and r don't play the same game.
4) H and p must play the same game. They could play backgammon or chess or they could be two-thirds of the domino group, so if H and someone other than p are playing the same game (or p and someone else), they must play dominoes.
5) m doesn't play dominoes.

**19** (D) Try Rule 5—both (A) and (C) violate it by having m play dominoes. Rule 4 looks helpful—H and p play the same game, but all the remaining choices, (B), (D), and (E) comply. Rule 3 tells us that G and r can't play the same game—(E) has them together. Rule 2 says we need a senior in each game. (B) has F and H, two seniors both playing dominoes and no senior playing chess, so (B) is out.

**20** (D) Neither k nor r is a senior and we need a senior for each game—and only dominoes has three people playing it. Who can be the senior? It can't be H, since H is with p. It can't be G either since G and r can't play the same game, so it's F. F, k, and r are playing dominoes, making (D) correct.

**21** (A) Since r is lowercase we know that the other backgammon player must be a senior. G and r can't play together, so G's out. Since H and p are together, it can't be H. It must be F, so F and r are playing backgammon.

Now go to your largest unit—the Hp unit. Either H and p are the entire chess group or two-thirds of the domino group. If they play chess, G, m, and k play dominoes but m can't play dominoes, so this won't work and H and p must play dominoes. With F in backgammon and H in dominoes the other senior, G, must play chess with m, and k must play dominoes with H and p. When r plays backgammon, there's only one grouping possible, so (A), one, is the correct answer for this question.

**22** (B) Which group can't play the same game? What about H and r ? Remember when H is with someone else, p comes along so we'd have H, p, and r together, and they'd have to play dominoes. That would leave, say, F and m playing backgammon and G and k playing chess—no problem, so (A) can't be our answer. Nix (E), p and r, since we know that H, p, and r playing dominoes is okay. What about (B)? Well, k and m are both lowercase, and we need a capital for each, so k, m, plus a capital would play dominoes (since there are three of them). But m can't play dominoes, so k and m can't play together, making (B) correct for Question 22.

For the record, F and m, (C), would be fine. We could have F and m playing backgammon, G and k playing chess and H, p, and r playing dominoes. We've seen (D)'s suggestion of G and m before. G and m could play backgammon, F and k chess, and H, p, and r dominoes. The impossible pair is (B), the correct answer.

**23** **(D)** According to the passage, when foreign aid money is tied, nation A gives money to nation B with the understanding that B will use the money only to buy A's products. That way, nation A makes most of its money back. The author says that European nations are phasing out this practice in order to avoid criticism leveled at other donors, "notably Japan." The inference to be drawn here is that Japan has been criticized for tying its foreign aid, so (D) is the inference we're looking for.

(A) isn't inferable because the passage discusses only *one* non-European nation, Japan, and its foreign aid policy. (E) says the same thing, that non-European nations are out for their own profit—one comment about Japan doesn't let you make sweeping inferences about non-European nations.

Choices (B) and (C) make statements of opinion—(B) about the role of ethical considerations and (C) about how to help underdeveloped countries—the author doesn't make any policy recommendations so (B) and (C) are wrong.

**24** **(D)** The author argues that we must accept inconvenience if we want to secure the well-being of our world. Most pollution is caused by vehicle fuel and, according to the author, it "must be cut regardless of the costs." That's best summarized by (D). We must do what's necessary, no matter how drastic and costly, to save the environment.

The closest choice is probably (B), but the if/then statement in (B) argues that a lower rate of car use would be sufficient to drastically reduce pollution. The author doesn't say that driving less is *sufficient* to cut pollution, but rather that it is *necessary* to cut pollution. (C) brings in the use of fuel by industry, which is outside the scope here. (A)'s saying that we've got to go back to the nineteenth century is too extreme to describe this argument. Finally, (E) states a causal relationship not implied in the stimulus—that people overuse their cars because they don't care about the environment. Again, (D) is correct.

**25** **(A)** When the commissary serves fish on workdays, all the actors eat there. When the commissary doesn't serve fish on workdays, none of the actors eat there. What happens on a nonworkday? We don't know. So you're asked what it means when all the actors are eating in the commissary. One possibility is that it's a workday and they're serving fish, but there's still the question of nonworkdays. If all we know is that the actors are eating in the commissary, it's a workday and fish is served or it's not a workday and fish may or may not be served on nonworkdays. No choice says exactly this, but (A) comes the closest. (A) gives you three possibilities—that it's not a workday, that the commissary is serving fish, which would have to be true on a workday, or both, that it's a nonworkday and fish is being served. So (A) is the correct answer for this question.

(E) was tricky—it lists only one of the possible types of days when the actors could be found in the commissary, the workday with fish. (B) also doesn't say anything about nonworkdays. (C) and (D) have the opposite problem, claiming that any day the actors are in the commissary is a nonworkday, but we know that's not true because the actors always eat in the commissary on workdays when they're serving fish. (A) is correct.

## Game 6: Questions 26–29

*The Action*
A lock has to be opened by pressing a combination of symbols. Each combination has five symbols: four letters and one number.

*The Rules*
1) This rule sets limits on the game—you'll be working with two basic options. Option 1 is the first situation described, where the number is second in the sequence. Option 2 is the second situation, where the number is the third symbol in the sequence.
2) Put a mark underneath the fourth and fifth space in each option.

3) We're dealing with Option 2, the one with the number in the third position. In Option 2, the fifth symbol must be either *B* or *D*, so we can write that under the fifth space in Option 2, *B* or *D* only.

4) The third symbol is a letter so you're dealing with, Option 1. In that combination there can't be any *F*s or *G*s.

5) There are different ways to take note of this—some of you may have chosen to circle the rule, others of you might have put something into your scratch work. Just don't forget it!

**Recap:** In Option 1, the number appears in the second place, there can't be an *F* or a *G*, and the fourth and fifth letters can't be the same. In Option 2, the number is in the third place, the fifth must be *B* or *D*, and the fourth place and the fifth place can't be the same. And the overall rule for the game is that the first letter has to be the letter that's closest to the beginning of the alphabet.

**26** **(D)** The quickest way to get through this is to take the rules and check the choices against them. Rule 1 eliminates (E) since it has the number in the fourth position. (C) can be thrown out because it has *G* in the fourth and the fifth positions—a Rule 2 no-no. Move on to Rule 3: The only one left with a number in the third position is (A) and (A) obeys Rule 3. Rule 4 applies to (B) and (D) because it talks about having a number in the second position—you can't have any *F*s or *G*s and (B) violates that rule with an *F* in the first position. Rule 5 eliminates (A). The letter *B* at the end of (A) violates Rule 5. (A) begins with the letter *E*, meaning that all the rest of the letters must appear later in the alphabet than *E*, and *B* doesn't. That leaves correct choice (D).

**27** **(E)** You can eliminate (B) and D) right off—numbers only appear in the second or the third position. Then (C) goes, since you can't start a sequence with *Y*—think about the alphabet—*X*, *Y*, *Z*. Only one letter comes after *Y*, so you'd be left with only one letter to fill the rest of the sequence, and

Rule 2 says that you can't have the fourth and fifth symbols the same. That leaves with (A), *F*, and (E), *E*. Seeing the *F* should make you suspicious—in Option 1 you can't use *F* at all, and in Option 2, where you've got the number in third place. In Option 2 you must end the sequence with *B* or *D*. If you start with *F*, you begin with a letter later in the alphabet than *B* or *D*, violating Rule 5. So *F* can't begin the sequence in Option 2 and *E*, (E), is the correct answer.

**28** **(A)** You're told about a combination with *B* first and *G* fourth. When you see *G*, you know you'll be dealing with Option 2 only because Option 1 can't contain *G*s. In Option 2, *B* is first, and you don't know what's second. The number is third, *G* is fourth, and fifth is either *B* or *D*, since in Option 2 fifth is either *B* or *D*. You've used *B* first, so you're left with only *D* for the fifth position. Your sequence has *B* first, you don't know what's second, a number third, *G* fourth, and *D* fifth. *D* has to be fifth and only (A) gives you that option, so it's correct.

**29** **(D)** The first thing is to figure out why the combination isn't acceptable. You have a number third so it's Option 2. You end with *B* or *D* and this one ends with *F*, so we need to switch that *F* for a *B* or a *D* and make the sequence correct. (A) offers to replace *F* with *B* but remember Rule 5—the first symbol must be closest to the beginning of the alphabet. If you replace *F* with *B* you break that rule because the sequence begins with *C*. The only way to put *B* at the end of this and still have an acceptable sequence would be to change the *C* to an *A* but you can't do that, so (A) won't work. Skim down to (D), replace the *F* with a *D*, which works with the rules for Option 2, the sequence ends with a *D*, and *D* comes later in the alphabet than *C*, so you're obeying Rule 5. So (D) is correct.

As for the others, if you do (B) and reverse the *C* and *P* you have Option 2 ending with an *F*—not acceptable. With (C) you reverse the *Q* and the 8 and you have Option 1 with the number second—but you can't have an *F* in Option 1, so (C) won't work. Finally, (E)

says replace the *C* with an *A*. Well, we talked about that when we were talking about (A). If you did (A) and (E) together you'd have an acceptable sequence but replacing the *C* with an *A* does not solve the problem of having the *F* at the end which isn't acceptable when the number is third. So (D) is correct.

**30** (E) The first sentence is evidence: some scientists argue that our planet may support more sources of protein than we think if presently unfished areas have as many fish in them as do the areas presently fished. The author then concludes that we can provide protein to the whole world even if population grows at its present rate. But his conclusion isn't expressed conditionally, and his evidence is. He's just *assuming* that there are as many fish in the unfished part of the ocean as there are in the fished part. Furthermore, he's assuming that the scientists are right, that those fish would mean the planet supports more protein than we believe. To conclude that we can feed the hungry masses, the author must assume that we can get the fish in the unfished areas, but maybe those areas are unfished because we can't fish them. Since we need to weaken the argument, we need an answer choice that contradicts one of these assumptions. Correct choice (E) denies the last one. Choice (E) says it will take 30 years before we can fish those areas, so we can't ensure the availability of protein to everyone over the next two decades.

As for the others, (A) supplies the view of some scientists that fish are less plentiful in the unfished areas. This isn't as damaging as (E). (B) is close, but the cost of the technology isn't as damning an obstacle as its availability. (C) focuses on cost. The author doesn't argue that the world can be fed *cheaply*. As for (D), cutting the population growth certainly doesn't weaken the argument. So (E) is correct.

**31** (A) It's possible for travelers to enter and remain in the Republic for anywhere from one to 59 days, but there's at least one condition for stays of longer than seven days. Although it's possible to stay for more than seven days, if you do so, you need a special visa. Correct choice (A) is simply a statement in which the antecedent, or if-clause, of the original is affirmed and the consequent, or then-clause, flows from it, just as it's supposed to. If a traveler wants to stay 14 days, then a special visa is required. This jibes perfectly with the if/then statement in the stimulus, so (A) it is.

(B) and (D) are wrong because each implies that some travelers don't need visas. We don't know that travelers staying fewer than seven days don't need anything. Maybe all travelers to the Republic need visas of some kind, so neither (B) nor (D) must be true. (C) fails by bringing up the topic of whether or not people have the visas they require. All the stimulus tells us is when a special visa is required. (E) comes out of thin air. Nothing precludes the possibility that every person in the Republic needs a visa, even those just passing through, so (E) isn't inferable from the stimulus, and (A) is correct.

**32** (B) The conclusion here is that the U.S. economy continues to grow and prosper. As evidence, the author cites the expansion over the last 15 years of the service sector, where last year alone 500,000 Americans found employment. She assumes that this growth correlates to growth in the economy. But what if declines in other sectors offset the growth in service? If, as correct choice (B) says, growth in the service sector can be at least partly attributed to a decline in the manufacturing and heavy industry sectors, then growth in the service sector can't be a reliable indicator of growth in the overall economy.

(A) tends to support the conclusion—job offers imply health, contributing to a sense that the economy isn't in bad shape. (C) doesn't do much to affect the author's conclusion. Just because the American economy isn't sluggish doesn't mean it's growing and prospering. (D) can be eliminated because the author is claiming that the American economy is prospering—she isn't claiming that it's prospering more than ever. Finally, (E) weakens the argument a bit, suggesting that some of the evidence for the claim of economic growth and health isn't as central as the author believes. But using the service sector as a barometer of economic growth may be valid, regardless of the doubt (E) casts on how much of that growth is caused by the service sector. Since (E)'s ability to weaken the argument is dubious while (B)'s is certain, it's (B) for this question.

## Game 7: Questions 33–37

### The Action
Three bells, a high, a medium, and a low, and eight rings. You ring the low bell three times, the medium bell three times, and the high bell two times.

### The Rules
1) The sixth ring is the medium bell—put it in.
2) You'll have to split the low rings up—they will always be separated by medium and high rings.
3) The two high bells will stick together throughout the game.

**33** **(B)** Starting with Rule 1, (C) puts a low bell sixth, which can't be true. Rule 2 won't let us ring the low bell twice in succession, so dump (D) and (E). And Rule 3 eliminates (A) by splitting up the high bells, leaving us with (B), the correct answer.

**34** **(E)** We have to ring the high bell fifth, so we've got to ring the other high bell fourth—the two high bells have to stay together and we've got the medium bell ringing sixth. Now we have to split up the low bells. We'll have to put two before this high-high-medium set, and one after. So we'll put one low first, one low third, then fill the space between with a medium. The beginning looks like this—low-medium-low-high-high-medium. You've got one low and one medium left. Does it matter which goes seventh and which eighth? No, either way would be acceptable. (A), the low bell is first, yes. (B) the medium bell is second, yes. (C), the low bell is third, yes. (D), the high bell is fourth, yes.

(E), the low bell is rung seventh—it could be true, but it could be eighth. So (E) could be true, but it doesn't have to be true, so it's correct.

**35** **(D)** We're told that we have a medium bell fourth and we know that there's a medium bell sixth. Sketching it out, we have eight spots for bells to be rung, and medium bells fourth and sixth. When can't the high bell be rung? Remember when we're talking about the high bell, we're talking about both high bells because they stay together. So you can't ring a high bell in five because there's no room for the other high bell next to it.

(A) puts the high bell first, and you'd ring the other high bell second and split up the low bells third, fifth, and seventh. (B) puts the high bell second and you can use the same sequence and ring a high bell second. (C) puts a high bell third, the other high bell second, and splits up the low bells by placing one first, one fifth, and one seventh. And (E) puts the high bell eighth. You can ring the other high bell seventh and still split up the lows by placing one first, one third, and one fifth. So (D) is the correct answer.

**36** **(D)** If you sketch out a sequence, one of the things you can see is that the third, fourth, and fifth group buts up against the medium bell in sixth. So all high and medium bells would be unacceptable in third, fourth, and fifth because you'd have a solid group of high and medium in the center and no way to split up those low bells on the ends. (D) has a high in third, a medium in fourth, and a medium in fifth, and it's the correct answer.

As for the wrong choices, (A) has high, medium, and low in third, fourth, and fifth. That works if we put a low first, the other high second, next to the high bell in third, and a medium and a low in seventh and eighth, if the high bells are together and the lows are split up. (B) has low, medium, and low, in third, fourth, and fifth. That makes it easy to split up the lows—we can put the third one in first and we still have two spaces at the end to keep the two highs together. (C) has the two highs in third and fourth and a low in fifth. We put a low first and a medium second next to the high in space three. That leaves seventh and eighth to put the other low and the other medium. Finally, (E) has high, low, and medium in third, fourth, and fifth. You put the high bell in second so it's next to first and third, and you put one low first and the other in seventh or eighth, with the other medium to keep them split up. (D) is correct.

**37** (C) (A) mentions ringing the high bell first. This may have "rung a bell" because, having done Questions 9 and 10, we've discussed whether or not it's possible to ring the high bell first—yes, it's acceptable. If you remembered that, you don't need to work out a sequence again. Let's skip to (D)—it says the high bell is fourth—you know that this is all right from Question 9. How about (E), ringing the low bell fifth? When we worked on Question 10 in trying out the possibilities we put the low bell fifth, so you know that this is acceptable. (B) says the low bell is rung second—what I did was put the low bell second and the medium first, put the two highs third and fourth, a low fifth, medium sixth, low seventh, medium eighth. That's acceptable, so (C) is correct—you can't ring the medium bell third. If you have a medium bell ringing third and another sixth, you have three groups of two spaces, first and second, fourth and fifth, seventh and eighth. One of those pairs has to contain the high bells but then you have three low bells to split up, and no way to do that. So the correct answer is (C).

## Game 8: Questions 38–42

*The Action*

Try a simple tack—break it into two flow charts, one following the Priority 1 mail and one following the Priority 2 mail—it's actually much simpler.

Information overload? Here's a breakdown: six cities, two types of memos, and the basic idea that they're sent from the head office to the branches. The second introductory paragraph: any branch that receives a memo from the head office has to pass it on to at least one other branch. The other branch can pass it on but it doesn't have to.

The real key to your work on this game is the second set of rules about which branches can send memos to which other branches. Look at the last rule—it says that Fresno can't send memos to any other branches. What that means in terms of the game is something very simple: Fresno is a dead end. Let's look at the questions.

**38** (B) One thing to notice is that you have to consider both Priority 1 and Priority 2, because both are sent from home to Atlanta. Check out both flow charts, and you notice that when memos go to Atlanta, in both cases, the next place they go is to Caracas. So the memos must leave Atlanta and go to Caracas, and that makes (B) correct. All of the wrong choices are only "could be trues"—you could send the memo on to Beijing, you could send it on to Dakar, to Edinburgh, to Fresno —but you don't have to.

**39** (E) Four of the choices describe routes of travel that the memo *could* have followed and one describes a route that the memo *could not* have followed and that's (E), a Priority 2 memo initially sent to Beijing. Take a look at the Priority 2 flowchart—start at the home office, send the memo to Beijing, and then send it where? The only place that you can send it is Fresno and Fresno is a dead end. So it can't be a memo sent from Edinburgh to

Fresno, so (E)'s correct. All the others work. (A), you can send a Priority 1 memo from Atlanta to Caracas to Beijing to Edinburgh to Fresno. (B), you can send a Priority 1 memo to Dakar to Caracas to Beijing to Edinburgh and then to Fresno. (C) is fine, a Priority 1 memo can be sent to Dakar, and then to Caracas, Beijing, Edinburgh, and Fresno. (D) is also fine, a Priority 2 memo can be sent to Atlanta to Caracas to Dakar to Edinburgh and then to Fresno.

**40** **(A)** If it wasn't originally sent to Atlanta, where was it sent? With Priority 2, the only places a memo can go from home are Atlanta and Beijing. If it didn't go to Atlanta, it went to Beijing. This will ring a bell because we're following the same path that we followed in the last question. The only place a Priority 2 memo can go after Beijing is Fresno, a dead end. Only two branches, Beijing and Fresno, could have seen the memo, and (A) is correct.

**41** **(C)** If the memo didn't go through Atlanta, where did it go? A Priority 1 memo would go to Dakar and a Priority 2 memo would go to Beijing. We want it to end up in Edinburgh—does that ring a bell? In Priority 2 we're dealing with the same path—a Priority 2 memo starting at home and going to Beijing then goes to Fresno, a dead end, so it can't do what this question asks. So all you have to do is concentrate on your Priority 1 system and see how a memo would go from Dakar to Edinburgh. After it goes to Dakar, the only place it can go is to Caracas, and from Caracas you could send it back to Dakar—but you want it to move toward Edinburgh. Send it to Beijing and the only place it can go is Edinburgh. So you take a Priority 1 memo and send it from home to Dakar to Caracas to Beijing then to Edinburgh. The question asks you how many branches saw this memo besides Edinburgh. Dakar, Caracas, and Beijing, that's three, and the answer is (C).

**42** **(D)** Here you'll have to try out both Priority 1 and Priority 2 memos. (A) asks if you can go from Atlanta to Caracas to Beijing. Yes, in both Priority 1 and Priority 2. (B) talks about going from Atlanta to Caracas to Beijing to Edinburgh. You know that both Priority 1 and Priority 2 you can go from Atlanta to Caracas to Beijing. Can you keep going to Edinburgh? Yes, in Priority 1—that's where you go from Beijing with Priority 1 memos. So (B) won't do it. As for (C), in Priority 2 you can go from Atlanta to Caracas to Dakar to Edinburgh. (D) suggests sending a memo from Beijing to Edinburgh to Fresno. A Priority 1 memo can't go to Beijing from the head office. The only way to get a Priority 1 memo to Beijing is through Atlanta or Dakar to Caracas and then on to Beijing. So (D) can't be the complete path of a Priority 1 memo from the home office because it can't start in Beijing.

As far as Priority 2 goes, when a Priority 2 memo leaves the head office and goes to Beijing, the only other place it can go is Fresno, the dead end. (D) describes a path that's impossible for both Priority 1 and Priority 2, so it's correct. (E) suggests sending from Dakar to Caracas to Beijing. That works in Priority 1; you can start in the home office, go to Dakar to Caracas to Beijing.

## Game 9: Questions 43–47

*The Action*
You have to sequence trophies on Shelves 1, 2, and 3, from top to bottom.

*The Rules*
2) Rule 2 seems to be the most helpful so let's look at it first. *F* must be on the shelf immediately above the shelf that *L* is on. You have two basic options. In Option 1 you place *F* on Shelf 1 and L on Shelf 2. With Option 2 you put *F* on Shelf 2 and *L* on Shelf 3.
1) In Option 1, we can write next to Shelf 2 "no *J*," and in Option 2, we can write next to Shelf 3 "no *J*."
3) No shelf can hold all three bowling trophies.
4) *K* can't be on Shelf 2—that's for either option.

# 43

**(B)** *G* and *H* are on Shelf 2, so if you remember that three bowling trophies can't be on the same shelf, this tells us that we must work with Option 1. If you put *G* and *H* on Shelf 2 in Option 2, you'd be breaking Rule 3—you'd have all three bowling trophies on the same shelf. So you'll have *F* on Shelf 1, and *L*, *G*, and *H* on Shelf 2. What must be true? Take a look at (B), *L* is on Shelf 2. Yes, we just went through the deduction whereby you realize you must use Option 1 in which *F* is on Shelf 1 and *L* is on Shelf 2. So (B) is the correct answer.

# 44

**(D)** Right away we realize that you can't use Option 2 here because Option 2 already has a tennis trophy on Shelf 3, *L*, so you will work with Option 1, *F* on the first shelf and *L* on the second shelf. You know that neither *J* nor *K* can appear on Shelf 2 in Option 1. *J* and *K* are tennis trophies, so if the question specifies that you can't have a tennis trophy on Shelf 3 and you can't have these two trophies on Shelf 2, then the only place for them is on Shelf 1. In other words, *K* and *J* must be on the same shelf, so (D) is correct.

# 45

**(C)** This question is directing you to Option 2, because you already know that *J* isn't allowed on Shelf 2 in Option 1. With Option 2 you know that *F* must appear on Shelf 2, so (C) is correct.

# 46

**(D)** In only one option can Shelf 1 remain empty, Option 2. The rest of the question says, "Which of the following must be false?" which means "Which of the following arrangements won't work?" First, let's look at the basic situation. We have Option 2 and we have *F* on 2 and *L* on 3, and Shelf 1 remains empty. That tells us that we can do something with *J* and *K*. We know in Option 2 that *J* can't go on Shelf 3 and Shelf 1 is empty, so the only other place for it is Shelf 2. We know that *K* can't be on Shelf 2 and Shelf 1 is empty, so the only home for *K* is Shelf 3. So we have Shelf 1 empty, Shelf 2 with *F* and *J*, and Shelf 3 with *L* and *K*. What to do with *G*

and *H*? The only thing we can't do is put them on Shelf 2 because that would violate Rule 3. So if we keep them together we have to put them on Shelf 3. If we split them up, we can put *G* on 2 and *H* on Shelf 3 or vice versa.

(A), can we put *H* and *F* on the same shelf? Sure, we've already said we can put one of *G* and *H* on Shelf 2 and one on Shelf 3. (B), can we put exactly three trophies on Shelf 2? Sure, we just did with (A). We put *F*, *J*, and *H* together on Shelf 2 and that left us with *L*, *K*, and *G* together on Shelf 3. (C)—can we put *G* and *H* on the same shelf? Yes, as long as they're on Shelf 3 and not on Shelf 2. (D), can we put exactly two trophies on Shelf 3? We have on Shelf 3, *L* and *K*. To have exactly two trophies on Shelf 3, we would put both *G* and *H* somewhere else and we can't put *G* and *H* together on Shelf 2 because that would violate Rule 3. So (D) is our answer here—it's the thing we can't do. (E), can we put *G* and *K* on the same shelf? Yes, whether *G* is alone or together with *H*, it's possible to do this.

# 47

**(A)** This is hard because the if-clause doesn't narrow it down to one of the two options. *L* and *G* can be on the same shelf in both options, which makes your work more complicated. In both options there's just one empty shelf—in Option 1 it's Shelf 3, and in Option 2 it's Shelf 1. Let's see if we can make any more deductions about both options. In Option 1, if we have to leave Shelf 3 empty, we can figure out what to do with *K* and *J* because they can't be on Shelf 2 and Shelf 3 is empty, so Shelf 1 has *F*, *K*, and *J* and Shelf 2 has *L* and *G* and the only thing left is *H*, on either Shelf 1 or Shelf 2. In Option 2 we know that *K* can't be on Shelf 2, and Shelf 1 has to be empty, so the only place for *K* is Shelf 3. *J* can't be on Shelf 3 in Option 2, and Shelf 1 is empty, so *J* is on Shelf 2. So we end up with *F* and *J* on Shelf 2, *L*, *K*, and *G* on Shelf 3 and Shelf 1 empty, and *H* is a floater.

For the answer to be correct, it must be true in both options—you hit pay dirt right away, because (A) is correct. It says if *H* is on Shelf 3, then *J* is on Shelf 2. The only way to put *H* on Shelf 3 is Option 2, where

Shelf 3 is open. You can put *H* on Shelf 3, and in Option 2, *J* is on Shelf 2, so (A)'s correct. (B) describes *K* and *L* as being on the same shelf, but that's true only in Option 2. (C) says if *H* is on Shelf 2, *J* is on Shelf 3, but *J* is never on Shelf 3. (D) has *F* and *K* on the same shelf; that's true in Option 1 only and not in Option 2. And (E) has *J* on Shelf 2. That's Option 2, but it goes on to say that *H* is on Shelf 1, and in Option 2 Shelf 1 is empty. Again, (A) is correct.

**48** **(E)** What if someone prefers the look of finished furniture over the look of painted furniture? Would that factor outweigh the person's desire to reduce work time and costs? We don't know—the author assumes that only the three factors he discusses—work time, cost, and longevity—determine a person's decision to paint rather than to finish. (E) says more or less the same thing and is our answer. As for (A), the author concludes that some people might prefer painting because it costs less and it saves work time, not because it is necessarily better than finishing. (B) is a distortion of the author's conclusions. The author needn't assume that most people will consider saving time and cost more important than longevity. (C) is wrong because it falls outside the scope. The discussion is limited only to people who will paint or finish—it doesn't include people who will do neither. As for (D), the author doesn't assume that work time, cost, and longevity are equally important factors in deciding whether to paint or to finish. Choice (E) is correct.

**49** **(C)** We need to find evidence that will strengthen the zoologists' conclusion, so we want to establish some connection between cubs living in captivity and an inability to hunt successfully in the wild. (C) does the trick—if cubs raised in captivity could hunt successfully in the wild, it would suggest that aggressive play is not a factor in learning to hunt. But (C) demonstrates that Cowonga lion cubs raised in captivity can't hunt successfully in the wild. Unless there are other differences, the aggressive play could

very well be the cause of this. (A) doesn't strengthen a connection between hunting and the lack of aggressive play—maybe the wild cubs would be equally successful at hunting if they didn't play aggressively. As for (B), that other predatory animals also engage in aggressive play when young doesn't mean that this play is necessary for successful hunting in later life. (D) is irrelevant—just because the skills used in play are similar to the skills necessary for hunting doesn't mean that cubs learn the hunting skills through play. And (E) doesn't strengthen the zoologists' conclusion—it simply repeats the part of the evidence they cite in support of their argument. So (C) is correct.

**50** **(A)** Two assumptions hold this argument together. First, the author decides that the survey means that the student body has become more religious. Then she decides that this is what has reduced cheating. So we'll look for a choice that suggests that either increased attendance at religious services or reduced cheating could be attributed to factors other than these. We get the former in (A). If most students attend services for social reasons, then this majority isn't attending because of increased religiosity, and this would destroy the author's primary assumption. (B) would *strengthen* the author's argument since it sums up her second assumption. If the students had really become religious, the author would be justified in asserting that the religiosity was a factor in the decrease of cheating. (C) lists the change in exam procedures made 15 years ago, but the survey compares attendance today with attendance 10 years ago, and the author's implicitly speaking of the last decade. (D) tries to attack the author's evidence, positing that not all students responded to the survey. But a survey just needs a sufficiently representative sample. (E) takes us way out of the ballpark—who said cheating was a major problem? All we know is that it's been massively reduced. The answer is (A).

# Appendixes

Appendixes

# APPENDIX A

# Root List

The Kaplan Root List can boost your knowledge of GRE-level words, and that can help you get more questions right. No one can predict exactly which words will show up on your test, but there are certain words that the test makers favor. The Root List gives you the component parts of many typical GRE words. Knowing these words can help you because you may run across them on your GRE. Also, becoming comfortable with the types of words that pop up will reduce your anxiety about the test.

Knowing roots can help you in two more ways. First, instead of learning one word at a time, you can learn a whole group of words that contain a certain root. They'll be related in meaning, so if you remember one, it will be easier for you to remember others. Second, roots can often help you decode an unknown GRE word. If you recognize a familiar root, you could get a good enough grasp of the word to answer the question.

## Kaplan Tip

Most of the words we use every day have their origins in simple roots. Once you know the root, it's much easier to figure out what a strange word means.

Take a look through this appendix. Many of the roots are easy to learn, and they'll help you on the test.

# The Kaplan Root List

❑ A, AN—not, without
amoral, atrophy, asymmetrical, anarchy, anesthetic, anonymity, anomaly

❑ AB, A—from, away, apart
abnormal, abdicate, aberration, abhor, abject, abjure, ablution, abnegate, abortive, abrogate, abscond, absolve, abstemious, abstruse, annul, avert, aversion

❑ AC, ACR—sharp, sour
acid, acerbic, exacerbate, acute, acuity, acumen, acrid, acrimony

❑ AD, A—to, toward
adhere, adjacent, adjunct, admonish, adroit, adumbrate, advent, abeyance, abet, accede, accretion, acquiesce, affluent, aggrandize, aggregate, alleviate, alliteration, allude, allure, ascribe, aspersion, aspire, assail, assonance, attest

❑ ALI, ALTR—another
alias, alienate, inalienable, altruism

❑ AM, AMI—love
amorous, amicable, amiable, amity

❑ AMBI, AMPHI—both
ambiguous, ambivalent, ambidextrous, amphibious

❑ AMBL, AMBUL—walk
amble, ambulatory, perambulator, somnambulist

❑ ANIM—mind, spirit, breath
animal, animosity, unanimous, magnanimous

❑ ANN, ENN—year
annual, annuity, superannuated, biennial, perennial

❑ ANTE, ANT—before
antecedent, antediluvian, antebellum, antepenultimate, anterior, antiquity, antiquated, anticipate

❑ ANTHROP—human
anthropology, anthropomorphic, misanthrope, philanthropy

❑ ANTI, ANT—against, opposite
antidote, antipathy, antithesis, antacid, antagonist, antonym

❑ AUD—hear
audio, audience, audition, auditory, audible

❑ AUTO—self
autobiography, autocrat, autonomous

❑ BELLI, BELL—war
belligerent, bellicose, antebellum, rebellion

❑ BENE, BEN—good
benevolent, benefactor, beneficent, benign

❑ BI—two
bicycle, bisect, bilateral, bilingual, biped

❑ BIBLIO—book
Bible, bibliography, bibliophile

❑ BIO—life
biography, biology, amphibious, symbiotic, macrobiotics

❑ BURS—money, purse
reimburse, disburse, bursar

❑ CAD, CAS, CID—happen, fall
accident, cadence, cascade, deciduous

❑ CAP, CIP—head
captain, decapitate, capitulate, precipitous, precipitate

❑ CAP, CAPT, CEPT, CIP—take, hold, seize
capable, capacious, recapitulate, captivate, deception, intercept, precept, inception, anticipate, emancipation, incipient, percipient

❑ CARN—flesh
carnal, carnage, carnival, carnivorous, incarnate

❑ CED, CESS—yield, go
cease, cessation, incessant, cede, precede, accede, recede, antecedent, intercede, secede, cession

❑ CHROM—color
chrome, chromatic, monochrome

❑ CHRON—time
chronology, chronic, anachronism

❑ CIDE—murder
suicide, homicide, regicide, patricide

❑ CIRCUM—around
circumference, circumlocution, circumnavigate, circumscribe, circumspect, circumvent

❑ CLIN, CLIV—slope
incline, declivity, proclivity

❑ CLUD, CLUS, CLAUS, CLOIS—shut, close
conclude, reclusive, claustrophobia, cloister, preclude, occlude

❑ CO, COM, CON—with, together
coeducation, coagulate, coalesce, coerce, cogent, cognate, collateral, colloquial, colloquy, commensurate, commodious, compassion, compatriot, complacent, compliant, complicity, compunction, concerto, conciliatory, concord, concur, condone, conflagration, congeal, congenial, congenital, conglomerate, conjure, conjugal, conscientious, consecrate, consensus, consonant, constrained, contentious, contrite, contusion, convalescence, convene, convivial, convoke, convoluted, congress

❑ COGN, GNO—know
recognize, cognition, cognizance, incognito, diagnosis, agnostic, prognosis, gnostic, ignorant

❑ CONTRA—against
controversy, incontrovertible, contravene

❑ CORP—body
corpse, corporeal, corpulence

❑ COSMO, COSM—world
cosmopolitan, cosmos, microcosm, macrocosm

❑ CRAC, CRAT—rule, power
democracy, bureaucracy, theocracy, autocrat, aristocrat, technocrat

❑ CRED—trust, believe
incredible, credulous, credence

❑ CRESC, CRET—grow
crescent, crescendo, accretion

❑ CULP—blame, fault
culprit, culpable, inculpate, exculpate

❑ CURR, CURS—run
current, concur, cursory, precursor, incursion

❑ DE—down, out, apart
depart, debase, debilitate, declivity, decry, deface, defamatory, defunct, delegate, demarcation, demean, demur, deplete, deplore, depravity, deprecate, deride, derivative, desist, detest, devoid

❑ DEC—ten, tenth
decade, decimal, decathlon, decimate

❑ DEMO, DEM—people
democrat, demographics, demagogue, epidemic, pandemic, endemic

❏ DI, DIURN—day
diary, diurnal, quotidian

❏ DIA—across
diagonal, diatribe, diaphanous

❏ DIC, DICT—speak
diction, interdict, predict, abdicate, indict, verdict

❏ DIS, DIF, DI—not, apart, away
disaffected, disband, disbar, disburse, discern, discordant, discredit, discursive, disheveled, disparage, disparate, dispassionate, dispirit, dissemble, disseminate, dissension, dissipate, dissonant, dissuade, distend, differentiate, diffidence, diffuse, digress, divert

❏ DOC, DOCT—teach
doctrine, docile, doctrinaire

❏ DOL—pain
condolence, doleful, dolorous, indolent

❏ DUC, DUCT—lead
seduce, induce, conduct, viaduct, induct

❏ EGO—self
ego, egoist, egocentric

❏ EN, EM—in, into
enter, entice, encumber, endemic, ensconce, enthrall, entreat, embellish, embezzle, embroil, empathy

❏ ERR—wander
erratic, aberration, errant

❏ EU—well, good
eulogy, euphemism, euphony, euphoria, eurythmics, euthanasia

❏ EX, E—out, out of
exit, exacerbate, excerpt, excommunicate, exculpate, execrable, exhume, exonerate, exorbitant, exorcise, expatriate, expedient, expiate, expunge, expurgate, extenuate, extort, extremity, extricate, extrinsic, exult, evoke, evict, evince, elicit, egress, egregious

❏ FAC, FIC, FECT, FY, FEA—make, do
factory, facility, benefactor, malefactor, fiction, fictive, beneficent, affect, confection, refectory, magnify, unify, rectify, vilify, feasible

❏ FAL, FALS—deceive
false, infallible, fallacious

❏ FERV—boil
fervent, fervid, effervescent

❏ FID—faith, trust
confident, diffidence, perfidious, fidelity

❏ FLU, FLUX—flow
fluent, flux, affluent, confluence, effluvia, superfluous

❏ FORE—before
forecast, foreboding, forestall

❏ FRAG, FRAC—break
fragment, fracture, diffract, fractious, refract

❏ FUS—pour
profuse, infusion, effusive, diffuse

❏ GEN—birth, class, kin
generation, congenital, homogeneous, heterogeneous, ingenious, engender, progenitor, progeny

❏ GRAD, GRESS—step
graduate, gradual, retrograde, centigrade, degrade, gradation, gradient, progress, congress, digress, transgress, ingress, egress

☐ GRAPH, GRAM—writing
biography, bibliography, epigraph, grammar, epigram

☐ GRAT—pleasing
grateful, gratitude, gratis, ingrate, congratulate, gratuitous, gratuity

☐ GRAV, GRIEV—heavy
grave, gravity, aggravate, grieve, aggrieve, grievous

☐ GREG—crowd, flock
segregate, gregarious, egregious, congregate, aggregate

☐ HABIT, HIBIT—have, hold
habit, inhibit, cohabit, habitat

☐ HAP—by chance
happen, haphazard, hapless, mishap

☐ HELIO, HELI—sun
heliocentric, helium, heliotrope, aphelion, perihelion

☐ HETERO—other
heterosexual, heterogeneous, heterodox

☐ HOL—whole
holocaust, catholic, holistic

☐ HOMO—same
homosexual, homogenize, homogeneous, homonym

☐ HOMO—man
homo sapiens, homicide, bonhomie

☐ HYDR—water
hydrant, hydrate, dehydration

☐ HYPER—too much, excess
hyperactive, hyperbole, hyperventilate

☐ HYPO—too little, under
hypodermic, hypothermia, hypochondria, hypothesis, hypothetical

☐ IN, IG, IL, IM, IR—not
incorrigible, indefatigable, indelible, indubitable, inept, inert, inexorable, insatiable, insentient, insolvent, insomnia, interminable, intractable, incessant, inextricable, infallible, infamy, innumerable, inoperable, insipid, intemperate, intrepid, inviolable, ignorant, ignominious, ignoble, illicit, illimitable, immaculate, immutable, impasse, impeccable, impecunious, impertinent, implacable, impotent, impregnable, improvident, impassioned, impervious, irregular, invade, inaugurate, incandescent, incarcerate, incense, indenture, induct, ingratiate, introvert, incarnate, inception, incisive, infer

☐ IN, IL, IM, IR—in, on, into
infusion, ingress, innate, inquest, inscribe, insinuate, inter, illustrate, imbue, immerse, implicate, irrigate, irritate

☐ INTER—between, among
intercede, intercept, interdiction, interject, interlocutor, interloper, intermediary, intermittent, interpolate, interpose, interregnum, interrogate, intersect, intervene

☐ INTRA, INTR—within
intrastate, intravenous, intramural, intrinsic

☐ IT, ITER—between, among
transit, itinerant, reiterate, transitory

☐ JECT, JET—throw
eject, interject, abject, trajectory, jettison

☐ JOUR—day
journal, adjourn, sojourn

☐ JUD—judge
judge, judicious, prejudice, adjudicate

❑ JUNCT, JUG—join
junction, adjunct, injunction, conjugal, subjugate

❑ JUR—swear, law
jury, abjure, adjure, conjure, perjure,
jurisprudence

❑ LAT—side
lateral, collateral, unilateral, bilateral,
quadrilateral

❑ LAV, LAU, LU—wash
lavatory, laundry, ablution, antediluvian

❑ LEG, LEC, LEX—read, speak
legible, lecture, lexicon

❑ LEV—light
elevate, levitate, levity, alleviate

❑ LIBER—free
liberty, liberal, libertarian, libertine

❑ LIG, LECT—choose, gather
eligible, elect, select

❑ LIG, LI, LY—bind
ligament, oblige, religion, liable, liaison, lien,
ally

❑ LING, LANG—tongue
lingo, language, linguistics, bilingual

❑ LITER—letter
literate, alliteration, literal

❑ LITH—stone
monolith, lithograph, megalith

❑ LOQU, LOC, LOG—speech, thought
eloquent, loquacious, colloquial, colloquy, soliloquy, circumlocution, interlocutor, monologue,
dialogue, eulogy, philology, neologism

❑ LUC, LUM—light
lucid, illuminate, elucidate, pellucid, translucent

❑ LUD, LUS—play
ludicrous, allude, delusion, allusion, illusory

❑ MACRO—great
macrocosm, macrobiotics

❑ MAG, MAJ, MAS, MAX—great
magnify, majesty, master, maximum, magnanimous, magnate, magnitude

❑ MAL—bad
malady, maladroit, malevolent, malodorous

❑ MAN—hand
manual, manuscript, emancipate, manifest

❑ MAR—sea
submarine, marine, maritime

❑ MATER, MATR—mother
maternal, matron, matrilineal

❑ MEDI—middle
intermediary, medieval, mediate

❑ MEGA—great
megaphone, megalomania, megaton, megalith

❑ MEM, MEN—remember
memory, memento, memorabilia, reminisce

❑ METER, METR, MENS—measure
meter, thermometer, perimeter, metronome,
commensurate

❑ MICRO—small
microscope, microorganism, microcosm,
microbe

❑ MIS—wrong, bad, hate
misunderstand, misanthrope, misapprehension, misconstrue, misnomer, mishap

❑ MIT, MISS—send
transmit, emit, missive

❑ MOLL—soft
mollify, emollient, mollusk

❑ MON, MONIT—warn
admonish, monitor, premonition

❑ MONO—one
monologue, monotonous, monogamy, monolith, monochrome

❑ MOR—custom, manner
moral, mores

❑ MOR, MORT—dead
morbid, moribund, mortal, amortize

❑ MORPH—shape
amorphous, anthropomorphic, metamorphosis, morphology

❑ MOV, MOT, MOB, MOM—move
remove, motion, mobile, momentum, momentous

❑ MUT—change
mutate, mutability, immutable, commute

❑ NAT, NASC—born
native, nativity, natal, neonate, innate, cognate, nascent, renascent, renaissance

❑ NAU, NAV—ship, sailor
nautical, nauseous, navy, circumnavigate

❑ NEG—not, deny
negative, abnegate, renege

❑ NEO—new
neoclassical, neophyte, neologism, neonate

❑ NIHIL—none, nothing
annihilation, nihilism

❑ NOM, NYM—name
nominate, nomenclature, nominal, cognomen, misnomer, ignominious, antonym, homonym, pseudonym, synonym, anonymity

❑ NOX, NIC, NEC, NOC—harm
obnoxious, noxious, pernicious, internecine, innocuous

❑ NOV—new
novelty, innovation, novitiate

❑ NUMER—number
numeral, numerous, innumerable, enumerate

❑ OB—against
obstruct, obdurate, obfuscate, obnoxious, obsequious, obstinate, obstreperous, obtrusive

❑ OMNI—all
omnipresent, omnipotent, omniscient, omnivorous

❑ ONER—burden
onerous, onus, exonerate

❑ OPER—work
operate, cooperate, inoperable

❑ PAC—peace
pacify, pacifist, pacific

❑ PALP—feel
palpable, palpitation

❑ PAN—all
panorama, panacea, panegyric, pandemic, panoply

❏ PATER, PATR—father
paternal, paternity, patriot, compatriot, expatriate, patrimony, patricide, patrician

❏ PATH, PASS—feel, suffer
sympathy, antipathy, empathy, apathy, pathos, impassioned

❏ PEC—money
pecuniary, impecunious, peculation

❏ PED, POD—foot
pedestrian, pediment, expedient, biped, quadruped, tripod

❏ PEL, PULS—drive
compel, compelling, expel, propel, compulsion

❏ PEN—almost
peninsula, penultimate, penumbra

❏ PEND, PENS—hang
pendant, pendulous, compendium, suspense, propensity

❏ PER—through, by, for, throughout
perambulator, percipient, perfunctory, permeable, perspicacious, pertinacious, perturbation, perusal, perennial, peregrinate

❏ PER—against, destruction
perfidious, pernicious, perjure

❏ PERI—around
perimeter, periphery, perihelion, peripatetic

❏ PET—seek, go toward
petition, impetus, impetuous, petulant, centripetal

❏ PHIL—love
philosopher, philanderer, philanthropy, bibliophile, philology

❏ PHOB—fear
phobia, claustrophobia, xenophobia

❏ PHON—sound
phonograph, megaphone, euphony, phonetics, phonics

❏ PLAC—calm, please
placate, implacable, placid, complacent

❏ PON, POS—put, place
postpone, proponent, exponent, preposition, posit, interpose, juxtaposition, depose

❏ PORT—carry
portable, deportment, rapport

❏ POT—drink
potion, potable

❏ POT—power
potential, potent, impotent, potentate, omnipotence

❏ PRE—before
precede, precipitate, preclude, precocious, precursor, predilection, predisposition, preponderance, prepossessing, presage, prescient, prejudice, predict, premonition, preposition

❏ PRIM, PRI—first
prime, primary, primal, primeval, primordial, pristine

❏ PRO—ahead, forth
proceed, proclivity, procrastinator, profane, profuse, progenitor, progeny, prognosis, prologue, promontory, propel, proponent, propose, proscribe, protestation, provoke

❏ PROTO—first
prototype, protagonist, protocol

❑ PROX, PROP—near
approximate, propinquity, proximity

❑ PSEUDO—false
pseudoscientific, pseudonym

❑ PYR—fire
pyre, pyrotechnics, pyromania

❑ QUAD, QUAR, QUAT—four
quadrilateral, quadrant, quadruped, quarter,
quarantine, quaternary

❑ QUES, QUER, QUIS, QUIR—question
quest, inquest, query, querulous, inquisitive,
inquiry

❑ QUIE—quiet
disquiet, acquiesce, quiescent, requiem

❑ QUINT, QUIN—five
quintuplets, quintessence

❑ RADI, RAMI—branch
radius, radiate, radiant, eradicate, ramification

❑ RECT, REG—straight, rule
rectangle, rectitude, rectify, regular

❑ REG—king, rule
regal, regent, interregnum

❑ RETRO—backward
retrospective, retroactive, retrograde

❑ RID, RIS—laugh
ridiculous, deride, derision

❑ ROG—ask
interrogate, derogatory, abrogate, arrogate, arrogant

❑ RUD—rough, crude
rude, erudite, rudimentary

❑ RUPT—break
disrupt, interrupt, rupture

❑ SACR, SANCT—holy
sacred, sacrilege, consecrate, sanctify, sanction,
sacrosanct

❑ SCRIB, SCRIPT, SCRIV—write
scribe, ascribe, circumscribe, inscribe, proscribe,
script, manuscript, scrivener

❑ SE—apart, away
separate, segregate, secede, sedition

❑ SEC, SECT, SEG—cut
sector, dissect, bisect, intersect, segment, secant

❑ SED, SID—sit
sedate, sedentary, supersede, reside, residence,
assiduous, insidious

❑ SEM—seed, sow
seminar, seminal, disseminate

❑ SEN—old
senior, senile, senescent

❑ SENT, SENS—feel, think
sentiment, nonsense, assent, sentient, consensus,
sensual

❑ SEQU, SECU—follow
sequence, sequel, subsequent, obsequious, obse-
quy, non sequitur, consecutive

❑ SIGN—mark, sign
signal, designation, assignation

❑ SIM, SEM—similar, same
similar, semblance, dissemble, verisimilitude

❑ SIN—curve
sine curve, sinuous, insinuate

❑ SOL—sun
solar, parasol, solarium, solstice

❑ SOL—alone
solo, solitude, soliloquy, solipsism

❑ SOMN—sleep
insomnia, somnolent, somnambulist

❑ SON—sound
sonic, consonance, dissonance, assonance,
sonorous, resonate

❑ SOPH—wisdom
philosopher, sophistry, sophisticated, sophomoric

❑ SPEC, SPIC—see, look
spectator, circumspect, retrospective, perspective,
perspicacious

❑ SPER—hope
prosper, prosperous, despair, desperate

❑ SPERS, SPAR—scatter
disperse, sparse, aspersion, disparate

❑ SPIR—breathe
respire, inspire, spiritual, aspire, transpire

❑ STRICT, STRING—bind
strict, stricture, constrict, stringent, astringent

❑ STRUCT, STRU—build
structure, construe, obstruct

❑ SUB—under
subconscious, subjugate, subliminal, subpoena,
subsequent, subterranean, subvert

❑ SUMM—highest
summit, summary, consummate

❑ SUPER, SUR—above
supervise, supercilious, supersede, superannuated, superfluous, insurmountable, surfeit

❑ SURGE, SURRECT—rise
surge, resurgent, insurgent, insurrection

❑ SYN, SYM—together
synthesis, sympathy, synonym, syncopation, syn-
opsis, symposium, symbiosis

❑ TACIT, TIC—silent
tacit, taciturn, reticent

❑ TACT, TAG, TANG—touch
tact, tactile, contagious, tangent, tangential,
tangible

❑ TEN, TIN, TAIN—hold, twist
detention, tenable, tenacious, pertinacious,
retinue, retain

❑ TEND, TENS, TENT—stretch
intend, distend, tension, tensile, ostensible,
contentious

❑ TERM—end
terminal, terminus, terminate, interminable

❑ TERR—earth, land
terrain, terrestrial, extraterrestrial, subterranean

❑ TEST—witness
testify, attest, testimonial, testament, detest,
protestation

❑ THE—god
atheist, theology, apotheosis, theocracy

❑ THERM—heat
thermometer, thermal, thermonuclear,
hypothermia

❏ TIM—fear, frightened
timid, intimidate, timorous

❏ TOP—place
topic, topography, utopia

❏ TORP—stiff, numb
torpedo, torpid, torpor

❏ TORT—twist
distort, extort, tortuous

❏ TOX—poison
toxic, toxin, intoxication

❏ TRACT—draw
tractor, intractable, protract

❏ TRANS—across, over, through, beyond
transport, transgress, transient, transitory,
translucent, transmutation

❏ TREM, TREP—shake
tremble, tremor, tremulous, trepidation, intrepid

❏ TURB—shake
disturb, turbulent, perturbation

❏ UMBR—shadow
umbrella, umbrage, adumbrate, penumbra

❏ UNI, UN—one
unify, unilateral, unanimous

❏ URB—city
urban, suburban, urbane

❏ VAC—empty
vacant, evacuate, vacuous

❏ VAL, VAIL—value, strength
valid, valor, ambivalent, convalescence, avail,
prevail, countervail

❏ VEN, VENT—come
convene, contravene, intervene, venue, conven-
tion, circumvent, advent, adventitious

❏ VER—true
verify, verity, verisimilitude, veracious, aver,
verdict

❏ VERB—word
verbal, verbose, verbiage, verbatim

❏ VERT, VERS—turn
avert, convert, pervert, revert, incontrovertible,
divert, subvert, versatile, aversion

❏ VICT, VINC—conquer
victory, conviction, evict, evince, invincible

❏ VID, VIS—see
evident, vision, visage, supervise

❏ VIL—base, mean
vile, vilify, revile

❏ VIV, VIT—life
vivid, vital, convivial, vivacious

❏ VOC, VOK, VOW—call, word
vocal, equivocate, vociferous, convoke, evoke,
invoke, avow

❏ VOL—wish
voluntary, malevolent, benevolent, volition

❏ VOLV, VOLUT—turn, roll
revolve, evolve, convoluted

❏ VOR—eat
devour, carnivore, omnivorous, voracious

# APPENDIX B

# Math Reference

The math on the GRE covers a lot of ground—from basic algebra to symbol problems to geometry.

Don't let yourself be intimidated. We've highlighted the 100 most important concepts that you need and listed them in this appendix. Although you probably learned most of this stuff in high school, this list is a great way to refresh your memory.

The GRE math tests your understanding of a relatively limited number of mathematical concepts. It is possible to learn all the math you need to know for the GRE in a short time. In fact, you've seen it all before. Listed on the following pages are 100 things you need to know for the GRE, divided into three levels.

Level 1 is the most basic. You couldn't answer any GRE math questions if you didn't know Level 1 math. Most people preparing to take the GRE are already pretty good at Level 1 math. Look over the Level 1 list below just to make sure you're comfortable with the basics.

Level 2 is the place for most people to start their review of math. These skills and formulas come into play quite frequently on the GRE, especially in the medium and hard questions. If you're like a lot of students, your Level 2 math is probably rusty.

Level 3 is the hardest math you'll find on the GRE. These are skills and formulas that you might find difficult. Don't spend a lot of time on Level 3 if you still have gaps in Level 2. But once you've about mastered Level 2, then tackling Level 3 can put you over the top.

---

## Level 1
### (Math You Probably Already Know)

**1. How to add, subtract, multiply, and divide WHOLE NUMBERS**

**2. How to add, subtract, multiply, and divide FRACTIONS**

**3. How to add, subtract, multiply, and divide DECIMALS**

**4. How to convert FRACTIONS TO DECIMALS and DECIMALS TO FRACTIONS**

**5. How to add, subtract, multiply, and divide POSITIVE AND NEGATIVE NUMBERS**

### 6. How to plot points on the NUMBER LINE

### 7. How to plug a number into an ALGEBRAIC EXPRESSION

### 8. How to SOLVE a simple EQUATION

### 9. How to add and subtract LINE SEGMENTS

### 10. How to find the THIRD ANGLE of a TRIANGLE, given the other two angles

## Level 2
## (Math You Might Need to Review)

### 11. How to use PEMDAS

When you're given an ugly arithmetic equation, it's important to know the order of operations. Just remember PEMDAS (as in "Please excuse my dear Aunt Sally"). What PEMDAS means is this:
Clean up **Parentheses** first; then deal with **Exponents**; then do the **Multiplication** and **Division** together, going from left to right; and finally do the **Addition** and **Subtraction** together, again going from left to right.

**Example:**

$9 - 2 \times (5 - 3)^2 + 6 \div 3 =$

Begin with the parentheses: $9 - 2 \times (2)^2 + 6 \div 3$.

Then do the exponent: $9 - 2 \times 4 + 6 \div 3$.

Now do multiplication and division from left to right: $9 - 8 + 2$.

Finally, do addition and subtraction from left to right:

$9 - 8 + 2 = 1 + 2 = 3$

### 12. How to use the PERCENT FORMULA

Identify the part, the percent, and the whole.

$$Part = percent \times whole$$

> **HINT: You'll usually find the part near the word *is* and the whole near the word *of*.**

**Example:** (Find the part)

What is 12 percent of 25?

**Setup:**

Part $= \frac{12}{100} \times 25 = 3$

**Example:** (Find the percent)

45 is what percent of 9?

**Setup:**

$45 = $ Percent $\times 9 = 5 \times 9$

Percent $= 5 \times 100\% = 500\%$

**Example:** (Find the whole)

15 is $\frac{3}{5}$ percent of what number?

**Setup:**

$\frac{3}{5}$ percent $= \frac{3}{500}$

$15 = \frac{3}{500} \times$ whole

Whole $= 2,500$

### 13. How to use the PERCENT INCREASE/DECREASE FORMULAS

Identify the original whole and the amount of increase/decrease.

$$Percent\ increase = \frac{amount\ of\ increase}{original\ whole} \times 100\%$$

$$Percent\ decrease = \frac{amount\ of\ decrease}{original\ whole} \times 100\%$$

**Example:**

The price goes up from $80 to $100. What is the percent increase?

**Setup:**

Percent increase = $\frac{20}{80} \times 100\% = 25\%$

---

**HINT: Be sure to use the original whole—not the new whole—for the base.**

---

## 14. How to predict whether a sum, difference, or product will be ODD or EVEN

Don't bother memorizing the rules. Just take simple numbers like 1 and 2 and see what happens.

**Example:**

If $m$ is even and $n$ is odd, is the product $mn$ odd or even?

**Setup:**

Say $m = 2$ and $n = 1$.
$2 \times 1$ is even, so $mn$ is even.

## 15. How to recognize MULTIPLES OF 2, 3, 4, 5, 6, 9, and 10

- 2: Last digit is even.
- 3: Sum of digits is a multiple of 3.
- 4: Last two digits are a multiple of 4.
- 5: Last digit is 5 or 0.
- 6: Sum of digits is a multiple of 3 and last digit is even.
- 9: Sum of digits is a multiple of 9.
- 10: Last digit is 0.
- 11: Sum of digits is a multiple of 3 and last two digits are a multiple of 4.

## 16. How to find a COMMON FACTOR

Break both numbers down to their prime factors to see what they have in common. Then multiply the shared prime factors to find all common factors.

**Example:**

What factors greater than 1 do 135 and 225 have in common?

**Setup:**

First find the prime factors of 135 and 225. $135 = 3 \times 3 \times 3 \times 5$, and $225 = 3 \times 3 \times 5 \times 5$. The numbers share $3 \times 3 \times 5$ in common. Thus, aside from 3 and 5, the remaining common factors can be found by multiplying 3, 3, and 5 in every possible combination: $3 \times 3 = 9$, $3 \times 5 = 15$, and $3 \times 3 \times 5 = 45$.

## 17. How to find a COMMON MULTIPLE

The product is the easiest common multiple to find. If the two numbers have any factors in common, you can divide them out of the product to get a lower common multiple.

**Example:**

What is the least common multiple of 28 and 42?

**Setup:**

The product $28 \times 42 = 1,176$ is a common multiple, but not the least. $28 = 2 \times 2 \times 7$, and $42 = 2 \times 3 \times 7$. They share a 2 and a 7, so divide the product by 2 and then by 7. $1,176 \div 2 = 588$. $588 \div 7 = 84$. The least common multiple is 84.

## 18. How to find the AVERAGE

$$Average = \frac{sum\ of\ terms}{number\ of\ terms}$$

**Example:**

What is the average of 3, 4, and 8 ?

**Setup:**

Average $= \frac{3+4+8}{3} = \frac{15}{3} = 5.$

## 19. How to use the AVERAGE to find the SUM

$$Sum = (average) \times (number\ of\ terms)$$

**Example:**

17.5 is the average (arithmetic mean) of 24 numbers. What is the sum?

**Setup:**

Sum $= 17.5 \times 24 = 420$

## 20. How to find the AVERAGE of CONSECUTIVE NUMBERS

The average of evenly spaced numbers is simply the average of the smallest number and the largest number. The average of all the integers from 13 to 77, for example, is the same as the average of 13 and 77:

$$\frac{13 + 77}{2} = \frac{90}{2} = 45$$

## 21. How to COUNT CONSECUTIVE NUMBERS

The number of integers from $A$ to $B$ inclusive is $B - A + 1$.

**Example:**

How many integers are there from 73 through 419, inclusive?

**Setup:**

$419 - 73 + 1 = 347$

---

**HINT: Don't forget to add 1.**

---

## 22. How to find the SUM OF CONSECUTIVE NUMBERS

$$Sum = (average) \times (number\ of\ terms)$$

**Example:**

What is the sum of the integers from 10 through 50, inclusive?

**Setup:**

Average $= (10 + 50) \div 2 = 30$

Number of terms $= 50 - 10 + 1 = 41$

Sum $= 30 \times 41 = 1,230$

## 23. How to find the MEDIAN

Put the numbers in numerical order and take the middle number. (If there's an even number of numbers, the average of the two numbers in the middle is the median.)

**Example:**
What is the median of 88, 86, 57, 94, and 73?

**Setup:**
Put the numbers in numerical order and take the middle number:

$$57, 73, 86, 88, 94$$

The median is 86. (If there's an even number of numbers, take the average of the two in the middle.)

## 24. How to find the MODE

Take the number that appears most often. For example, if your test scores were 88, 57, 68, 85, 98, 93, 93, 84, and 81, the mode of the scores is 93 because it appears more often than any other score. (If there's a tie for most often, then there's more than one mode.)

## 25. How to find the RANGE

Simply take the difference between the highest and lowest values. Using the previous example, if your test scores were 88, 57, 68, 85, 98, 93, 93, 84, and 81, the range of the scores is 41, the difference between the highest and lowest values (98 – 57 = 41).

## 26. How to use actual numbers to determine a RATIO

To find a ratio, put the number associated with *of* on the top and the word associated with *to* on the bottom.

$$Ratio = \frac{of}{to}$$

The ratio of 20 oranges to 12 apples is $\frac{20}{12}$, or $\frac{5}{3}$.

## 27. How to use a ratio to determine an ACTUAL NUMBER

Set up a proportion.

**Example:**
The ratio of boys to girls is 3 to 4. If there are 135 boys, how many girls are there?

**Setup:**
$$\frac{3}{4} = \frac{135}{x}$$
$$3 \times x = 4 \times 135$$
$$x = 180$$

## 28. How to use actual numbers to determine a RATE

Identify the quantities and the units to be compared. Keep the units straight.

**Example:**

Anders typed 9,450 words in $3\frac{1}{2}$ hours. What was his rate in words per minute?

**Setup:**

First convert $3\frac{1}{2}$ hours to 210 minutes. Then set up the rate with words on top and minutes on bottom:

$$\frac{9,450 \text{ words}}{210 \text{ minutes}} = 45 \text{ words per minute}$$

---

**HINT: The unit before *per* goes on top, and the unit after *per* goes on the bottom.**

---

## 29. How to deal with TABLES, GRAPHS, AND CHARTS

Read the question and all labels extra carefully. Ignore extraneous information and zero in on what the question asks for. Take advantage of the spread in the answer choices by approximating the answer wherever possible.

## 30. How to count the NUMBER OF POSSIBILITIES

In most cases, you won't need to apply the combination and permutation formulas on the GRE. The number of possibilities is generally so small that the best approach is just to write them out systematically and count them.

**Example:**

How many three-digit numbers can be formed with the digits 1, 3, and 5?

**Setup:**

Write them out. Be systematic so you don't miss any: 135, 153, 315, 351, 513, 531. Count them: six possibilities.

## 31. How to calculate a simple PROBABILITY

$$Probability = \frac{number\ of\ favorable\ outcomes}{total\ number\ of\ possible\ outcomes}$$

**Example:**

What is the probability of throwing a 5 on a fair six-sided die?

**Setup:**

There is one favorable outcome—throwing a 5. There are 6 possible outcomes—one for each side of the die.

$Probability = \frac{1}{6}$

## 32. How to work with new SYMBOLS

If you see a symbol you've never seen before, don't freak out: it's a made-up symbol. Everything you need to know is in the question stem. Just follow the instructions.

## 33. How to MULTIPLY POLYNOMIALS

First multiply to eliminate all parentheses. Each term inside one parentheses is multiplied by each term inside the other parentheses. All like terms are then combined.

**Example:**

$$(3x^2 + 5x)(x - 1) =$$
$$3x^2(x - 1) + 5x(x - 1) =$$
$$3x^3 - 3x^2 + 5x^2 - 5x =$$
$$3x^3 + 2x^2 - 5x$$

## 34. How to FACTOR certain POLYNOMIALS

Learn to spot these classic factorables:

$$ab + ac = a(b + c)$$
$$a^2 + 2ab + b^2 = (a + b)^2$$
$$a^2 - 2ab + b^2 = (a - b)^2$$
$$a^2 - b^2 = (a - b)(a + b)$$

## 35. How to solve for one variable IN TERMS OF ANOTHER

To find $x$ "in terms of" $y$: isolate $x$ on one side, leaving $y$ as the only variable on the other.

## 36. How to solve an INEQUALITY

Treat it much like an equation—adding, subtracting, multiplying, and dividing both sides by the same thing. Just remember to reverse the inequality sign if you multiply or divide by a negative number.

**Example:**
Rewrite $7 - 3x > 2$ in its simplest form:

**Setup:**

$7 - 3x > 2$. Subtract 7 from both sides:
$7 - 3x - 7 > 2 - 7$.
So $-3x > -5$. Now divide both sides by $-3$, and remember to reverse the inequality sign:

$$x < \frac{5}{3}$$

## 37. How to handle ABSOLUTE VALUES

The *absolute value* of a number $n$, denoted by $|n|$, is defined as $n$ if $n \geq 0$ and $-n$ if $n < 0$. It's also referred to as the distance from zero to the number on the number line:

$$|-5| = 5$$

If $|x| = 3$, then $x$ could be 3 or $-3$.

**Example:**
If $|x - 3| < 2$, what is the range of possible values for $x$?

**Setup:**

$|x - 3| < 2$, so $(x - 3) < 2$ and $-(x - 3) < 2$.
So $x - 3 < 2$ and $x - 3 > -2$.
So $x < 2 + 3$ and $x > -2 + 3$.
So $x < 5$ and $x > 1$.
So $1 < x < 5$.

## 38. How to TRANSLATE ENGLISH INTO ALGEBRA

Look for the key words and systematically turn phrases into algebraic expressions and sentences into equations.

Here's a table of key words that you may have to translate into mathematical operations:

| Operation | Key Words |
|---|---|
| Addition | sum, plus, and, added to, more than, increased by, combined with, exceeds, total, greater than |
| Subtraction | difference between, minus, subtracted from, decreased by, diminished by, less than, reduced by |
| Multiplication | of, product, times, multiplied by, twice, double, triple, half |
| Division | quotient, divided by, per, out of, ratio of __ to __ |
| Equals | equals, is, was, will be, the result is, adds up to, costs, is the same as |

**HINT: Be extra careful of the order you place numbers in when subtraction is called for.**

## 39. How to find an ANGLE formed by INTERSECTING LINES

Vertical angles are equal. Adjacent angles add up to 180°.

$$a = c$$
$$b = d$$
$$a + b = 180°$$
$$a + b + c + d = 360°$$

## 40. How to find an angle formed by a TRANSVERSAL across PARALLEL LINES

All the acute angles are equal. All the obtuse angles are equal. An acute plus an obtuse equals 180°.

**Example:**

$\ell_1$ is parallel to $\ell_2$
$$e = g = p = r$$
$$f = h = q = s$$
$$e + q = g + s = 180°$$

## 41. How to find the AREA of a TRIANGLE

$$Area = \frac{1}{2}(base)(height)$$

**Example:**

**Setup:**
Area $= \frac{1}{2}(5)(8) = 20$

---

**HINT: You might have to construct an altitude, as we did in the triangle above.**

---

## 42. How to work with ISOSCELES TRIANGLES

Isosceles triangles have two equal sides and two equal angles. If a GRE question tells you that a triangle is isoceles, you can bet that you'll need to use that information to find the length of a side or a measure of an angle.

## 43. How to work with EQUILATERAL TRIANGLES

Equilateral triangles have three equal sides and three 60° angles. If a GRE question tells you that a triangle is equilateral, you can bet that you'll need to use that information to find the length of a side or a measure of an angle.

## 44. How to work with SIMILAR TRIANGLES

In similar triangles, corresponding angles are equal and corresponding sides are proportional. If a GRE question tells you that triangles are similar, you'll probably need that information to find the length of a side or the measure of an angle.

## 45. How to find the HYPOTENUSE or a LEG of a RIGHT TRIANGLE

*Pythagorean theorem: $a^2 + b^2 = c^2$*

---

**HINT: Most right triangles on the GRE are "special" right triangles (see below), so you can often bypass the Pythagorean theorem.**

---

## 46. How to spot "SPECIAL" RIGHT TRIANGLES

*3-4-5*
*5-12-13*
*30-60-90*
*45-45-90*

---

**HINT: Learn to spot "special" right triangles—the less you have to calculate the Pythagorean theorem, the more time you save.**

---

### 47. How to find the PERIMETER of a RECTANGLE

$$Perimeter = 2(length + width)$$

**Example:**

**Setup:**

Perimeter = 2(2 + 5) = 14

### 48. How to find the AREA of a RECTANGLE

$$Area = (length)(width)$$

**Example:**

**Setup:**
Area = 2 × 5 = 10

### 49. How to find the AREA of a SQUARE

$$Area = (side)^2$$

**Example:**

**Setup:**

Area = $3^2$ = 9

### 50. How to find the AREA of a PARALLELOGRAM

$$Area = (base)(height)$$

**Example:**

**Setup:**
Area = 6 × 4 = 24

### 51. How to find the AREA of a TRAPEZOID

A trapezoid is a quadrilateral having only two parallel sides. You can always drop a line or two to break the figure into a rectangle and a triangle or two triangles. Use the area formulas for those familiar shapes. You could also apply the general formula for the area of a trapezoid:

$$Area = (Average\ of\ parallel\ sides) \times (height)$$

**Example:**

**Setup:**

Area of rectangle = 8 × 5 = 40

Area of triangle = $\frac{1}{2}$(4 × 5) = 10

Area of trapeziod = 10 × 5 = 50

> **HINT: Any time you're asked to find the area of an unfamiliar shape, try dropping lines to break it into familiar shapes that you can work with.**

## 52. How to find the CIRCUMFERENCE of a CIRCLE

$$Circumference = 2\pi r$$

**Example:**

**Setup:**

Circumference = $2\pi(5) = 10\pi$

## 53. How to find the AREA of a CIRCLE

$$Area = \pi r^2$$

**Example:**

**Setup:**
Area = $\pi \times 5^2 = 25\pi$

## 54. How to find the DISTANCE BETWEEN POINTS on the coordinate plane

If two points have the same $x$'s or the same $y$'s—that is, they make a line segment that is parallel to an axis—all you have to do is subtract the numbers that are different.

**Example:**

What is the distance from (2, 3) to (−7, 3)?

**Setup:**

The $y$'s are the same, so just subtract the $x$'s.

$$2 - (-7) = 9$$

If the points have different $x$'s and different $y$'s, make a right triangle and use the Pythagorean theorem.

**Example:**

What is the distance from (2, 3) to (−1, −1)?

**Setup:**

It's a 3-4-5 triangle!

$PQ = 5$

---

**HINT: Look for "special" right triangles.**

---

## 55. How to find the SLOPE of a LINE

$$Slope = \frac{rise}{run} = \frac{change\ in\ y}{change\ in\ x}$$

**Example:**

What is the slope of the line that contains the points (1, 2) and (4, −5)?

**Setup:**

Slope = $\frac{2 - (-5)}{1 - 4} = -\frac{7}{3}$

# Level 3 (Math You Might Find Difficult)

## 56. How to determine COMBINED PERCENT INCREASE/DECREASE

Start with 100 and see what happens.

**Example:**

A price rises by 10 percent one year and by 20 percent the next. What's the combined percent increase?

**Setup:**

Say the original price is $100.

Year one: $100 + (10% of 100) = 100 + 10 = 110.

Year two: 110 + (20% of 110) = 110 + 22 = 132.

From 100 to 132—That's a 32 percent increase.

## 57. How to find the ORIGINAL WHOLE before percent increase/decrease

Think of a 15 percent increase over $x$ as $1.15x$ and set up an equation.

**Example:**

After decreasing by 5 percent, the population is now 57,000. What was the original population?

**Setup:**

.95 × (Original Population) = 57,000

Original Population = 57,000 ÷ .95 = 60,000

## 58. How to solve a SIMPLE INTEREST problem

With simple interest, the interest is computed on the principal only and is given by:

$$interest = (principal) \times (interest\ rate^*) \times (time^{**})$$

\*     expressed as a decimal
\*\*    expressed in years

**Example:**

If $12,000 is invested at 6 percent simple annual interest, how much interest is earned after 9 months?

**Setup:**

$$(12,000) \times (.06) \times \left(\frac{9}{12}\right) = \$540$$

## 59. How to solve a COMPOUND INTEREST problem

If interest is compounded, the interest is computed on the principal as well as on any interest earned. To compute compound interest:

$$(final\ balance) = (principal) \times (1 + \frac{interest\ rate}{C})^{(time)(C)}$$

where $C$ = the number of times compounded annually

**Example:**

If $10,000 is invested at 8 percent annual interest, compounded semiannually, what is the balance after 1 year?

**Setup:**

Final balance

$$= (10,000) \times \left(1 + \frac{.08}{2}\right)^{(1)(2)}$$

$$= (10,000) \times (1.04)^2$$

$$= \$10,816$$

> **HINT: Often on the GRE, you don't have to do the work of calculating compound interest. Try calculating the simple interest and looking for the answer that's just a little bit larger.**

## 60. How to solve a REMAINDERS problem

Pick a number that fits the given conditions and see what happens.

**Example:**

When $n$ is divided by 7, the remainder is 5. What is the remainder when $2n$ is divided by 7 ?

**Setup:**

Find a number that leaves a remainder of 5 when divided by 7. A good choice would be 12. If $n = 12$, then $2n = 24$, which, when divided by 7, leaves a remainder of 3.

## 61. How to solve a DIGITS problem

Use a little logic—and some trial and error.

**Example:**

If $A$, $B$, $C$, and $D$ represent distinct digits in the addition problem below, what is the value of $D$ ?

$$
\begin{array}{r}
AB \\
+\ BA \\
\hline
CDC
\end{array}
$$

**Setup:**

Two 2-digit numbers will add up to at most something in the 100s, so $C = 1$. $B$ plus $A$ in the units' column gives a 1, and since it can't simply be that $B + A = 1$, it must be that $B + A = 11$, and a 1 gets carried. In fact, $A$ and $B$ can be just about any pair of digits that add up to 11 (3 and 8, 4 and 7, etcetera), but it doesn't matter what they are, they always give you the same thing for $D$ :

$$
\begin{array}{r}
47 \\
+74 \\
\hline
121
\end{array}
\qquad
\begin{array}{r}
83 \\
+38 \\
\hline
121
\end{array}
$$

## 62. How to find a WEIGHTED AVERAGE

Give each term the appropriate "weight."

**Example:**

The girls' average score is 30. The boys' average score is 24. If there are twice as many boys as girls, what is the overall average?

**Setup:**

$$
\text{Weighted Avg.} = \frac{1 \times 30 + 2 \times 24}{3} = \frac{78}{3} = 26
$$

---

**HINT: Don't just average the averages.**

---

## 63. How to find the NEW AVERAGE when a number is added or deleted

Use the sum of the terms of the old average to help you find the new average.

**Example:**

Michael's average score after four tests is 80. If he scores 100 on the fifth test, what's his new average?

**Setup:**

Find the original sum from the original average:
$$\text{Original sum} = 4 \times 80 = 320$$
Add the fifth score to make the new sum:
$$\text{New sum} = 320 + 100 = 420$$
Find the new average from the new sum:
$$\text{New average} = \frac{420}{5} = 84$$

## 64. How to use the ORIGINAL AVERAGE and NEW AVERAGE to figure out WHAT WAS ADDED OR DELETED

Use the sums.

*Number added = (new sum) − (original sum)*

*Number deleted = (original sum) − (new sum)*

### Example:

The average of five numbers is 2. After one number is deleted, the new average is −3. What number was deleted?

### Setup:

Find the original sum from the original average:

Original sum = 5 × 2 = 10

Find the new sum from the new average:

New sum = 4 × (−3) = −12

The difference between the original sum and the new sum is the answer.

Number deleted = 10 − (−12) = 22

## 65. How to find an AVERAGE RATE

Convert to totals.

$$Average\ A\ per\ B = \frac{Total\ A}{Total\ B}$$

### Example:

If the first 500 pages have an average of 150 words per page, and the remaining 100 pages have an average of 450 words per page, what is the average number of words per page for the entire 600 pages?

### Setup:

Total pages = 500 + 100 = 600

Total words = 500 × 150 + 100 × 450 = 120,000

$$Average\ words\ per\ page = \frac{120,000}{600} = 200$$

To find an average speed, you also convert to totals.

$$Average\ speed = \frac{total\ distance}{time}$$

### Example:

Rosa drove 120 miles one way at an average speed of 40 miles per hour and returned by the same 120-mile route at an average speed of 60 miles per hour. What was Rosa's average speed for the entire 240-mile round trip?

### Setup:

To drive 120 miles at 40 mph takes 3 hours. To return at 60 mph takes 2 hours. The total time, then, is 5 hours.

$$Average\ speed = \frac{240\ miles}{5\ hours} = 48\ mph$$

---

**HINT: Don't just average the rates.**

---

## 66. How to solve a WORK PROBLEM

In a work problem, you are given the rate at which people or machines perform work individually, and asked to compute the rate at which they work together (or vice versa). The work formula states: The inverse of the time it would take everyone working together equals the sum of the inverses of the times it would take each working individually. In other words:

$$\frac{1}{r} + \frac{1}{s} = \frac{1}{t}$$

where $r$ and $s$ are, for example, the number of hours it would take Rebecca and Sam, respectively to complete a job working by themselves, and $t$ is the number of hours it would take the two of them working together.

**Example:**

If it takes Joe 4 hours to paint a room and Pete twice as long to paint the same room, how long would it take the two of them, working together, to paint the same room, if each of them works at his respective individual rate?

**Setup:**

Joe takes 4 hours, so Pete takes 8 hours; thus:

$$\frac{1}{4} + \frac{1}{8} = \frac{1}{t}$$

$$\frac{1}{4} + \frac{1}{8} = \frac{3}{8} = \frac{1}{\frac{8}{3}}$$

So it would take them $\frac{8}{3}$ hours, or 2 hours 40 minutes, to paint the room together.

## 67. How to determine a COMBINED RATIO

Multiply one or both ratios by whatever you need to in order to get the terms they have in common to match.

**Example:**

The ratio of $a$ to $b$ is 7:3. The ratio of $b$ to $c$ is 2:5. What is the ratio of $a$ to $c$?

**Setup:**

Multiply each member of $a{:}b$ by 2 and multiply each member of $b{:}c$ by 3 and you get $a{:}b$ = 14:6 and $b{:}c$ = 6:15. Now that the $b$'s match, you can just take $a$ and $c$ and say $a{:}c$ = 14:15.

## 68. How to solve a DILUTION or MIXTURE problem

In dilution or mixture problems, you have to determine the characteristics of the resulting mixture when substances with different characteristics are combined. Or, alternatively, you have to determine how to combine substances with different characteristics to produce a desired mixture. There are two approaches to such problems—the straightforward setup and the balancing method.

**Example:**

If 5 pounds of raisins that cost $1.00 per pound are mixed with 2 pounds of almonds that cost $2.40 per pound, what is the cost per pound of the resulting mixture?

**Setup:**

The straightforward setup:

$5(1.00) + 2(2.40) = 9.80$

The cost per pound is $\frac{9.80}{7}$ = $1.40

**Example:**

How many liters of a solution that is 10 percent alcohol by volume must be added to 2 liters of a solution that is 50 percent alcohol by volume to create a solution that is 15 percent alcohol by volume?

**Setup:**

The balancing method:

Make the weaker and stronger (or cheaper and more expensive, etc.) substances balance. That is: (percent/price difference between the weaker solution and the desired solution) × (amount of weaker solution) = (percent/price difference between the stronger solution and the desired solution) × (amount of stronger solution).

In this case:

$n(15 - 10) = 2(50 - 15)$

$n \times 5 = 2(35)$

$n = \frac{70}{5} = 14$

So 14 liters of the 10 percent solution must be added.

---

**HINT: The balancing method is also effective on weighted average questions.**

---

## 69. How to solve a GROUP problem involving BOTH/NEITHER

Some GRE word problems involve two groups with overlapping members, and possibly elements that belong to neither group. It's easy to identify this type of question because the words "both" and/or "neither" appear in the question. These problems are quite easy if you just memorize the following formula:

$$Group_1 + Group_2 + Neither - Both = Total$$

### Example:

Of the 120 students at a certain language school, 65 are studying French, 51 are studying Spanish, and 53 are studying neither language. How many are studying both French and Spanish?

### Setup:

$65 + 51 + 53 - Both = 120$

$169 - Both = 120$

$Both = 49$

## 70. How to solve a GROUP problem involving EITHER/OR CATEGORIES

Other GRE word problems involve groups with distinct "either/or" categories (male/female, blue collar/white collar, etc.). The key to solving this type of problem is to organize the information in a grid.

### Example:

At a certain professional conference with 130 attendees, 94 of the attendees are doctors and the rest are dentists. If 48 of the attendees are women, and $\frac{1}{4}$ of the dentists in attendance are women, how many of the attendees are male doctors?

### Setup:

To complete the grid, each row and column adds up to the corresponding total:

|        | Doctors | Dentists | Total |
|--------|---------|----------|-------|
| Male   | 55      | 27       | 82    |
| Female |         | 9        | 48    |
| Total  | 94      | 36       | 130   |

After you've filled in the information from the question, simply fill in the remaining boxes until you get the number you are looking for—in this case, that 55 of the attendees are male doctors.

## 71. How to work with FACTORIALS

You may see a problem involving factorial notation. If $n$ is an integer greater than 1, then $n$ factorial, denoted by $n!$, is defined as the product of all the integers from 1 to $n$. In other words:

$2! = 2 \times 1 = 2$

$3! = 3 \times 2 \times 1 = 6$

$4! = 4 \times 3 \times 2 \times 1 = 24$, etc.

By definition, $0! = 1! = 1$.

Also note: $6! = 6 \times 5! = 6 \times 5 \times 4!$, etc. Most GRE factorial problems test your ability to factor and/or cancel.

### Example:

$$\frac{8!}{6! \times 5!} = \frac{\cancel{8} \times 7 \times \cancel{6!}}{\cancel{6!} \times 5 \times \cancel{4} \times 3 \times \cancel{2} \times 1} = \frac{7}{15}$$

## 72. How to solve a PERMUTATION problem

Factorials are useful for solving questions about permutations, i.e., the number of ways to arrange elements sequentially. For instance, to figure out how many ways there are to arrange 7 items along a shelf, you would multiply the number of possibilities for the first position times the number of possibilities remaining for the second position, and so on—in other words: $7 \times 6 \times 5 \times 4 \times 3 \times 2 \times 1$, or $7!$.

If you're asked to find the number of ways to arrange a smaller group that's being drawn from a larger group, you can either apply logic or you can use the permutation formula:

$$P = \frac{n!}{(n-k)!}$$

where $n$ = (# in the larger group) and $k$ = (# you're arranging).

### Example:

Five runners run in a race. The runners who come in first, second, and third place will win gold, silver, and bronze medals respectively. How many possible outcomes for gold, silver, and bronze medal winners are there?

### Setup:

Any of the 5 runners could come in first place, leaving 4 runners who could come in second place, leaving 3 runners who could come in third place, for a total of $5 \times 4 \times 3 = 60$ possible outcomes for gold, silver, and bronze medal winners. Or, using the formula:

$$P = \frac{5!}{(5-3)!} = \frac{5!}{2!} = 5 \times 4 \times 3 = 60$$

## 73. How to solve a COMBINATION problem

If the order or arrangement of the smaller group that's being drawn from the larger group does NOT matter, you are looking for the numbers of combinations, and a different formula is called for:

$$C = \frac{n!}{k!(n-k)!}$$

Where $n$ = (# in the larger group) and $k$ = (# you're choosing)

### Example:

How many different ways there are to choose 3 delegates from 8 possible candidates?

### Setup:

$$C = \frac{8!}{3! \times 5!} = \frac{8 \times 7 \times 6 \times 5!}{3 \times 2 \times 1 \times 5!} = 56$$

So there are 56 different possible combinations.

## 74. How to solve a MULTIPLE-EVENT PROBABILITY problem

Many hard probability questions involve finding the probability of a certain outcome after multiple events (a coin being tossed several times, etc.). These questions come in two forms: those in which each individual event must occur a certain way, and those in which individual events can have different outcomes.

To determine multiple-event probability where each individual event must occur a certain way:

• Figure out the probability for each individual event.

• Multiply the individual probabilities together.

### Example:

If 2 students are chosen at random from a class with 5 girls and 5 boys, what's the probability that both students chosen will be girls?

**Setup:**

The probability that the first student chosen will be a girl is $\frac{5}{10} = \frac{1}{2}$, and since there would be 4 girls left out of 9 students, the probability that the second student chosen will be a girl is $\frac{4}{9}$. Thus the probability that both students chosen will be girls is $\frac{1}{2} \times \frac{4}{9} = \frac{2}{9}$.

To determine multiple-event probability where individual events can have different outcomes:

- Find the *total number of possible outcomes* by determining the number of possible outcomes for each individual event and multiplying these numbers together.

- Find the *number of desired outcomes* by listing out the possibilities.

**Example:**

If a fair coin is tossed 4 times, what's the probability that at least 3 of the 4 tosses will come up heads?

**Setup:**

There are 2 possible outcomes for each toss, so after 4 tosses there are a total of $2 \times 2 \times 2 \times 2 = 16$ possible outcomes.

List out all the possibilities where "at least 3 of the 4 tosses" come up heads:

    H, H, H, T

    H, H, T, H

    H, T, H, H

    T, H, H, H

    H, H, H, H

So there's a total of 5 possible desired outcomes. Thus, the probability that at least 3 of the 4 tosses will come up heads is $\frac{\text{number of desired outcomes}}{\text{number of possible outcomes}} = \frac{5}{16}$.

## 75. How to deal with STANDARD DEVIATION

Like mean, mode, median, and range, standard deviation is a term used to describe sets of numbers. Standard deviation is a measure of how spread out a set of numbers is (how much the numbers deviate from the mean). The greater the spread, the higher the standard deviation. You'll never actually have to calculate the standard deviation on test day, but here's how it's calculated:

- Find the average (arithmetic mean) of the set.

- Find the differences between the mean and each value in the set.

- Square each of the differences.

- Find the average of the squared differences.

- Take the positive square root of the average.

Although you won't have to calculate standard deviation on the GRE, you may be asked to compare standard deviations between sets of data, or otherwise demonstrate that you understand what standard deviation means.

**Example:**

High temperatures, in degrees Fahrenheit, in 2 cities over 5 days:

| September | 1 | 2 | 3 | 4 | 5 |
|-----------|-----|-----|-----|-----|-----|
| City *A* | 54 | 61 | 70 | 49 | 56 |
| City *B* | 62 | 56 | 60 | 67 | 65 |

For the 5-day period listed, which city had the greater standard deviation in high temperatures?

## Setup:

Even without trying to calculate them out, one can see that City $A$ has the greater spread in temperatures, and therefore the greater standard deviation in high temperatures. If you were to go ahead and calculate the standard deviations following the steps described above, you would find that the standard deviation in high temperatures for City $A = \sqrt{\frac{254}{5}} \approx$ 7.1, while the same for City $B = \sqrt{\frac{74}{5}} \approx 3.8$ .

## 76. How to MULTIPLY/DIVIDE POWERS

Add/subtract the exponents.

**Example:**

$x^a \times x^b = x^{(a + b)}$
$2^3 \times 2^4 = 2^7$

**Example:**

$\frac{x^c}{x^d} = x^{(c - d)}$

$\frac{5^6}{5^2} = 5^4$

## 77. How to RAISE A POWER TO A POWER

Multiply the exponents.

**Example:**

$(x^a)^b = x^{ab}$
$(3^4)^5 = 3^{20}$

## 78. How to handle ZERO POWERS

Zero raised to any power equals zero.

**Example:**

$0^4 = 0^{12} = 0^1 = 0$

Any number raised to the 0 power equals 1.

**Example:**

$3^0 = 15^0 = (0.34)^0 = 345^0 = \pi^0 = 1$

The lone exception is 0 raised to the 0 power, which is *undefined*.

## 79. How to handle NEGATIVE POWERS

A number raised to the exponent $-x$ is the reciprocal of that number raised to the exponent $x$.

**Example:**

$5^{-3} = \frac{1}{5^3} = \frac{1}{5 \times 5 \times 5} = \frac{1}{125}$
$n^{-1} = \frac{1}{n}$, $n^{-2} = \frac{1}{n^2}$, and so on.

## 80. How to handle FRACTIONAL POWERS

Fractional exponents relate to roots. For instance, $x^{\frac{1}{2}} = \sqrt{x}$ .

Likewise, $x^{\frac{1}{3}} = \sqrt[3]{x}$, $x^{\frac{2}{3}} = \sqrt[3]{x^2}$, and so on.

---

**HINT: The rules for multiplying powers, dividing powers, and raising powers to powers also apply nicely to negative, zero, and fractional exponents.**

---

**Example:**

$4^{\frac{1}{2}} = \sqrt{4} = 2$

$(x^{-2})^{\frac{1}{2}} = x^{(-2)(\frac{1}{2})} = x^{-1} = \frac{1}{x}$

## 81. How to handle CUBE ROOTS

The cube root of $x$ is just the number that multiplied by itself 3 times (i.e., cubed) gives you $x$. Both positive and negative numbers have one and only one cube root, denoted by the symbol $\sqrt[3]{\phantom{x}}$, and the cube root of a number is always the same sign as the number itself.

**Example:**

$(-5) \times (-5) \times (-5) = -125$, so $\sqrt[3]{-125} = -5$

$\frac{1}{2} \times \frac{1}{2} \times \frac{1}{2} = \frac{1}{8}$, so $\sqrt[3]{\frac{1}{8}} = \frac{1}{2}$

## 82. How to ADD, SUBTRACT, MULTIPLY, and DIVIDE ROOTS

You can add/subtract roots only when the parts inside the $\sqrt{\phantom{x}}$ are identical.

**Example:**

$$\sqrt{2} + 3\sqrt{2} = 4\sqrt{2}$$
$$\sqrt{2} - 3\sqrt{2} = -2\sqrt{2}$$

$\sqrt{2} + \sqrt{3}$—cannot be combined.

To multiply/divide roots, deal with what's inside the $\sqrt{\phantom{x}}$ and outside the $\sqrt{\phantom{x}}$ separately.

**Example:**

$(2\sqrt{3})(7\sqrt{5}) = (2 \times 7)\,(\sqrt{3 \times 5}) = 14\sqrt{15}$

$\dfrac{10\sqrt{21}}{5\sqrt{3}} = \dfrac{10}{5}\sqrt{\dfrac{21}{3}} = 2\sqrt{7}$

## 83. How to SIMPLIFY A SQUARE ROOT

Look for perfect squares (4, 9, 16, 25, 36...) inside the $\sqrt{\phantom{x}}$. Factor them out and "unsquare" them.

**Example:**

$$\sqrt{48} = \sqrt{16} \times \sqrt{3} = 4\sqrt{3}$$
$$\sqrt{180} = \sqrt{36} \times \sqrt{5} = 6\sqrt{5}$$

## 84. How to solve certain QUADRATIC EQUATIONS

Forget the quadratic formula. Manipulate the equation (if necessary) into the "_____ = 0" form, factor the left side, and break the quadratic into two simple equations.

**Example:**

$$x^2 + 6 = 5x$$
$$x^2 - 5x + 6 = 0$$
$$(x - 2)(x - 3) = 0$$
$$x - 2 = 0 \text{ or } x - 3 = 0$$
$$x = 2 \text{ or } 3$$

**Example:**

$$x^2 = 9$$
$$x = 3 \text{ or} -3$$

---

**HINT: Watch out for $x^2$.**
**There can be two solutions.**

## 85. How to solve MULTIPLE EQUATIONS

When you see two equations with two variables on the GRE, they're probably easy to combine in such a way that you get something closer to what you're looking for.

**Example:**

If $5x - 2y = -9$ and $3y - 4x = 6$, what is the value of $x + y$?

**Setup:**

The question doesn't ask for $x$ and $y$ separately, so don't solve for them separately if you don't have to. Look what happens if you just rearrange a little and "add" the equations:

$$\begin{array}{r} 5x - 2y = -9 \\ -4x + 3y = \phantom{-}6 \\ \hline x + y \phantom{=} = -3 \end{array}$$

---
**HINT: Don't do more work than you have to. Look for the shortcut.**

---

## 86. How to solve a SEQUENCE problem

The notation used in sequence problems scares many test takers, but these problems aren't as bad as they look. In a sequence problem, the $n$th term in the sequence is generated by performing an operation, which will be defined for you, on either $n$ or on the previous term in the sequence. Familiarize yourself with sequence notation and you should have no problem.

**Example:**

What is the difference between the fifth and fourth terms in the sequence 0, 4, 18, . . . whose $n$th term is $n^2(n - 1)$?

**Setup:**

Use the operation given to come up with the values for your terms:

$n_5 = 5^2(5 - 1) = 25(4) = 100$

$n_4 = 4^2(4 - 1) = 16(3) = 48$

So the difference between the fifth and fourth terms is $100 - 48 = 52$.

---
**HINT: Many GRE sequence problems invite you to backsolve.**

---

## 87. How to solve a FUNCTION problem

You may see classic function notation on the GRE. An algebraic expression of only one variable may be defined as a function, $f$ or $g$, of that variable.

**Example:**

What is the minimum value of the function $f(x) = x^2 - 1$?

**Setup:**

In the function $f(x) = x^2 - 1$, if $x$ is 1, then $f(1) = 1^2 - 1 = 0$. In other words, by inputting 1 into the function, the output $f(x) = 0$. Every number inputted has one and only one output (although the reverse is not necessarily true). You're asked to find the minimum value, so how would you minimize the expression $f(x) = x^2 - 1$? Since $x^2$ cannot be negative, in this case $f(x)$ is minimized by making $x = 0$: $f(0) = 0^2 - 1 = -1$, so the minimum value of the function is $-1$.

## 88. How to handle GRAPHS of FUNCTIONS

You may see problem that involves a function graphed onto the $xy$-coordinate plane, often called a "rectangular coordinate system" on the GRE. When graphing a function, the output, $f(x)$, becomes the $y$-coordinate. For example, in the previous example, $f(x) = x^2 - 1$, you've already determined 2 points, $(1, 0)$ and $(0, -1)$. If you were to keep plugging in numbers to determine more points and then plotted those points on the $xy$-coordinate plane, you would come up with something like this:

This curved line is called a *parabola*. In the event that you should see a parabola on the GRE (it could be upside down or squatter or more elongated than the one shown), you will most likely be asked to choose which equation the parabola is describing. These questions can be surprisingly easy to answer. Pick out obvious points on the graph, such as $(1, 0)$ and $(0, -1)$ above, plug these values into the answer choices, and eliminate choices that don't jibe with those values until only one answer is left.

## 89. How to handle LINEAR EQUATIONS

You may also encounter linear equations on the GRE. A linear equation is often expressed in the form

$$y = mx + b, \text{ where:}$$

• $m$ = the slope of the line = $\frac{rise}{run}$.

For instance, a slope of 3 means that the line rises 3 steps for every 1 step it makes to the right. A positive slope slopes up from left to right. A negative slope slopes down from left to right. A slope of zero (e.g., $y = 5$) is a flat line.

• $b$ = the $y$-intercept (where the line passes the $y$-axis).

**Example:**

The graph of the linear equation $y = -\frac{3}{4}x + 3$ is:

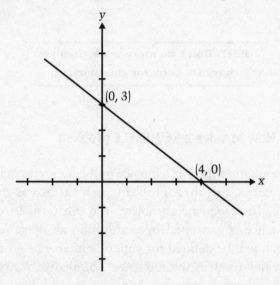

**Note:** The equation above could also be written in the form $3x + 4y = 12$.

To get a better handle on an equation written in this form, you can solve for $y$ to write it in its more familiar form. Or, if you're asked to choose which equation the line is describing, you can pick obvious points such as $(0, 3)$ and $(4, 0)$ above, and use these values to eliminate answer choices until only one answer is left.

## 90. How to find the *x*- and *y*-INTERCEPTS of a line

The *x*-intercept of a line is the value of *x* where the line crosses the *x*-axis. In other words, it's the value of *x* when *y* = 0. Likewise, the *y*-intercept is the value of *y* where the line crosses the *y*-axis, i.e., the value of *y* when *x* = 0, also the value *b* when the equation is in the form: *y* = *mx* + *b*. For instance, in the line shown in the previous example, the *x*-intercept is 4 and the *y*-intercept is 3.

## 91. How to find the MAXIMUM and MINIMUM lengths for a SIDE of a TRIANGLE

If you know two sides of a triangle, you know that the third side is between the difference and the sum.

**Example:**

The length of one side of a triangle is 7. The length of another side is 3. What is the range of possible lengths for the third side?

**Setup:**
The third side is greater than the difference (7 − 3 = 4) and less than the sum (7 + 3 = 10).

## 92. How to find one angle or the sum of all the ANGLES of a REGULAR POLYGON

*Sum of the interior angles in a polygon with n sides =*
*(n − 2) × 180*

*Degree measure of one angle in a regular polygon with*
*n sides =* $\frac{(n-2) \times 180}{n}$

**Example:**

What is the measure of one angle of a regular pentagon?

**Setup:**

Plug *n* = 5 into the formula:

Degree measure of one angle =

$$\frac{(5-2) \times 180}{5} = \frac{540}{5} = 108$$

## 93. How to find the LENGTH of an ARC

Think of an arc as a fraction of the circle's circumference.

$$Length\ of\ arc = \frac{n}{360} \times 2\pi r$$

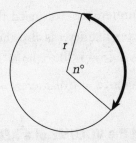

## 94. How to find the AREA of a SECTOR

Think of a sector as a fraction of the circle's area.

$$Area\ of\ sector = \frac{n}{360} \times \pi r^2$$

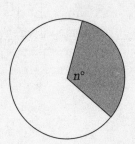

## 95. How to find the dimensions or area of an INSCRIBED or CIRCUMSCRIBED FIGURE

Look for the connection. Is the diameter the same as a side or a diagonal?

**Example:**

If the area of the square is 36, what is the circumference of the circle?

**Setup:**

To get the circumference, you need the diameter or radius. The circle's diameter is also the square's diagonal, which (it's a 45-45-90 triangle!) is $6\sqrt{2}$.

$$\text{Circumference} = \pi(\text{diameter}) = 6\pi\sqrt{2}$$

## 96. How to find the VOLUME of a RECTANGULAR SOLID

$$Volume = length \times width \times height$$

## 97. How to find the SURFACE AREA of a RECTANGULAR SOLID

To find the surface area of a rectangular solid, you have to find the area of each face and add them together. Here's the formula.

$Surface\ area =$
$2(length \times width + length \times height + width \times height)$

## 98. How to find the DIAGONAL of a RECTANGULAR SOLID

Use the Pythagorean theorem twice, unless you spot "special" triangles.

**Example:** What is the length of *AG* ?

**Setup:** Draw diagonal *AC*.

*ABC* is a 3-4-5 triangle, so *AC* = 5. Now look at triangle *ACG:*

*ACG* is another special triangle, so you don't need to use the Pythagorean theorem. *ACG* is a 45-45-90, so *AG* = $5\sqrt{2}$.

## 99. How to find the VOLUME of a CYLINDER

$$Volume = \pi r^2 h$$

## 100. How to find the VOLUME of a SPHERE

$$Volume = \frac{4}{3}\pi r^3$$

# How Did We Do? Grade Us.

Thank you for choosing a Kaplan book. Your comments and suggestions are very useful to us. Please answer the following questions to assist us in our continued development of high-quality resources to meet your needs.

The title of the Kaplan book I read was: _____

My name is: _____

My address is: _____

_____

My e-mail address is: _____

What overall grade would you give this book?      (A)   (B)   (C)   (D)   (F)

How relevant was the information to your goals?    (A)   (B)   (C)   (D)   (F)

How comprehensive was the information in this book?  (A)   (B)   (C)   (D)   (F)

How accurate was the information in this book?     (A)   (B)   (C)   (D)   (F)

How easy was the book to use?                      (A)   (B)   (C)   (D)   (F)

How appealing was the book's design?               (A)   (B)   (C)   (D)   (F)

What were the book's strong points? _____

How could this book be improved? _____

Is there anything that we left out that you wanted to know more about?

Would you recommend this book to others?   ☐ YES      ☐ NO

Other comments: _____

_____

_____

Do we have permission to quote you?   ☐ YES      ☐ NO

Thank you for your help.
Please tear out this page and mail it to:

Managing Editor
Kaplan, Inc.
888 Seventh Avenue
New York, NY 10106

**KAPLAN®**

Thanks!

# About Kaplan

## KAPLAN TEST PREPARATION & ADMISSIONS

With 3,000 classroom locations throughout the U.S. and abroad, Kaplan has served more than three million students in its classes over the past 60-plus years. Kaplan's nationally-recognized programs for roughly 35 standardized tests include entrance exams for secondary school, college and graduate school as well as English language and professional licensing exams. Kaplan also offers private tutoring and one-on-one admissions guidance and is a leader in test prep for computerized exams. Kaplan is the first major player to provide online test prep to students across the globe, as well as admissions courses and other resources at **www.kaptest.com.**

## SCORE! LEARNING, INC.

SCORE! Learning, Inc. is a national provider of customized learning programs for students. SCORE! Educational Centers help students in K-10 build confidence along with academic skills in a motivating, sports-oriented environment after school and on weekends. SCORE! Prep provides in-home, one-on-one tutoring for high school academic subjects and standardized tests. SCORE! Educational Centers and SCORE! Prep share a highly personalized approach, proven educational techniques, and the goal of cultivating a love of learning in children.

## THE KAPLAN COLLEGES

The Kaplan Colleges system (**www.kaplancollege.edu**) is a collection of institutions offering an extensive array of online and traditional educational programs for working professionals who want to advance their careers. Learners will find programs leading to bachelor and associates degrees, certificates and diplomas in fields such as business, IT, paralegal studies, legal nurse consulting, criminal justice and financial planning. The Kaplan Colleges system includes Concord Law School (**www.concordlawschool.com**), the nation's only online law school, offering J.D., Executive J.D. and LL.M. degrees for working professionals, family caregivers, students in rural communities, and others whose circumstances prevent them from attending a fixed facility law school.

## QUEST EDUCATION CORPORATION

Kaplan's Quest Education unit (**www.questeducation.com**) is a leading provider of post-secondary education. Quest offers bachelor and associate degrees and diploma programs designed to provide students with the skills necessary to qualify them for entry-level employment. Programs are primarily in the fields of healthcare, business, information technology, fashion and design.

## KAPLAN PUBLISHING

Kaplan Publishing, in a joint venture with Simon & Schuster, publishes more than 150 titles on test preparation, admissions, education, career development, and life skills. Kaplan Publishing emerged as a leader in sales of books for statewide assessments with the publication of dozens of new state test titles. Books are offered in traditional paper form, pre-packaged with computer software, and now in e-book form.

## KAPLAN INTERNATIONAL

Kaplan International (**www.kaptest.com**) provides students and professionals with intensive English instruction, university preparation, test preparation programs, housing and activities at 12 city and campus centers in the U.S. and Canada. Kaplan also has a strong presence overseas with 41 centers in 18 countries outside of the United States.

## KAPLAN COMMUNITY OUTREACH

Kaplan Community Outreach provides educational resources and opportunities to thousands of economically disadvantaged students annually. Kaplan joins forces with numerous nonprofit groups, educational institutions, government agencies, and other grass-roots organizations on a variety of local and national support programs. These programs help students and professionals from a variety of backgrounds achieve their educational and career goals.

## KAPLAN PROFESSIONAL

The Kaplan Professional companies (**www.kaplanprofessional.com**) provide licensing and continuing education, training, certification, professional development courses, and compliance tracking for securities, insurance, financial services, legal, IT, and real estate professionals and corporations. Offering an array of educational tools, from on-site training and classroom instruction to nearly 200 online courses and programs, Kaplan Professional serves professionals who must maintain licenses and comply with regulatory mandates despite busy travel schedules and work obligations.

- **Dearborn Financial Services** provides innovative education and compliance solutions to the financial services industry, including registration services, firm element needs analysis and training plan development, securities and insurance prelicensing training, continuing education, and compliance management services, in classes nationwide, online and via books and software.

- **Dearborn Trade Publishing** publishes approximately 250 titles specializing in finance, business management and real estate, plus well-read consumer real estate books to help homebuyers, sellers and real estate investors make informed decisions.

- **Dearborn Real Estate Education** is the leading real estate content provider for real estate schools and associations, offering practical prelicensing and continuing education training materials on appraisal, home inspection, property management, brokerage, ethics, law, sales approaches, and contracts, and an online real estate campus at **RECampus.com.**

- **Perfect Access Speer** is a leader in software education and consulting, bringing both traditional and e-learning solutions to its clients in the legal, financial, and professional services industries.

- **The Schweser Study Program** offers training tools for the Chartered Financial Analyst (CFA®) examination, with a comprehensive product line of study notes, audiotapes, videotapes, flashcards and live seminars that are developed and taught by a top-notch faculty.

- **Kaplan Professional Real Estate Schools** provide real estate licensing and continuing education programs through live classroom instruction, Internet-based learning, and correspondence courses, to help real estate professionals acquire the skills needed to meet state licensing and educational requirements.

- **Self Test Software** is a world leader in exam simulation software and preparation for technical certifications including Microsoft, Oracle, Cisco, Novell, Lotus, CIW and CompTIA, serving businesses and individuals seeking to attain vendor-sponsored certification.

- **Call Center Solutions** provides assessment and training services to the call center industry.

# Want more information about our services, products or the nearest Kaplan center?

**1** **Call our nationwide toll-free numbers:**

**1-800-KAP-TEST** for information on our test prep courses, private tutoring and admissions consulting

**1-800-KAP-ITEM** for information on our books and software

**2** **Connect with us online:**
On the web, go to:
**www.kaptest.com**

**3** **Write to:**

Kaplan
888 Seventh Avenue
New York, NY 10106

# CD-ROM Installation and Technical Support

Congratulations! You've purchased the best test-prep software on the market, the software that's more fun than an abacus and more educational than an overhead projector. Kaplan's CD-ROM is the most comprehensive, instructive, and entertaining software product in the field of test prep to arrive since . . . well, since the dawn of humankind!

In this software, you get:

- Interactive Lessons detailing the famed Kaplan approaches to each question type
- Full-length and Practice Tests, so that you can try out your new skills as you move through the sessions
- Your own personalized study plan based on your needs
- Vocabulary and math flashcards
- Invaluable admissions information and more!

This CD provides the tools that will help you devise your own personal test-taking plan. Each test you take is closely analyzed, with detailed feedback on your strategic performance. Naturally, every question comes with a complete explanation. And our detailed scoring charts will track your progress on every type of question. Only Kaplan offers this range of features essential for successful test performance.

## Installation Instructions

1. Start your PC and Windows.
2. Insert the CD into the CD-ROM drive.
3. From the Start menu, choose RUN and type d:\gresetup.exe (where d: is your CD-ROM drive).

Please note: This CD-ROM is Windows-compatible only.

## Tech Support

If you have any questions or problems, you can call our tech support line at (503) 968-4058. You can speak to a tech support rep between the hours of 9 A.M. and 9 P.M. EST Monday through Friday, and between 9 A.M. and 8 P.M. EST Saturday and Sunday, or you can leave a message and a rep will get back to you the following business day.

## Copyright and Permission Notices

# Minimum System Requirements

Operating System:          Windows® 98, 98SE, NT 4.0, 2000, ME, XP
CPU Type and Speed:        Pentium® 266 MHz or higher
Hard Drive Space:          15 MB
Memory:                    8 MB
Graphics:                  640 x 480 thousands of colors (millions recommended)
CD-ROM Speed:              4X or higher

Note: Internet connection required for the Web features of the program

## SOFTWARE LICENSE/DISCLAIMER OF WARRANTIES

1. ACCEPTANCE. By using this compact disc you hereby accept the terms and provisions of this license and agree to be bound hereby.

2. OWNERSHIP. The software contained on this compact disc, all content, related documentation and fonts (collectively, the "Software") are all proprietary copyrighted materials owned by Kaplan, Inc. ("Kaplan") or its licensors.

3. LICENSE. You are granted a limited license to use the Software. This License allows you to use the Software on a single computer only. You may not copy, distribute, modify, network, rent, lease, loan, or create derivative works based upon the Software in whole or in part. The Software is intended for personal usage only. Your rights to use the Software and this License shall terminate immediately without notice upon your failure to comply with any of the terms hereof.

4. RESTRICTIONS. The Software contains copyrighted material, trade secrets, and other proprietary material. In order to protect them, and except as permitted by applicable legislation, you may not decompile, reverse engineer, disassemble, or otherwise reduce the Software to human-perceivable form.

5. LIMITED WARRANTY; DISCLAIMER. Kaplan warrants the compact disc on which the Software is recorded to be free from defects in materials and workmanship under normal use for a period of ninety (90) days from the date of purchase as evidenced by a copy of the receipt. Kaplan's entire liability and your exclusive remedy will be replacement of the compact disc not meeting this warranty. The Software is provided "AS IS" and without warranty of any kind, and Kaplan and Kaplan's licensors EXPRESSLY DISCLAIM ALL WARRANTIES, EXPRESS OR IMPLIED, INCLUDING THE IMPLIED WARRANTIES OF MERCHANTABILITY OR FITNESS FOR A PARTICULAR PURPOSE. FURTHERMORE, KAPLAN DOES NOT WARRANT THAT THE FUNCTIONS CONTAINED IN THE SOFTWARE WILL MEET YOUR REQUIREMENTS, OR THAT THE OPERATION OF THE SOFTWARE WILL BE UNINTERRUPTED OR ERROR-FREE, OR THAT DEFECTS IN THE SOFTWARE WILL BE CORRECTED. KAPLAN DOES NOT WARRANT OR MAKE ANY REPRESENTATIONS REGARDING THE USE OR THE RESULTS OF THE USE OF THE SOFTWARE IN TERMS OF THEIR CORRECTNESS, ACCURACY, RELIABILITY, OR OTHERWISE, UNDER NO CIRCUMSTANCES, INCLUDING NEGLIGENCE, SHALL KAPLAN BE LIABLE FOR ANY DIRECT, INDIRECT, PUNITIVE, INCIDENTAL, SPECIAL OR CONSEQUENTIAL DAMAGES, INCLUDING, BUT NOT LIMITED TO, LOST PROFITS OR WAGES, IN CONNECTION WITH THE SOFTWARE EVEN IF KAPLAN HAS BEEN ADVISED OF THE POSSIBILITY OF SUCH DAMAGES. CERTAIN OF THE LIMITATIONS HEREIN PROVIDED MAY BE PRECLUDED BY LAW.

6. EXPORT LAW ASSURANCES. You agree and certify that you will not export the Software outside of the United States except as authorized and as permitted by the laws and regulations of the United States. If the Software has been rightfully obtained by you outside of the United States, you agree that you will not re-export the Software except as permitted by the laws and regulations of the United States and the laws and regulations of the jurisdiction in which you obtained the Software.

7. MISCELLANEOUS. This license represents the entire understanding of the parties, may only be modified in writing, and shall be governed by the laws of the State of New York.

**KAPLAN**